RELIGION AND MENTAL HEALTH

Religion and Mental Health

Edited by

John F. Schumaker

New York   Oxford
OXFORD UNIVERSITY PRESS
1992

Oxford University Press

Oxford   New York   Toronto
Delhi   Bombay   Calcutta   Madras   Karachi
Kuala Lumpur   Singapore   Hong Kong   Tokyo
Nairobi   Dar es Salaam   Cape Town
Melbourne   Auckland

and associated companies in
Berlin   Ibadan

Copyright © 1992 by Oxford University Press, Inc.

Published by Oxford University Press, Inc.
200 Madison Avenue, New York, NY 10016

Oxford is a registered trademark of Oxford University Press

Library of Congress Cataloging-in-Publication Data
Religion and mental health / edited by John F. Schumaker.
p. cm.   Includes index.
ISBN 0-19-506985-4
1. Psychology, Religious.   2. Mental health—Religious aspects.
I. Schumaker, John F., 1949–
BL53.R435   1992
291.1′78322—dc20   92-3775

1 3 5 7 9 8 6 4 2
Printed in the United States of America
on acid-free paper

Contents

Contributors, vii

Introduction, 3
John F. Schumaker

I Historical Perspectives

1. The Psychopathology of Religion: European Historical Perspectives, 33
   Jacob A. Belzen
2. Religion and the Mental Health of Women, 43
   Robert A. Bridges and Bernard Spilka
3. Mental Health Consequences of Irreligion, 54
   John F. Schumaker
4. Religion and Sexual Adjustment, 70
   John D. Shea

II Affective and Cognitive Consequences

5. Religiosity, Depression, and Suicide, 87
   Steven Stack
6. Religion, Anxiety, and Fear of Death, 98
   Peter Pressman, John S. Lyons, David B. Larson, and John Gartner
7. Sin and Guilt in Faith Traditions: Issues for Self-Esteem, 110
   Ralph W. Hood, Jr.
8. Religion and Rationality, 122
   James E. Alcock
9. Religion and Self-Actualization, 132
   Joseph B. Tamney
10. Religiosity, Meaning in Life, and Psychological Well-Being, 138
    Kerry Chamberlain and Sheryl Zika

11. Religion, Neuroticism, and Psychoticism, 149
    Leslie J. Francis

III   Psychosocial Dimensions

12. Religon and Mental Health in Early Life, 163
    Edward P. Shafranske

13. Religion and Mental Health in Later Life, 177
    Harold G. Koenig

14. Religion and Marital Adjustment, 189
    Gary L. Hansen

15. Crime, Delinquency, and Religion, 199
    William Sims Bainbridge

16. Religion and Substance Use, 211
    Peter L. Benson

17. Religious Orientation and Mental Health, 221
    Kevin S. Masters and Allen E. Bergin

18. Mental Health of Cult Consumers: Legal and Scientific Controversy, 233
    James T. Richardson

19. Religious Diagnosis in Evaluations of Mental Health, 245
    H. Newton Malony

IV   Cross-Cultural Perspectives

20. Religion as a Mediating Factor in Culture Change, 259
    Erika Bourguignon

21. Buddhism and Mental Health: A Comparative Analysis, 270
    Gary Groth-Marnat

22. Religious Experience and Psychopathology:
    Cross-Cultural Perspectives, 281
    Raymond H. Prince

23. Religious Ritual and Mental Health, 291
    Janet L. Jacobs

24. Content and Prevalence of Psychopathology in World Religions, 300
    David Greenberg and Eliezer Witztum

    Index, 315

Contributors

James E. Alcock is Professor of Psychology at Glendon College, York University, in Toronto, Canada.

William Sims Bainbridge is Professor and Chairman of the Department of Sociology and Anthropology at Towson State University, near Baltimore, Maryland.

Jacob A. Belzen is an Associate Professor at Titus Brandsma Instituut, University of Nijmegen, The Netherlands.

Peter L. Benson is President of Search Institute in Minneapolis, Minnesota.

Allen E. Bergin is Professor and Director of Clinical Psychology at Brigham Young University in Provo, Utah.

Erika Bourguignon is Professor Emeritus of Anthropology at Ohio State University, in Columbus, Ohio.

Robert A. Bridges is the Adult Outpatient Clinic Director for Addiction, Treatment and Recovery at St. Luke's Hospital in Denver, Colorado. He is also Adjunct Professor at the University of Denver and the Metropolitan State College in Denver.

Kerry Chamberlain is a Senior Lecturer in Psychology at Massey University, in Palmerston North, New Zealand.

Leslie J. Francis is Mansel Jones Fellow at Trinity College, Carmarthen, Wales.

John Gartner is a Clinical Assistant Professor of Psychology at The Johns Hopkins University, in Baltimore, Maryland.

David Greenberg is a psychiatrist and Director of the Jerusalem Mental Health Center, in Jerusalem, Israel.

Gary Groth-Marnat is a Lecturer in Psychology at Curtin University, in Perth, Australia.

Gary L. Hansen is an Associate Extension Professor of Sociology at the University of Kentucky, in Lexington, Kentucky.

Ralph W. Hood, Jr. is Professor of Psychology at the University of Tennessee at Chattanooga.

Janet L. Jacobs is Assistant Professor of Women's Studies at the University of Colorado, Boulder.

Harold G. Koenig is Assistant Professor of Psychiatry at Duke University Medical Center in Durham, North Carolina.

David B. Larson is an Associate Professor of Psychiatry on the Clinical Faculty of Duke University Medical Center in Durham, North Carolina.

John S. Lyons is Associate Professor of Psychology at Northwestern University Medical School in Chicago, Illinois.

H. Newton Malony is Professor of Psychology in the Graduate School of Psychology at Fuller Theological Seminary, Pasadena, California.

Kevin S. Masters is Assistant Professor of Psychological Science at Ball State University, in Muncie, Indiana.

Peter Pressman is a doctoral candidate in clinical psychology at Northwestern University Medical School, in Chicago, Illinois.

Raymond H. Prince is Director of the Division of Social and Transcultural Psychiatry at McGill University, Montreal, Canada.

James T. Richardson is Professor of Sociology and Judicial Studies at the University of Nevada, Reno.

John F. Schumaker is Senior Lecturer in Psychology, Department of Psycho-Social Health Studies, at the University of Newcastle, in Newcastle, Australia.

Edward P. Shafranske is Associate Professor of Psychology, Graduate School of Education and Psychology, Pepperdine University, in Culver City, California.

John D. Shea is a Senior Lecturer in Psychology at the University of Newcastle, in Newcastle, Australia.

Bernard Spilka is Professor of Psychology at the University of Denver, in Denver, Colorado.

Steven Stack is Professor of Sociology at Wayne State University, in Detroit, Michigan.

Joseph B. Tamney is Professor of Sociology at Ball State University, in Muncie, Indiana.

Eliezer Witztum is a Senior Psychiatrist at the Jerusalem Mental Health Center, in Jerusalem, Israel.

Sheryl Zika is a doctoral candidate in psychology at Massey University, in Palmerston North, New Zealand.

RELIGION AND MENTAL HEALTH

Introduction

John F. Schumaker

Religion and mental health are two topics that continue to intrigue specialists and lay people alike. Each has been viewed in any number of lights, and ample controversy surrounds both areas of study. The same is true for the ways in which religion and mental health are thought to relate to one another, which is precisely the subject matter of this book.

Many people have ventured the argument that religion is generally beneficial to mental health. Among the numerous rationales to support this position is that religion (1) reduces existential anxiety by offering cognitive structure whereby pacifying explanations and attributions serve to order an otherwise chaotic world; (2) offers a sense of hope, meaning, and purpose along with a resultant sense of emotional well-being; (3) provides a reassuring fatalism that enables one to better withstand suffering and pain; (4) affords solutions to a wide array of situational and emotional conflicts; (5) partially solves the disturbing problem of mortality by way of afterlife beliefs; (6) gives people a sense of power and control through association with an omnipotent force; (7) establishes self-serving and other-serving moral guidelines, while suppressing self-destructive practices and lifestyles; (8) promotes social cohesion; (9) offers a well focused social identity and satisfies belongingness needs by uniting people around shared understandings; and (10) provides a foundation for cathartic collectively enacted ritual. Such a list of purported functions reminds one of Pruyser's (1971) assertion that, psychologically, religion is equivalent to an elaborate human "rescue operation" (p. 80).

Some people would want to qualify these and other claims about the purported ability of religion to act in the service of mental health, while others would disagree altogether with the notion that religion constitutes psychological "rescue." In fact, a number of individuals have elaborated on the ways in which religion (or some types of religion) can be detrimental to psychological health. Among other things, it has been argued that religion has the potential to: (1) generate unhealthy levels of guilt; (2) promote self-denigration and low self-esteem by way of beliefs that devalue our fundamental nature, or aspects of our nature; (3) establish a foundation for the unhealthy repression of anger; (4) create anxiety and fear by way of beliefs in punishment (e.g., hell) for our "evil" ways; (5) impede self-direction and a sense of internal control, while acting as an obstacle to personal growth and autonomous functioning; (6) foster dependency, conformity, and suggestibility, with a resultant over-reliance on forces or groups external to oneself; (7) inhibit the expression of sexual feelings, and pave the way for sexual maladjustment; (8) encourage the view that the world is divided into camps of mutually exclusive "saints" and "sinners" which, in turn, increases hostility and lowers tolerance toward the "other"; (9) instill an ill-founded paranoia concerning malevolent forces that threaten one's moral integrity; and (10) interfere with rational and critical thought.

Certain theoretical approaches have even considered religion *itself* to be a direct expression of either mental illness or mental health. For example, Spiro (1965) asked, "How can we be sure that religious behavior is not abnormal behavior, requiring psychiatric, rather than sociocultural analysis?" (p. 100). He justified this question on the grounds that religion involves serious impairment of psychological functioning in the form of (1) cognitive distortion in which logically unfounded beliefs are entertained as true; (2) perceptual distortion wherein stimuli are perceived as something other than what they are; and (3) affective distortion that is associated with religious activity and experience. Spiro concluded that religion should be regarded as "absolute insanity" that serves as health-giving culturally constituted defense mechanisms (also see Schumaker, 1990, 1991). Ellis (1975) depicted religion as "mental sickness . . . that *must* make you self-depreciating and dehumanized" (p. 440). Then there is Freud's (1964/1927) frequently cited allegation that religion is a "universal neurosis" which spares us "the task of forming a personal neurosis" (p. 77). By sharp contrast, people of differing persuasions have viewed religion as a direct display of optimal reality contact and psychological health. From this view have emerged various psychotherapies that employ religion to ameliorate psychological disturbance.

A large proportion of thinkers take a well-reasoned middle ground, maintaining that religion has the *potential* to be either positive or negative in its effects on mental health. They claim that religion is subject to endless variations in structure, content, and orientation, all of which serve to establish any particular religion as a psychological asset or liability, or neither. In this vein, Roberts (1953) wrote that religion can be health-giving and beneficial, or inhibiting and pathological. Spilka, Hood, and Gorsuch (1985) concluded that religion can serve several different functions. It can safeguard mental health by acting as a haven from life's difficulties, or it can be a hazard by infusing people with "abnormal mental content and abnormal motives" (Spilka et al., 1985, p. 305). They add that religion has the potential to be a "therapy" but that religion itself can "sponsor the expression of psychological abnormality" (p. 291).

This book was not approached with the intention of resolving the argument in an either-or fashion. In fact, the contributors themselves come from various backgrounds and have widely differing personal views about religion. Instead, this volume strives to present some recent theory and research that promises to enhance understanding of the complex interface between religion and mental health. Although a great deal remains to be learned, the past decade has afforded a large corpus of work in this area. It has also seen a general resurgence of investigative interest in the myriad of relationships between religion and various specific dimensions of mental health.

In the course of their respective chapters in this book, many contributors make reference to the research limitations that have plagued this area of study. Most studies are correlational in nature, making it impossible to draw conclusions about the impact of religion on mental health or the impact of a person's mental health status on religious belief. In many cases, ill-conceived sample selection makes meaningful generalization difficult or impossible. A great many studies have employed college students as the sample population, while others included in their samples only people who were religious or who were members of a church. Very little research has used experimental methodologies that permit mental health comparisons between individuals of widely varying religious intensities. This is a serious problem since it is becoming apparent that the relationship of religion to mental health is not a linear one. In fact, Masters and Bergin (chapter 17) raise the possibility that small amounts of religion may do nothing but "bug" people, while other investigators have suggested that only very high levels of religion are associated with significant mental health advantages. Completely irreligious people are an especially neglected group, and we have yet to appreciate the ways in which a very low level of religious belief/involvement relates to psychological adjustment. Likewise, not enough attention has been paid to religiosity among populations with specific patterns of psychopathology. The sparsity of longitudinal research limits understanding of the interaction between religion and mental health variables as people progress through the life cycle.

Other research shortcomings reveal themselves in this book, limitations that should inhibit any tendency to rush toward definitive statements and final conclusions. Nevertheless increased awareness of the need to upgrade the quality of research on religion and mental health has resulted in improved research methods that continue to become more sophisticated. As new patterns begin to emerge, long-standing confusions and contradictions are becoming clarified.

Much of the historical difficulty in understanding the interconnectedness between religion and mental health lies in the extremely broad nature of these constructs. Each can be defined in any number of ways. What is clear above all else is that the relationship between religion and mental health is largely dependent upon the definitions one chooses. In fact, some definitions differ so dramatically from one another that the actual valence of the relationship between religion and mental health can shift. Since this is an ongoing complication, we might consider briefly some of the ways in which the two concepts have been circumscribed.

Conceptualizing Religion

It is generally conceded that religion must be understood as a multidimensional form of behavior, and also one that has almost endless potential modes of expression. This point is made explicitly by Wilson (1978) who wrote that "Religion is not a homogenous whole. Individuals who are religious in one respect might not be in another . . . religion is multidimensional" (p. 442).

The different definitions of religion tend to emphasize selected aspects of the overall process. For example, Spiro (1966) stressed social involvement with deities in describing religion as "an institution consisting of culturally patterned interaction with culturally postulated superhuman beings" (p. 96). Such definitions have been criticized on the grounds that some religions (e.g., Buddhism) do not involve obvious deities. By contrast, Smith (1978) focused on intrapersonal elements in defining religion as "a dialectical process between the mundane and the transcendent . . . whose locus is in the personal faith and lives of men and women, not altogether observable and not to be confined within any intelligible limits" (p. 187).

Lenski (1963) highlighted the cognitive and ritualistic aspects of religion in defining religion as "a system of beliefs about the nature of the force(s) ultimately shaping man's destiny, and the practices associated therewith, shared by members of a group" (p. 331). Religion was viewed by Geertz (1966) largely in terms of meaning and motivation and the methods by which these are integrated in action systems: "Religion is a system of symbols which acts to establish powerful, pervasive and long-lasting moods and motivations . . . by formulating conceptions of a general order of existence and clothing these conceptions with such an aura of factuality that the moods and motivations seem uniquely realistic" (p. 4).

Religion is sometimes understood within the context of the existential dilemmas into which the human being is born. For instance, Bellah (1971) postulated that religion and its related rituals were a direct consequence of the fundamentally problematic nature of existence. Accordingly, religion is "that symbolic form through which man comes to terms with the antimonies of his being" (Bellah, 1971, p. 50). Allport (1950) also emphasized existential concerns and goals when he described religion as "a man's audacious bid to bind himself to creation and the Creator. It is his ultimate attempt to enlarge and to complete his own personality by finding the supreme context in which he rightly belongs." (p. 142). Likewise, Erikson (1958) described religion as an ordering force capable of offering a meaningful translation of "the exceeding darkness which surrounds man's existence, and the light which pervades it beyond all discrete comprehension" (p. 21).

As Giddens (1989) noted regarding the multifaceted nature of religion, all religions share certain common elements. They all involve a set of *symbols* which invoke feelings of reverence or awe. These are associated with *rituals* which, in turn, are practiced by people who entertain a specific *belief*. Glock (1962) put forward a five-part model of religion consisting of the following dimensions: (1) ideological (a person's *beliefs*); (2) intellectual (information and knowledge about faith, scriptures, etc.); (3) ritualistic (overt, institutional actions culturally defined as "religious"); (4) periential (direct knowledge of ultimate reality arising from religious emotion and/or experience); and (5) consequential (the secular effects of the other four dimensions of religious involvement).

Fromm's (1950) definition of religion addressed the cognitive, interactional, and ritualistic dimensions of religion in defining it as "a system of ideas, norms, and rites that satisfy a need that is rooted in human existence, the need for a system of orientation and an object of devotion" (see Funk, 1982, p. 294).

While some of the above definitions might be useful, controversy will certainly continue to surround the nearly impossible task of delineating what is meant by religion. Some thinkers, such as Allport (1967), have suggested that the concept of "religion" is too broad for discriminating use. Even so, for the purpose of empirical study, many researchers have found it necessary to somehow make the concept of religion operational so that its relation to mental health can be studied. Without question, knowledge has increased considerably through the resulting quantitative analysis in this area. However, for practical purposes, many studies have quantified religion in such a way that they do not take into account its multidimensional nature.

Some research has used range or intensity of religious belief as the primary measure, thus concentrating on the cognitive dimension of religion. Other studies have measured religion on the basis of frequency of church attendance or degree of participation in church-related activities. Such measures might allow assessment of the relative benefits of social affiliation and ritual enactment in the religious context, but care must be taken not to generalize beyond the limits of the specific index of religiosity. In fact, King and Hunt (1975) assert that there are as many as 21 different factors that make up religiosity. So, in drawing conclusions about the relationship of religion to mental health, it should be remembered that most studies only deal with a small number of these factors, and sometimes only a single factor.

A great deal more work is necessary to more exactly delineate religious factors. The same is true with regard to the different "types" or "kinds" of religion that have emerged in the literature. For instance, a distinction is often made between "intrinsic" and "extrinsic" religion, a basic dichotomy deriving from the work of Allport and Ross (1967). Although these types of religion are themselves a subject of debate, *intrinsic religiousness* usually refers to religion as a "meaning-endowing framework" (Donahue, 1985) that constitutes some sort of *end* in a person's life. By contrast, extrinsic religion is usually regarded as a *means,* or more specifically, a self-serving vehicle by which to achieve comfort and to adapt to social convention. See Masters and Bergin (chapter 17, this volume) for a detailed discussion of the development of the intrinsic-extrinsic dichotomy, and for an overview of the relationships between different religious orientations and mental health.

Much of the motivation underlying recent typologies has stemmed from the desire to separate "healthy" religion from "unhealthy" religion. This dates back at least as far as William James (1902), who differentiated between "healthy-mindedness" and the "sick soul." Allport (1950) extended his theory of mature versus immature personality to include the concepts of mature and immature religion. He described mature, or healthy, religion as "a disposition, built up through experience, to respond favorably . . . to conceptual objects and principles that the individual regards as of ultimate importance in his own life, and as having to do with what he regards as permanent or central in the nature of things" (Allport, 1950, p. 56). Allport's efforts to separate healthy from unhealthy religion were then further developed in the distinction between intrinsic and extrinsic religion (Allport & Ross, 1967).

The intrinsic-extrinsic dichotomy was extended by Batson and Ventis (1982) to include a generally positive religious orientation in the form of "quest." Their rationale for this stemmed from their feeling that Allport's dichotomy did not leave room for a mature type of religiosity entailing "skepticism of traditional orthodox religious answers, and a sense of incompleteness and tentativeness" (p. 236). They also wrote of the quest orientation that it is an "open-ended and questioning" type of religion, one that "involves honestly facing existential questions in all their complexity, while resisting clear-cut, pat answers" (p. 150).

Adorno, Frenkel-Brunswik, Levinson, and Sanford (1950) contrasted "serious" religion with "neutralized" religion. Serious religion was thought to be healthier since it revolved around personally experienced belief, whereas neutralized religion was used "to gain some immediate practical advantage or to aid in the manipulation of other people" (Adorno et al., 1950, p. 733). In a somewhat similar way, Ashbrook (1966) distinguished between "moral commitment" and "calculative involvement."

Erich Fromm (1950) argued for a qualitative division between "humanistic" and "authoritarian" religion. Of these, humanistic religion was seen to be healthier since it centered on human strength and the virtue of *self-realization*. In this religious mode, God was viewed as a symbol of humankind's *own* power and not as an entity having power *over* human beings. By contrast, in authoritarian religion, human beings allow themselves to be controlled by a deity that is regarded as deserving of reverence, worship, and obedience. In Fromm's words, "the main virtue of this type of religion is obedience, its cardinal sin is disobedience" (p. 35).

Allen and Spilka (1967) contrasted "committed" and "consensual" forms of religiosity. Of these two, committed religion was more health-giving since it entailed "a high sense of perspective combined with a flexible approach to faith and life" (Spilka & Werme, 1971, p. 465). This pattern of religious involvement was thought to be more likely to provide life meaning, expressive emotional outlets, and therapeutic resolution of personal and situational conflict. On the other hand, consensual religion was described as less conducive to psychological health since such religionists were "marked by a shallow and restrictive mode of thinking which results in a simple conformist orientation to life" (Spilka & Werme, 1971, p. 465). In the process, the individual becomes a mere extension of conventional cultural dictates, which leads to suppression of personal feeling and emotion.

Pruyser (1977) contrasted "healthy religion" with "neurotic religion," or what he referred to as the potentially "seamy side of religion" (p. 329). More recently, Spilka (1989) drew on General Attribution Theory in classifying religion as either "functional" or "dysfunctional" in nature. In that dichotomy, religion served a functional role if it fostered attributions that met a person's need for meaning, self-esteem, and a sense of personal control. Additionally, this kind of religion was seen to contain religious meanings that furthered freedom and advanced a person's potential and development. Conversely, Spilka wrote that dysfunctional religion involves religious meanings "that lead to dogmatism, restrict thought and limit freedom and opportunity, distort reality, separate people, and arouse fear and anxiety" (p. 6).

Much of this book deals with the specific conditions under which religion is either beneficial, detrimental, or of no consequence in relation to mental health. Given the highly complex and mulitdimensional nature of religion, the reader should appreciate that it is not possible to arrive at a single, all-embracing conclusion. Certain individual, social, or situational factors will reveal religion's "functional" side, whereas religion's "dysfunctional" side will be apparent when other factors are in place.

Conceptualizing Mental Health

Allport (1967) made the cogent observation that, in the broadest sense, all human life is "psychologically marginal" (p. 83). Consequently, to say that someone is "mentally healthy" may be to ignore the ongoing psychological struggles and adjustment problems that are an inevitable feature of human existence. Conversely, to conclude that a person somehow lacks mental health is almost certain to ignore the many ways in which that individual operates effectively and in accord with guidelines for appropriate behavior.

Like religion, there are many ways to understand and define "mental health." The construct overlaps with that of "mental disturbance" (or mental illness) in that both usually assume a continuum (or set of continua) along which it is possible to gauge degrees of mental health or ill-health. Yet, it is an exceedingly slippery concept that is inextricably tied to the equally elusive concept of "normality." Some of the difficulty in coming to terms with the notion of normality can be traced to the language used to describe and judge behavior. We usually attach *primary* meaning to the word "abnormal," which in turn inclines us to define "normal" as "not abnormal." The same is true for the vast array of words that imply abnormality.

For instance, our vocabulary would allow us quite easily to describe a person who is compulsive, the reason again being that "compulsive" has primary meaning. But most people would be at a loss to adequately describe someone who is "normal" on the basis of *not* being compulsive. Furthermore, it is insufficient to depict normality in this case as the opposite of compulsiveness. A person who is the opposite of compulsive could be equally maladjusted (maybe uncontrollably "expulsive," as Freud described that trait). In general, then, our system of language predisposes us to depict normality and mental health as extensions of our conceptions (and verbalizations) of abnormality and mental ill-health. For this reason, most treatises on "mental health" are at least partially contextualized in terms of behaviors deemed to be abnormal, or mentally unhealthy.

The situation is further complicated by the numerous ways in which abnormality can be defined and understood. These include: (1) personal suffering; (2) maladaptiveness, wherein a behavior interferes with individual or social well-being; (3) irrationality or incomprehensibility; (4) unpredictability and/or loss of control; (5) unconventionality; (6) observer discomfort; or (7) violation of moral or ideal standards (Rosenhan & Seligman, 1984). Moreover, in the context of cross-cultural variations in normative behavior, the actual concepts of normality and abnormality become virtually useless.

Some humanistically oriented thinkers have urged us to recognize that normality (in the sense of being not abnormal) does not necessarily imply that one is living in a healthy or satisfying manner. Jahoda (1958) referred to "positive mental health" while Rosenhan and Seligman (1984) preferred the term "optimal living." Both allow mental health to be evaluated according to degrees of positive attributes, such as personal growth and development, autonomous functioning, self-love, environmental competence, degree of insight and wisdom, the exercise of rationality, the realization of one's potential, the joy derived from life, and so forth. The concept of "self-actualization" (Maslow, 1971; Rogers, 1961) embraces many of these healthy qualities (see chapter 9, this volume, by Joseph B. Tamney).

A conceptualization of mental health (or its lack) is additionally hampered by the existence of distinctly different schools of thought in psychology and related fields of study. Each has a somewhat different notion of what underlies mental health, and each has a different view on the way that psychological health expresses itself behaviorally. Without spelling these out in detail, their disparate assertions mean that religion's perceived influence on mental health will vary depending upon the school of thought that one endorses. The reason for this is obvious. In one school, the behaviors considered indicative of mental health may relate closely to the behavioral ideals within society's dominant religion(s). By contrast, the mentally "healthy" behaviors of another theoretical school may be at relative odds with religion's behavioral ideals. Stated otherwise, religion may engender behaviors and attitudes that are consonant with mental health for some psychological schools, but not others.

One might speculate, for example, that religion is more likely to be viewed as having a deleterious effect on mental health when humanistic definitions of mental health are employed. In defending such a hypothesis, one could isolate key features of humanistic mental health, such as *self*-actualization, *self*-fulfillment, *self*-knowledge, *self*-determination, emancipation from external sources of control, and so forth. It could then be argued that at least some types of religion (e.g., fundamentalist Christianity) foster behaviors and behavioral ideals that are somewhat incompatible with humanistic models of optimal psychological health.

Batson and Ventis (1982) demonstrated quite clearly that the way in which one defines mental health will, to some extent, determine how religion *appears* to affect mental health. They analyzed the *direction* of the relationship between religion and mental health by applying seven different definitions for mental health. Whether mental health was positively related, negatively related, or unrelated to religion was determined by the mental health criteria employed. Their work indicated that humanistic criteria of mental health (e.g., self-actualization, self-acceptance) are more likely than other sets of criteria to depict religion as detrimental to psychological health. It has since been shown, however, that the relationship between religion and humanistic mental health criteria (e.g., self-actualization) changes as a function of specific religious orientations (Watson, Hood, & Morris, 1984; Watson, Morris, & Hood, 1990).

Instead of identifying themselves with a single definition, many mental health professionals have come to view mental health as a *composite* of emotion, cognition, perception, and sensation. In any one person, this composite translates into a pattern of experience and behavior by which to assess that person's *overall* state of psychological health. But, in viewing mental health as a composite, one would expect to find a considerable amount of variation among the numerous factors that contribute to the totality of mental health/ill-health. Therefore everyone's psychological world probably contains both "healthy" and "unhealthy" elements. Furthermore, as this volume will reveal, there is no reason to suspect that religion will relate similarly to all subcomponents of mental health.

It seems unrealistic to expect that definitive conclusions will ever be possible concerning religion and all-encompassing conceptions of mental health. A more reasonable approach assumes that mental health is, in fact, a constellation of variables that have differing relationships to religion. In line with this logic, the present volume is structured in such a way that religion is discussed in relation to specific dimensions of behavior. It will become apparent that religion (and the different types of religion) has a much different effect on some areas of functioning than others.

Before proceeding, however, let us briefly examine the conclusions of previous attempts to summarize the relationships between religion and mental health.

Previous Reviews

Different approaches have been used in an effort to synthesize and generalize about the relationships between religion and mental health. In some reviews, this relationship was summarized in terms of a finite number of factors related to mental health and situational adjustment. Other people preferred to group large numbers of studies, regardless of mental health category, in trying to uncover broader, more wide-ranging connections between religion (and religious types) and mental health.

Argyle and Beit-Hallahmi

In a chapter from *The Social Psychology of Religion,* Argyle and Beit-Hallahmi (1975/1958) reviewed empirical studies on what they termed "religion and personal adjustment." Of direct concern here are their conclusions about the associations of religion with (1) overall "personal adequacy," (2) ability to adjust to life crises, (3) suicide potential, (4) alcohol use/abuse, and (5) crime and delinquency.

On the matter of the relationship of religion to "personal adequacy," these investigators arrived at two generalizations: (1) in student populations, religiosity is related to personal *inadequacy;* (2) in adults (and especially the elderly) participation in public religious activities is *positively* related to measures of personal adjustment. They cautioned that these generalizations were based on correlational data, so they reserved judgment about the direction of causation. However, they did comment on their conclusion that religious orthodoxy was associated with better overall adjustment, or adequacy. In this regard, Argyle and Beit-Hallahmi speculated that the positive relationship between personal adjustment and formal religious participation can be explained on the basis that (1) a certain degree of personal functioning is a prerequisite for this and other forms of social participation, and (2) once involved, the group itself affords its members support, companionship, and a sense of identity and belonging.

Argyle and Beit-Hallahmi did not arrive at a clear conclusion regarding the ability of religion to function as an effective coping mechanism during times of situational crisis. While some research showed religion to be marginally helpful during crisis, they wrote, "Evidently, most people do not turn to the church, though they do resort to prayer, when emotionally disturbed" (p. 141). In addition, they saw reason to suspect that religion is being used less and less as a source of support during periods of crisis.

This review concluded that there was "some evidence" that religious involvement is associated with lower rates of suicide. However Argyle and Beit-Hallahmi did not find evidence that religious affiliation or degree of religiosity had a significant effect on likelihood of suicide attempts. According to their analysis, Protestants no longer have a higher risk of suicide than Catholics.

Research on religion and alcohol use led Argyle and Beit-Hallahmi to conclude that religion plays a role in the control of impulsive behavior, including alcohol consumption. They cited the possible exception of extremely strict religions which demand absolute abstinence. In their view, a "rebellion" response may explain the higher rates of alcoholism for people from such backgrounds.

Argyle reviewed research related to delinquent behavior, church membership, and church attendance. However, the findings were mixed and they did not generalize about that relationship. These reviewers also summarized research relating criminal activity to religious affiliation, but concluded that many previously cited differences could be understood in terms of social class variations.

James E. Dittes

Dittes's review chapter in *The Handbook of Social Psychology* (Vol. 5) (1969) is somewhat controversial since it operates from the assumption that people with "weak egos" are attracted to religion and that religion generally is associated with "deficiencies of personality" (p. 636). While conceding that religion can serve people in times of need, he stated that religion is associated with personal inadequacy, intellectual inadequacy, hypersuggestibility, and "desperate and generally unadaptive defensive maneuvers" (p. 636).

Dittes analyzed several studies dealing with religion and self-esteem and found contradictory results. If there was a trend regarding self-esteem, he added, it was that religion was "correlated with indices of pathology and deficiency" (p. 637).

According to Dittes's interpretation of the research, religion was also associated with unhealthy levels of dependency, as well as a pathological degree of suggestibility. He offered three potential explanations for religion's relationship to aberrant suggestibility: (1) hypersuggestibility represented a "general personal weakness or frustration" (p. 639) that sought and found support in the form of religion; (2) it indicated an "inhibition of personal initiative and a submissiveness to authority, reminiscent of 'superego' religion;" and (3) inordinately suggestible people might be drawn to institutional religion which is conventional and part of the cultural *status quo.*

In terms of research related to religion, personality constriction, and the use of defense mechanisms, Dittes commented that "a generally consistent correlation has been reported between orthodox religious commitment and a relatively defensive, constricted personality" (p. 639). The limited research available at the time prevented him from extending this generalization into the areas which he labeled "mental illness," "intropunitiveness," and "extrapunitiveness."

Victor D. Sanua

Sanua's research review in the *American Journal of Psychiatry* (1969) covered mental health variables under the headings of "psychological adjustment" and "deviancy and social pathology." In addition, he reviewed empirical work on the relationship between religion and personality, with specific focus given to prejudice, authoritarianism, and humanitarianism. At the outset, he made the sweeping statement that "the contention that religion as an institution has been instrumental in fostering general well-being, creativity, honesty, liberalism, and other qualities has not been supported by empirical data" (p. 1203).

With specific regard to religion and "psychological adjustment," Sanua concluded that "most studies show no relationship between religiousness and mental health, while others point out that the religious person may at times show greater anxiety and at times less anxiety" (p. 1206). He cited the lack of clear patterns as reason for additional research. Sanua made passing reference to the intrinsic-extrinsic religious dichotomy of Allport and Ross (1967), while advancing the view that "intrinsic" religion carried more psychology benefits at both the individual and collective levels. He even speculated about the possibility of restructuring religious education in such a way that would maximize the "intrinsic" orientation and minimize the "extrinsic" orientation.

On the subject of "deviancy and social pathology," Sanua examined a small and divergent body of research related to delinquency, antisocial behavior, alcoholism, and "moral integration of the community" (as measured by concern for the welfare of one's neighbors). In most instances, Sanua reaffirmed his general theme, namely that there is no convincing evidence that religion serves to deter deviancy or social pathology. This can be seen in his summational statement that "the evidence regarding the relationship between social pathology and religion points out that the latter may not necessarily fulfill the function ascribed to it—namely, that of an integrating force in society and a contributor to the mental health of the members of that society" (p. 1207). Despite what he termed this "startling" conclusion, he reiterated the need for further research in this subject area.

Rodney Stark

In an article in *Review of Religious Research,* Rodney Stark (1971) challenged the "hoary proposition . . . that religion is associated with psychopathology" (p. 165). After discounting the theory and logic sustaining this proposition, he analyzed the "scarce, dated, and usually very inferior" (p. 167) research in this area. He grouped studies into four categories: (1) religion and mental illness; (2) religion and psychic inadequacy; (3) religion and neurotic distrust; and (4) religion and authoritarianism.

Stark's analysis of data on outpatient mental patients revealed that psychiatric patients were far more likely than "normal" individuals to be of "no religious affiliation," more likely to view religion as "unimportant," and less likely to belong to a church congregation. He concluded that those data constituted support for his hypothesis "that mental illness and religious commitment are *negatively* related" (p. 169).

Stark constructed a measure of "psychic inadequacy" using data from a large United States national survey. Items in the survey measured degree of worry, proneness to loneliness, lack of self-perceived coping ability, and so forth. Four religious denomination groups were included in the analysis and, in each case, Stark found a *negative* relationship between religious commitment and psychopathology. Specifically, Stark deduced that "persons scoring high on psychic inadequacy are *less* likely to be high on religious orthodoxy than are persons scoring low on psychic inadequacy" (p. 169). However, Stark did concede that a time-order issue precluded a final decision regarding the direction of the relationships involved. That is, it remained unclear whether psychological health was the end result or the source of religious commitment.

Stark's conclusions about "neurotic distrust" were very similar to those for "psychic inadequacy." He concluded his survey analysis by saying that people with high degrees of neurotic distrust were significantly less likely to be high on religious orthodoxy, and to attend church regularly (regardless of religious denomination).

Stark's review led him to the overall conclusion that "whether psychopathology is measured by clinical diagnosis of severe impairment or by more inclusive and less severe survey indices, there is a negative relationship with religious commitment" (pp. 170–71). He further deduced that conventional expressions of religion were not a product of psychological processes. Rather, argued Stark, "psychopathology seems to *impede* the manifestation of conventional religious beliefs and activities" (p. 175).

Russell J. Becker

In a chapter from the book *Research on Religious Development*, Becker (1971) summarized the interaction of religion and psychological functioning while grouping previous research as follows: (1) religious belief studies; (2) religious practice studies; (3) religious feeling and subjective experience studies; (4) religious knowledge studies; and (5) religious effects (the "consequential" dimension) studies. However, in each case, he pointed to research shortcomings and methodological problems that precluded any definitive conclusions.

Becker did comment, very tentatively, that "certain favorable correlations" existed between religious identity/activity and psychological health as measured by "absence of mental illness and neurotic symptoms" (p. 415). But he tempered this by remarking that "the attempt to find detailed points of relationship between positive psychological traits and religion has produced very few clues" (p. 415).

Gary Lea

A review by Gary Lea (1982), which appeared in the *Journal of Religion and Health,* highlighted some of the methodological inadequacies that have plagued the study of religion and mental health. Among these was his observation that all but two percent of studies have been *correlational* in nature, thus rendering meaningful interpretation very difficult. Attention was also drawn to inadequate sampling techniques wherein subjects were drawn entirely from student groups or populations of religious people. In addition, Lea criticized many studies for failing to control for a wide range of demographic variables, such as socioeconomic status, sex, age, and ethnic background.

While Lea's review was not organized around clearly circumscribed categories of religion or mental health variables, he nonetheless arrived at some general conclusions about the previous two decades of research on this subject. Of direct relevance to the interface of religion and mental health were the following conclusions: (1) religiosity is detrimental to personal adjustment in students, but positively related to psychological health in adults, and especially the elderly (i.e., the previous summation by Argyle & Beit-Hallahmi, 1975/1958); (2) religiosity does not relate significantly to either social deviancy or moral behavior; (3) the hallmark of "healthy" religion is "social responsibility, and relatedness to other parts of life and to a being greater than oneself, however defined" (p. 347); and (4) "unhealthy" religion involves a preoccupation with guilt-generating concerns (e.g., sin, imperfection, one's "evil" nature), as well as "rigidity with respect to healthy sexual and emotional functioning, and idiosyncratic and literal interpretation of religious symbolism" (p. 347).

C. Daniel Batson and W. Larry Ventis

Batson and Ventis (1982) devoted a chapter of their book *The Religious Experience* to a review of religion and mental health. Their strategy was to condense numerous different measures of mental health into seven categories: (1) absence of mental illness (i.e., lack of symptoms); (2) appropriate social behavior; (3) freedom from worry and guilt; (4) personal competence and control; (5) self-acceptance and self-actualization; (6) unification and organization; and (7) openmindedness and flexibility. They then grouped previous studies of religion and mental health according to these seven sets of mental health criteria. This allowed Batson and Ventis to ascertain the *valence* of the relationship between religion and mental health as a function of the type of definition used to specify mental health.

Batson and Ventis demonstrated that the relationship between religion and mental health changes in relation to one's definition of mental health. More specifically, they found that religion tends to have a positive effect on mental health when mental health is defined in the traditional sense as an absence of psychological symptoms. However, when employing other definitions, they found that religion was more likely to be associated with impaired psychological functioning. This was especially the case when mental health was defined according to (1) personal competence and control; (2) self-acceptance or self-actualization; and (3) openmindedness and flexibility. The direction of the relationship was unclear in the other categories.

This review also attempted to establish the relative merits of intrinsic, extrinsic, and quest orientations in relation to the above-mentioned conceptions of mental health. The extrinsic religious orientation tended to have a negative relationship to mental health. In terms of specific definitions of mental health, extrinsic religion had a negative relationship to appropriate social behavior, freedom from worry and guilt, personal competence and control, and openmindedness and flexibility.

Intrinsic religion was shown to be positively related to all seven sets of mental health criteria. A scarcity of available data caused these reviewers to refrain from making firm conclusions regarding the "quest" orientation.

The lack of data in some mental health categories is one reason that the Batson and Ventis summation should be viewed with some caution. Additionally, theoretical and interpretive problems arise when one collapses a large number of mental health variables into a limited group of definitional categories. Unwittingly, one could easily include in the same category variables that have opposing relationships to religion. Another problem is that some of their definitions are themselves almost impossible to define. For example, concepts such as "unification" or "flexibility" or "competence" can have any number of meanings.

Allen E. Bergin

Bergin (1983) provided a review and "critical evaluation" of the relationship of religiosity and mental health in an article in the journal *Professional Psychology: Research and Practice.* This entailed a meta-analysis of 24 selected studies from the period 1951–1979.

Bergin presented his review as evidence against the contentious assertion of Ellis (1980) who wrote of people that "the less religious they are, the more emotionally healthy they will be" (p. 637). In the words of Bergin, his review offered "no support for the preconception that religiousness is necessarily correlated with psychopathology" (p. 170). In fact, only 23 percent of the effects examined showed a negative relationship between religion and mental health.

This review offered more support for claims that religion is beneficial to mental health. Bergin found that 47 percent of his selected research outcomes showed a positive relationship between religious and mental health variables, whereas a zero relationship was obtained in 30 percent of cases. However, this changed somewhat when only statistically significant results were included. When this was done, 77 percent showed no significant relationship between religion and mental health, 17 percent had a positive relationship, and 6 percent had a negative relationship.

Bergin concluded that religion is "a complex phenomenon with numerous correlates and consequences" (p. 170), most of which cannot be explained simply.

Bergin stated that the confusing mixture of positive and negative results were indicative of religion's multidimensional nature. In his view, the slight positive relationship between religion and mental health may be a deceptive *average* that disguises powerful relationships between *specific* religious and mental health variables. Of this, Bergin wrote that "positive effects of some *kinds* of religiosity are being balanced by negative effects of other kinds, which yield unimpressive or ambiguous average effects" (p. 180).

I. Reed Payne, Allen E. Bergin, Kimberly A. Bielema, and Paul H. Jenkins

In a review article appearing in *Prevention in Human Services,* I. Reed Payne and coworkers (1991) summarize religion in relation to the domains of (1) psychological adjustment; (2) social conduct; and (3) mental illness. Their overriding conclusion is that religion (or more specifically intrinsic/internalized religion) is a generally positive force in all of these areas. In contrast, extrinsic religion is depicted as putting up impediments to optimal functioning in each of these areas. It is argued that differential findings in terms of the intrinsic-extrinsic religious modes serve to dispel the "uniformity myth," the myth that all religious beliefs, practices, and commitments have an equal impact on psychological and psychosocial processes.

With regard to religion and psychological adjustment variables, Payne and his colleagues conclude that (intrinsic) religion tends to relate positively to a subjective sense of well-being, as well as measures of self-esteem. In examining religion's effect on mental health across the life span, their literature analysis leads them to describe religion as a promoter of mental health at all stages of life. However, they do not disregard the possibility that, in some cases, religious belief/activity can strengthen maladaptive defenses while offering only temporary escape from emotional conflict. A subsection is included to emphasize further the need to understand the interaction of religion and mental health in the context of healthy (i.e., intrinsic) and unhealthy (i.e., extrinsic) religious orientations.

On the matter of social conduct, the review considers the effect of religion on family functioning, premarital sex, alcohol and drug abuse, and suicide. While acknowledging certain limiting factors, the authors ascertain that religious affiliation/involvement shows a consistent positive correlation with a variety of prosocial behaviors. Specifically, they interpret available evidence as indicative of religious ability to foster marital adjustment, mitigate marital conflict and divorce, and enhance overall family cohesion. Religion is also portrayed as a socialization agent capable of inhibiting premarital sexual behavior and permissive sexual attitudes, while also serving as a potent deterrent to alcohol and drug abuse. According to the authors, available research points to an overall inverse relationship between suicide and degree of religious belief and involvement.

Payne and coworkers describe as ambiguous the relationship between undifferentiated religion and indexes of mental illness. They state that the studies conducted on truly disturbed populations can be divided into (1) those showing a disturbance among the more religious and (2) those showing no relationship between religion and disturbance. They add that this pattern bears a general resemblance to that found with normal populations, but they observe that mental illness has yet to be studied in relation to religious subtypes (e.g., intrinsic, extrinsic).

This review culminates with a series of generalizations and speculations about healthy religion. Most of these concur with Clinebell's (1970) analysis of religion as a "sleeping giant" (p. 46) with vast untapped potential to prevent psychological maladjustment, while simultaneously fostering positive mental health and personal growth.

John Gartner, David B. Larson, and George D. Allen

In their article in *Journal of Psychology and Theology,* Gartner, Larson, and Allen (1991) reviewed research on religion and twenty-one different measures of mental health. After doing so, they created three categories reflecting either a positive, negative, or ambiguous relationship between religion and mental health.

Those mental health variables that had a positive association with religiosity included suicide risk, drug usage, alcohol abuse, delinquent behavior, divorce and marital satisfaction, psychological well-being, and depression. Physical health and longevity were also found to be positively related to religion. Moreover, this review indicated that participation in religious activities and religiously-based psychotherapeutic interventions tended to be followed by improvement in psychological functioning.

Religion was found to relate negatively to five mental health variables: authoritarianism, self-actualization, suggestibility/dependency, temporal lobe epilepsy, and dogmatism/tolerance of ambiguity/rigidity. It revealed mixed findings for religion's relationship to six dimensions of mental health. Among these were anxiety, psychosis, self-esteem, sexual disorders, prejudice, and intelligence/education.

According to these researchers, many of the discrepant and contradictory findings are the result of the ways in which we measure both religion and mental health. They pointed out that most studies that reported a negative relationship between religion and mental health tended to rely on "soft" mental health measures (i.e., paper and pencil tests). By contrast, they observed that studies showing a positive relationship were more likely to use "hard variables" such as suicide rates, objective measures of drug and alcohol use, rates of delinquency, and so forth. This concurred with the findings of Bergin (1983) and Donahue (1985), who also observed that studies linking religion and psychopathology tended to use "intrapsychic" measures of mental health, while behavioral measures were more typical of research which found religion to be an asset to psychological health.

A few additional patterns derived from this review. For example, the authors concluded that a lack of religious commitment was associated with disorders of "impulse control," (e.g., antisocial behavior, suicide, drug and alcohol abuse). On the other hand, religious involvement increased the likelihood of "over-control" problems, such as "rigidity." They also concluded that certain measures of religious behavior (most notably church attendance and other forms of religious participation) were more strongly related to mental health than religiosity as measured by attitude scales. This, they added, was especially true in cases where positive relationships were reported between religion and mental health. Finally, Gartner, Larson, and Allen noted that the intrinsic-extrinsic dichotomy can be useful in explaining a number of apparently inconsistent findings in this area.

Organization and Content of this Volume

This book is divided into four sections. The first, titled "Historical Perspectives," includes chapters that trace the development of thought on the subject of religion and mental health. In addition, this section includes chapters that cover specialized subject areas within a larger historical framework.

Part I

Chapter 1. Jacob A. Belzen provides historical background of European views on the relationship between religion and psychological disturbance. This area of study, labeled the "Psychopathology of Religion," chronicles the historical dualism that has existed regarding the supposed causes of aberrant behavior. With Hippocrates and Aristotle as starting points, Belzen recounts the ways in which spiritual and/or somatic origins have been postulated in an effort to understand culturally deviant patterns of behavior. In the process he distinguishes between two broad schools of thought, namely the "psychicists" and the "somaticists." The former stressed the unity of body and soul, a stance that precluded the possibility that mental illness was only a manifestation of defective bodily processes.

By contrast, the "somaticists" argued for a dualism of body and soul, but one in which the soul was deemed impervious to dysfunction. As Belzen shows, this paved the way for monistic materialism and reductionistic theories that accounted for mental disturbance in strictly physical terms. He brings this discussion forward in time and shows how contemporary theories (e.g., psychoanalysis, phenomenology, historical-cultural theory) address the age-old differentiation of spirit ("psyche") and body ("soma"). Belzen concludes his analysis with a general discussion and critique of the way in which various psychological schools have dealt with the matter of religion.

Chapter 2. Robert A. Bridges and Bernard Spilka write about religion with special reference to the mental health of women. They call attention to the ways in which the majority of world religions (including Judaism, Christianity, Islam, Hinduism, and Buddhism) have placed women in a secondary position to men. They maintain that, as an integral part of the religio-cultural heritage of many nations, this organization of sex roles has been a major cause of conflict, frustration, stress and mental disorder among women. With special reference to the Judeo-Christian tradition, Bridges and Spilka offer a general perspective on religion and mental health that emphasizes the human needs for meaning, control, and self-esteem. They discuss scripture, theology, and psychological research and theory in showing how religion offers negative meanings to women, thus reducing their sense of personal control and lowering their self-esteem. According to these authors, the result may be depression, agoraphobia, and other adjustment problems that disproportionately affect women. However, Bridges and Spilka do not discount the complexity of religion or the ways in which it can enhance mental health. They conclude with a discussion of new and constructive theological developments as well as some new directions for research related to religion and women's psychological health.

Chapter 3. John F. Schumaker examines theory and research concerning the mental health consequences of irreligion. The chapter begins with a discussion of the prevalence of irreligion in various societies, as well as some demographic factors that are related to irreligiosity. Space is devoted to theories which attempt to explain modern irreligion. It is pointed out that irreligion in its present form did not exist prior to the eighteenth century, and that its emergence was the result of several social developments originating at that time. Although mental health studies of irreligious people are rare and methodologically flawed, available evidence suggests that very low levels of irreligiosity are associated with increased symptoms of psychopathology. Schumaker attempts to explain this historically in terms of the "cognitive crisis" brought about by an absence of transcendent explanation, as well as the important source of group-enacted ritual which irreligious people lack. Mention is given to the "private" (or improvised) types of "religion" that irreligious people often substitute for traditional modes of religiosity. However, he points out that such religious surrogates are less conducive to psychological health than their more conventional religious counterparts. Schumaker concludes by noting the ways in which traditional religion itself has changed and partially succumbed to irreligious forces. The result is that religious people are themselves partially divested of age-old pathways to mental health.

Chapter 4. John D. Shea gives a historical discussion of the relationship between religion and sexual expression/adjustment. He examines the pagan origins of Christian antipathy to sex, noting the break from the mainstream tolerance of diverse sexual experience in the ancient world. Reference is made to the ways in which church rules about sex became more specific, with certain key figures adding their own qualities to the message of repression. Shea observes that the medical profession, spurred on by an extraordinary commitment to its Christian origins, eventually joined Christianity in the repression of sexuality. It introduced a body of pseudo-scientific nonsense, including the infamous theory of masturbatory insanity which condemned people (and especially women) to another couple of centuries of sexual fear and anxiety.

Shea takes the topic into the twentieth century and offers data that demonstrate a direct association between Christian religious conviction and sexual inhibition, with the consequences extending into the areas of marriage, the experience of childbirth, and childrearing. He also uses the data to argue that changes in sexual experience during the twentieth century can be interpreted as a move away from the limitations imposed by Christian beliefs and teachings. In Shea's analysis, the weakened influence of the Christian church has also weakened its power to destroy the binding force in human intimate relationships. Yet he cautions that it may be some time before a stable new sexual philosophy will replace the sexual negativism of Christianity. Shea refers to certain non-Christian religions which offer more sex-positive models of sexuality.

Part II

The seven chapters of Part II examine religion in relation to different aspects of emotion and cognition.

Chapter 5. Steven Stack's chapter discusses the relationships between religiosity, depression, and suicide. His literature review shows that recent research has not supported Durkheim's theory that religions with a high number of rules and activities (e.g., Catholicism) are relatively more effective in reducing suicide risk. Stack describes a second theory, developed in the early 1980s, that targets certain specific beliefs as more effective than others in deterring suicide. One example might be the belief that those who persevere will be rewarded with a favorable afterlife. Stack's review shows that a slight majority of recent studies support such a theory. He also elaborates on a new "networks" perspective wherein it is contended that religion will have its greatest impact in an area where it has been historically strong, and where it has developed an infrastructure of supportive networks for its constituents. However, he also comments on certain contradictions in available research in this area. Stack's research review suggests that religion is able to muster a protective shield against depression. However, he calls for large scale epidemiological work in this area, especially in light of the nonrepresentative samples that were typically used in this research area.

Chapter 6. The interactions of religion, anxiety, and fear of death are the focus of this chapter by Peter Pressman, John S. Lyons, David B. Larson, and John Gartner. They make the observation that anxiety, like religion, is a ubiquitous and insufficiently understood phenomenon. Their analysis of the confusing literature on the linkages between religion and anxiety suggests that religion has the potential to increase or decrease anxiety, depending on various factors. Some of the discrepancies in the research are explained in terms of the forms of religiousness that were chosen for study. For example, they cite evidence that somatic manifestations of anxiety correlate negatively with religious participation of a public nature, but positively with private religiosity. They describe age as another variable that might mediate the value of religion in relation to the regulation of anxiety. It is also suggested that different religious orientations (e.g., intrinsic versus extrinsic) correlate differently with the experience of anxiety.

Pressman and colleagues also describe the rather complicated relationship between religion and death anxiety. They cite research that indicates that religiosity has an effect on certain aspects of death anxiety, but possibly not the global construct of "death anxiety" as that term is generally defined. In this context, they discuss "fear of the unknown" (i.e., what happens after death) in terms of religious motivation. They also raise the possibility that there is a curvilinear relationship between religion and death anxiety, with extremes of religiosity being associated with lower levels of anxiety. These authors conclude with a discussion of various methodological problems that have made it difficult to understand the influence of religion on anxiety, including death anxiety. Specific guidelines for future research are outlined in an effort to promote more rigorous and potentially fruitful methods of investigation in this area.

Chapter 7. Ralph W. Hood, Jr., integrates a diverse literature on sin, guilt, and shame within different faith traditions, while concentrating on implications for self-esteem. In so doing, Hood makes reference to empirical, psychoanalytic, and phenomenological studies in this area. Hood draws attention to the crude measures of religiosity that have characterized empirical research, and observes that no consistent relationship between religion and self-esteem emerges when religion is measured globally. However, patterns do appear when more sophisticated measures of religion are employed. For example, intrinsic religion is associated with positive self-esteem and lower levels of guilt. By contrast, extrinsic religion is related to poorer self-esteem and enhanced guilt feelings.

Hood also discusses these variables in relation to God images while showing that intrinsic religion is associated with benevolent God images, less guilt, and increased self-esteem. On the other hand, extrinsic religion relates to punitive God images, more guilt, and lower self-esteem. Hood also examines the psychoanalytic and phenomenological literature, as well as the hermeneutical work on St. Augustine's *Confessions.* Hood concludes with empirical clarifications indicating that, within faith traditions, guilt, sin, and self-esteem operate in a complex manner. In this regard, he writes that the religiously devout (especially the intrinsic type) are allowed to experience both guilt and relief from guilt, thereby paving the way for enhanced self-esteem.

Chapter 8. James E. Alcock discusses the relationship between religion and rationality. He notes that religion continues to play a central role in the lives of many millions of people around the world. Alcock adds that, in our era of science and technology, supernatural belief (both religious and nonreligious) survives because it gives meaning to life and offers relief from anxiety, including existential anxiety. It is argued that most people partition their beliefs so that religious principles rarely intrude into domains where rationality is most efficacious. However, Alcock notes that, for some, religion dominates everything, not only jeopardizing rational thought and behavior, but sometimes also producing detrimental effects on their psychological well-being. In this regard, he observes that fundamentalism, dogmatism, and authoritarianism, rather than religion per se, constitute the real threats to Reason.

Chapter 9. Joseph B. Tamney expounds on the relationship between religion and self-actualization, both at the level of the individual and society. It is pointed out that Maslow's ideal (i.e., self-actualized) person is not anti-spiritual. In fact, as Tamney explains, Maslow's truly healthy person is priestlike, mysticlike, and godlike. Nonetheless, we are reminded that Maslow did consider organized religion to be an obstacle to self-actualization. This reflects the difficulty in reconciling religion based on belief in a transcendent deity with a model of mental health wherein the ultimately healthy person is seen as godlike in nature. Tamney reviews empirical research that shows a consistent negative relationship between religiosity and measures of self-actualization. However, Tamney notes that most studies failed to measure directly those Christian attributes that are incongruent with self-actualization.

While again noting that Maslow did not regard self-actualizers as anti-religious, Tamney stresses the importance of analyzing the effects of specific religious traditions on the self-actualization process. He also discusses self-actualization in the context of a cultural shift toward "postmaterialism," one that facilitates self-actualization on a large scale, but also one whereby traditional religion diminishes in importance. He summarizes his own research, which reveals that self-actualization is least valued by Christian Rightists since they actively reject the goals of self-actualization. Tamney also mentions the possibility that religion can indirectly influence self-actualization by swaying public opinion and shaping structural and cultural conditions.

Chapter 10. Kerry Chamberlain and Sheryl Zika present research findings on the relationship between religiosity, psychological well-being, and meaning in life.

They write that meaning in life can be conceptualized as an integral part of religiosity, as a component of well-being, or as an independent construct. They argue that religion may provide one, among many, possible sources of meaning in life, and that meaning is best considered as a separate construct.

Chamberlain and Zika elaborate on two of their own studies, the first of which involved mothers of young children as well as a group of elderly people. Religiosity was found to have a limited positive association with well-being, one that was reduced when meaning in life was controlled for. Confirmation of this finding came from the second study, which used two religious groups (Roman Catholics and Pentecostals), as well as a multidimensional measure of religiosity. They conclude that religiosity may influence well-being more strongly as the salience of religion increases, and that any association of religiosity with well-being may have its route through meaning.

Chapter 11. Leslie J. Francis reviews research related to religion and the Eysenckian constructs of neuroticism and psychoticism. He begins with a discussion of fundamental issues related to the definition of religion and mental health, and what it is that constitutes a positive or negative relationship between the two. With these in mind, Francis presents psychometric equations utilizing Eysenck's dimensional model of personality, according to which neurotic and psychotic disorders lie towards the extreme poles of two orthogonal dimensions of normal personality. He then reviews theoretical and empirical relationships between religion and these two variables. Francis draws the overall conclusion that there is no evidence to suggest that religious people experience lower levels of mental health, but some clear evidence that they enjoy higher levels of mental health. Specifically, Francis's research review shows a consistent inverse relationship between religion and psychoticism, and a consistent absence of a relationship between religion and neuroticism.

Part III

The eight chapters in Part III deal with religion and different dimensions of behavior that involve both social and psychological elements.

Chapter 12. Edward P. Shafranske reviews theoretical and empirical perspectives on the role that religion serves in the mental health of children. In pointing out that religion is an important element in the lives of most children, he writes that, within childhood, religion should be viewed as a complex, multidimensional experience that includes religious representations, beliefs, attributions, and practices. In Shafranske's analysis, these interrelated features are a determining factor with regard to a child's sense of self and others, and the code of prescribed and proscribed behaviors that a child assumes. In addition, they are an essential aspect of the attributions and systems of social support that promote coping and adaptation to developmental transitions and life challenges.

However, Shafranske observes that religion also has the potential to be destructive to the mental health of children. On this subject, he makes reference to critical and sadistic God representation, as well as belief systems that condemn humaneness and offer no tolerance for the vicissitudes of childhood existence. Shafranske also writes that certain specific religious orientations are more conducive than others to the psychological well-being of children.

Chapter 13. Harold G. Koenig writes about religion and mental health among the elderly, noting that religious beliefs and activities are very common in older populations. Koenig dispels the notion that religion is equivalent to neurosis or aberrant thinking, while describing ways in which religious cognitions and behaviors can assist the elderly in coping with life stress and change. His analysis reveals that, among older adults involved in the Judeo-Christian religious tradition, both cross-sectional and longitudinal studies tend to reveal a positive relationship between religiousness, well-being, and absence of symptoms (e.g., anxiety, depression). But Koenig also acknowledges that the relationship between religion and mental health is a complex one that is affected by physical health, socioeconomic circumstances, and various psychodynamic processes. He observes that the elderly are sometimes reluctant to talk openly about their religious experiences. Yet, despite these and other potential difficulties, Koenig makes the case that much more research is needed in this area.

Chapter 14. The chapter by Gary L. Hansen concerns itself with religion and marital adjustment. He reviews the secularization hypothesis as well as studies that suggest that, despite secularization, religion continues to exert an influence on marital adjustment and family life generally. Hansen's analysis of research on this subject leads him to the conclusion that religiosity is associated with higher levels of marital adjustment. In turn, this is related positively to a number of other factors, or "rewards." Hansen also concludes that higher levels of religiosity appear to explain the fact that individuals in same-faith marriages show better marital adjustment than those in interfaith marriages. His chapter also shows that religion has a significant impact on social psychological processes in families. Hansen offers possible explanations for these findings and discusses the implications for family scholars and mental health practitioners.

Chapter 15. William Sims Bainbridge deals with religion in relation to crime and delinquency. He observes that, in the past, sociologists of deviance have tended to ignore religion while assuming that religion was powerless to constrain human behavior. However, Bainbridge cites recent studies that reveal significant inverse relationships between religiousness and several kinds of crime and delinquency. But, as Bainbridge also observes, religion loses its power in this regard if it is not embedded in a moral community. Yet, even without social support, he shows that religion can deter promiscuous sexuality, illegal drug use, and excessive alcohol consumption.

Bainbridge is able to demonstrate that crimes (e.g., larceny) are deterred by religion only when the surrounding community is religious. But religion is shown to be incapable of preventing the passionate outburst that is so often the cause of murder. In his conclusion, Bainbridge states that the potentially beneficial effect of religion is more social than psychological, and that this effect depends on the social bonds of church membership more than on individual faith.

Chapter 16. Peter L. Benson reviews and evaluates the impressive volume of research dealing with religion, alcohol, marijuana, tobacco, and other drug use. He gives a detailed description of religion's inhibiting role and the way in which this can generalize to multiple demographic subgroups and across multiple measures of religion and substance abuse. Benson documents the manner in which religion is associated with lower levels of substance use, and compares the power of religion in this regard to other social and psychological factors. He notes that previous efforts to explain religion's ability to inhibit substance use have relied exclusively on religion's role as a social control mechanism. However, Benson argues that we must also consider the manner in which religion can promote the kinds of personal and social resources that, in turn, can function to inhibit substance use.

Among the personal resources promoted by religion are academic achievement, prosocial values, and social competence. The inhibiting social resources mentioned by Benson include family harmony, parent-child communication, and parental support. He makes the point that institutional religion may increase access to these resources. Consequently, religion not only inhibits substance use by its direct pronouncements against use, but also indirectly through the promotion of personal and environmental assets that deter risk-taking. Benson finishes by citing the need to examine more closely how the religious dimension of life can be useful in dealing with problematic areas of behavior.

Chapter 17. Kevin S. Masters and Allen E. Bergin devote their chapter to the relationships between mental health and different religious orientations. These include intrinsic and extrinsic modes of religion as originally set out by Gordon Allport, as well as the quest mode introduced by Batson and Ventis (1982). After reviewing the literature in this area, Masters and Bergin draw several conclusions. Among them are these: (1) intrinsic religiosity is generally related to positive mental health, whereas extrinsic religiosity is related to poor mental functioning; (2) measures of intrinsic religiosity are *not* simply a reflection of social desirability; (3) while the quest dimension has added to our thinking and research, questions remain regarding its theoretical foundations and empirical correlates; (4) certainty of belief or lack of conflict *may* be more important to well-being than religion per se; (5) synchrony between religious values and behaviors is more likely to lead to positive outcomes than is disparity between them; and (6) much more sophisticated and precise research is needed, particularly relating content of religious beliefs with mental health.

Chapter 18. James T. Richardson writes about the mental status of cult consumers and examines the controversy about whether mental illness is associated with participation in different new religions, or cults. He focuses on one key episode involving a series of legal actions in the 1970s over the mental competence of a participant in ISKCON (International Society for Krishna Consciousness). In this case, the participant's father was a well-known psychiatrist whose subsequent writings gave impetus to the effort to define involvement as indicative of psychopathology. The principal expert witness was then, and continues to be, a prominent legitimator of the anti-cult movement, one which promotes the theory that cult participants have been brainwashed and that they are under the influence of mind control. Richardson describes how more contemporary brainwashing theorists are making use of the Diagnostic and Statistical Manual in attempting to equate mental illness and participation in various new religions. His chapter cautions against such practices, while noting their implications for society generally.

Chapter 19. H. Newton Malony discusses the issue of religious diagnosis in relation to mental health, as well as the treatment of psychopathology. He maintains that much confusion concerning the impact of religion on psychological health is due to problems of definition. Malony observes that, at varying times, religion has been defined in negative terms (absence of illness), positive terms (achievement of an ideal state), and in the context of "normal" behavior (adjustment to a culture). Moreover, he argues that studies showing negative or nonexistent relationships between religion and psychological adjustment are typically flawed by definitional deficiencies wherein theology is conceived too narrowly.

The Religious Status Interview and the Religious Status Inventory are offered as psychometrically sound instruments capable of assessing optimal religious functioning. Their use indicates that good Christian functional theology is consistently associated with positive mental health. Malony also provides some initial thoughts on ways that religious diagnosis can be useful in prescribing effective treatment plans for a variety of pathological symptoms. He concludes that, although research in the area of religious diagnosis is in the early stages, it is a viable activity that can be a useful adjunct to current methods of psychological evaluation.

Part IV

Part IV contains five chapters that discuss the interaction of religion and mental health in a wide cross-cultural context.

Chapter 20. Erika Bourguignon examines two examples of reactions to culture change, while placing these in a religious context. These demonstrate that religion is multiform and that its role in culture change is variable and dependent on a host of factors. In some instances, it may be a creative innovative adaptation that seeks to modify society. Such movements, which have come to be termed "revitalization movements" and "crisis cults," are rooted in the founders' personal distress as well as society's disorganization. They constitute attempts at healing the self and society.

Other reactions to culture change are personal expressions of distress (exemplified by "mass hysteria") are phrased in traditional terms (e.g., spirit possession), but they do not lead to personal or social resolution. Bourguignon addresses the issue of the diversity that exists in multicultural or cross-cultural situations, while pointing out that the distinction between religion and psychopathology is difficult to draw. She also shows that, while religion can act as a coping strategy, it can also create its own problems, especially through the imposition of strong social controls.

Chapter 21. Gary Groth-Marnat writes about Buddhism in the context of mental health issues, while comparing the psychological benefits of Buddhism to those of other world religions. He observes that Buddhism can be understood, not only as a religion, but also as a practical system by which to achieve change and growth. Moreover, many of the prescriptions for personal change advocated by Buddhism are consistent with traditional conceptions of mental health. According to Groth-Marnat, the essential tenets of Buddhism revolve on the principle of nonattachment, both to the physical world and the self. Although sometimes viewed as negative by Westerners, the realization of nonattachment and cessation of self leads to greater joy, compassion, flexibility, acceptance, fullness, and other healthy attributes.

Groth-Marnat discusses some of the specific techniques by which the Buddhist ideals of mental health are achieved. These include meditation, teaching stories, rational analysis, and koans. An analysis of the empirical literature indicates that such strategies constitute effective methods by which to reduce anxiety (including death anxiety), heighten insight and awareness, increase empathy, enhance one's self-esteem, and improve cognitive performance.

Chapter 22. The chapter by Raymond H. Prince deals with religious experience and psychopathology from a cross-cultural perspective. He develops the argument that religious experiences have a considerable overlap with phenomena designated as psychiatric disorders, and that this close kinship is especially apparent with cultures outside the Western world. Prince draws on specific examples from Korea, India, and Western culture in demonstrating that highly similar mental and behavioral states may be considered religious in some cultural settings, while in others they are designated as mental illness.

With reference to people who experience these unusual mental states, he shows that they are sometimes channeled into socially valuable roles. But Prince notes that this requires that a culture attach meaning to the mental phenomena and also that institutional support be provided to the individual having the experiences. Mention is also made to other factors that serve to determine if an experience is regarded as religious and positive or psychotic and negative.

Chapter 23. Janet L. Jacobs presents a cross-cultural analysis of religious ritual and mental health. She describes the cathartic effects of religious ritual and examines the relational quality of religious rites as emotions are released and expressed through attachment and connection to significant others. Drawing on anthropological data and social-psychological theory, Jacobs explores the emotions of shame, grief, and anger in the context of rites of confession, mourning, and confrontation. Her chapter includes the ritual practices of tribal cultures as well as those of contemporary industrial societies. Jacobs concludes that religious ceremony and ritual functions to mitigate anxiety and deal effectively with other problematic emotional states. However, she emphasizes that the primary mental health benefits of ritual are closely tied to the relational aspects of the ritual process, ones that act to validate and encourage the healthy expression of a wide range of human emotions.

Chapter 24. David Greenberg and Eliezer Witztum review research concerning the prevalence and content of psychopathology in different world religions. They point out the methodological flaws that plague this line of study, while commenting on recent research indicating that socioeconomic status and level of social support may help to explain the differing rates of mental disturbance across religions. Greenberg and Witztum give additional focus to two specific components of religion, creed (i.e., beliefs) and cultus (i.e., ceremonies and rituals), and the ways in which they become manifested in psychopathological symptoms. They provide a comparative analysis of religious possession, glossolalia, and obsessive-compulsive disorder while discussing the conditions under which these are deemed pathological. Spiritism, santeria, and Jewish mysticism are presented as religious belief systems that have the therapeutic potential to offer normalization (via meaning and support) to people suffering from mild forms of psychopathology.

References

Adorno, T.W., Frenkel-Brunswik, E., Levinson, D.J., & Sanford, R.N. (1950). *The authoritarian personality.* New York: Norton.

Allen, R.O., & Spilka, B. (1967). Committed and consensual religion: A specification of religion-prejudice relationships. *Journal for the Scientific Study of Religion, 6,* 191–206.

Allport, G.W. (1950). *The individual and his religion.* New York: Macmillan.

Allport, G.W. (1967). Behavioral science, religion, and mental health. In D. Belgum (Ed.), *Religion and medicine* (pp. 83–95). Ames, Iowa: Iowa State University Press.

Allport, G.W., & Ross, J.M. (1967). Personal religious orientation and prejudice. *Journal of Personality and Social Psychology, 5,* 432–443.

Argyle, M., & Beit-Hallahmi, B. (1975). *The social psychology of religion.* London: Routledge & Kegan Paul. (Original work published 1958.)

Ashbrook, J.B. (1966). The relationship of church members to church organizations. *Journal for the Scientific Study of Religion, 5,* 397–419.

Batson, C.D., & Ventis, W.L. (1982). *The religious experience.* New York: Oxford University Press.

Becker, R.J. (1971). Religion and psychological health. In M.P. Strommen (ed.), *Research on religious development* (pp. 391–421). New York: Hawthorn Books.

Bellah, R.N. (1971). The historical background of unbelief. In R. Caporale & A. Grumelli (Eds.), *The culture of unbelief* (pp. 39–52). Berkeley, CA: University of California Press.

Bergin, A.E. (1983). Religiosity and mental health: A critical reevaluation and meta-analysis. *Professional Psychology: Research and Practice, 14,* 170–184.

Clinebell, H.J. (1970). The local church's contribution to positive mental health. In H.J. Clinebell (Ed.), *Community mental health: The role of Church and Temple.* Nashville, TN: Abingdon Press.

Dittes, J.E. (1969). The psychology of religion. In G. Lindzey & E. Aronson (Eds.), *The handbook of social psychology* (vol. 5) (pp. 602–659). Reading, MA: Addison-Wesley.

Donahue, M.J. (1985). Intrinsic and extrinsic religiousness: Review and meta-analysis. *Journal of Personality and Social Psychology, 48,* 400–419.

Ellis, A. (1975). The case against religion: A psychotherapist's view. In B. Ard (Ed.), *Counseling and psychotherapy: Classics on theories and issues.* Palo Alto, CA: Science & Behavior Books.

Ellis, A. (1980). Psychotherapy and atheistic values: A response to A.E. Bergin's "Psychotherapy and religious values." *Journal of Consulting and Clinical Psychology, 48,* 635–639.

Erikson, E.H. (1958). *Young man Luther.* New York: W.W. Norton.

Freud, S. (1964). *The future of an illusion.* New York: Anchor Books. (Original work published 1927.)

Fromm, E. (1950). *Psychoanalysis and religion.* New Haven, CT: Yale University Press.

Funk, R. (1982). *Erich Fromm: The courage to be human.* New York: Continuum.

Gartner, J., Larson, D.B., & Allen, G.D. (1991). Religious commitment and mental health: A review of the empirical literature. *Journal of Psychology and Theology, 19,* 6–25.

Geertz, C. (1966). Religion as a cultural system. In M. Banton (Ed.), *Anthropological approaches to the study of religion* (pp. 1–46). New York: Praeger.

Giddens, A. (1989). *Sociology.* Cambridge, UK: Polity Press.

Glock, C.Y. (1962). On the study of religious commitment. *Religious Education Research Supplement, 57,* 98–110.

Jahoda, M. (1958). *Current concepts of positive mental health.* New York: Basic Books.

James, W. (1902). *The varieties of religious experience.* New York: Longmans, Green.

King, M.B., & Hunt, R.A. (1975). Measuring the religious variable: A national replication. *Journal for the Scientific Study of Religion, 14,* 13–22.

Lea, G. (1982). Religion, mental health, and clinical issues. *Journal of Religion and Health, 21,* 336–351.

Lenski, G. (1963). *The religious factor.* New York: Anchor Books.

Maslow, A.H. (1971). *The farther reaches of human behavior.* New York: Viking.

Payne, I.R., Bergin, A.E., Bielema, K.A., & Jenkins, P.H. (1991). Review of religion and mental health: Prevention and the enhancement of psychosocial functioning. *Prevention in Human Services, 9,* 11–40.

Pruyser, P.W. (1971). A psychological view of religion in the 1970s. *Bulletin of the Menninger Clinic, 35,* 77–97.

Pruyser, P.W. (1977). The seamy side of current religious beliefs. *Bulletin of the Menninger Clinic, 41,* 329–348.

Roberts, D. (1953). Health from the standpoint of Christian faith. In P. Maves (Ed.), *The church and mental health.* New York: Charles Scribners & Sons.

Rogers, C. (1961). *On becoming a person.* Boston: Houghton Mifflin.

Rosenhan, D.L., & Seligman, M.E.P. (1984). *Abnormal psychology.* New York: W.W. Norton.

Sanua, V.D. (1969). Religion, mental health, and personality: A review of empirical studies. *American Journal of Psychiatry, 125,* 1203–1213.

Schumaker, J.F. (1990). *Wings of Illusion.* Cambridge, UK: Polity Press (in USA, Buffalo, NY: Prometheus Books).

Schumaker, J.F. (1991). The adaptive value of suggestibility and dissociation. In J.F. Schumaker (Ed.), *Human suggestibility: Advances in theory, research, and application* (pp. 108–131). New York and London: Routledge.

Smith, W.C. (1978). *The meaning and end of religion.* London: SPCK.

Spilka, B. (1989). Functional and dysfunctional roles of religion: An attributional approach. *Journal of Psychology and Christianity, 8,* 5–15.

Spilka, B., Hood, R.W., Jr., & Gorsuch, R.L. (1985). *The psychology of religion.* Englewood Cliffs, NJ: Prentice-Hall.

Spilka, B., & Werme, P.H. (1971). Religion and mental disorder: A research perspective. In M.P. Strommen (Ed.), *Research on religious development: A comprehensive handbook* (pp. 462–481). New York: Hawthorne.

Spiro, M.E. (1965). Culturally constituted defense mechanisms. In M.E. Spiro (Ed.), *Context and meaning in cultural anthropology.* New York: Free Press.

Spiro, M.E. (1966). Religion: Problems of definition and explanation. In M. Banton (Ed), *Anthropological approaches to the study of religion* (pp. 85–126). London: Tavistock.

Stark, R. (1971). Psychopathology and religious commitment. *Review of Religious Research, 12,* 165–176.

Watson, P.J., Hood, R.W., Jr., & Morris, R.J. (1984). Religious orientation, humanistic values, and narcissism. *Review of Religious Research, 25,* 257–264.

Watson, P.J., Morris, R.J., & Hood, R.W., Jr. (1990). Intrinsicness, self-actualization, and the ideological surround. *Journal of Psychology and Theology, 18,* 40–53.

Wilson, J. (1978). *Religion in American society: The effective presence.* Englewood Cliffs, NJ: Prentice-Hall.

I

HISTORICAL PERSPECTIVES

1

The Psychopathology of Religion: European Historical Perspectives

Jacob A. Belzen

Nearly inextricable with human culture, religion has woven itself into the very existence of the human being throughout a long and complex history. As such, a culture theory can only abstractly distinguish religion as an "ideological system" from techno-economics, social structure, and individual personality (Kaplan & Manners, 1972). Everywhere and in multivarious forms, religion reveals itself in the histories of cultures. It has inspired the highest and the best in people. On our travels we admire temples and cathedrals. In concert halls we enjoy the compositions of religious themes, and in museums we devote ourselves to so-called religious art. At the same time, however, the history of religion has been a sad tale wherein it has constituted, legitimized, and enforced inequitable relations in the spheres of labor and society. Whereas religion has at times promoted people's best, it has also defamed and oppressed people, and it has persecuted other-believers and nonbelievers.

Besides the impossibility of evaluating scientifically the truth of religious statements, it is difficult to formulate general propositions as research progresses. A wide variety of opposing views can be seen to exist on nearly all topics in this area of study. This is also the case with regard to the subject matter of this chapter, the "psychopathology of religion." This term refers to the subdiscipline of both psychology and psychiatry, which studies religious behaviors that are judged to be deviant in nature. We can discern several positions here. Religion is sometimes seen as having nothing whatsoever to do with psychopathology. Other theoretical formulations consider religion to be a major pathogenic factor. In some cases, religion is thought to prevent mental disturbance, while in others, it has to be unmasked as one of the symptoms of ill health. To make any justifiable and worthwhile statement in this field, however, it is vital to examine carefully what *this* particular religious form means with *this* particular person having *this* particular disorder. Such a statement should not be viewed as an evasive maneuver to avoid taking a theoretical stand that concerns the exact relationship between religion and mental illness. On the contrary, it is a qualified stance that was reached only after a long history in which virtually every possible position has been defended.

33

The Focus

Exciting and bizarre stories could be told about many individual forms of religious mania (an outdated term). One could also point to religiously colored "psychic epidemics," such as the well-known flagellants in the late Middle Ages, who beat themselves bloody during their pilgrimages. Another chapter in history is the religious care for the insane, with its counterpart of exorcism, witch-hunting and other now abhorred practices. However, these subjects are not the focus of this chapter. Rather, I will concentrate on the scientific enterprise called "psychopathology of religion," including a brief review of the different viewpoints that have led various thinkers to theorize about pathological forms of religiosity.

The scope has to be restricted even more, however, as the phrase "psychopathology of religion" can be understood in several ways. Different methodological viewpoints lead to different conceptions of this particular area of study. This chapter does not deal with religious examples of different psychopathological diseases (one of the most current understandings of the term). Also, it will not discuss seemingly pathological examples of religious behavior such as the experience of being possessed, glossolalia, visions, and stigmata (another way that the term can be understood). Instead, I will concentrate on one particular fundamental methodological viewpoint, namely, the pertinacious dualism with regard to the *genesis* of religious psychopathology. This dualism may manifest itself as an opposition between natural and supernatural causes of mental illness, but also as a differentiation of somatic and psychic determinants. Although the topic is treated in historical perspective, this should not suggest that unilinear progress has been made. Yet, there have been some developments, as well as a succession of dominant viewpoints, that can be historically situated. Some of these viewpoints remain influential.

Antiquity and the Middle Ages

Contrary to popular opinion, the dualism with regard to the genesis of religious psychopathology is certainly not an achievement of modernity. In nearly all historic and contemporary cultures, one finds two different explanations for remarkable or deviant behavioral phenomena, and for illness in general: natural causes and supernatural ones (Hole, 1977; Bromberg, 1975; Howells, 1975). Both explanations appear in such classic texts as the Bible. There is knowledge about somatic determinants of psychic phenomena (e.g., dreams). But one can also read that the condition of the Old Testament king, Saul, was understood as the work of a nonhuman evil spirit, external to Saul. In Greek mythology, psychological disturbance was also seen as something coming from outside the individual, caused by gods.

In the history of medicine, it is generally accepted that the *Corpus Hippocraticum* was a first scientific highlight. Hippocrates tried to explain states of mind, and even psychological types, by means of variations in the mixture of bodily fluids. Hippocrates is also recognized as the debunker of all kinds of "obscure" causes of illness. In his thinking, illness was interpreted strictly somatically, with deviations explained in terms of processes in the body. More "psychological" approaches still resembled "demonological" interpretations: illness as the result of something that influenced the person from outside, acting on body and soul. This external force was often thought to be the work of a demon or the result of demonic influences. Illness then was seen as something that existed independent of the human being, alien to the essence of human nature. In Aristotles's writings, the dualism is also found in strictly somatic interpretations of mental disorders on the one hand, and interpretations based on psychic influences on the other hand.

In the Middle Ages, the field of medicine was far less "dark" than is often assumed. People certainly lived with angels and demons, and exorcism did exist. But there also existed a range of somatically oriented "theories" and treatments (Beek, 1974). Even so, Christian influences saw demonological interpretations gain prominence during the Middle Ages. The works of Albertus Magnus (see, Kopp, 1933), for example, dealt with the classic hippocratic approach as well as with the possibility of demonic causes of mental illness. Natural, somatic, psychological and supernatural interpretations coexisted without excessive conflict. P. E. Huston (see, Siegler & Osmond, 1974, p. x) tells of a diagnostic "trick" that was used to differentiate epileptic attacks caused by demonic influences from those due to natural causes. Words from the Bible were whispered into the ear of the victim. If the attack stopped, it was considered to be a case for the clergyman, since the devil could not bear to hear these words and therefore left the body. If the attack did not stop, the patient had to be treated by a physician.

Psychicists versus Somaticists

Two related developments have been responsible for more recent conceptions: the introduction of the experiment in medical science and the Enlightenment. Experimental methodology allowed medical knowledge to progress enormously in those domains that were accessible to experimental investigation. In turn, other approaches and viewpoints were discredited due to a lack of scientific rigor. One consequence of the Enlightenment was an increased emphasis on the transcendental nature of the deity and the divine sphere, leading to positions such as deism. In terms of scientific inquiry, the consequences were that one did not have to deny God and his activity. But it was no longer necessary to introduce these as variables in empirical research. God exists, demons too perhaps, but (so reasoning goes) mental illness is not caused by supernatural or extra-natural influences. This became an important and widespread point of view.

As could be expected, before such consensus was reached, considerable quarrelling took place. The controversy was fought out primarily in German countries, and was known as the debate between Psychicists (Psychiker) and Somaticists (Somatiker). These groups opposed each other because of their differing anthropological presuppositions. The psychicists emphasized the unity of body and soul, with an independent soul and the body as the instrument of the soul. Mental illness that emanated from the body was impossible in this view; a defective body could only hinder the correct activity or manifestation of the soul. Only something "psychic" could cause disturbances of the soul.

In contrast, the somaticists defended a dualism of soul and body. Accordingly, illness was never a matter of only the soul or only the body, but rather an infliction of the animated body. It was thought that the soul was impervious to illness. Mental illness was a disturbance of the form of the (animated) body, as was implied in the Aristotelian underpinnings of their position. For scientific research and patient care, this meant that one had to search for the still unknown, but presumably somatic, bases of the psychic symptoms. However, it also meant that, ultimately, these dualists would adopt a methodological monistic materialism. In addition to the notion of the "animated" body they did use the concept of the soul. But to them this was the object of religion and metaphysics (and eventually psychology), and not a useful construct for a scientific understanding of psychopathology (Verwey, 1985). Thus, they severely criticized Heinroth (1818, 1822), the best known representative of the psychicists. Heinroth had defined the nature of mental illness as "unfreedom" and a consequence of sin and/or guilt.[1] According to the somaticists, he confused psychiatric and moral-religious categories in an irresponsible way.

While an entire history of the debate is beyond the scope of this chapter, it is sufficient to say that the somaticists were victorious. The methodological priority given to research of the body would later be expressed in Wilhelm Griesinger's (1872/1844) theoretical proposition that diseases of the mind are diseases of the brain.[2] The psychiatry at universities (which Karl Jaspers [1913] strictly differentiated from the psychiatry in asylums) developed more in a materialistic direction. It understood science according to the Galilean tradition and wanted psychiatry to share in the prestige of the natural sciences.

The Rise of Somatically Oriented Psychiatry

By the end of the nineteenth century, the above development was praised in leading German handbooks of the time. When von Krafft Ebing (1883) reviewed the history of psychiatry, he stated that the view of psychiatry as a natural science had liberated it from the "one-sided metaphysical and psychological school" that extended from the Middle Ages. He mentioned Heinroth and Ideler as major representatives of this "mystical-pious school" (p. 46).[3] Von Krafft Ebing also wrote that psychiatry had finally, "after severe struggle gained her rightful place among the natural sciences and purified herself from the last philosophical and metaphysical rests" (p. 47). He attributed this to the work of people from "natural science who fought this spiritualistic, ethical and psychological school" (p. 46). To von Krafft Ebing, psychiatric disturbance was an "element of the diseases of the brain and the nerves" (p. 1). He did not want to speak of "diseases of the soul," but preferred to describe "mental illness" as the principal object of psychiatry.

Clearly, the somatically oriented school was a reaction to the preceding psychical and ethical schools. There were extreme representatives such as Meynert (see, Zilboorg, 1941) in Vienna (one of Freud's teachers, by the way). He even opposed the use of the word "psychiatry," because one should deal with the "soma" rather than "psyche." Thus a somatic reductionism appeared in psychiatry. Less scientific attention was devoted to psychological aspects such as the life history of the patient, personal experiences, emotions and behavior, situational factors, and so forth. It is clear that the psychopathology of religion could not flourish in such an atmosphere.

Contrary Motions Searching for the Soul: Psychoanalysis

By demystifying the demonological interpretation of mental illness, scientific psychiatry had also lost much of its empathy for the patient.[4] One of the most important figures in the countermovement was Sigmund Freud, who focused on the patient's subjective experiences while trying to take seriously the stories and symptoms of these people. It was a stroke of genius when he stated that things were as the patient experienced them. That is, the patient was really in the grasp of dark and unknown powers. However, these powers were not of a supernatural nature. Instead, they were seen as intra-psychic and of human origin. By translating the former religious language into psychological language, one can see how demonology expressed psychic reality symbolically. It was a psychic reality that existed in hidden desires, anxieties, and deceptions of the censure mechanisms (Vergote, 1988). When the patient asserted being possessed by the devil, this was not an incidental nonsense uttered by an afflicted brain using the accidental idiom of its surroundings. The statement contained sense, but it was a sense that had to be discovered. With the rise of psychoanalysis, the older demonology could suddenly be revaluated as an earlier form of the same search and the same desire for insight into the mentally disturbed individual. For the psychopathology of religion, this was a great step forward. It showed that it was possible to understand all kinds of aberrant religious emotions and behavior in terms of a dysfunctional psyche.

As so often happens, however, the scale tipped. Freud and many of his followers could not avoid the temptation of making the new insight as all-embracing as the older demonological one. That is, once mental illness was shown to be a matter of psychological (rather than supernatural) order, could it not be the case with religion as a whole? Using a long string of analogies, Freud (1959/1907) made several bold statements. He compared religious practices to the obsessive actions of the neurotic patient.[5] Beyond that, since compulsive neurosis supposedly stemmed from feelings of guilt about insufficient control of sexual and/or selfish desires, he asked if religion was also derived from guilt. Freud answered this question affirmatively. Early in our history, human religion came into being because of feelings of guilt about the murder of the (prehistoric) father (Freud, 1955/1913). Also, Freud (1961/1927) interpreted personal religiosity in terms of life-long "universal transference" and the need for a strong father. God was the exalted father of people's childhood. While Freud's essays on culture and religion were well-crafted and compelling, they transgressed flagrantly the frontiers of professional competence. A cultural phenomenon such as religion cannot originate in the psyche of the individual. Many thinkers hold the opposite view, namely that the individual has to be understood from an analysis of culture.

Even though the new psychological insights introduced by psychoanalysis proved fruitful, they were obscured by the fact that religion was still being evaluated according to prescientific biases. This was also true of the study of psychopathology. Freud's analyses were excessively critical of religion as a result of ontological and anthropological arguments. Unnecessary storms of protest emerged. For a long time psychoanalysis was repressed in religious circles. As is well known, other psychoanalysts tried to safeguard religion from Freud's critique by defending the position that religion belongs to human nature, and that it is even a criterion for mental health (e.g., Jung, Maeder, Fromm). However, they were only working from a different anthropological model, and their work proved to be just as biased as that of Freud. This was no step forward for the methodology of psychopathological research.

Phenomenology

The methodological frontiers were better guarded by another psychological school that tried to replace the one-sidedness of the biomedical psychiatry with psychological approaches. The philosopher Karl Jaspers (1913) was an important figure in early stages of the so-called phenomenological movement in psychiatry (see, Spiegelberg, 1972, 1982). Again, the focus turned to the patient and subjective experience. The phenomenologists, following Dilthey (1964/1894), searched for appropriate methods to explore the nature of the psyche. They represented an alternative approach to the psychological research methods associated with the tradition of the natural sciences. With regard to the psychopathology of religion, Jaspers spoke of a "methodological insight" that recognizes that all knowledge (including scientific knowledge) is determined by the conditions and means by which it was obtained. So knowledge is seen as always partial, and with boundaries. This also means that the religious phenomena (and "symptoms") have dual aspects. Religious behavior and experience have psychophysical dimensions that are accessible to psychological and psychopathological research. The religious essence, however, is inaccessible to this kind of research and has to be judged by theology or philosophy (Heimann, 1961). Incidentally, Freud (1961/1927) did not deny this. He even explicitly affirmed this methodological discernment, placing psychoanalysis in its modest place. But after Freud traced the supposed roots of religion he (from his ontological *a priori*) deemed religion to be *nothing but* its psychological roots. This was a clear case of a category mistake.

The phenomenological school paid more attention to religion than the somatically oriented school. Phenomenology could be, and usually is, combined with the former somatical orientation. One of the best known publications in this field was *Zur Einführung in die Religionspsychopathologie* (Introduction to the Psychopathology of Religion) by Kurt Schneider (1928). He started from an organic understanding of psychopathology and described the abnormal religious phenomena that occurred in the different clinical disorders. His book was intended to teach pastors to recognize pathologically determined forms of religion, and to allow them to collaborate with psychiatrists. Schneider made no definitive statements about the value or the genesis of the religious symptoms, and in this way offered less insight than the critical psychoanalytic school. On the other hand, he managed to avoid the sticky issue of whether religion and religiosity should be evaluated positively or negatively, and whether it should be considered a manifestation of human nature.

The Historical-Cultural Psychological Perspective

In recent decades, a historical-cultural perspective has been elaborated in psychology. This perspective strives to do justice to human history by viewing the human being as a cultural and historical creature who is born into a culture and a religion. These are considered to be objective phenomena that exist *prior* to the individual. As such, people are absorbed into the culture and, consequently, bear its characteristics. In this model, personal vicissitudes sometimes cause people to become psychologically "misspent" and unable to be integrated adequately into the objective culture and its religion. This perspective has the advantage of being modest and empirically oriented. It does not assume that human beings are *by nature* either religious or nonreligious. Rather, it supposes that we can *become* religious or nonreligious, and that it is this process that has to be investigated. To learn whether a particular behavior, language, or sentiment is psychopathological in nature, this perspective takes a double approach. It turns to the culture concerned for a "verdict" about religion and other matters. The representatives of the individual's (religious) culture should tell whether a particular religious manifestation is normal or not. Thus this perspective avoids the problem of labeling as "pathological" behaviors with which the researcher is not acquainted, ones that might be appropriate within a religious (sub)culture. This cultural aspect of the perspective derives its inspiration from descriptive phenomenology. The second approach is a *psycho*pathological one that makes reference to psychological standards and not to the content of behavior or experience. Instead, it investigates whether the psychological roots of any particular behavior or experience are pathological in nature. This second (historical) approach was inspired by psychoanalysis: where and how things went wrong in the individual's (early) psycho-history.

Thus, research in the psychopathology of religion requires analysis at two levels: (1) the common religious convictions and behavior of all participants of the culture concerned and (2) the individual organization of life within the collective system. Accordingly, it is only possible to make statements with regard to an individual in a specific, historical culture. Furthermore, to make such statements one must be acquainted with the human psychic structure, as well as the culture in which the afflicted person participates. This position is defended very eloquently in the work of the psychologist-theologian-philosopher Antoine Vergote, emeritus professor from the University of Louvain, Belgium. He attained a preliminary synthesis by combining phenomenological and modern psychoanalytical insights with historical and anthropological data. In his book *Guilt and Desire,* Vergote (1988) provided a fine psychological analyses of, among other things, the mystical experiences of Theresa of Avila, the voices of Jeanne d'Arc, and the visions and stigmata of Thérèse Neumann.

Conclusion

We now arrive at our point of departure and the realization that one cannot give general *a priori* formulations concerning the relationship between religion and psychopathology. One must always consider the individual person in describing the interface between religion and psychological symptoms. I hope this short exploration has illustrated a little of the long and often very difficult way in which this formulation was reached.

All kinds of viewpoints have been defended over the course of history, and all types of reasoning and practices have existed. Nevertheless, some progress has been made. On the whole, the blunt *a priori* statements have been left behind. It is more generally recognized that specific religious practices can be harmful to one individual while being beneficial to another. Also, certain kinds of religious devotion may be a sign of genuine mental health with one person, but a manifestation of infantile restraint or clinical disturbance in another. With regard to mental health, empirical research shows that religion can be a haven, a hazard, a therapy, an expression or a suppression of mental pathology (Spilka, Hood, & Gorsuch, 1985). The old question of whether religion is right or wrong, and whether it is the cause or remedy for mental disease, has proved fruitless. Too much apology for their own religious position was mixed up with those who attempted to provide the answers. We have noticed that different psychoanalysts, although working with the same research methods, have judged opposedly on religion, according to their different anthropologies. Phenomenologists tried to avoid a judgment on this issue and described religion in the greater clinical context while circumventing questions concerning the value or the impact of these religious forms. More satisfying, however, seems to be the historical-psychological position where there *is* a verdict whether the observed religious phenomena are pathological or not. But this verdict is left to the appropriate experts: to the religious culture or community concerned. The mental health professional only tries to understand how these (deviant) religious phenomena came into being and whether their psychological roots are pathological in nature. On the other hand, however, we have to realize that spiritual health does not necessarily correlate with psychological understanding of health. Therefore, from a psychological point of view, behavior that is accepted or even encouraged by the religious culture can be nonetheless structured in a pathological way. Perhaps it is best to relegate these matters to the critics of culture and religion but not to what has here been described as the psychopathology of religion.

Notes

1. Heinroth further pleaded for a classification of clinical pictures on the basis of psychological criteria. If he had not spoken of *guilt*, but of *feelings* of guilt, historians of science would have regarded him as a forerunner of psychoanalysis.

2. Griesinger is often regarded as a metaphysical materialist. This is not right. His way of regarding mental diseases as diseases of the brain was a methodological reduction: he conceived of mental disease as the result of a disease of the brain, not as nothing-but-disease of the brain.

3. The psychiatrist K. W. Ideler had great interest in the psychopathology of religion. He wrote books like *Der Religiöse Wahnsinn erläutert durch Krankengeschichten* (Religious Madness Explained by Histories of the Disease) (1847) and *Versuch einer Theorie des religiösen Wahnsinns* (Attempt at a Theory of Religious Madness) (1850).

4. This does not suggest that psychiatrists with a biomedical orientation did not (and do not) pay enough attention to their patients as human beings. The care for the patient was often as good as possible. And in the religious regard, pastors worked in asylums, religious

services were held, and so forth. However, these elements of care were not part of the psychiatric "method."

5. Contrary to what is often assumed, Freud did *not* regard religion as such to be a neurosis. He only compared religion and neurosis methodologically. He even stated that being religious could prevent an individual neurosis. However, religion as such might in his opinion be the *cultural* counterpart of a neurosis.

References

Beek, H.H. (1974). *Waanzin in de Middeleeuwen. Beeld van de gestoorde en bemoeienis met de zieke.* Hoofddorp: Septuaginta.

Bromberg, W. (1975). *From shaman to psychotherapist: A history of the treatment of mental illness.* Chicago: Henry Regnery.

Dilthey, W. (1964). *Gesammelte Schriften,* Band V (pp. 139–241). Stuttgart: Teubner. (Original work published 1894.)

Freud, S. (1959). Obsessive actions and religious practices. In *The standard edition of the complete psychological works,* vol. IX (pp. 116–127). London: Hogarth Press. (Original work published 1907.)

Freud, S. (1955). Totem und Tabu. In *The standard edition of the complete psychological works,* vol. XIII (pp. 1–162). London: Hogarth Press. (Original work published 1913.)

Freud, S. (1961). The future of an illusion. In *The standard edition of the complete psychological works,* vol. XXI (pp. 2–58). London: Hogarth Press. (Original work published 1927.)

Griesinger, W. (1872). Recension über: M. Jacobi. In W. Griesinger, *Gesammelte Abhandlungen,* Band I (pp. 80–106). Berlin: Hirschwald. (Original work published 1844.)

Heimann, H. (1961). Religion und Psychiatrie. In: H.W. Gruhle, R. Jung, W. Mayer-Gross & M. Müller (Eds.), *Psychiatrie der Gegenwart: Forschung und Praxis,* Band III (pp. 471–493). Berlin: Springer.

Heinroth, J. Chr. A. (1818). *Lehrbuch der Störungen des Seelenlebens oder der Seelenstörungen und ihrer Behandlung.* Leipzig: Vogel.

Heinroth, J. Chr. A. (1822). *Lehrbuch der Anthropologie.* Leipzig: Vogel.

Hole, G. (1977). *Der Glaube bei Depressiven. Religionspsychopathologische und klinisch-statistische Untersuchung.* Stuttgart: Enke.

Howells, J.G. (Ed.) (1975). *World history of psychiatry.* London: Baillière Tindall.

Ideler, K.W. (1847). *Der religiöse Wahnsinn erläutert durch Krankengeschichten.* Halle: Schwetschke.

Ideler, K.W. (1850). *Versuch einer Theorie des religiösen Wahnsinns.* Halle: Schwetschke.

Jaspers, K. (1913). *Allgemeine Psychopathologie.* Berlin: Springer.

Kaplan, D., & Manners, R.A. (1972). *Culture theory.* London: Prentice-Hall.

Kopp, P. (1933). Psychiatrisches bei Albertus Magnus. *Zeitschrift für die gesamte Neurologie und Psychiatrie, 147,* 50–60.

Krafft-Ebing, R. von. (1883). *Lehrbuch der Psychiatrie.* Stuttgart: Enke.

Schneider, K. (1928). Zur Einführung in die Religionspsycho-pathologie. Tübingen: Mohr.

Siegler, M., & Osmond, H. (1974). *Models of madness, models of medicine.* New York: Macmillan.

Spiegelberg, H. (1972). *Phenomenology in psychology and psychiatry.* Evanston, IL: Northwestern University Press.

Spiegelberg, H. (1982). *The phenomenological movement: A historical introduction.* Den Haag: Mouton.

Spilka, B., Hood, R.W., & Gorsuch, R.L. (1985). *The psychology of religion: An empirical approach.* New Jersey: Prentice-Hall.

Vergote, A. (1988). *Guilt and desire: Religious attitudes and their pathological derivatives.* New Haven, CT: Yale University Press.

Verwey, G. (1985). *Psychiatry in an anthropological and biomedical context: Philosophical presuppositions and implications of German psychiatry, 1820–1870.* Dordrecht/Boston: Reidel.

Zilboorg, G. (1941). *A history of medical psychology.* New York: Norton.

2

Religion and the Mental Health of Women

Robert A. Bridges and Bernard Spilka

The Historical-Cultural Context

Whether the religious heritage be Judeo-Christian, Islamic, Hindu, or Buddhist, its institutional forms have bound people into coherent social orders. To achieve this end, existing social, political, and economic structures have been sacralized and therefore legitimated. Among the most central of such considerations is the relationship between the sexes. For example, the perspectives of Judaism, Christianity, and Islam, have been described as "uncompromisingly male monotheistic" (Gaba, 1987, p. 190). Power and authority are clearly vested in men: the position of women is secondary. This pattern also holds for Buddhism and Hinduism. With religious backing, the sexual stratification of society is pervasive and regarded as the natural state of affairs. The psychosocial ramifications of such systematic patterning have yet to be fully appreciated.

Relative to our concern, the evidence for sex-linked genetic and physiological bases for psychological problems is weak and contradictory. Attention has therefore focused on the organization of sex roles within these religiocultural systems as the major factor in the prevailing sexual configuration of mental disorder (Basow, 1980). Theory avers that the stress accompanying the female sex role largely accounts for the female pattern of mental problems (Makosky, 1980; Miller & Mothner, 1981). One may further theorize that religion contributes both to the creation of these difficulties and, in some instances, their alleviation.

Empirical data to assess this viewpoint is lacking for non-Western religions and is far from complete for Judaism and Christianity. Nevertheless, enough information exists to clarify the current situation and identify research needs.

The Religious Background of Sex Roles

The stage was set for a religious justification of the dominant cultural pattern of gender relations in Genesis, initially by the story of woman being created after man and from a rather minor part of his anatomy. It concludes with the myth of the Fall of humanity from grace, which connotes woman as the cause of all subsequent evil, sin, and suffering. Female "weakness" and corporeality came to represent the "lower nature" in contradistinction to the "higher" spiritual nature of man. Scripture and subsequent theology thus legitimize patriarchal society and masculine control.

Even with this beginning, one should not assume that the Bible only pictures the female in negative or subservient terms. Nevertheless, the laws and customs of ancient Hebrew society are reflected in the persistence of patrilineality, patrilocality, and patriarchy. Roles such as the good wife, mother, and supporter of the husband are extolled. Woman as homemaker is complemented by masculine decision-making and power (Bird, 1974).

After some initial indications of liberalism toward women, early Christianity, selectively using St. Paul as a guide, began to "put women in their subordinate place." As part of this development, the early church Fathers often seemed to be projecting their own sexual conflicts onto women (Ruether, 1972). Virginal asexuality became the approved female condition; sexual activity, even when a woman was married, was regarded, at best, as a necessary evil. Women were considered the source of immorality and corruption, and therefore they needed restriction and control by men and, of course, the church (Reineke, 1989).

Protestantism, through Luther, reestablished marriage as an honorable state ordained by God which, by absolute prescription, confined women to the home, child-bearing, and child-rearing. Contemporary mainstream religion, particularly in its conservative forms, still authenticates these inequalities by reference to scripture and theology (McLaughlin, 1974). Similar views prevail in such non-Western religious traditions as Buddhism, Hinduism, and Islam (Bancroft, 1987; Reineke, 1989).

Religion as a Source of Disorder in Women: Theological Influences

As noted, scripture and theology, historically and contemporaneously, legitimate a patriarchal sociocultural system. Divine validation of such a gender-based hierarchical order endows it with the force of natural law. Biblically, females were invariably classified as virgin, wife, mother, widow, slave, or harlot. Within these roles, there is neither the power nor the religious sanction for a woman to be self-determining. A system of sexual dualism is posited in which she is defined as naturally inferior, hence lacking the authentic selfhood that characterizes the male (Ruether, 1975). In other words, the masculinization of religion leads to a conception of "ideal health" as also masculine. This is theologically grounded in Aquinas, who argued that "only the male represents the fullness of human potential, whereas woman by nature is defective physically, morally, and mentally. . . . The male represents wholeness of human nature, both in himself and as head of the woman" (Ruether, 1985, p. 45).

Meaning and status for the woman, both in the biblical past and today, is primarily determined by her sexual agency, reproductivity, relationship to males, and labor and service to others (Ruether, 1983). The seeds of powerlessness are thus sown, and the solution is to be dependent upon and obedient to the male.

Ruether (1983) notes that there is a "tendency to correlate femaleness with the lower part of human nature in a hierarchical scheme. . . . Since the lower part of the self is seen as the source of sin. . . . Femaleness becomes linked with the sin-prone part of the self" (p. 93). Inferiority is now compounded with sin and guilt as the natural female state.

Women, Religion, and Mental Disorder

Sex Differences in Mental Disorder

Though the question of whether women are overrepresented in mental hospital populations is debatable (Hyde & Rosenberg, 1976), the majority of studies reveal a higher incidence of disturbance for women than for men (Dohrenwend & Dohrenwend, 1969). These differences are due in large part to depression rates for women that are two to six times greater than for men (Weissman & Klerman, 1977). Such variations hold for women of all ages and are found in both the United States and Europe (Plancherel, Bolognini, Rossier, & Bettschart, 1990).

In addition to depression, women exceed men in the specific phobic reaction known as agoraphobia. This fear or dread of open areas is said to account for 50–60 percent of all phobic reactions. The percentage of females in nine samples of agoraphobics ranged from 63 percent to 100 percent (Brehony, 1983). Because of these high frequencies, various researchers have labeled this disorder "housebound housewives," or "discontented housewives" (Brehony, 1983, p. 115).

Women also suffer disproportionately from eating disorders. For example, rates of anorexia nervosa for women are 20 times those for men (Coleman, Butcher, & Carson, 1984). Similar statistics hold for bulimia and weight problems.

Sexual responsivity is another area in which women seem to show high rates of frustration and dysfunction (Basow, 1980; Millett, 1978). Female sexual performance is often unsatisfactory, and associated with negativism, fear, guilt, and shame.

Though a fair amount of research has been reported on the association of religion with mental disorder, very few studies have focused on women. In the following pages, because of the patterning of the literature, we will primarily stress the relationship of religion to depression.

Diagnostic Biases

Confounding this picture of sex differences and mental pathology is evidence that the criteria professionals use to diagnose mental disorders place women at a disadvantage (Kaplan, 1983). Conceptually, clinicians see the healthy male as the equivalent of the healthy adult, but this is not true for females. For the latter, the use of an "adjustment" criterion implies that "for a woman to be healthy . . . she must adjust to and accept the behavioral norms for her sex, even though these behaviors are generally less socially desirable and considered to be less healthy for the generalized competent mature adult" (Broverman, Broverman, Clarkson, Rosenkrantz, & Vogel, 1970, p. 6).

The Religious Context of Sex Differences in Mental Illness

Our position is that the Judeo-Christian heritage is operative, implicitly if not explicitly, in the lives of those in Western culture. The fact that 95–97 percent of Americans affirm a belief in God, 63 percent are formally affiliated with religious institutions, and 41 percent attend services weekly suggests the continuing reinforcement of traditional perspectives regarding males and females (Spilka, Hood, & Gorsuch, 1985). The views of both psychological and psychiatric professionals, as well as the behavior and thinking of lay people, have been formed by our religio-cultural background. In most instances, sex-role stereotypes remain unquestioned if not unrecognized. Even into the "nineteenth century, Eve's role in the fall from grace was considered an adequate explanation for any pains women might be more likely to suffer" than men (Nolan-Hoeksema, 1990, p. 14). Such stereotyping and concomitant "disorders" may still be operative within the diagnostic framework of the DSM-IIIR. For example, Landrine (1989) found that the diagnosis of personality disorders "represents the role/role stereotype of the specific group that tends to receive the [diagnostic] label most often" (p. 331). Illustrative is the fact that the diagnosis of histrionic and dependent personality disorders overwhelmingly appears among women while antisocial disorders are primarily attributed to men. Among classical Freudians, the diagnosis of gender identity disorder of childhood and atypical gender disorder is often applied to girls and women, but seldom to boys or adult men (Kaplan, 1983).

A General Perspective on Religion and Mental Health

Recent work suggests that three motives, or "desires," underlie people's attempts to cope with the world (Spilka, Shaver, & Kirkpatrick, 1985; Taylor, 1983). These are: (1) a need for meaning, based on a desire to make sense out of what takes place; (2) a need to maintain or enhance one's sense of control or power, and to master each situation; and (3) a need to maintain or enhance one's sense of esteem, and to feel adequate and valued. We feel that religion satisfies these needs, both positively and negatively.

The Need for Meaning

Of special significance here is Clark's assertion that "religion more than any other human function satisfies the need for meaning in life" (1958, p. 419). Scripture and theology therefore define the parameters of life with meanings that carry divine sanction. These include male and female roles.

The Need for Control

It almost goes without saying that power and control are central considerations in religion. People often feel that they can exert a measure of control over seemingly impossible situations through participation in religious ritual and prayer. By such means they hope to influence God to solve their problems. Whether or not objective reality can be changed (primary control), the individual has gained the "illusion of control," the way one looks at the world (secondary control) (Weisz, Rothbaum, & Blackburn, 1984).

On one level, religion offers women the same "illusion of control" to which men have access. Paradoxically, it concurrently denies them much real control over their lives by advocating restrictive female sex roles.

The Need for Esteem

Negative views of the self are inevitable when the religious message is that women are the cause of all sin and evil, that they are corrupting influences, and that they need to be limited to certain low status positions. Therefore, to the degree that such ideas are internalized by women, a heightened potential for developing mental disorder should be present.

Women, Stress, and Religion: General Considerations

We theorize that frustration, conflict, and stress result from undesirable meanings, powerlessness, and low self-esteem. In fact, these can be viewed as mediate stressors. Religion, however, can work in the opposite direction. It can also offer ennobling meanings that buttress women against role stresses, provide ritualistic and ceremonial avenues to apparent power, and suggest models and activities that elevate self-esteem. The roles religion may play are far more complex than may be initially suggested.

Religion as a Source of Disorder in Women

Female Socialization: Religion, Role, and Guilt

The religiocultural bases of mental disorder are realized in socialization practices that inculcate high levels of powerlessness and guilt in women. Some potential adverse effects of these characteristics have been demonstrated experimentally by Wallington (1973), who realized that people who engage in wrongdoing often attempt to compensate for any harm that might have been done. Specifically, Wallington theorized that, if no opportunity was available for such redress, wrongdoers might even punish themselves to atone for their "sin." Creating a situation in which transgression was likely to occur, she observed that females manifested significantly more self-aggression than males. In addition, Wallington found behavioral and cognitive signs of depression in the transgressing subjects.

Basow (1980) cited supportive work indicating that girls learn to internalize anger and be self-critical. Wallington also noted research showing that girls are more likely than boys to use self-punishment as a means of reducing guilt and anxiety about parental punishment.

Hints of the role of religion abound in this work. Bateman and Jensen (1958) found that religiosity is positively associated with intropunitiveness. Hypothetically, this suggests that most religious parents may not be inclined to employ extra-punitive physical discipline in child rearing. Aronfreed (1968) observed that psychological control techniques such as withdrawal of love and guilt induction are more likely than physical means to elicit self-aggression or intropunitiveness in children. One such procedure has been cited by Nunn (1964), in which parents form a "coalition with God." The deity becomes an ally in order to control children. This could open a door to considerable guilt and anxiety. A socialization avenue to potential depression is thus identified as religion counsels intropunitive modes of handling frustration and conflict. Methods like these are also more apt to be applied to girls than boys.

In essence, as McGuire (1987) observed, "religious symbols and images . . . shape the individual's gender role concept" (p. 97). This socializes women into their "appropriate" roles, and these constitute the basis of female self-identity. The frame of reference for self-evaluation becomes "I am a good girl/daughter/woman/mother/wife" (p. 97). Deviation from these role expectations may create guilt feelings, and negative self-evaluation. The woman might respond with self-blame, "proof that she is wrong, and moreover 'abnormal'" (Miller, 1986, p. 130).

Religious Meanings: Some Negative Implications

The above socialization practices convey meanings that deny empowerment to women. They learn roles that their faith states are the lot of the female in life. Empirical support for this position is evidenced in positive correlations between religious commitment among Catholics and Jews and the acceptance of traditional female roles (Holter, 1970). Ammerman (1987), in her study of Protestant fundamentalists, reported similar findings, but also cited material illustrating the internalization of frustration and anger by women. The rule "for keeping the peace in their homes is that in the end wives must give in rather than cause too much trouble" (p. 144). She noted how the strict religious norms of this group keep some women "in or near a state of depression" (p. 145). Brehony (1983) indicated the reinforcement of the approved "homebound behavior" (p. 119) as a factor in the development of agoraphobia.

Accepting such roles because of religious doctrine may result in pathological self-destructive passivity. For example, Hathaway-Clark (1980) found that battered women are usually highly religious, and this orientation supports their victimization. One might also consider the "patriarchal democracy" (Eaton & Weil, 1955, p. 30) that characterizes certain religious communities such as the Hutterites. In these groups, women have fewer opportunities than men to express aggression. The result is a greater internalization of frustration by women, a factor that could explain the finding that four-fifths of all Hutterite "psychoneurotics" are women

(Eaton & Weil, 1955, p. 121). It should be added that depression was the most frequent neurotic manifestation.

A central but subtle meaning that may contribute to these adverse responses on the part of women is the dominant God concept advocated in many other cultures. God is not gender free, but clearly male, and this masculinity is identified with both power and perfection. Foster and Keating (1990) claimed that this image is advantageous for men, but detrimental to women. When religious people attempt to identify with the deity, this is easier for males, allowing them higher esteem than is true for females. Other research suggests a partial way out of this dilemma (Nelsen, Cheek, & Au, 1985), since women are more likely to perceive the male God as a supportive healer than as a punishing figure. Guilt may be assuaged and anxiety reduced, but the essential meaning of classical doctrine is still present.

The Denial of Female Empowerment

Meanings imply personal control, and negative messages convey a sense of reduced mastery and power. Traditional religion explicitly transmits such ideas to devout women, and even with less awareness to those reared in conventional homes who may not be religious.

Religiously sponsored and culturally approved female roles are evidently active in the development of mental disorder among women. Rothblum (1983) claimed that the problem begins early in life, since "women are socialized to be unassertive, passive, or helpless, all of which behaviors lead to depression rather than action under stress" (p. 88). Weinraub and Brown (1983) observed the sex typing of occupations that takes place, sometimes as early as three years of age. Males tend to be assigned to jobs and tasks that connote power, while female careers are frequently associated with less competence and control. The net effect of this set of images is to present young girls and women with weak and powerless role models.

Among married women, employment seems to increase their sense of adequacy. Even so, actual control may be questionable since their outside job is usually added to their responsibilities as wife, mother, and homemaker. Being a "superwoman" adds greatly to stress, and middle-age depression is a correlate of these extra duties (Basow, 1980). It is possible that some religionists, including extremely devout women, see abnormality as punishment for deviance from God's plan. Whether psychopathology develops seems to be a function of the coping history of the woman. The prevailing explanation employs a "learned helplessness" model in which the customary female role implies dependency, and lack of competence and mastery in any broad sense (Klerman & Weisman, 1980; Radloff, 1980).

These are notable risk factors for depression. An appropriate hypothesis suggests that a woman's religiosity should correlate positively with these perceptions of inadequacy. A corollary stance would have religious women spiritually justifying these views. For example, Douglas (1965) noted that ministers' wives "may *alleviate* these feelings through a sense of the worth of the goals to which they have committed themselves" (p. 76). In addition, "they would like the freedom to *give* of themselves, rather than feeling that they must toe the line of someone else's expectations" (p. 183). The issue of personal control is evidently a central theme in the resistance to or development of disorder.

By definition, depression is consonant with low self-esteem. As we have seen, the stereotyped sex roles purveyed by our religiocultural heritage usually deny women real control over their lives. Helplessness is the main lesson that is learned. The result is that women who perceive themselves as stereotypically feminine demonstrate low self-esteem (Spence, Helmreich, & Stapp, 1975).

Deviation from established norms (classical religious prescriptions) can, however, work to the advantage of women. Messer and Harter (1986) observed that married mothers who hold full-time jobs possess more positive self-images on seven different aspects of self-concept than comparable women who are full-time homemakers; this despite the additional stress they face combining home and job.

Arguments similar to those advanced above could be applied to the other psychological problems mentioned earlier, particularly where control over one's body is concerned. These would appear to be especially applicable to eating disorders and sexual dysfunction. In sum, however, one should take seriously Cortes's admonition that "underlying most, if not all, psychological problems, probably there is also a theological or religious problem" (1965, p. 315).

Beneficial Impact of Religion on Female Mental Health

Though we have emphasized those aspects of religion that foster psychological difficulties and disturbance, it must also be noted that "religion represents an important resource for efforts to prevent significant personal and social problems" (Maton & Pargament, 1987, p. 161). Religion can thus play a pivotal role in a woman's struggle to attain meaning, control, and esteem.

Generally, the evidence is strongly against the proposition that religious commitment and psychopathology are positively associated (Spilka, Hood, & Gorsuch, 1985). In a major study of 2500 American women, Shaver, Lenauer, and Sadd (1980) showed that strong religiousness was related to enhanced mental and physical health. Glass (1971) observed that religiously active college women were less prone to anxiety than their counterparts who did not practice religion. Social support from church members, along with strong belief in a just deity and world, may be important factors here. While a few studies have found positive relationships between neuroticism and religiosity in female subjects (e.g., Brown, 1987), such results tend to be in the minority.

Religion often seems to act as a buffer against stress. Hayden and Gross (1990) reported positive relationships between religious belief and God images with the ability to tolerate chronic pain. Religion also offers constructive explanations that improve self-esteem and strengthen one's sense of personal self-control for cancer patients and their families, and also for widows during bereavement (Spilka, Hood, & Gorsuch, 1985).

A number of clinicians demonstrated how religion can alleviate depression by helping to deal with anger, improving self-concept, and by reducing guilt, loneliness, paranoid thinking, and interpersonal anxiety (Andreason, 1972; Crockett, 1977; Silverstone, 1956; Stoudenmire, 1976). Insofar as depression and suicide go together, religion appears to counter the latter (Spilka, Hood, & Gorsuch, 1985). Though pastoral counseling and therapy have been effective for many problems, we would caution against the utilization of procedures and doctrines that may ease the difficulty in the short run while maintaining the damaging images and prescriptions discussed earlier.

The dominant role of religion throughout history, and even in contemporary culture has not offered females positive ways by which to enhance their self-identity and self-esteem, or to improve their sense of control. Yet, there is much research and theory that shows how religion may suppress mental disorder, socialize people against it, and act as a haven or even a therapy (Spilka, Hood, & Gorsuch, 1985).

Conclusions and Recommendations

Working from scriptural, theological, and empirical data, we have claimed that the principal role of traditional religion relative to the sexes has been to endow men with power and esteem. In contrast, woman's legacy has emphasized dependency and helplessness. Concurrently, religion contains content and mechanisms that may act as buffers against female conflict and disorder. Modern feminist developments in theology offer constructive alternatives to past ideas, but have yet to gain broad acceptance and understanding.

Research specifically devoted to religion and mental health/disorder in women is very scarce. A broad program that treats faith as multidimensional needs to be instituted, since no work along these lines appears to have been conducted. Classical and modern theologies can provide fruitful theoretical frameworks for such research. In turn, it may be possible to integrate these with attributional, self-concept, and control theory perspectives from psychology. There is much here of both conceptual and pragmatic significance for both the individual and mass society. It calls for a program of *action research* that is long overdue.

References

Ammerman, N.T. (1987). *Bible believers: Fundamentalists in the modern world.* New Brunswick, NJ: Rutgers University Press.

Andreason, N.J.C. (1972). The role of religion in depression. *Journal of Religion and Health, 11,* 153–166.

Aronfreed, J. (1968). *Conduct and conscience: The socialization of internal control over behavior.* New York: Academic.

Bancroft, A. (1987). Women in Buddhism. In U. King (Ed.), *Women in the world's religions, past and present* (pp. 81–104). New York: Paragon House.

Basow, S.A. (1980). *Sex-role stereotypes: Traditions and alternatives.* Monterey, CA: Brooks/ Cole.

Bateman, M.M., & Jensen, J.S. (1958). The effect of religious background on modes of handling anger. *Journal of Social Psychology, 47,* 133–141.

Bird, P. (1974). Images of women in the Old Testament. In R.R. Ruether (Ed.), *Religion and sexism: Images of woman in the Jewish and Christian traditions* (pp. 41–88). New York: Simon and Schuster.

Brehony, K.A. (1983). Women and agoraphobia: A case for the etiological significance of the feminine sex-role stereotype. In V. Franks & E.D. Rothblum (Eds.), *The stereotyping of women: Its effects on mental health* (pp. 112–128). New York: Springer.

Brown, L.B. (1987). *The psychology of religious belief.* London: Academic.

Broverman, I.K., Broverman, D.M., Clarkson, F.E., Rosenkrantz, P.E., & Vogel, S.R. (1970). Sex-role stereotypes and clinical judgments of mental health. *Journal of Consulting and Clinical Psychology, 34,* 1–7.

Clark, W.H. (1958). *The psychology of religion.* New York: Macmilian.

Coleman, J.C., Butcher, J.N., & Carson, R.C. (1984). *Abnormal psychology and modern life,* seventh ed., Glenview, IL: Scott, Foresman.

Cortes, J.B. (1965). Religious aspects of mental illness. *Journal of Religion and Health, 4,* 315–321.

Crockett, M.W. (1977). Depression in middle-aged women. *Journal of Pastoral Care, 31,* 47–55.

Dohrenwend, B.P., & Dohrenwend, B.S. (1969). *Social status and psychological disorder.* New York: Wiley.

Douglas, W. (1965). *Ministers' wives.* New York: Harper & Row.

Eaton, J.W., & Weil, R.J. (1955). *Culture and mental disorders.* Glencoe, IL: The Free Press.

Foster, R.A., & Keating, J.P. (1990, November). *The male God-Concept and self-esteem: A theoretical framework.* Paper presented at the Convention of the Society for the Scientific Study of Religion, Virginia Beach, Virginia.

Gaba, C.R. (1987). Women and religious experience among the Anlo of West Africa. In U. King (Ed.), *Women in the world's religions, past and present* (pp. 177–195). New York: Paragon House.

Glass, K.D. (1971). *A study of religious belief and practice as related to anxiety and dogmatism in college women.* Unpublished Doctoral Dissertation, University of Tennessee.

Hathaway-Clark, C. (1980, April). *Multidimensional locus of control in battered women.* Paper presented at the Convention of the Rocky Mountain Psychological Association, Tucson, Arizona.

Hayden, J. & Gross, R. (1990, August). *Religious and affective dimensions of chronic pain.* Paper presented at the Convention of the American Psychological Association, Boston, Massachusetts.

Holter, H. (1970). *Sex roles and social structure.* Oslo: Universitetsforlaget.

Hyde, J.S., & Rosenberg, B.G. (1976). *Half the human experience.* Lexington, MA: Heath.

Kaplan, M. (1983). A woman's view of DSM-III. *American Psychologist, 38,* 786–803.

Klerman, G.L., & Weissman, M.M. (1980). Depressions among women: Their nature and causes. In M. Guttentag, S. Salasin, & D. Belle (Eds.), *The mental health of women* (pp. 57–92). New York: Academic.

Landrine, H. (1989). The politics of personality disorder. *Psychology of Women Quarterly, 13,* 325–339.

Makosky, V.P. (1980). Stress and the mental health of women: A discussion of research and issues. In M. Guttentag, S. Salasin, & D. Belle (Eds.), *The mental health of women* (pp. 111–127). New York: Academic.

Maton, K.I., & Pargament, K.I. (1987). The roles of religion in prevention and promotion. In L.A. Jason, R.D. Felner, R. Hess, & J. M. Mortisugu (Eds.), *Communities: Contributions from allied disciplines* (pp. 161–205). New York: Haworth.

McGuire, M.B. (1987). *Religion: The social context,* second ed. Belmont, CA: Wadsworth.

McLaughlin, E.C. (1974). Equality of souls, inequality of sexes: Women in medieval theology. In R.R. Reuther (Ed.), *Religion and sexism: Images of woman in the Jewish and Christian traditions* (pp. 213–266). New York: Simon and Schuster.

Messer, B., & Harter, S. (1986). *Manual for the Adult Self-Perception Profile.* Denver, CO: University of Denver.

Miller, J.B. (1986). *Toward a new psychology of women,* second ed. Boston: Beacon.

Miller, J.B., & Mothner, I. (1981). Psychological consequences of sexual inequality. In E.

Howell & M. Bayes (Eds.), *Women and mental health* (pp. 41–50). New York: Basic Books.

Millett, K. (1978). *Sexual politics.* New York: Ballantine.

Nelsen, H.M., Cheek, N.H. Jr., & Au, P. (1985). Gender differences in images of God. *Journal for the Scientific Study of Religion, 24,* 396–402.

Nolan-Hoeksema, S. (1990). *Sex differences in depression.* Stanford CA: Stanford University Press.

Nunn, C.Z. (1964). Child-control through a coalition with God. *Child Development, 35,* 417–432.

Plancherel, B., Bolognini, M., Rossier, L., & Bettschart, W. (1990). The life-style and health of 20 year-old young people. *Acta Paedopsychiatrica, 53,* 1–14.

Radloff, L.S. (1980). Risk factors for depression: What do we learn from them? In M. Guttentag, S. Salasin, & D. Belle (Eds.), *The mental health of women* (pp. 93–109). New York: Academic.

Reineke, M.J. (1989). Out of order: A critical perspective on women in religion. In J. Freeman (Ed.), *Women: A feminist perspective,* fourth ed. (pp. 395–413). Mountain View, CA: Mayfield.

Rothblum, E.D. (1983). Sex-role stereotypes and depression in women. In V. Franks & E.D. Rothblum (Eds.), *The stereotyping of women* (pp. 83–111). New York: Springer.

Ruether, R.R. (1972, September). *St. Augustine's penis: Sources of mysogynism in Christian theology and prospects for liberation today.* Paper presented at the International Congress of Learned Societies in the Field of Religion, Los Angeles, California.

Ruether, R.R. (1975). *New woman, new earth: Sexist ideologies and human liberation.* Minneapolis, MN: Winston.

Ruether, R.R. (1983). *Sexism and God talk: Towards a feminist theology.* Boston: Beacon.

Ruether, R.R. (1985). *To change the world: Christology and cultural criticism.* New York: Crossroad.

Shaver, P., Lenauer, M., & Sadd, S. (1980). Religiousness, conversion, and subjective well-being: The "healthy-minded" religion of modern American women. *American Journal of Psychiatry, 137,* 1563–1568.

Silverstone, H. (1956). *Religion and psychiatry.* New York: Twayne.

Spence, J.T., Helmreich, R., & Stapp, J. (1975). Ratings of self and peers on sex-role attributes and their relation to self-esteem. *Journal of Personality and Social Psychology, 32,* 29–39.

Spilka, B., Hood, R.W. Jr., & Gorsuch, R.L. (1985). *The psychology of religion: An empirical approach.* Englewood Cliffs, NJ: Prentice-Hall.

Spilka, B., Shaver, P., & Kirkpatrick, L. (1985). General attribution for the psychology of religion. *Journal for the Scientific Study of Religion, 24,* 1–20.

Stoudenmire, J. (1976). The role of religion in the depressed housewife. *Journal of Religion and Health, 15,* 62–67.

Taylor, S.E. (1983). Adjustment to threatening events: A theory of cognitive adaptation. *American Psychologist, 38,* 1161–1173.

Wallington, S.A. (1973). Consequences of transgression: Self-punishment and depression. *Journal of Personality and Social Psychology, 28,* 1–7.

Weinraub, M., & Brown, L.M. (1983). The development of sex-role stereotypes in children: Crushing realities. In V. Franks & E.D. Rothblum (Eds.), *The stereotyping of women: Its effect on mental health* (pp. 30–58). New York: Springer.

Weissman, M.M., & Klerman, G.L. (1977). Sex differences and the epidemiology of depression. *Archives of General Psychiatry, 34,* 98–111.

Weisz, J.R., Rothbaum, F.M., & Blackburn, T.C. (1984). Standing out and standing in: The psychology of control in America and Japan. *American Psychologist, 39,* 955–969.

3

Mental Health Consequences of Irreligion

John F. Schumaker

Irreligion has been conceptualized in a number of ways. Campbell (1971) wrote that irreligion can be marked by either indifference or hostility. In this way, irreligion could encompass "a-religion" as well as "anti-religion." According to Demerath (1969), however, irreligion implies an aggressive rejection of religion that often includes active patterns of counter-belief. Campbell (1977) contrasted "reactive" with "developmental" types of irreligion. Reactive irreligion amounts to a total negation of religion, whereas developmental irreligion is less directly hostile toward specific doctrines and more of an "ultimate extension of the reformative principles within religion itself" (p. 343). Campbell noted that hostile reactive types of irreligion were more characteristic of the nineteenth century, which witnessed many organized efforts to actively combat religion. Today, according to Campbell, we tend to see developmental or "Protestant" irreligion, which blends with radical theology. For the purpose of this chapter, the term *irreligion* is used rather loosely to describe extremely low levels of religious belief and involvement, regardless of degree of hostility/passivity.

While acknowledging definitional difficulties, Vernon (1968) offered evidence that irreligion has been increasing in most, but not all, societies of the world for at least the past century. More specifically, Duke and Johnson (1989) observed that people seem to be falling away from Christian and tribal religions at a considerably faster rate than Hinduism, Buddhism, and Muslim religions. They add that, despite apparent increases in irreligion, the majority of world societies contain less than 3 percent of people who profess irreligiosity. Also, societies with irreligion rates in excess of 10% often have Marxist governments that actively suppress religion. Notable exceptions include Japan, France, Germany, Sweden, and the Netherlands.

The relationship between religion and irreligion is a complex and paradoxical one. Some researchers have pointed out that increases in irreligion do not necessarily correspond to equal declines of religion (Hartel & Nelson, 1974; Roof, 1985). Sometimes religion appears to remain relatively steady in the face of rising rates of irreligion, a phenomenon that might relate to a greater willingness by people to express religious doubt or even unbelief.

Irreligion varies somewhat in relation to such factors as age, sex, social class, and occupational category. For instance, irreligion is more common in men (Argyle, 1958; Gee & Veevers, 1989), a consistent finding, which Moberg (1962) explained in terms of women's role as "culture-bearers" (p. 399). Veevers and Cousineau (1980) described the apparent curvilinear relationship between age and irreligion, with irreligion most common in the middle years of life. Wuthnow (1985) reviewed the relationship between irreligion and occupation and found support for the widely held opinion that irreligiosity is more common in the scientific professions. However, he also found some of the highest rates of irreligiosity in certain professions in the humanities and social sciences that are regarded as exceptionally nonscientific (e.g., philosophy). Irreligion also tends to be more prevalent in urban, as compared to rural, areas (Veevers & Cousineau, 1980).

Sources of Modern Irreligion

Many explanations have been put forth about the modern "epidemic" of irreligion. It is often claimed that there have been recurrent waves of unbelief, doubt, and infidelity throughout history. One might even speak of previous "secular ages," or ages of "spiritual crisis." But historians tend to regard modern irreligion as unique. Prior to the early part of the nineteenth century, irreligion had never become an established, and even accepted, position among the masses. It was largely confined to the societal elites, and it constituted what Campbell (1971) termed "a form of upper-class delinquency, . . . tolerated because it constituted no real challenge to the established belief system or threat to the power structure of society" (p. 2).

There is some consensus that factors contributing to contemporary irreligion were the outgrowth of an educated elite from the seventeenth century onward, as well as increased literacy beginning in the early nineteenth century. This latter development was thought to be responsible for the emergence of anti-authoritarianism, including religious authority. Specific developments along these lines in nineteenth century France led to unparalleled degrees of irreligion among the French working class. Neusch (1982) traced the roots of modern irreligion to the seventeenth century, while stating that it was not until the eighteenth century that it became a social force. According to Neusch, God became "morally impossible," intolerable as an obstacle to newly perceived freedoms, useless from a scientific viewpoint, and "metaphysically superfluous" (pp. 27–28).

Turner (1985) maintained that the modern variety of religious unbelief was virtually nonexistent in the middle ages. He depicted modern irreligion as a "near thing" in the sense that growing modern belief (including more sophisticated theologies and increasing church membership) almost repelled the rising tide of unbelief. Turner referred to both intellectual and moral sources of unbelief. There was an "intellectual crisis of belief in God" (Turner, 1985, p. 202) wherein the tighter principles of knowledge in the nineteenth century made religious "knowledge" less credible.

The "moral crisis" was a process whereby religious belief became morally repulsive, even "sinful" (Turner, 1985, pp. 202–204). Not only had it become intellectually reprehensible to accept religious beliefs in the absence of sufficient evidence, but religion itself became immoral. Of this, Turner wrote:

> God seemed not merely implausible but blasphemous. In a world of pain, no humanitarian could with entire comfort worship its Creator. This dilemma had become, by the later nineteenth century, especially excruciating. Many believers had attributed to God their concern to ease human suffering; church leaders had joined in divinizing humanitarianism. And now the very principles thus sanctified turned on their baptizers. God became the victim of those who insisted on His human tenderness. (Turner, 1985, p. 207)

Together, the interplay between the different humanizing trends formed a new foundation by which individual and societal needs could be met, or at least partially met.

One could describe the influence of certain organized nineteenth-century irreligion movements in Britain and America, such as the Secularist Movement, the Positivist Movement, organized Agnosticism, the Ethical Movement, the Free Religion Movement in America, the Religion of Humanity, and the various other humanistic movements (Campbell, 1971; Lightman, 1987). Also, it would be possible to detail the effects of noteworthy irreligion spokespeople, such as Ludwig Feuerbach (the "father of modern atheism," according to Neusch, 1982), Karl Marx, and Friedrich Nietzsche. But let us instead turn to the matter at hand, namely the impact of irreligion on individual and collective mental health.

Dearth of Empirical Evidence

There is an extreme sparsity of research specifically devoted to irreligion in relation to mental health. In part, this may stem from the difficulties involved in locating reasonably sized samples of irreligious subjects. Another problem is that many studies of supposedly nonreligious people do not use stringent criteria in classifying subjects as nonreligious.

Some studies labeled subjects as "nonreligious" if they did not attend church. But such an approach is flawed by the fact that one can be highly religious without attending church services. Other investigators have classified people as "nonreligious" if they gave "none" in response to a question about religious affiliation. But Vernon (1968) showed that only a relatively small percentage (23 percent) of religious "nones" described themselves as atheistic. Beyond that, 20 percent of the "nones" claimed that they felt themselves to be in the presence of God! So it is clear that a sample of religious "nones" cannot be studied as if they were all irreligious.

After eliminating studies with the above shortcomings, one is left with very few hard data relating irreligion to mental health. But a few studies warrant mention here since they did attempt to locate samples of people who were minimally religious, if not actively irreligious. As such, they represent some initial steps in our understanding of the connections between mental health and extremely low levels of religiosity.

Crawford, Handal, and Weiner (1989) isolated 39 people of "low" religious intensity and compared their mental health ratings to "medium" and "high" religious subjects. They used the Langer Symptom Survey (LSS), a 22-item epidemiological screening measure of psychological symptoms (Langer, 1962). Many of these symptoms were drawn from the Minnesota Multiphasic Personality Inventory (Dohlstrem & Welsh, 1960) and the Neuropsychiatric Screening Adjunct (Star, 1950). Crawford et al. found that "low religion" subjects had significantly more symptoms of mental disturbance than "high religious" subjects. In fact, mean LSS scores were nearly twice as high for "low religion" subjects (M = 3.85) as there were for their "high religion" counterparts (M = 2.08). It is interesting to note that "medium" religion subjects scored at nearly the exact level as "low religion" subjects on the LSS.

Crawford's team administered two other measures of psychological adjustment for purposes of comparison on the basis of degree of religiosity. One was the Flanagan Life Satisfaction Scale (FLSQ; Flanagan, 1978), which assesses life satisfaction across 15 life domains. Results showed that "low religion" subjects had significantly *lower* reported life satisfaction than "high religion" subjects, with "medium" subjects again scoring at the same level as "low" subjects. Another test was the Saint Louis University Role Functioning Inventory (SLURFI), which indicates how satisfying people find their lives in six social role categories, and also how high they rate their hopes and expectations for the future (Weiner & Margolis, 1984). Like the other two tests, the SLURFI showed "low religion" (and "medium religion") subjects to be significantly less psychologically adjusted than the "high religion" subjects.

Handal, Black-Lopez, and Moergen (1989) conducted a similar study using a sample of black women from Missouri. They too used the LSS while dividing subjects into "high," "medium," and "low" religious intensity. The "low" religion subjects were found to have far more LSS symptoms than either "medium" or "high" subjects. Unlike the Crawford et al. (1989) study, no significant difference was found between "medium" and "high" religious subjects. Of particular interest in this study was the exceptionally high mean LSS score (M = 5.07) for the "low religion" subjects. A score of 4.0 on the LSS is considered the cut-off point for psychological distress of "clinical" proportions.

Schumaker (1987) also used the LSS in comparing the mental health ratings of 40 "highly nonreligious" and 40 "highly religious" subjects, classified on the basis of extreme scores on the Religion Subscale of the Tobacyk and Milford (1983) Paranormal Belief Scale (PBS). The highest possible score on the PBS Religion Subscale is 20, which indicates strong belief in traditional concepts such as God, heaven and hell, the Devil, and life after death. The lowest possible score was four out of twenty, indicating staunch unbelief in those concepts. Subjects were classified as strongly religious if they scored 18 or more out of twenty, and highly nonreligious if they scored between four and six. When comparing the LSS mental health ratings of religious and nonreligious subjects, the findings were strikingly similar to those of the previously mentioned studies. Low religious subjects had significantly more symptoms of psychological disturbance (LSS mean = 4.2) than their highly religious counterparts (LSS mean = 2.9).[1] No "medium" religious group was included.

In assessing religion's influence on "worthwhileness of life," Hadaway and Roof (1978) established five subject groups on the basis of importance of religious faith, including a "not at all important" group. Subjects who attached no importance to religious faith perceived their lives as significantly less worthwhile than individuals for whom faith was "extremely important." However, subjects in the middle ranges of the faith continuum tended to score no higher than nonreligious subjects. Hadaway and Roof (1978) concluded that, while most people view their lives as worthwhile, "an exceptionally strong religious faith may make the difference in whether an individual feels that life is *very* worthwhile" (p.300).

The often cited Midtown Manhattan Study (Srole, Langer, Michael, Opler, & Rennie, 1962) compared mental health ratings across different religious denominations, but it did not use irreligious subjects in that comparison. However, that study did find that higher rates of psychological disturbance were characteristic of people who had made a shift from organized religion to "no religion." Of course, such a finding does not establish the direction of causation. Rather than "no religion" being the cause of psychopathology, it may be that psychopathology interferes with the ability to experience and express religion.

Rodney Stark (1971) assessed degree of religiosity in a group of outpatients from an American mental health clinic, as well as a group of matched control subjects. He then compared the percentages of people from both groups who fell into different categories (i.e., degrees) of religious commitment. One of the categories included people who stated that religion is "not important at all" to them. Stark found that "nonreligion" was significantly more prevalent in the outpatient sample. In fact, there were four times as many outpatients as controls in the nonreligious category. Almost identical results were obtained by outpatient/control comparisons made in a "no religious affiliation" category. The difference, while in the same direction, was not as great when the two groups were compared in the category containing people who did *not* belong to a church. Stark also reported that there were over five times as many religious "nones" in the outpatient sample as in the control sample (16 percent and 3 percent, respectively). Not surprisingly, Stark concluded that "these data support the hypothesis that mental illness and religious commitment are *negatively* related (p. 169). Of course, these latter findings must be viewed in the context of the above-mentioned limitations of religious "none" research.

The findings of Rokeach and Kemp (1960) contradict the proposition that irreligion has a deleterious influence on mental health, or at least one dimension of mental health. They found that a group of 15 "nonbelievers," as they were called, had significantly *lower* anxiety levels than their Catholic and Protestant counterparts. In a similar study, Rokeach and Kemp (1960) found that a group of six "unbelievers" had significantly lower anxiety levels than Catholic and Jewish subjects, but roughly the same level as Protestants. See Pressman, Lyons, Larson, and Gartner (Chapter 6, this volume) for a detailed discussion of the complex relationship between religion and anxiety.

All of these studies suffer from methodological problems that are beyond the scope of this chapter, but together they begin to suggest that *irreligion-prone* individuals might be predisposed to symptoms of psychological disturbance. Such a generalization assumes the traditional definition of mental health as an absence of mental illness. Most of the above research made use of this admittedly narrow conception of mental health. It should be noted that the picture appears to change as one begins to define mental health more "humanistically" in terms of self-actualization, self-awareness, autonomous functioning, creativity, openmindedness, flexibility, personal control and competence, and the like. In fact, Batson and Ventis (1982) demonstrated that religion is associated with *increased* psychopathology when such definitions are employed. Conversely, and in accord with the above evidence, they found that religion is related to *fewer* signs of disturbance when mental health is defined as an absence of psychopathological symptoms.

Historical Background

Given the general inadequacy of existing empirical knowledge, let me turn to some historical developments that have resultant mental health ramifications for irreligious and religious people alike. Important changes have taken place concerning the three categories of religious variables set out by Ellison, Gay, and Glass (1989). These are (1) religious belief and knowledge, (2) type and strength of identification with a *majority* religious community, and (3) level of participation in sanctioned religious ritual. In the following paragraphs mental health issues will be addressed with regard to each category, at both the collective and individual levels. It will become apparent that optimal psychological adjustment has become more difficult for all members of affected societies, including so-called religious people. But it will be argued that these problems manifest themselves to an even greater degree in individuals who have abandoned majority-sanctioned religion altogether. In the process, mention will be given to the present day "cognitive crisis," the psychological pitfalls of religious privatization and improvization, and the mental health liabilities posed by the fading of collectively enacted ritual.

Cognitive Crisis

Historically, religion entailed cognitions that provided an *ultimate* foundation and *absolute* meaning. These were *unreasonable,* but effective, mechanisms by which to transcend and transform earthly reality. In the past, as Marty (1971) observed, we even enjoyed the luxury of spatial transcendence, with God *up there* and humankind *down here.* Over the past two hundred years, however, we have seen a process of "*self*-absolutization" (Molnar, 1980, p. 134), along with a gradual divinization of ourselves and our earthly home. God, humankind, and nature have come into closer union and, as a result, we have seen the debut of relatively more *reasonable* cognitions by which to comprehend ourselves and the world. In former ages, religious cognitions tended to serve as "a bar to the exercise of free rationality" (La Barre, 1972, p. 1). More recently, religion has been infiltrated by relatively "informed" cognitive sets that leave a great many questions unanswered, and many problems unsolved. This led Marty (1971) to conclude that "the God of explanation is dead today" (p. 180). More specifically, "cognitive truth" is dead and being replaced by more immediate and potentially apocalyptic modes of consciousness (Marty, 1971, p. 115).

Molnar (1980) observed that human divinization and self-absolutization dethrones a transcendent God, and forces explanation to be circumscribed by the self and this-world experience. But Molnar saw this "dead-end street," as he termed it, as an unhealthy form of "eternal role-playing followed by emptiness instead of anticipated exaltation" (p.180). The "human absolute," wrote Molnar, "creates a frightful spiritual and political vacuum around his throne" (p. 180).

It has been pointed out that "enlightened," or secularized, religions tend to be in far worse organizational shape than "unenlightened" ones (Kelley, 1972). Stark (1985) explained this phenomenon in terms of the internal structural failure that occurs when religious systems become "too worldly and too emptied of supernaturalism" (p. 145). This, he added, accounts for diminished levels of commitment and participation in "too worldly" religions. But we might also speak of *individual* organization in relation to degree of enlightenment. In the same way that entire religious institutions begin to collapse under the weight of this-world explanation, *personal* integration may also suffer as a consequence of "enlightened" understandings. Of course, irreligious individuals would be especially prone to personal disorganization if, in fact, supernaturalism is a requisite ingredient for optimal psychological integrity.

In this vein, Bellah (1971a) reminded us that only a *transcendental* perspective can offer hope for an effective reinterpretation of empirical reality. The prospect that transcendent cognitions are important to mental health led Wilson (1971) to write that human beings will *always* need superempirical reassurances, nonrational fantasy outlets, and supernatural benefits and dispensations. But, once again, these and related mental health advantages are only transferred to people along a pathway of *unnatural* and *unthinkable* cognitions. Therefore, it could be argued that many irreligious people face a "crisis" as a result of cognitive sets that are at least partially constrained by empirical reality.

Pérez-Esclarin (1980) described the "post-religious" view of the world as "immanentist, scientific, and secular" (p. 102). This compares, he said, to the traditional world view as transcendental, mythological, and sacral. Likewise, Vahanian (1961) observed that God has been "domesticated" and metamorphized into someone better suited to our own measure. Turner (1985) highlighted the psychological costs of self-conscious religion. Furthermore, he blamed contemporary irreligion on the church leaders themselves, since they "too often forgot the *transcendence* essential to any worthwhile God" (p. 267). He added that "they committed religion *functionally* to making the world better in human terms and *intellectually* to modes of knowing God fitted only for understanding this world . . . [but by] trying to meet the challenge of modernity, they virtually surrendered to it" (p. 267).

In that fine analysis we see the problem. More and more people fell away from religion when its new "human" perspective made it no more useful as an explanatory tool than purely earthbound ones. Adherents to modern explanationless religion were themselves affected. They too became psychological captives of a "literal and circumscribed reality . . . which is precisely and classically, to be trapped in hell ... without transcendence, without manner, and without the devastating power of the sacred" (Bellah, 1971b, p. 155).

Irreligion and this-world religion fail as an interpretive system. As Bellah (1971a) realized, *this* world is the problem. One invites psychological trouble by trying to define, or redefine, this world according to its own unsavory mode of operation. Parsons (1971) acknowledged this when he wrote that "the world as such is in its very nature *never* the transcendentally defined ideal" (p. 217). As will be seen in the next section, there are ways to partially compensate for irreligion and this-world religion. Historically, however, *functional* religions have served as mental health benefactors by offering *nonordinary* cognitions by which to compete with self-consciousness and this-world knowledge. In failing to draw on conventional transcendent "proofs," people are destined to pay a mental health price. The general waning of transcendent religious cognitions may have condemned many "post-religious" people to Bellah's (1971a) mental hell in the form of *literal* reality.

Another problem emerged as religion descended over time to better accommodate human needs and wishes. Unlike worldly modes of religion, this-world religion is unstable and potentially transparent. As Glock and Stark (1965) realized, humanistic perspectives that commit themselves to "determinate statements about the empirical world" (p.11) are more vulnerable to disconfirmation than transcendent other-world conceptions. Of course, religious disconfirmation could be expected to generate considerable stress and upheaval, both at the level of the individual and society.

Some individuals and groups, most notably the organized Humanists, deny the need for superempirical "answers" (e.g., Kurtz, 1986). It has even been suggested that humanity would be safer from itself without superempirical mental constructions (e.g., Bowker, 1986; Schumaker, 1990). Yet it is probable, as Bellah (1971a) proposed, that our fragmented and disorganized culture, as well as its so-called mental health crisis, is owing in part to the depletion of credible *transcending* and nondisconfirmable religious cognitions.

Today many people find themselves in the cognitive limbo known as "agnosticism." But Malinowski observed that agnosticism is a "tragic and shattering state of mind" that has brought upon us an unsettling "Age of Longing" (see Lightman, 1987, p. 2). Organized agnosticism flourished for a while in the nineteenth century but began to wane as early as the 1890s. At its peak, it had an "optimistic, forward-looking, religious element" (Lightman, 1987, p. 181) that undoubtedly met certain cognitive, social, and spiritual needs. But Lightman chronicled the demise of agnosticism as an organized movement, while writing that "the death of the agnostic god of science transformed the faith of agnosticism into a frustrated and despairing doubt longing for faith" (p. 182).

The active and well-organized atheist movements of that period also provided some *absolute* (albeit earthbound) answers, and even transcendence in the form of a highly exaggerated veneration for descendence. But official atheism also declined, leaving modern atheists without even the subcultural stamp of approval that was once readily available. While one must recognize the "religious" nutrients that some people extract from present-day atheist groups, modern atheism (like agnosticism) is sorely lacking as an officially sanctioned position. In the absence of social sanction, irreligion does not substitute well for religion. Consequently, there are only *islands* of understanding, ones that are inextricably pulled toward Bellah's mental hell.

Religious Privatization and Improvization

Despite its supposed decline, there is an indefatigable quality about religion. This becomes apparent if one adopts a definition of religion sufficiently broad to be able to speak of religion at the subcultural or individual levels. In this regard, Stark (1985) described the "countervailing responses" that are triggered following phases of religious decline. Similarly, Duke and Johnson's data dispelled the notion that secularization is a linear process (1989). They found that, in the majority of cases, decline in the dominant religion is eventually followed by the appearance of several *minority* religions. Beckman (1976) attested to religion's remarkable resilience in describing how atheistic societies are able to adjust to religious repression by creating religious subcultures that act to challenge the source of the repression.

Schumaker (1990, 1991) assumed a very broad definition of religion in describing it as an adaptive *imperative* that is closely linked to the unique biological underpinnings of human consciousness. While many thinkers balk noisily at the prospect of a biology of religion, the fact remains that religion is a remarkably enduring feature of human behavior. In this regard, most people today continue to reach out, as always, for superempirical reconstructions of ordinary reality. In fact, our current "decline in religion" may be better understood as a process of religious *privatization* whereby belief (and related ritual) become separated from an organized referent body. Additionally, Machovec (1971) may have been correct in saying that irreligious people are best understood as "other believers" (p.99).

The concept of "substitutionism" is rooted in a functionalist view of religion and assumes that the disappearance of one religious attachment will be replaced by a *functional alternative*. Eliminationists tend to renounce the potential benefits of religion and to argue that no substitutory action is needed, or indeed desirable. My own functionalist leanings are such that I find the prospect of religious eliminationism rather implausible. Furthermore, I do not feel that one has to look far to see the diffusion of small-scale "private" religion that has paralleled the disintegration of organized religion. Religion and irreligion alike have undergone deinstitutionalization, leading Campbell (1977) to conclude that many people today are *their own* theologians (or atheists).

It is not true that irreligious people do not accept other superempirical premises. In fact, Emmons and Sobal (1981) studied a group of religious "nones" and found that they were significantly more likely than religious people to endorse nonreligious "paranormal" beliefs (e.g., astrology, numerology, witches, clairvoyance, etc). Their overall conclusion was that nonreligious systems of transcendent belief are capable of serving as *functional alternatives* to "mainstream" religion. This was substantiated by Bainbridge and Stark (1981a, 1981b), who studied religious "nones" and found that they were *more* likely than any other group to accept "deviant" supernatural and magical propositions. These researchers also demonstrated that many cult movements consist of disproportionately large numbers of formerly irreligious people (Stark & Bainbridge, 1984). One could also speak of the current upsurgence of "pop," "new age," and other nonconventional religious systems (e.g., Alcock, 1981), while asserting that their increased prevalence is also in response to religious deinstitutionalization.

Luckmann (1967) is well-known for his theory of "invisible religion," whereby *privatized* belief systems will arise in response to a waning of organized religion. These can take the form of semi-organized "secular religions" or highly subjective personal "religions." Bellah (1971a) used the term "civic religion" while arguing that the face of religion can change, but religion can never disappear. People have written about a large number of substitutionist "religions," including nationalism, Marxism, liberal and scientific humanism, scientism, the "religion of black power," acquisitionism, charity-ism, the "religion of health," corporation worship, and Hollywood Star worship. Peter Berger considered Western society's exceedingly high valuation of the "Virtue of Childhood" as an example of contemporary religious substitutionism (see Isambert, 1971, p. 149).

If substitutionism theory is correct, one should accept the possibility that, through religious improvization, surrogate religions can serve many of the functions of conventional religion. But Bellah (1971b) remarked that *several* religious substitutes may be necessary in the course of meeting a person's needs, which leads to the serious problem of *integrating* all these various signals (p. 151). Additionally, Glock (1971) raised the possibility that substitute religions are unable to produce social integration in the same manner as conventional religions.

Even more central to the issue of mental health is the fact that improvised religion has *minority* status. Religion's superempirical, or "unnatural," premises are dependent upon group endorsement. They are *patterned* and *normalized* by way of mass sanctioning. In this respect, the "religion" of irreligious people is often a futile attempt to use *abnormal* (i.e., non-normalized) methods to achieve psychological adjustment.

Berger (1969) wrote about the growing number of people who today must make sense of the world *without the benefits of religious interpretation* (p. 108). It may be, as suggested earlier, that religious surrogates can act as *partial* functional alternatives. Even so, without the normalizing influence of social sanction, improvised religion cannot provide the mental health benefits historically derived from conventional religious systems. Turner (1985) commented that "reality kicks our self-esteem" (p. 264) in the absence of majority-sanctioned religion. Furthermore, the problem is not resolved completely when attempts are made to organize irreligion, or minority religion. Demerath and Thiessen (1966) saw such efforts as nothing more than "spitting against the wind" (p. 674), since these "deviant" groups are organizationally precarious by their very nature.

It is not only irreligious people who lack the benefits of organizational normalization of their chosen religion. History has seen organizational breakdown *within* existing religious organizations. Neusch (1982) spoke of the "modern crisis of religion" as a crisis of *principle* in the sense that, more and more, religion has become more *self*-centered while operating in the absence of any "universally accepted organizing principle" (p. 215). Contemporary religion's "strong note of *innerness*"

(Luckmann, 1971, p. 47) is, in my view, a defensive reaction to the experience of the non-normalized character of improvized private religions. On this subject, Turner (1985) wrote that, in the past, traditional religion offered a "web of *shared* assumptions" that provided a frame for an *agreed-upon* universe. But he added that, today, this web has partially unraveled. According to Turner, religion no longer serves as a traditional linchpin and, as a result, *our culture now lacks a center.* More and more, in Turner's view, this demands that individuals define their own meaning with their own "deviant" theologies. He felt that this has predisposed contemporary people to the *angst,* despair, and unceasing yearning so prevalent today.

Eclipse of Religious Ritual

Although typically bizarre by appearance, ritual is a very powerful sustainer of mental health, as well as a method by which to prevent the onset, or progression, of psychological disturbance. Also, the therapeutic use of ritual in the healing process has been well documented by behavioral and medical anthropologists. Ritual theorists have argued that religious ritual can help to cope with fear, anxiety, frustration, uncertainty, trauma, and alienation (e.g., Ahler & Tamney, 1964; also see Chapter 23 in this volume, by Janet L. Jacobs). Rituals can combat feelings of insignificance and provide a solution to the problem of mortality. Durkheim (1961) wrote of the power of rituals as they combine with myth to support social structure, and to affirm and retain the general sense of reality of people within any functional society. In this regard, Hong (1981) provided empirical support for the theory that religion's ritual component is able to reduce "anomia," a term that refers to the "personal level of normlessness" (p. 243) experienced by people.

In his classic essay on the dynamics of ritual, Thomas Scheff (1977) argued that ritual performs a function that is vital to mental health. It enables the human being to cope with universal emotional threats by offering a mechanism to achieve necessary *distance from one's emotions.* While Scheff's theory is not without controversy, it fits well with much that has been observed with regard to repression and cathartic behavior as mechanisms of affective release. According to Scheff, those people who can no longer avail themselves of collective ritual will run a continual risk of being *underdistanced* from their emotions.

As Giddens (1989) pointed out, collective ritual is a defining feature of all religion. In fact, traditional religion has been the historical center for group-enacted ritual. Therefore, one could speculate that irreligious people lack a very important source of group ritual, which places them at risk of being emotionally "underdistanced." Yet proponents of substitutionism argue convincingly that highly differentiated secular ritual can substitute for institutionalized religious ritual. Some even speak of "atheistic ritual," which in every way resembles religious ritual, except of course that the ritual does not have meaning with regard to the existence of a deity (Apostel, 1981).

But the problem with privatized or "unofficial" ritual is that ritual actions (as we saw with religious cognitions) are normalized by collective participation. As Apostel (1981) noted, ritual is useless and meaningless when viewed from an external source. Beyond that, *individually* enacted ritual would be considered highly pathological in most cases. The same holds true for the attributions people would attach to their own *personal* rituals. The overall effect would be to inhibit the degree to which a person would indulge themselves with ritual, thereby depriving that individual of key mental health benefits.

Conversely, Apostel (1981) wrote that collective ritual action constitutes an important mode of affiliation whereby communication takes place among participants. Common convictions are reinforced and the rituals are embellished with status and specific symbolic meaning. When rituals become "normal" through group endorsement, they are valuable for purposes of overall social cohesion. But Apostel may be right in saying that collectively sanctioned ritual also has the potential to be destructive at the social level. The same has been argued more generally about religion (Bowker, 1986; Schumaker, 1990). Also, Scheff (1977) pointed out that, in excess, ritual can become counter-productive by *over-distancing* a person from the experience of emotion. But this does not change the fact that, in a suitable collective context, ritual is highly functional and the source of many mental health advantages.

While distinctly irreligious people may lack the health-giving benefits of majority-enacted ritual, recent history has also seen the decline of ritual within organized religion. Although majority religion was the traditional base for much of the ritual that has served us throughout history, Ninian Smart (1985) observed that there has been a shift away from ritual dimensions of religion. According to Smart, complex and everyday religious ritual has lost much of its former magical function. He added that, even within religious circles, there has been the emergence of more *individuastic* and *informal* versions of ritual, ones that parallel the overall informalization and privatization of religion. Furthermore, Smart predicted that a growing emphasis on personal and experiential modes of "religion" will continue to replace the group-enacted rituals that were previously contextualized by normative myths. Therefore, it may be that many religious people today are nearly as "underdistanced" emotionally as their irreligious counterparts.

Concluding Comments

Some people have depicted religion as destructive to mental health on the grounds that it breeds intolerance, prejudice, personality constriction, self-denigration, dependency and hypersuggestibility, diminished sense of autonomy, loss of critical thinking ability, and so forth (e.g., Alcock, 1981; Ellis, 1975; Dittes, 1971). However, that overall conclusion requires a much broader definition of mental health than the traditional one espoused here. I would argue that the above categories of behavior are better understood as predictable *side effects* of religion, or as features of what Spilka (1987) described as "dysfunctional" modes of religion.

In my view, irreligion (as well as most improvised religion) divests people of certain age-old pathways to psychological health. As was seen, these pathways exist in the areas of cognition, social affiliation, and collective action. But I also offered support for Demerath's (1969) observation that religious and irreligious people alike are disadvantaged in this age of "post-religion." It does seem, as Demerath noted, that the religion of many people today is half-hearted, and that they are often religious by mere imitation and habit. Even among supposedly religious church-going people, Demerath (1969) sees a "restless, skeptical, and emotionalized probing" (p. 202). In a similar way, Harvey Cox (1971) wrote about the profound hypocrisy of contemporary religious people in concluding that they "do not really have a living belief motivating their lives, giving them hope, and uniting them with the rest of mankind" (p. 93). Likewise, Smart (1969) described how, in contemporary times, it is easy for religious ritual to become an "empty shell" that is acted out mechanically and without sentiment, thus making it devoid of many of its traditional benefits.

Therefore, it may be that comparative studies of mental health among the religious and irreligious amount to a comparison of people with varying degrees of psychological disturbance. Naroll (1983) demonstrated that *average* mental health varies greatly from one society to another. He explained this in terms of his concept of the "moral net," and theorized that societies with intact moral nets should have better mental health, on average, than societies in which this net is weakened. According to Naroll, socially sanctioned religious beliefs and rituals are an important feature of the moral net. Consequently, erosion of conventional religious systems serves to unravel the moral net, one effect being lessened psychological health in *all* members of that society.

Erich Fromm (1968) wrote similarly that an entire culture can become "insane" if it no longer functions in order to meet *human* needs. According to Fromm, any intact or "sane" society should have, among other things, a system of *group-endorsed* myth and ritual (i.e., religion) that operates to satisfy basic needs such as transcendence, orientation, and belonging. Despite the fact that a high proportion of people still identify themselves with aspects of religion, Fromm regarded Western society as a highly irreligious, as well as an extremely "insane," one. In *To Have or To Be,* Fromm (1976) painted a bleak picture of our "collective neurosis" wherein *Having* is the new God, and consumption the new ritual base. In the process, we have become "a society of notoriously unhappy, lonely, anxious, depressed, destructive, and dependent people who are glad when we have killed the time we are trying so hard to save" (pp. 5–6). There may be some unfortunate truth in his provocative summation that "in the nineteenth century the problem was that *God is dead;* in the twentieth century the problem is that *man is dead*" (Fromm, 1976, p. 360). Furthermore, this may apply *almost* equally to people who are still able to take psychological advantage of our ailing religion.

Notes

1. The Schumaker (1987) study contains a misprint. Lines 12–14 should read: "Nonreligious subjects had significantly higher scores (M = 4.2) than religious subjects (M = 2.9) on the LMHS (t = 2.0, p <.05)."

References

Alcock, J. (1981). *Science or magic?* New York: Pergamon.

Ahler, J.G., & Tamney, J.B. (1964). Some functions of religious ritual in a catastrophe. *Sociological Analysis, 25,* 212–230.

Apostel, L. (1981). Mysticism, ritual, and atheism. In L. Apostel, R. Pinxten, R. Thibau, & F. Vandamme (Eds.), *Religious atheism?* Gent, Belgium: E. Story-Scientia.

Argyle, M. (1958). *Religious behavior.* London: Routledge & Kegan Paul.

Bainbridge, W.S., & Stark, R. (1981a). The consciousness reformation reconsidered. *Journal for the Scientific Study of Religion, 20,* 1–16.

Bainbridge, W.S., & Stark, R. (1981b). Friendship, religion, and the Occult. *Review of Religious Research, 22,* 313–327.

Batson, C.D., & Ventis, W.L. (1982). *The religious experience: A social-psychological perspective.* Oxford and New York: Oxford University Press.

Beckman, B.M. (1976). Religious survival in an atheistic society: A Soviet dilemma. *Michigan Academician, 8,* 349–358.

Bellah, R.N. (1971a). The historical background of unbelief. In R. Caporale & A. Grumelli (Eds.), *The culture of unbelief.* Berkeley, CA: The University of California Press.

Bellah, R.N. (1971b). Toward a definition of unbelief. In R. Caporale & A. Grumelli (Eds.), *The culture of unbelief.* Berkeley, CA: The University of California Press.

Berger, P.L. (1969). *The sacred canopy.* Garden City, NY: Doubleday.

Bowker, J.W. (1986). The burning fuse: The unacceptable face of religion. *Zygon, 21,* 415–438.

Campbell, C. (1971). *Toward a sociology of irreligion.* New York: Macmillan.

Campbell, C. (1977). Analyzing the rejection of religion. *Social Compass, 24,* 339–346.

Cox, H. (1971). Variations in perspective on secularization and unbelief. In R. Caporale & A. Grumelli (Eds.), *The culture of unbelief.* Berkeley, CA: The University of California Press.

Crawford, M.E., Handal, P.J., & Weiner, R.L. (1989). The relationship between religion and mental health/distress. *Review of Religious Research, 31,* 16–22.

Demerath, N.J. (1969). Irreligion, a-religion, and the rise of the religion-less church: Two case studies in organized convergence. *Sociological Analysis, 30,* 191–203.

Demerath, N.J., & Thiessen, V. (1966). On spitting against the wind: Organizational precariousness and American irreligion. *American Journal of Sociology, 71,* 674–687.

Dittes, J.E. (1971). Religion, prejudice, and personality. In M.P. Strommen (Ed.), *Research on religious development.* New York: Hawthorn Books.

Dohlstrem, W.G., & Welsh, G.S. (1960). *An MMPI handbook.* St. Paul, MN: North Central.

Duke, J.T., & Johnson, B.L. (1989). The stages of religious transformation: A study of 200 nations. *Review of Religious Research, 30,* 209–224.

Durkheim, E. (1961). *The elementary forms of religious life.* New York: Collier.

Ellis, A. (1975). The case against religion: A psychotherapists view. In B. Ard (Ed.), *Counseling and psychotherapy.* Palo Alto, CA: Science & Behavior Books.

Ellison, C.G., Gay, D.A., & Glass, T.A. (1989). Does religious commitment contribute to life satisfaction? *Social Forces, 68,* 100–123.

Emmons, C.F., & Sobal, J. (1981). Paranormal beliefs: Functional alternatives to mainstream religion? *Review of Religious Research, 22,* 301–312.

Flanagan, J.C. (1978). A research approach to improving our quality of life. *American Psychologist, 33,* 126–147.

Fromm, E. (1968). *The sane society.* London: Routledge & Kegan Paul.

Fromm, E. (1976). *To have or to be.* New York: Harper & Row.

Gee, E.M., & Veevers, J.E. (1989). Religiously unaffiliated Canadians: Sex, age, and regional variations. *Social Indicators Research, 21,* 611–627.

Giddens, A. (1989) *Sociology.* Cambridge: Polity Press.

Glock, C.Y. (1971). The study of unbelief: Perspectives on research. In R. Caporale & A. Grumelli (Eds.), *The culture of unbelief* (pp. 53–75). Berkeley, CA: University of California Press.

Glock, C.Y., & Stark, R. (1965). *Religion and society in tension.* Chicago: Rand McNally.

Hadaway, C.K., & Roof, W.C. (1978). Religious commitment and the quality of life in American society. *Review of Religious Research, 19,* 295–307.

Handal, P.J., Black-Lopez, W., & Moergen, S. (1989). Preliminary investigation of the relationship between religion and psychological distress in black women. *Psychological Reports, 65,* 971–975.

Hartel, B.R., & Nelson, H.M. (1974). Are we entering a post-Christian era? Religious belief and attendance in America, 1957–1968. *Journal for the Scientific Study of Religion, 13,* 409–419.

Hong, L.K. (1981). Anomia and religiosity: Some evidence for reconceptualization. *Review of Religious Research, 22,* 233–244.

Isambert, F. (1971). Toward a definition of unbelief. In R. Caporale & A. Grumelli (Eds.), *The culture of unbelief.* Berkeley, CA: The University of California Press.

Kelley, D.M. (1972). *Why conservative churches are growing.* New York: Harper & Row.

Kurtz, P. (1986). *The transcendental temptation.* Buffalo, NY: Prometheus Books.

Langer, T.S. (1962). A twenty-one item screening scale score of psychiatric symptoms indicating impairment. *Journal of Health and Human Behavior, 3,* 269–276.

La Barre, W. (1972). *The ghost dance: Origins of religion.* New York: Harper & Row.

Lightman, B. (1987). *The origins of agnosticism.* Baltimore and London: Johns Hopkins University Press.

Luckmann, T. (1967). *The invisible religion.* London: Collier-Macmillan.

Luckmann, T. (1971). Belief, unbelief, and religion. In R. Caporale & A. Grumelli (Eds.), *The culture of unbelief.* Berkeley, CA: The University of California Press.

Machovec, M. (1971). Round table discussion. In R. Caporale & A. Grumelli (Eds.), *The culture of unbelief.* Berkeley, CA: The University of California Press.

Marty, M. (1971). Responses to Bellah. In R. Caporale & A. Grumelli (Eds.), *The culture of unbelief.* Berkeley, CA: The University of California Press.

Moberg, D.O. (1962). *The church as a social institution.* New Jersey: Prentice-Hall.

Molnar, T. (1980). *Theists and atheists: A typology of non-belief.* The Hague, the Netherlands: Mouton.

Naroll, R. (1983). *The moral order.* London: Sage Publications.

Neusch, M. (1982). *The sources of modern atheism.* New York: Paulist Press.

Parsons, T. (1971). Belief, unbelief, and disbelief. In R. Caporale & A. Grumelli (Eds.), *The culture of unbelief* (pp. 207–245). Berkeley, CA: University of California Press.

Pérez-Esclarin, A. (1980). *Atheism and liberation.* London: SCM Press.

Rokeach, M., & Kemp, C.G. (1960). Open and closed systems in relation to anxiety and childhood experience. In M. Rokeach, *The open and closed mind* (pp. 347–365). New York: Basic Books.

Roof, W.C. (1985). The study of social change in religion. In P.E. Hammond (Ed.), *The sacred in a secular age* (pp. 75–89), Berkeley, CA: University of California Press.

Scheff, T.J. (1977). The distancing of emotion in ritual. *Current Anthropology, 18,* 483–505.

Schumaker, J.F. (1987). Mental health, belief deficit compensation, and paranormal beliefs. *Journal of Psychology, 121,* 451–457.

Schumaker, J.F. (1990). *Wings of Illusion.* Cambridge: Polity Press (in USA, Buffalo, NY: Prometheus Books).

Schumaker, J.F. (1991). The adaptive value of suggestibility and dissociation. In J.F. Schumaker (Ed.), *Human suggestibility: Advances in theory, research, and application* (pp. 108–131). New York and London: Routledge.

Smart, N. (1969). The religious experience of mankind. New York: Charles Scribner's Sons.

Smart, N. (1985). The future of religions. *Futures, 17,* 24–33.

Spilka, B. (1987). Functional and dysfunctional roles of religion. *Journal of Psychology and Christianity, 8,* 5–15.

Srole, L., Langer, T., Michael, S.T., Opler, M.K., & Rennie, T.A. (1962). *Mental health in the metropolis* (vol. 1). New York: McGraw-Hill.

Star, S.A. (1950). The screening of psychoneurotics in the army: Technical development of a test. In S.A. Stouffer (Ed.), *Measurement and prediction* (pp. 486–547). Princeton, NJ: Princeton University Press.

Stark, R. (1971). Psychopathology and religious commitment. *Review of Religious Research, 12,* 165–176.

Stark, R. (1985). Church and sect. In P.E. Hammond (Ed.), *The sacred in a secular age* (pp. 134–149). Berkeley, CA: University of California Press.

Stark, R., & Bainbridge, W.S. (1984). *The future of religion.* Berkeley, CA: University of California Press.

Tobacyk, J., & Milford, G. (1983). Belief in paranormal phenomena: Assessment development and implications for personality functioning. *Journal of Personality and Social Psychology, 44,* 1029–1037.

Turner, J. (1985). *Without God, without creed: The origins of unbelief in America.* Baltimore and London: The Johns Hopkins University Press.

Vahanian, G. (1961). *The death of God.* New York: George Braziller.

Veevers, J.E., & Cousineau, D.F. (1980). The heathen Canadians: Demographic correlates of nonbelief. *Pacific Sociological Review, 23,* 199–216.

Vernon, G.M. (1968). The religious "nones": A neglected category. *Journal for the Scientific Study of Religion, 2,* 219–229.

Weiner, R.L., & Margolis, R. (1984). *Chronic pain, pain manageability, and role functioning.* Unpublished manuscript, Saint Louis University, Department of Psychology, Saint Louis, Missouri.

Wilson, B. (1971). Unbelief as an object of research. In R. Caporale & A. Grumelli (Eds.), *The culture of unbelief.* Berkeley, CA: The University of California Press.

Wuthnow, R. (1985). Science and the sacred. In P.E. Hammond (Ed.), *The sacred in a secular age* (pp. 187–203). Berkeley, CA: University of California Press.

4

Religion and Sexual Adjustment

John D. Shea

Christianity has been unremittingly hostile to sex (Bullough, 1976). Since sexual behavior involves emotions that are sometimes profound, we might expect that such hostility would have harmful consequences for psychological stability. Evaluating the effects of religion on contemporary sexual behaviors is a relatively straightforward task, and it has been addressed by several research studies in this century. For instance, in *Sexual Behaviour in the Human Male,* Kinsey, Pomeroy, and Martin (1948) proposed that "there is nothing in the English-American social structure which has had more influence upon present day patterns of sexual behaviour than the religious backgrounds of that culture" (p. 465).

Estimating the psychological distress or the personal misery caused by Christianity's hostility to sex is more difficult. If we consider those people prosecuted and punished for sexual sins or crimes in Christian communities, we might conservatively estimate the number of castrations, whippings, incarcerations, burnings, beheadings, hangings, and other executions attributable directly to Christian teaching to be in the millions. Presumably such punitive actions, which continue to the present time, are actually distressing to the people who are punished, but perhaps we can go further in the search for Christianity's effects.

Patton (1988) argues that Catholicism has caused its adherents severe psychological damage and suffering in the form of shame, guilt, fear, and anxiety related to sex, ultimately leading in many cases to anger, depression, and rage. He suggests that there have been billions of victims over the past two thousand years and uses contemporary evidence to substantiate his case. While a plausible case might be constructed, applicable to a greater or lesser degree to other Christian communities, finding evidence of actual behavioral outcomes, particularly with regard to previous historical periods, is more difficult.

The enthusiastic, even fanatical, anti-sexual writings and self-mutilating behaviors of early Christian leaders encourage speculation about their sanity. Considering their followers, we might wonder whether the attacks on sexuality, especially female sexuality, had destabilizing and destructive effects on marital relationships, on the birthing experience, and on the quality of nurturance that mothers and fathers were able to offer their children. However, our conclusions would for the most part be mere guesswork. In some respects, the task is made easier because anti-sexual attitudes probably reached their peak in the last century. Thus examination of changes that have taken place since that time gives some indication of the success of Christianity in inhibiting sexual behaviors. A first step is to understand the comprehensiveness of the Christian attack on sexuality, and the degree to which this diverged from preceding cultures, including Judaism. Where there are similarities between our own and earlier cultures, it may be that we are looking at the source of our own values; where there are differences, we might wonder at the forces that produced those changes.

Ancient Societies

An enduring and pervasive idea has been the view that women are little more than property. This was a position adopted by the civilizations of Babylon, Egypt, Greece, and the Jews. It was also the way among the Germanic tribes, who began to populate the Roman Empire as Christianity itself spread throughout much of Europe and the Near East. Women were considered the responsibility of their fathers or husbands, or some other male relative. They had economic value. Adultery, or fornication with an unmarried woman, were not sins against morality but offenses against the husband's or father's property that reduced the economic value of their women. Usually a husband had freedom to fornicate, but a wife could be severely punished, perhaps put to death, for the same thing. Generally free women were closely secluded and protected, female slaves were often available for the sexual use of the male head of the household and his sons, and concubinage was a common practice. A general misogyny is evident from Old Testament portrayals of women (Harris, 1984) and from Greek writings (Bullough, 1976).

Despite the inferior social position of women, it seems that women of ancient cultures were considered to have sexual drives and capacities equal to or greater than those of men. However, they usually had much less opportunity to put this idea to the test. Among the Greeks there was the persistent notion that the womb had an appetite for sex and childbearing, almost independent from the woman (Sevely, 1987). Jewish scriptural tradition presents women as having the more constant and aggressive sex drive. Exodus (21:10) mentions a husband's conjugal obligations in terms of frequency, and Deuteronomy (24:5) recognized women's sexuality by insisting on the duty of their husbands to satisfy them. In intercourse, women were supposed to achieve orgasm, and the best way a man could be certain of begetting a son was to bring his wife to orgasm before he himself achieved it (Bullough, 1976).

There was a near universal preference for the female superior position in intercourse in ancient Greece, Rome, and Egypt, judging by the art objects and materials and literature of the times (Kinsey, et al., 1948; Bullough, 1976). Considering the role of the female superior position in intercourse for increasing feelings of control and increasing the likelihood of women's coital orgasm, it does not seem unreasonable to assume that women had a better time in intercourse in ancient times than during most of the past two thousand years.

Marriage in ancient times was primarily for procreation. Among the Jews, marriage was virtually compulsory whether or not reproduction was possible. Generally wives were not acknowledged as being for companionship, except perhaps among the Jews. In Aristotle's discussion of friendship, he did not consider the relationship of husband and wife at all. As Demosthenes expressed it in the fourth century B.C.: "We resort to courtesans for our pleasures, keep concubines to look after our daily needs and marry wives to give us legitimate children and be the faithful guardians of our domestic hearths" (see Bullough, 1976, p. 98).

In sexual attitudes, the ancient Babylonians, Egyptians, Greeks, and Romans were very tolerant. Premarital and extramarital relations were tolerated for the male and often encouraged, as long as such behavior did not threaten the survival of the family. Both heterosexual and homosexual anal intercourse were common, though the latter may not have been greatly favored. Prostitution, male and female, was accepted and widely practiced, though homosexuality seems to have been considered demeaning. Apparently, masturbation was viewed as a natural substitute for the lack of sexual intercourse. The Greeks were more tolerant than others of homosexuality, especially in the context of a relationship with an adolescent boy. The Jews accepted virtually any sexual behavior within marriage as long as vaginal entry occurred, even if no conception was possible. The Hebrew Bible approved of marital sex for whatever joy it could bring (Ecclesiastes, 9:9). However, the Jews were antagonistic to nonmarital sex of any kind, being troubled by the waste of "generative seed" (Szasz, 1981). Consistent with a positive evaluation of procreative sex, premarital sex was tolerated, though virginity in a bride was highly regarded. The Christian era, influenced by pagan philosophies, brought the Western world a negativity to sex that is unique among the great cultures of history.

Pagan Asceticism

Persian ascetic religious ideas, like those in Greece, may have come ultimately from common Indo-European origins (Bullough, 1976). They became the predominant philosophy among the Persians from the sixth century B.C. after the religious triumph of Zoroaster. They spread to Egypt and Babylon with the Persian military conquests. Zoroastrianism probably strengthened Greek asceticism after Alexander the Great took over the Persian Empire in the later part of the fourth century B.C. Its influence on Christianity can be seen as late as the fourth century A.D. in the teachings of Augustine of Hippo.

A dominant theme was the conflict between the flesh and the spirit, with the triumph of the spirit seen as necessary for immortality. All aspects of sexual activity that did not lead to procreation were to be condemned and prohibited, as was intercourse with courtesans and prostitutes. Adultery and polygamy were disapproved of as well. Homosexual intercourse was a more serious sin than killing a righteous man. Masturbation, and even involuntary emission of male semen, were serious sins. The Persian correlation of sexual morality with religious salvation appeared also among the Greek ascetics before adoption by Christianity.

As Bullough (1976) noted, the ascetic, sex-negative undercurrent in Greek culture, recorded as early as the eighth century B.C. in Orphic cultic teachings, contrasts dramatically with the mainstream sex-positive attitudes of the Greeks. Like Zoroastrianism, Greek dualistic thought divided the world into the spiritual and the material and advocated a struggle against the corrupting influence of the flesh. The Greeks taught that the spiritual soul was undergoing punishment for sin imprisoned in the material body, but the soul could escape the domination of the flesh and immortality through ritual purity, and through purity as a way of life. The Orphics advocated sexual abstinence because they regarded sexual intercourse as polluting.

When it was first expressed, this ascetic viewpoint was not greatly influential, but it was a theme that persisted over many centuries (Bullough, 1976). It was taken up by Pythagoras in the sixth century B.C., then by Empedocles; by Democritus in the fifth century B.C., and by Epicurus in the fourth. Epicurus claimed that "sexual intercourse never benefitted any man" and that a good life could not result from "sexual intercourse with women" (see Bullough, 1976, p. 166). Plato was the most influential transmitter of many Pythagorean ideals. He taught that the soul, an immaterial agent, was superior to the body and was hindered by the body in its performance of the higher psychic functions of human life. Copulation lowered a man to the frenzied passions characteristic of beasts, and sexual desire was relegated to the lowest element of the psyche. The Cynics, dating from the fourth century B.C., and somewhat less influential, had similar views. When asked the right time to marry Diogenes said, "For young men, not yet; for old men, never" (see Bullough, 1976, p. 166). Zeno (340–265 B.C.), the founder of Stoicism, patterned his personal life after the Cynics, but appealed in particular for the application of reason in human affairs. Sexual passion was suspect, because it threatened reason. The use of sex for anything but procreation was considered contrary to nature.

Together these philosophies influenced the thinking of Philo in Alexandria in the first century B.C. He held that those who mated with their wives for sexual enjoyment were mere pleasure lovers, like "pigs or goats." All other forms of nonprocreative sex were also condemned, with homosexuality considered particularly offensive. Philo blamed women for the fall from the Garden of Eden. For women, spiritual progress meant giving up the nonrational female gender for the male gender, which was more rational and akin to mind and thought. Women could do best by remaining virgins. His ideas considerably influenced Christianity and the neo-Pythagorean and neo-Platonist revivals in the second and third centuries A.D.

At about the same time an ascetic trend emerged also among the Romans, strongly influenced by Stoic ideas. Seneca, the first-century A.D. Stoic, was later cited approvingly by St. Jerome as claiming that a "wise man ought to love his wife with judgment, not affection. Let him control his impulses and not be borne headlong into copulation. Nothing is fouler than to love a wife like an adulteress" (cited in Bullough, 1976, p. 167).

Following a similar position were the neo-Pythagoreans, and the neo-Platonists. Most notable was Plotinus, who lived and wrote during the third century A.D., gaining favor with the Roman Emperor. Plotinus taught that the key to human virtue lay in detachment from worldly (i.e., evil) desire. By implication, it was necessary to become indifferent to sex. His pupil, Porphyry, went further in condemning *any* kind of pleasure as sinful, including horseracing, theatergoing, dancing, eating meat, and, of course, sexual intercourse under any and all conditions.

Shortly before the millennium, there seem to have been some minority ascetic Jewish groups, no doubt influenced by these widespread ideas, including the Therapeutae "who were unusually severe in their discipline and life" (May, 1930, p. 39). In the time of Jesus, Judaism was more strict than in earlier times, and there existed one particular ascetic group, the Essenes, with whom he may have had close contact (Szasz, 1981). By about the second or third century A.D., more than a thousand years after its recorded appearance, Greek and Persian ascetic thought had become a very powerful movement, and it provided the context in which Christian ideas were to emerge.

Christian Asceticism

Pagan Greek and Persian ideas about the conflict of the body and soul, and the importance of sexual denial in particular, were enthusiastically embraced by the early Christians. The Stoic attention to nature, virtue, decorum, and freedom from excess were attractive to early Christian teachers, but current interpretations of Plato's ideas were the dominant force in early Christian thought (Bullough, 1976). Christianity adopted so many of the Platonic concepts that Justin Martyr, an early Christian teacher, frequently commented that Plato must have been versed in Christian prophecy, for he was a Christian before Jesus had appeared. The anti-sex attitudes of the pre-Christian pagan ascetics have endured through the vehicle of Christianity to shape Western sexual behavior even today.

Jesus, a Palestinian Jew, had few negative things to say about sex in his own teachings, though he did express concern about sexual excess, and preached against adultery, or even thinking about it, in both men and women. He disapproved of divorce, and seemed to favor celibacy for those who were capable. Indeed his statement that "there be eunuchs which have made themselves eunuchs for the kingdom of heaven's sake" (Matthew 19:11–12), was occasionally interpreted literally. Origen of Alexandria (died about A.D. 251–254), and other devout Christians went out into the desert and castrated themselves as an act of purification.

However, Jesus said very little else about sex, and it was St. Paul who created the basis for Christian attitudes from very limited offerings. His ideas, particularly the view that celibacy was a higher state than marriage, were contrary to mainstream Jewish ideas of the time. He said, "It is good for a man not to touch a woman" (I Corinthians, 7:1), "for to be carnally minded is death" (Romans, 8:5–8). However, if a man was weak and unable to resist sexual urges, "it is better to marry than to burn" (I Corinthians, 7:12). Thus marriage was a concession to human frailty, but it was not sinful.

Paul felt it was woman's fault that men were sexually aroused. Like Philo he gave special emphasis to the sin of Adam and Eve, and to the fault of Eve in this process; "And Adam was not deceived, but the woman being deceived was in the transgression" (I Timothy 1:11–15). From this it was not far to his teachings about the need for the strict subjugation of women, and the need for them to cover themselves to reduce their seductive powers.

Paul's views should be seen in their personal and historical context. Paul had been a man who persecuted the early followers of the "Messiah," and he had led a full sexual life (Tannahill, 1982). He had a dramatic conversion experience, a vision of "the risen Christ" which changed his way of life. He was a man driven by his intense beliefs, and probably by guilt for his early sins. He expressed strong negative feelings for his own body, and judged himself harshly. To add to this he believed that Christ's return was imminent. The intensity of his belief and the feeling of urgency about the need to spread Christian teachings drove him to missionary zeal, and efforts to diminish the significance of earthly satisfactions.

Later, Justin Martyr was so committed to a philosophy that associated virtue with sexual abstinence, he propounded the notion of the virgin birth of Jesus and spoke approvingly about living a life of continence, and the desire for self-castration (Bullough, 1976). Nearly as influential was his disciple, Tatian, the leader of a group known as the Encratites, or the "self-controlled." They taught that marriage was corruption, and prohibited sexual intercourse, intoxicants, and meats. For a time in the third century, the Syrian Church, influenced by these ideals, maintained that virginity was essential for the Christian life (Bullough, 1976).

Such anti-sex, anti-marriage, and anti-women ideas remained strong in the early church. Gregory of Nyssa, in the fourth century, dismissed marriage as a sad tragedy. St. Jerome (died A.D. 420) tolerated marriage only because it produced more virgins. He spoke of sexual intercourse as "unclean," and, after his own experiences in the desert, praised those who underwent self-castration (Pagels, 1988). Jerome asserted that a woman who remained virginal, serving Christ, "will cease to be a woman and will be called a man" (Bullough, 1976, p. 365).

St. Ambrose (died A.D. 397) similarly expressed contempt for marriage, especially when comparing it with virginity. He described intercourse as "a defilement." Ambrose too followed Philo's view of the inferiority of women. Not surprisingly, celibacy within the priesthood gradually became the norm in the Western church, though not in the East. In fact, the Eastern church was generally less negative about sex than the West. With the fading of the influence of the Gnostics and the pagan philosophies, the Western Christian church might also have become less hostile to sex if it had not been for St. Augustine. Pagels (1988) suggests that the obsessions of Augustine effected a metamorphosis in the church's world view.

Before he was a Christian, Augustine was a sexually indulgent, but guilt-ridden follower of the Babylonian religion Manichaeanism, which contained elements of Gnostic, Christian, Zoroastrian, and Greek ascetic ideas. In his personal life Augustine could not achieve the self-denial required to join the inner circle of the Elect though he struggled for this over an eleven-year period. He often begged God to release him from his "fetters of lust." He wrote, "I had prayed to you for chastity and said 'Give me chastity and continency, but do not give it yet.' For I was afraid that you would answer my prayer at once and cure me too soon of the disease of lust, which I wanted satisfied, not quelled" (Watts, 1919, pp. VII, VIII).

After first abandoning his long-term mistress and child, then taking a temporary mistress while waiting to be married to an underage girl, Augustine went through a crisis of conscience that led him to conversion to Christianity and the adoption of a life of celibacy. Given this process of development, the antagonism he expressed to women is not surprising. He said, "I do not see what other use a woman can be to man if the purpose of generating was eliminated;" and in speaking of his distrust of women he described them as "the most dangerous of all the serpents" (Newman, 1948, p. 455). Nothing so powerfully brought "the manly mind down from the heights than a woman's caresses and that joining of bodies without which one cannot have a wife" (p. 455). He decided that every concrete act of sexual intercourse was evil. The guilt was passed from parents to children, but could be removed by Baptism. Marriage and procreation could reduce but not eliminate the sin.

St. Augustine applied the test of procreation to determine those sexual acts that were "against nature." Any other sexual behavior involving the use of a member (i.e., organ) not granted for the purpose of procreation was wrong. Homosexuality and bestiality clearly failed the test, but in the church's eye so did intercourse in any position except the female on her back. So did any attempt to avoid conception, and to use any orifice except the vagina for intercourse. Western attitudes have been dominated by anti-sex concepts ever since those times. Pagels (1988) argues that Augustinian theory prevailed in the Christian church because it provided a kind of certainty, and people preferred to feel guilt concerning their sexual urges than to feel the helplessness of not knowing how to chart their spiritual destiny.

The Middle Ages and the Eventual Medico-Religious Attack on Sex

The Christian church in the West gradually increased its control over sexual practices. For instance, marriage was changed from a secular event to an occasion of sacramental importance, celebrated by a priest with much ritual (Bullough, 1976). The concept of the sin against nature, formulated by St. Augustine, was further elaborated, in particular by St. Thomas Aquinas (1225–1274), a woman hater who said women were good only for conception. He found that all sorts of sexual acts were against nature, as well as being contrary to right reason. In descending order of seriousness were, bestiality, homosexuality, sexual intercourse in any position other than face-to-face contact with the female on her back, and masturbation. Consent to the lustful act was as culpable as the act itself. Because sins against nature were sins against God, they were considered more serious than sins against other people, such as adultery, seduction, and rape. Procreation justified coitus, though otherwise it was sinful, even in marriage. The definitions of St. Thomas tended to dominate all thinking on sexual subjects to the end of the Middle Ages.

Evidence of fears about sex, women, and women's sexuality is provided by the growth in the manufacture and sale of chastity belts in the fifteenth century, and by the attacks on witches. Certain forms of sexual activity were equated with witchcraft. In particular it was feared that men and women would have sex with demons, in human form, with all sorts of awful health and social consequences. Bullough (1976) notes that accused witches were beheaded, hanged, whipped to death, and burned alive, possibly in the millions, by Catholics and Protestants alike.

There were some contradictory themes appearing in the Middle Ages. A new idea, the concept of romantic love, which eventually came to include sexual expression, represented a complete split with the Christian and pagan past. The revival of an old (Greek) idea was the portrayal of the nude, albeit female, in art. Despite the "official" attitudes, early European literature such as Boccaccio's *Decameron,* Chaucer's *Canterbury Tales,* and the writings of Rabelais, was often explicitly sexual, and expressed an attitude of enjoyment of sex, alongside an awareness of its "naughtiness" (Shorter, 1982). Pornography flourished, usually underground, especially during times of heightened sexual repression. Even sex manuals appeared, the most popular one in the English-speaking world from the seventeenth to the nineteenth century being called *Aristotle's Masterpiece.* This book recognized women's sexual needs, and gave attention to the clitoris in women's sexual arousal; "blowing the coals of these amorous fires" (Bullough, 1976, p. 473) would lead to greater satisfaction. Its great popularity suggests a change in the educated Westerner's acceptance of at least marital sex.

The Protestant reformers introduced modest changes to prevailing attitudes about sex and celibacy. Martin Luther (1488–1546), and John Calvin (1509–1564) both believed that compulsory celibacy was wrong. Both taught that sex was to be confined to marriage, but Luther continued to teach that the sex act is always "unclean." For Calvin, sexual intercourse was a pure, honorable and holy act, an institution of God. He saw companionship as the primary purpose for marriage. In both Protestant and Catholic countries, sins against nature became crimes against nature, though the Puritans in Britain and in New England, following Calvinist ideas, probably carried this the farthest.

In the eighteenth century, Rousseau and his colleagues argued for the removal of barriers to marriage and divorce, for the secularization of marriage, and the elimination of old restrictions on moral behavior, seeing them as issues of personal rather than state responsibility. The medical moralists cut the ground from under their feet.

The Medicalization of Morality

By the end of the seventeenth century, traditional sexual attitudes were being questioned in Europe. However, medical science provided a final, but exceedingly powerful, prop for the old values of sexual repression. As Szasz (1981) noted, European medicine concluded that sex was either a disease or an important cause of disease. For instance, some French physicians held the view that any sexual excitement in women was a "melancholic affliction," while others claimed that the open show of sexual desire was a sure sign of mental disease.

Foucault (1978) argued that medical views about sexuality were motivated primarily by the religious beliefs of their perpetrators. They had little to do with science. In particular, the Swiss doctor, Tissot propounded the theory of masturbatory insanity (Bullough & Bullough, 1977). Actually Tissot concluded that all sexual activity was potentially dangerous, but the most threatening activity was masturbation in young people because it was so difficult to control. Such waste of semen would lead to all manner of physical disorders, and mental cloudiness that could extend to madness. Medical authorities in various parts of the world soon made pronouncements about the "dangers" of masturbation. Benjamin Rush, the father of American psychiatry, French surgeon Claude-François Lallemand, French psychiatrist Jean Esquirol, and British psychiatrist Henry Maudsley, all wrote of the deadly dangers of masturbation. William Acton (1814–1875), the English physician, was equally worried about the loss of vital energy through marital sexual activity. He revealed that God had created females indifferent to sex to prevent the male's vital energy from being overly expended.

Efforts to prevent masturbation included the widespread use of chastity girdles, devices designed to prevent individuals from touching, looking at, or examining their genitals. There were devices for girls and boys, some of which relied on spikes or clamps to deter erection. Next, as standard remedies, came surgical procedures such as clitoridectomy for masturbation. A standard pediatric textbook, Luther E. Holt's *Diseases of Infancy and Childhood,* continued to recommend until the 1936 edition circumcision for boys and cauterization of the clitoris for girls (and in some cases surgical removal of the clitoris as well) as a cure for masturbation (Bullough & Bullough, 1977). Nonmedical writers flocked to join the anti-sex and anti-masturbation bandwagon, reflecting back to the community the distortions created by the medical profession.

Even Sigmund Freud (1856–1939), the founder of psychoanalysis, in some major respects was little more than a spokesman for the entrenched medico-religious sexual attitudes. He regarded excessive masturbation as a threat to full potency in marriage, and the probable cause of neuroses and even organic damage. To make things worse, Freud saw masturbation not only in sexual self-stimulation but also in all sorts of nongenital activities, even squeezing blackheads (Szasz, 1981). To become mature adults, women had to give up self-stimulation of the "inferior" clitoris and focus instead on stimulation of the vagina by a penis. Until the 1970s, psychiatry formally maintained the view that homosexuality was an illness that should be cured. It all looks very similar to the traditional Christian condemnation of "unnatural" sex.

The Sexual Revolution

The medico-religious moral crusade waged against the Western populace in the eighteenth and nineteenth centuries represents the climax of Christianity's suppression of sexuality. What is remarkable is that this intensely pervasive and ultimately powerful influence of religious teaching and belief, painstakingly created over the last two and a half thousand years, seems to have collapsed all at once with the advent of the twentieth century (Katchadourian, 1989; Robinson, 1976). There have been profound changes in individual experience, chronicled first in the Kinsey reports (1948, 1953), and later in a multitude of other surveys of sexual behavior. Also, legislative change appeared so that, in many Western countries, the capacity of the law to punish private sexual experience was significantly reduced. If there has been a sexual revolution, its first developments occurred early in this century.

In democratic societies, there were movements toward giving women the vote even before the turn of the century, and this democratic evolution probably helped change women's sexual experience. As Katchadourian (1989) observed, these changes were accelerated by the turmoil of World War I, the increased involvement of women in what had previously been men's work, improved contraception and increasing urbanization, and not least, the development of a sanitary pad that actually worked. Most striking was the increase in premarital sex across generations. The data of Kinsey et al. (1953) show that those women born before 1900 reported less than half as much premarital coital experience as those born in any subsequent decade. A similar effect was noted for premarital petting. Change appeared inevitable; "The failure of the church to treat sex and natural impulse with dignity and candor is the largest single fact in that disintegration of personal codes which confronts us in these hectic times" (Calverton & Schmalhausen, 1929, p. 11).

Kinsey et al. (1948) recommended comparison of human behavior with a suitable nonhuman group as a way of estimating the effects of religious suppression of sexuality. They suggested that the total sexual outlet in humans should have been about the same as other anthropoids, though even in males it was much reduced. Observed differences between people inactive or devout in their religion supported such conclusions. With regard to masturbation, Kinsey and his colleagues (1948, 1953) found that religion had a greater effect within female groups than among males. They did find that the more religious men, especially Orthodox Jews and practicing Catholics, masturbated less often, and religiously inactive Protestants the most. But among women these effects were even stronger.

Within the Kinsey data there were indications of increases in masturbation and nocturnal emissions for a younger generation compared with an older one. Later surveys suggested further profound changes had taken place with dramatic increases in the percentage of women masturbating and in the rate of masturbation especially among younger groups (Hunt, 1974). Religion still had strong inhibiting effects, but less clearly among younger respondents. Later surveys of the readers of various popular magazines suggested a picture of continuing change for women. They were starting masturbation much earlier (e.g., Wolfe, 1981), and many more were masturbating (Hite, 1976; Miller & Lief, 1976; Wolfe, 1981). These data may be an artifact of the samples, though they are similar to figures from the more conservative *Redbook* readers (Tavris & Sadd, 1978).

Similar patterns of change have been evident in heterosexual interactions. Amount of time spent in sexual foreplay increased between the Kinsey and Hunt studies. The average time for males to reach orgasm after vaginal entry increased from about two minutes in Kinsey's subjects to ten minutes for Hunt's respondents. The use of oral-genital techniques increased enormously between the Kinsey and Hunt studies so that in the 1970s they were used by more than 90 percent of younger samples (Hunt, 1974; Tavris & Sadd, 1978). There was a trebling of the use of the female superior sexual position (up to 75 percent) between Kinsey's data and Hunt's report. The estimated use of prostitutes by single males in the 1970s was no more than half what it was in the 1940s. The data suggest an enormous change within the space of a generation, and this change indicates the level of earlier inhibition.

Kinsey et al. (1953), showed that more females were reaching orgasm after some years of marriage than earlier generations, with steady increases apparent across successive generations. The religious backgrounds of the females in the sample had strongly and consistently affected their total sexual outlet, the percentage achieving orgasm and median frequencies of orgasm. Among the Catholic females who were married and aged from 21 to 25, the differences in rate of orgasm were greater than 2 to 1 for the inactive Catholics compared with devout Catholics. For both the females and males, strength of religious devotion was correlated with the incidence of various types of sexual activity. Devout religious observance prevented some of the females and males from ever engaging in certain types of sexual activity. There was less of almost all types of sexual activity except marital coitus among the more devout, and more among the less devout. In more recent studies, a negative relationship has been reported between religiosity and sexual restrictiveness. Lower frequencies of marital coitus and other aspects of sexual behavior, such as masturbation, premarital sex, and marital sexual variety, have been associated with religiosity in studies from different parts of the world (Alzate, 1978; Athanasiou, Shaver, & Tavris, 1970; Bayer, 1977; Bell, 1974; Murstein & Holden, 1979; reviewed by Reiss & Miller, 1979). This effect may be related to guilt generated by sexual feelings. Athanasiou et al. (1970) found that guilt was a fairly good negative predictor of frequency of sexual intercourse, evaluation of intercourse, and feeling of regret about premarital intercourse.

Western culture tends to view females as less sexually motivated than males. On the surface, the early research seemed to support this view. Males masturbated more, had more orgasms by any method, had more sexual partners, were more aroused by visual erotic material, and so on. Concerning this apparent sex difference, Kinsey et al. (1953) observed:

> The anatomy and physiology of sexual response and orgasm . . . do not show differences between the sexes that might account for the differences in their sexual responses. Females appear to be as capable as males of being aroused by tactile stimuli; they appear as capable as males of responding to the point of orgasm. Their responses are not slower than those of the average male if there is any sufficiently continuous tactile stimulation" (p. 688).

Consequently, the observed sex differences were assumed to be the result of learning. Masters and Johnson (1966) came to a similar conclusion after their observational studies. Schmidt and Sigusch (1973) suggested a cultural desexualization of women in Western societies. However, sex differences in general have reduced enormously over the past thirty to forty years, so that in some behaviors females now surpass males.

Studies with German adolescents and university students (Schmidt & Sigusch, 1970, 1973; Clement, Schmidt, & Kruse, 1984) point to a narrowing of sex differences since Kinsey's time, and a continuing rapid convergence of male and female sexual behaviors. By the latest of these studies, the difference in age of first masturbation, and rates of masturbation had reduced considerably; there were no differences in sexual mobility, females showed more liberal sexual attitudes than males, and there had been a reversal of the sex differences in age of first premarital experience. Females now began earlier and were more active than males.

Similar convergence of behavior and attitudes has been observed in other parts of the Western world. While Reiss (1960) found evidence of a double standard in attitudes and actual premarital sexual behaviors in American groups, later studies found no gender differences (e.g., DeLamater & MacCorquodale, 1979; Reiss &

Miller, 1979; Vener & Stewart, 1974; Walster, Walster, & Traupmann, 1978). In a group of Spanish university students, no sex differences in attitudes to premarital sex, masturbation, or homosexuality were observed, though Catholics were more disapproving of these behaviors (Lafuente-Benaches & Valcarel-Gonzalez, 1984). Among French university students, the value placed on virginity for females seemed to be decreasing and the mean age of first sexual encounter was the same (17 years) for both males and females (Bonierbale-Branchereau, 1985).

A valid estimate of the consequences for female sexual behavior of religious inhibitions must consider more than adult sexual interactions. Niles Newton (1973) has pointed out that adult females have at least three acts of interpersonal reproductive behavior; coitus, parturition, and lactation. All involve reproductive relationships between two individuals, the potential for intense emotionality, and similarity of physiological response. For instance, vaginal lubrication, uterine contraction, nipple erection, emotional feelings of tenderness and closeness, and sometimes orgasm, are associated with both lactation and intercourse. Newton suggests that religious factors have affected women's enjoyment of these other sexual responses just as they have negatively affected heterosexual interactions. She cites research showing that feelings of aversion for the breast-feeding act seem to be related to dislike of nudity and sexuality. Rossi (1973) concurs with Newton's suggestions adding that (Biblically-sanctioned) pain in labor, lack of enjoyment of pregnancy, and nausea during pregnancy are associated with poor sexual adjustment, and have been affected at all points by the repressive religiously prescribed sexual attitudes of Western communities. Just as challenging is her suggestion that the effective denial of sensual gratification in maternity may have weakened the bond between mother and child in Western societies.

Newton (1973) proposed that the intense emotions involved in orgasm are, in fact, a perfect model for operant conditioning of the attachment relationship, "the biologic foundation upon which patterns of family life are built" (p. 92). Destroy the pleasure of sex and you destroy an important element of the family bond. In support of this idea, she cites research indicating that lower female orgasm rates, and decreasing orgasmic responsiveness, are associated with marital unhappiness or with lower cooperativeness of relationships (Clark & Wallen, 1965; Gebhard, 1966; Hunt, 1974; Rainwater, 1966). Thus the consequences of the religious suppression of sex may extend beyond specifically sexual behaviors.

Another perspective for examining the impact of religion on sexuality comes from clinical work. Masters and Johnson (1974) outlined a link between strict religious upbringing and psychosexual dysfunction based on clinical observations of thousands of cases. However, experimental examination of this issue has not been enlightening so far. Hoch, Safir, Peres, and Shepher (1981) found male sex therapy patients came from more traditional religious homes, but Cole's study (1986) did not.

The practice of Catholic sexual orthodoxy has been related to more general psychopathology (Colton, 1979; Kennedy, 1971; Kurtz, 1972; Murphy, 1981; Patton, 1988). Sex guilt has been found to be highest among members of conservative denominations, and lowest among those individuals with no denomination (Peterson, 1964). However, it may be that religion provides a set of norms by which to live, thereby making life easier (Pagels, 1988; Wilson & Filsinger, 1986). Clark and Wallen (1965) found that religiosity reduced the impact of lack of sexual gratification on marital satisfaction among women. Hansen (1987) made similar observations, but noted that religion compensates for lack of rewards in a broad range of other areas too. Perhaps it is not surprising to find that religiosity has been associated with several dimensions of marital adjustment in a sample of Protestants who attend church, though satisfaction with expressions of affection and sex was not one of them (Wilson & Filsinger, 1986).

We can only speculate about future directions in sexual attitudes and behaviors. Throughout the Western world, AIDS education campaigns have had to face the paradoxical problem of giving unaccustomed explicit information about sex, and making nonjudgmental statements about homosexual lifestyles, while at the same time advising some restriction in sexual behaviors. This pressure for sexual conservatism conflicts with opposing pressures caused by the continuing problems of overpopulation. These forces may yet allow increasing tolerance of sexual variety and nonprocreative sex within stable relationships, which by itself represents a change in direction from the destructive limitations imposed first by Christianity, and then by its ideological ally, the medical profession, over the last two thousand years.

References

Alzate, H. (1978). Sexual behavior of Colombian female university students. *Archives of Sexual Behavior, 7,* 43–54.

Athanasiou, R., Shaver, P., & Tavris, C. (1970). Sex. *Psychology Today, 4,* 37–52.

Bayer, A.E. (1977). Sexual permissiveness and correlates as determined through interaction analyses. *Journal of Marriage and the Family, 39,* 29–40.

Bell, R.R. (1974). Religious involvement and marital sex in Australia and the United States. *Journal of Comparative Family Studies, 5,* 109–116.

Bonierbale-Branchereau, M. (1985). The first sexual encounter. *Genitif, 6,* 39–56.

Bullough, V.L. (1976). *Sexual variance in society and history.* New York: John Wiley & Sons.

Bullough, V.L., & Bullough, B. (1977). *Sin, sickness, and sanity.* New York: Garland Publishing.

Calverton, V.F., & Schmalhausen, S.D. (1929). *Sex in civilization.* New York: Citadel.

Clark, A., & Wallen, P. (1965). Women's sexual responsiveness and the duration and quality of their marriages. *American Journal of Sociology, 71,* 187–196.

Clement, U., Schmidt, G., & Kruse, M. (1984). Changes in sex differences in sexual behavior: A replication of a study on West German students (1966–1981). *Archives of Sexual Behaviour, 13,* 99–108.

Cole, M. (1986). Socio-sexual characteristics of men with sexual problems. *Sexual and Marital Therapy, 1,* 89–108.

Colton, H. (1979). A personal view of the sex revolution. In V. Bullough (Ed.), *Frontiers of Sex Research.* Buffalo, NY: Prometheus.

DeLamater, J., & MacCorquodale, P. (1979). *Premarital sexuality: Attitudes, relationships, behavior.* Madison, WI: University of Wisconsin Press.

Foucault, M. (1978). *The history of sexuality, vol. 1: An introduction.* New York: Pantheon Books.

Gebhard, P.H. (1966). Factors in marital orgasm. *Journal of Social Issues, 22,* 321–334.

Hansen, G.L. (1987). The effect of religiosity on factors predicting marital adjustment. *Social Psychology Quarterly, 50,* 264–269.

Harris, K. (1984). *Sex, ideology, and religion.* Wheatsheaf, NJ: Brighton.

Hite, S. (1976). *The Hite report.* New York: Macmillan.

Hoch, Z., Safir, M., Peres, Y., & Shepher, J. (1981). An evaluation of sexual performance: Comparison between sexually dysfunctional and functional couples. *Journal of Sex and Marital Therapy, 7,* 195–196.

Hunt, M. (1974). *Sexual behavior in the 1970s.* Chicago, IL: Playboy Press.

Katchadourian, H.A. (1989). *Fundamentals of human sexuality* (5th ed.). Fort Worth, TX: Holt Rinehart & Winston.

Kennedy, E. (1971). The guilt machine. In E. Kennedy (Ed.), *The people are the church.* New York: Image Books.

Kinsey, A.C., Pomeroy, W.B., & Martin, C.E. (1948). *Sexual behaviour in the human male.* Philadelphia: Saunders.

Kinsey, A.C., Pomeroy, W.B., Martin, C.E., & Gebhard, P.H. (1953). *Sexual behaviour in the human female.* Philadelphia: Saunders.

Kurtz, P. (1972). Tolerance versus repression. *Humanist, 32,* 34–35.

Lafuente-Benaches, J., & Valcarel-Gonzalez, P. (1984). Attitudes about sexuality in a sample of Valencian university students. *Psicologica, 5,* 81–89.

Masters, W.H., & Johnson, V.E. (1966). *Human sexual response.* Boston: Little Brown.

Masters, W.H., & Johnson, V.E. (1974). The role of religion in sexual dysfunction. In M. Calderone (Ed.), *Sexuality and human values.* New York: Association Press.

May, G. (1930). *Social control of sex expression.* London: Allen & Unwin.

Miller, W.R., & Lief, H.I. (1976). Masturbatory attitudes, knowledge, and experience: Data from the sex knowledge and attitude test (SKAT). *Archives of Sexual Behavior, 5,* 447–467.

Murphy, F. (1981). Sex and the Catholic church. *Atlantic Monthly, 247,* 44–51.

Murstein, B.I., & Holden, C.C. (1979). Sexual behavior and correlates among college students. *Adolescence, 14,* 625–639.

Newman, A.H. (1948). Translation of St. Augustine's "Concerning the nature of good." In W.J. Oates (Ed.), *Basic writings of St. Augustine.* New York: Random House.

Newton, N. (1973). Interrelationships between sexual responsiveness, birth, and breast feeding. In J. Zubin & J. Money (Eds.), *Contemporary sexual behavior: Critical issues in the 1970s* (pp. 77–98). Baltimore, MY: Johns Hopkins University Press.

Pagels, E. (1988). *Adam, Eve, and the serpent.* London: Random House.

Patton, M.S. (1988). Suffering and damage in Catholic sexuality. *Journal of Religion and Health, 27,* 129–142.

Peterson, J.A. (1964). *Education for marriage* (2nd ed.). New York: Scribner's.

Rainwater, L. (1966). Some aspects of lower class sexual behaviour. *Journal of Social Issues, 22,* 96–108.

Reiss, I.L. (1960). *Premarital sexual standards in America.* New York: Free Press.

Reiss, I.L., & Miller, B.C. (1979). Heterosexual permissiveness: A theoretical analysis. In W.R. Burr, R. Hill, F.I. Nye, & I.L. Reiss (Eds.), *Contemporary theories about the family: Vol. I, research based theories.* New York: Free Press.

Robinson, P. (1976). *The modernisation of sex.* New York: Harper & Row.

Rossi, A.S. (1973). Maternalism, sexuality, and the new feminism. In J. Zubin & J. Money (Eds.), *Contemporary sexual behavior: Critical issues in the 1970s* (pp. 145–173). Baltimore, MY: Johns Hopkins University Press.

Schmidt, V., & Sigusch, G. (1970). Sex differences in responses to psychosexual stimulation by films and slides. *Journal of Sex Research, 6,* 268–283.

Schmidt, V., & Sigusch, G. (1973). Women's sexual arousal. In J. Zubin & J. Money (Eds.), *Contemporary sexual behavior: Critical issues in the 1970s* (pp. 117–143). Baltimore, MD: Johns Hopkins University Press.

Sevely, J.L. (1987). *Eve's secrets: A new perspective on human sexuality.* London: Bloomsbury.

Shorter, E.A. (1982). *History of women's bodies.* New York: Basic Books.

Szasz, T. (1981). *Sex: Facts, frauds, and follies.* Oxford: Basil Blackwell.

Tannahill, R. (1982). *Sex in history.* New York: Stein & Day.

Tavris, C., & Sadd, D. (1978). *The Redbook report on female sexuality.* New York: Delacorte.

Vener, A.M., & Stewart, C.S. (1974). Adolescent sexual behavior in middle America revisited: 1970–1973. *Journal of Marriage and the Family, 36,* 728–735.

Walster, E., Walster, G.W., & Traupmann, J. (1978). Equity and premarital sex. *Journal of Personality and Social Psychology, 36,* 82–92.

Watts, W. (1919). *Translation of St. Augustine's "Confessions."* London: William Heinemann.

Wilson, M.R., & Filsinger, E.E. (1986). Religiosity and marital adjustment: Multidimensional interpretations. *Journal of Marriage and the Family, 48,* 147–151.

Wolfe, L. (1981). *The Cosmo report.* Toronto: Bantam.

II

AFFECTIVE AND COGNITIVE CONSEQUENCES

5

Religiosity, Depression, and Suicide

Steven Stack

The literature on the impact of religiosity on suicide and depression has pursued a number of recurrent themes. The social integration/regulation perspective of Durkheim (1966) has been the dominant theoretical link between religion and suicide; the sheer numbers of religious rituals and beliefs are seen as critical to suicide prevention (e.g., Stack, 1980; Kowalski, Faupel, & Starr, 1987). Others have contended that a few key aspects of religion may be enough to lower suicide risk (Stark, Doyle, & Rushing, 1983; Stack, 1983b); this is the religious commitment view. A relatively new "networks" approach explores factors such as the organizational aspects of religious bodies (hierarchical structure, primary group ties, and the like) in order to assess suicide risk (Pescosolido & Georgianna, 1989). This chapter reviews each of these theories and the empirical literature associated with them. It treats the special problem of religion and depression in a shorter section, and a conclusion provides a summary and suggestions for future research.

Religion and Suicide

Durkheim's (1966) classic work serves as the starting point for most sociological work on suicide. Subordination of the individual to group life constitutes the essence of Durkheim's (1966/1897) theory of integration and suicide. Accordingly, subordination makes life more meaningful, provides a sense of purpose through devotion to others and the ideology of group life, and distracts the individual from personal troubles, which might otherwise unleash suicidal tendencies (Durkheim, 1966). Examples of integrative subordination include parental devotion to children, subordination to a political cause, and subordination to religious teachings.

Turning to the issue of religion and suicide, two key dimensions of religious integration are beliefs and practices (Durkheim, 1966). The more numerous and strong these dimensions are, the greater the integration of the individual to group life and the lower the probability of suicide. The details of the religious dogmas and rituals are secondary. Durkheim used religious affiliation as a measure of religious integration. Protestants were thought to be much lower than Catholics in integration. Protestants were high in "free inquiry," a system of religious individualism lacking in subordination. A Protestant does not have to subordinate him/herself as much to collective rituals and beliefs, there being fewer of the latter in Protestantism. Durkheim did not list many examples of beliefs and practices found among Catholics but not among Protestants. However, these would have included (in the nineteenth century) meatless Fridays, confession, compulsory weekly church attendance, norms against divorce and remarriage, and prohibition of switching religions. As evidence supporting these assertions, Durkheim (1966) illustrates that, in the case of all five nations for which data were available, the suicide rate for Protestants was at least 50% higher than that for Catholics.

Tests of the Durkheimian Integration Model

Reanalyses of Durkheim's data have questioned his conclusions (e.g., Pope, 1976; Pope & Danigelis, 1981; Stark et al., 1983; Day, 1987). Three geographic regions where the suicide rate for Catholics was higher than that of Protestants were overlooked. Although Catholic regions were less economically developed than Protestants, no control was introduced for economic development resulting in a possible spurious relationship between religious affiliation and suicide (Pope, 1976). His assertion that the Church of England was responsible for the high suicide rate in Britain is mistaken since only a minority of English were church members (Stark et al., 1983).

Analyses of new data have yielded mixed results for the religious affiliation measure of religious integration. Micro-level studies comparing suicide rates of Catholics and Protestants are relatively uncommon, but the data we have is split (Maris, 1981; see, Stack, 1983b for a review). Much of this work is inconclusive since it fails to control for economic development or modernization, a factor also related to religious affiliation at the national level.

At the ecological level, for studies of a large number of nations, a bivariate relationship between Catholicism and suicide was found to be spurious once a control for modernization was included (Pope & Danigelis, 1981) or when a control for the divorce rate was incorporated (Stack, 1981). In a similar vein, research on the 50 states of the United States also found the bivariate relationship spurious once a control was incorporated for divorce (Stack, 1980). Further, analyses of urban data from early twentieth century America refuted Durkheim's theory (Bainbridge & Stark, 1982). Also, an analysis of Louisiana counties not only found that Catholicism offered no protection against suicide but also that it actually increased its incidence (Bankston, Allen, & Cunningham, 1983).

Finally, more recent studies of American counties have largely failed to support a Durkheimian theory. While one study does support a link between Catholicism and suicide (Faupel, Kowalski, & Starr, 1987), a second study by the same authors does not. Kowalski et al. (1987) employed exactly the same data set, but after adding four additional control variables (percent Protestant, sex ratio, educational diversity, and population size), the relationship between percent Catholic and suicide became nonsignificant. Breault (1988) reported that the greater the percent Catholic the lower the suicide rate. The percent Protestant was, however, more closely related to suicide than the percent Catholic. In addition, the percents

Lutheran, Methodist, and Southern Baptist were also associated with reductions in suicide. If Protestantism and specific Protestant denominations can reduce suicide, this is a sign that we need a new theory relating suicide to religion.

Theoretical interpretations of the findings from the early 1980s included the notion that Catholic levels of integration have been greatly reduced in the 80 years since Durkheim wrote his book entitled *Suicide.* For example, church attendance rates have nearly converged. Hence, we would expect differences in suicide rates to converge as well (e.g., Stack, 1980; 1982).

A Reformulation of the Religion-Suicide Link:
Religious Commitment and Suicide

Given the weight of the evidence against a simple operationalization of Durkheim's concept of religious integration, researchers developed new measures and theories of the more general impact of religion on suicide. That is, research began to look beyond the simple Protestant-Catholic operationalization of religious integration (e.g., Breault & Barkey, 1982; Breault, 1986). Others not only used new measures but also developed a new theory (e.g., Stark & Bainbridge, 1980; Stark et al., 1983; Stack, 1983b). Some debate also occurred over whether new measures of religion could realistically fit under a Durkheimian model (Breault & Barkey, 1983; Stack, 1983c).

Commitment to a few core religious beliefs may be all that is needed for a religious shield against suicide. The sheer number of religious beliefs may be unimportant, in spite of a Durkheimian theory to the contrary. A belief in the Virgin Birth, for example, is probably not as conducive to saving lives as belief in an afterlife as a reward for perseverance.

Stack (1983b) has outlined the principal propositions of a theory of religious commitment and suicide. Belief in an afterlife involving the promise of bliss can offset some of the adversity faced by people experiencing stress such as that associated with job loss, divorce, poor health and so on. Such suffering can be more readily endured if it is viewed as short-lived, a moment in time compared to eternity. Second, such suffering can be viewed as having a purpose; it may be part of God's will and/or function to teach us the value of perseverance per se. Third, a belief that God is watching and knows about our sufferings may make them more endurable. Fourth, religion offers a spiritual ranking or stratification system as an alternative to society's materialistic stratification system. Hence, one's sense of self-esteem can be built up through seeking spiritual success, especially if one is unsuccessful in society's pecking order. Fifth, a belief in a responsive God, one who hears and eventually will respond to prayer, may pull some people through adverse life circumstances. Sixth, religion often glorifies the state of poverty. The Bible, for example, teaches that it is easier for a camel to go through the eye of a needle than for a rich man to enter the Kingdom of God. As such, it assuages the suffering of some of the poor, a group with the highest incidence of suicide (e.g., Stack, 1982). Seventh, a belief in Satan fosters the subordination of self to the war against the devil, a spiritual war that can take on the functions of a great international military war. Both cases can develop a sense of unity against a common, external enemy; other beliefs like "Jesus walked on water," simply do not rouse the passions as does this belief. Finally, religions provide idealistic role models such as Job in the Bible. These figures endure enormous suffering, but do not resort to suicide. By example, they can reduce suicide potential in those who suffer from significant affliction. These eight features of religion are not meant to provide an exhaustive list of life-saving beliefs, but they do provide examples of how a few core beliefs might be enough to reduce suicide.

Early empirical work on religious commitment and suicide was based on large samples of nations, and used religious book production (as a percentage of all books) as an indicator of religiosity. Wuthnow (1977) defended this measure at length. It is associated with other dimensions of religiosity, including beliefs, organizational strength, ritual frequency, and membership. Using a sample of 25 industrial nations, Stack (1983b) found that the higher the religiosity the lower the suicide rate. This was especially true for female rates. Breault and Barkey (1982) analyzed the impact of religious publication rates on suicide in 42 nations and found a significant, life-saving effect. These investigations may, however, be marked by cross-sectional bias, since nations were investigated only at one point in time. In contrast, two time series analyses for Denmark and Norway showed no relationship between the religious publications variable and suicide for the 1950–1980 period (Stack, 1989, 1990).

Other investigations employed church membership rates as an index of religious commitment and used large cities as their unit of analysis. Stark et al. (1983) reported a negative correlation ($r = -0.36$) between church membership and the rate of suicide for a sample of large American metropolitan areas. This finding may be a function of inadequate controls. Bainbridge's findings (1989) depart from the Stark et al. (1983) investigation. In an analysis of 75 American Standard Metropolitan Statistical Areas, a strong zero-order association between church membership and suicide rates vanished when a control for another aspect of social solidarity was introduced: geographic mobility, a process thought to reduce attachments to group life.

Studies of American states are also mixed in their findings for a theory of religious commitment. One study reported significant church membership coefficients for each of four census years from 1950 to 1980 (Breault, 1986).[1] Girard (1988) found these associations to be spurious once a control for percent black was introduced. Breault (1988) accepted Girard's critique on this particular score.

A pair of studies on American counties provided support for the negative relationship between church membership and suicide rates (Breault, 1986, 1988). However, Breault (1988) introduced nine new "control variables," giving no explanation for their addition. It is not clear whether the religion-suicide link would be maintained without the addition of these new factors.

Two investigations employed church attendance as a measure of religiosity, a factor that can be interpreted from either a Durkheimian or a religious commitment view. Not only was this factor significant, it was also the most important variable in explaining the overall suicide rate and the suicide rate for the young. But no control was introduced for divorce in this study, so it needs to be read with caution

(Stack, 1983a). A second study indicated that religious commitment and familial integration were, in fact, indicators of a more general phenomenon of collectivism. Borrowing from recent developments in the sociology of religion (D'Antonio and Aldous, 1983), Stack (1985a) contended that religious trends in America were too closely associated with trends in another "collectivistic" institution, the family, to be analyzed separately. Together, however, as an index of collectivism, they proved to be a potent predictor of suicide.

Therefore, research in the religious commitment vein is split, but slightly supportive of the notion that religion lowers the suicide rate. A third stream of work attempted to specify what kinds of religion, and within what social contexts, have the most impact on suicide.

Further Reformulation: Religion and Suicide in Social Context

Some investigators contend that the link between religion and suicide can best be modeled within special social contexts. That is, religion may have an impact on suicide only in certain situations. For example, in the American hub of Catholicism, namely New England, Catholicism lowers suicide (Maris, 1981; Pescosolido, 1990), but in the southern context of Louisiana Catholicism offers no protective shield against suicide (Bankston et al., 1983). Historical factors in the development of religious strength may need to be taken into account to understand the conditions under which religion will, in fact, lower suicide.

Recent work on social contexts has stressed such factors as urban environment (Kowalski et al., 1987; Faupel et al., 1987); organizational features of religious denominations, such as encouragement of primary group ties with co-religionists (Pescosolido & Georgianna, 1989); population density that facilitates location of co-religionists (Pescosolido, 1990); and region of the nation, which relates to religious resources (Pescosolido, 1990). All of these contextual arguments can be viewed as an elaboration or modification, not a refutation, of Durkheim (e.g., see Pescosolido, 1990).

Faupel et al. (1987) drew on Durkheim's (1933) later work to construct an urban context theory of religion's influence on suicide. Durkheim contended that large urban areas have the greatest potential for social integration, providing the most important arena for mitigating social institutions. Fischer's (1982) observations bear this out. Urban dwellers are more apt than rural residents to form affiliations through friendships or other linkages such as voluntary associations, which have a mitigating effect on suicide. Consistent with their expectations, Faupel et al. (1987) found that there was a significant relationship between percent Catholic and suicide for the middle third and top third of counties (in size). The relationship is strongest for the middle third of counties. This may be because they were lacking the extensive kinship support systems found in rural counties, and also lacking the multiplicity of ties with voluntary associations characteristic of the most urban areas. Following Tittle and Welch (1983), the authors maintained that the middle group of counties had relatively weak social institutions, and that religion therefore played a stronger role there than in the most urban counties. However, a very similar investigation by the same writers produced somewhat different results. With a control entered for percent Protestant, percent Catholic affected suicide only for the middle group of counties (Kowalski et al., 1987).

A second social contextual argument consists of applying network theory to the problem of religion and suicide (Pescosolido & Georgianna, 1989). Contending that three socio-historical trends (evangelicalism, secularization, and ecumenicalism) have changed the relationship between society and religion since Durkheim's times, these authors argued that Durkheim's theory needs to be reformulated. An analysis of 27 major religious denominations, using data from 404 county groups (county sets with populations of 250,000 or more), revealed that Catholicism and some Protestant religions continued to protect against suicide. In addition, some Protestant denominations increased county group suicide rates.

An explanation was constructed around four major dimensions of religion in terms of network theory. Higher rates of church attendance are characteristic of Protestant denominations that are conservative, nonecumenical, whose teachings are in tension with societal culture, and whose power structure is non-hierarchical or congregational. This promotes a much greater incidence of friendship ties among their members than liberal, ecumenical, low tension, and hierarchical Protestant churches. The social bonds formed in the first type of structure provide more social support than the latter. Hence, the former have more intense "networks" of social support, which reduce suicide risk. Catholics follow the same patterns as the former group and, as such, have low suicide rates (Pescosolido & Georgianna, 1989).

One problem with the Pescosolido and Georgianna (1989) paper is that they relaxed standards of statistical significance, saying (and they are technically correct) that all observed differences were "real" given that they were studying a population. This was, however, true of just about all previous work based on aggregated suicide rates, since that work too studied populations. If, as in previous works, we use significance tests as a guide, most of the relationships in their tables are not "significant." In fact, only 5 of the 27 denomination coefficients were significant (Pescosolido & Georgianna, 1989). Even so, these five terms generally support their main thesis. Increased suicide was associated with mainline Episcopalians, whereas reduced suicide was found with Catholics, Reformed Churches, Evangelical Baptists, and Seventh Day Adventists.

Pescosolido (1990) developed her network theory while accounting for the contexts of region and population density as factors promoting religious social support systems. A region that has been the "historical hub" of a denomination is marked by a well-developed infrastructure (e.g., religious schools, hospitals, social clubs) that will promote networking and social support for members of that faith; a consequence is a lower suicide rate. Furthermore, areas of high population density foster a greater availability of co-religionists for social support, and for building or maintaining an infrastructure. As a corollary, such areas will have lower suicide rates as well. For example, Southern Jews are spread out, lacking a strong local infrastructure. As such, their opportunities for social support are relatively low and their suicide rate is high. The reverse is true for New England, the historical hub of American Judaism.

In an analysis of 404 county groups, Pescosolido (1990) found support for these premises. In addition to findings on Jews already discussed, results for Catholics were also consistent with networking theory. Catholicism had its greatest protective effect against suicide in the Northeast, but it aggravated suicide in the South, its weakest region of influence. The protective effect of many evangelical protestant groups is reversed in the Northeast, a region of weakness for these denominations. Exceptions to the general pattern were found as well, such as the prediction that the largest protective effect for institutional Lutherans would be found in their stronghold, the Midwest. This was not confirmed by the data. Overall, region exerted a larger protective effect than did the context of population density. Only 3 of 54 coefficients, about the same number we would expect by chance, met the requirements for statistical significance for the low- and medium-density county groups. For high-density county groups, 6 of 27 coefficients were significant, but two (evangelical Presbyterians and institutional Baptists) indicated an aggravating effect on suicide. Only four groups promoted decreased suicide: Catholics, Nazarenes, Unitarians, and evangelical Methodists.

Among the patterns found in Pescosolido's (1990) study, Catholicism was found to protect against suicide (1) when all 404 county groups were considered together, (2) in its "historical hub," and (3) in areas of high population density. The first and third of these findings conflicted with the observation of Kowalski et al. (1987), who used a greater array of control variables and analyzed all 3,108 counties, as opposed to 404 county groups. Further work is needed to explore these important discrepancies.

Religion and Depression

There are at least three ways in which religiosity might affect depression levels (Idler, 1987). The social cohesiveness hypothesis contends that a religion offers social support from religion-based social networks. Such support includes emotional, cognitive, and material benefits that can lower the risk of depression. The coherence hypothesis contends that religion lowers depression through fostering a sense of optimism and reducing a sense of fatalism. The theodicy hypothesis argues that religion alters potential negative perceptions of suffering, even viewing suffering in a positive light. Stack's (1983b) previously mentioned theory of religious commitment offers examples of this process. The three hypotheses are not mutually exclusive; in fact, they can operate simultaneously.

Most of the available research on the specific problem of depression is restricted to nonrepresentative samples of the American population such as students (Brown & Lowe, 1951; Mayo, Puryear, & Richek, 1969), the elderly (Idler, 1987), a bereaved parents' support group (Maton, 1989), the Midwest (Stack, 1985b), rural women (Hertsgaard & Light, 1984), and Mormon women (Spendlove, West, & Stanish, 1984). Studies which found no relationship include Stack (1985b) and Spendlove et al. (1984). Studies which document religious protection against depression include Brown and Lowe (1951), Hertsgaard and Light, (1984), Mayo et al. (1969), and Hathaway and Pargament (1990). McClure and Loden (1982) found that time spent in religious activities reduced depression as measured by the relevant scale on the MMPI, but that it was not highly useful to help one cope with life stresses. Idler (1987) found no evidence linking either public or private religion to male depression once a control was introduced for health status. Specifically, those who were less involved in religion were more depressed, not due to the lack of involvement, but to their tendency to have poorer physical health. For females, public religiousness (church attendance, having co-religionists as friends) lowered depression independent of the control variables. Private religiousness (self-reported level of religiosity and the perception that religion is "of help" to the individual) was unrelated to female depression. The weight of the limited evidence favors the theories arguing a negative relationship between religion and depression.

It is not very clear whether the results of these studies can be generalized to the American population as a whole. The only instance in which a systematic comparison can be made is Stack's (1985b) investigation where no relationship was found between religiosity and depression in the Midwest. A study that used a national random sample, as well as the same depression measures and controls, found a relationship for the nation as a whole (Martin & Stack, 1983). But that study also noted that the religious factor played only a minor role in explaining the variance in depression. Education level is five times more closely associated with the variance in depression than either church attendance or a belief in an afterlife (Martin & Stack, 1983).

Further reasons for caution in assessing the religion-depression link consists of work on closely associated mental health concepts. These include happiness, which might be considered the reverse of depression, and loneliness, which is a special dimension of depression. Often religion is unrelated, or marginally related, to these concepts. For example, none of four dimensions of religion (e.g., church attendance, belief in life after death) were related to happiness (Steinitz, 1980). Belief in a wrathful God increased loneliness, belief in God per se was unrelated to loneliness, while belief in a helpful God reduced loneliness (Schwab & Petersen, 1990). These findings also need to be read with caution due to the problem of nonrepresentative samples of the general population.

Conclusion

This chapter has reviewed the theory and research linking religion to suicide. Theories have stressed different aspects of religion, but all have contended that religion protects against suicide. Integration theory (Durkheim, 1966), based on the meanings that flowed from a large number of religious beliefs and practices, has not been supported by most recent investigations. In response, new theories have emerged. Religious commitment theory (e.g., Stack, 1983b) stresses the life-saving value of just a few core religious beliefs such as life after death. This theory has been supported by a slight majority of investigations using indicators such as church membership and religious publications as estimates of religiosity. A third category of theory emphasizes social contexts that mediate the religion-suicide link. Evidence suggests that religions with nonhierarchical structures and ones that promote primary relations are the ones that save lives (Pescosolido & Georgianna, 1989). Other work has found that religious denomination offers the most protection at its historical hub, a place where it has built up resources and credibility for its constituents. However, most of the 27 religious denominations studied bear no significant relationship to county suicide rates no matter what contextual networking factor is inspected (Pescosolido, 1990).

One central limitation of the work on religion and suicide is that it is based predominately on United States data. Some of the relevant theory based on religious heterogeneity (Pescosolido, 1990) cannot be tested in many other nations, including those with state religions. In contrast, the religious commitment perspective can be tested in the contexts of many other nations. While cross-sectional analysis has offered much evidence in support of this view (e.g., Breault & Barkey, 1982), time series models within a single nation have not done so (e.g., Stack, 1990). As Pescosolido (1990) pointed out, the United States continues to rank at the top of the list of industrial countries in religiosity indicators. It may be that the relatively low levels of religiosity in other more secularized nations may be inadequate to have a significant effect on the incidence of suicide.

Tittle and Welch (1983) have argued that religion affects deviant behavior the most when other institutions are weak. Consequently, the American case is ripe for a religious effect on suicide. American institutions often stand out as rather low on the list of industrial nations. For example, we typically have the highest rates of divorce and unemployment. Voter turnout, which is an index of the political institution's vitality, is also the lowest. The proportion of our labor force that belongs to unions is one of the lowest (e.g., see, Stack, 1990). In this context, religion may indeed save lives. When other institutions are strong, however, people are under less stress, and possibly have less need for religion. In such a case, religious trends may not influence suicidal behavior. More comparative research is needed to address these issues.

Micro-level research on depression and suicide tends to document a negative relationship. While religion insulates people against depression in these studies, they need to be taken with some caution since most are based on nonrepresentative samples of the American population such as students and members of support groups. Further work is needed on national random samples, or large-scale epidemiological surveys drawing on a cross section of the population. Nevertheless, the general existing findings interface quite well with the research on suicide. If further research finds that religion lowers depression, we have another solid basis for expecting religion to lower suicide at the group level as well.

Notes

1. Breault (1986) mistakenly used a two-tailed significance test and dismissed coefficients with t-ratios in the −1.9 range as insignificant.

References

Bainbridge, W.S. (1989). The religious ecology of deviance. *American Sociological Review, 4*, 288–295.

Bainbridge, W.S., & Stark, R. (1982). Suicide, homicide and religion. *Annual Review of the Social Sciences of Religion, 5,* The Hague, Netherlands: Mouton.

Bankston, W.B., Allen, H.D., & Cunningham, D.S. (1983). Religion and suicide: A research note on sociology's 'one law.' *Social Forces, 62,* 521–528.

Breault, K.D. (1986). Suicide in America: A test of Durkheim's theory of religious and family integration, 1933–1980. *American Journal of Sociology, 92,* 628–656.

Breault, K.D. (1988). Beyond the quick and dirty: Reply to Girard. *American Journal of Sociology, 93,* 1479–1486.

Breault, K.D., & Barkey, K. (1982). A comparative analysis of Durkheim's theory of egoistic suicide. *Sociological Quarterly, 23,* 321–331.

Breault, K.D., & Barkey, K. (1983). Reply to Stack. *Sociological Quarterly, 24,* 629–632.

Brown, D.G., & Lowe, W.L. (1951). Religious beliefs and personality characteristics of college students. *Journal of Social Psychology, 33,* 103–129.

D'Antonio, W., & Aldous, J. (1983). *Families and religions.* Beverly Hills, CA: Sage.

Day, L. (1987). Durkheim on religion and suicide: A demographic critique. *Sociology, 21,* 449–461.

Durkheim, E. (1966). *Suicide.* New York: Free Press. (Original work published 1897).

Durkheim, E. (1933). *The division of labor in society.* New York: Macmillan.

Faupel, C.E., Kowalski, G.S., & Starr, P.D. (1987). Sociology's one law: Religion and suicide in the urban context. *Journal for the Scientific Study of Religion, 26,* 523–534.

Fischer, C.S. (1982). *To dwell among friends: Personal networks in town and city.* Chicago: University of Chicago Press.

Girard, C. (1988). Church membership and suicide reconsidered: Comment on Breault. *American Journal of Sociology, 93,* 1471–1479.

Hathaway, W.L., & Pargament, K.I. (1990). Intrinsic religiousness, religious coping, and psychosocial competence. *Journal for the Scientific Study of Religion, 29,* 423–441.

Hertsgaard, D., & Light, H. (1984). Anxiety, depression and hostility in rural women. *Psychological Reports, 55,* 673–674.

Idler, E.L. (1987). Religious involvement and the health of the elderly. *Social Forces, 66,* 226–238.

Kowalski, G.S., Faupel, C., & Starr, P.D. (1987). Urbanism and suicide: A study of American counties. *Social Forces, 66,* 85–101.

Maris, R. (1981). *Pathways to suicide.* Baltimore: Johns Hopkins University Press.

Martin, J., & Stack, S. (1983). The effect of religiosity on alienation. *Sociological Focus, 16,* 65–76.

Maton, K.I. (1989). The stress-buffering role of spiritual support: Cross sectional and prospective investigations. *Journal for the Scientific Study of Religion, 28,* 310–323.

Mayo, C.C., Puryear, H.B., & Richek, H.G. (1969). MMPI correlates of religiousness in late adolescent college students. *Journal of Nervous and Mental Disease, 149,* 381–385.

McClure, R.F., & Loden, M. (1982). Religious activity, denomination membership, and life satisfaction. *Psychology: A Quarterly Journal of Human Behavior, 19,* 12–17.

Pescosolido, B. (1990). The social context of religious integration and suicide: Pursuing the network explanation. *Sociological Quarterly, 31,* 337–357.

Pescosolido, B., & Georgianna, S. (1989). Durkheim, suicide, and religion. *American Sociological Review, 54,* 33–48.

Pope, W. (1976). *Durkheim's Suicide: A classic reanalyzed.* Chicago: University of Chicago Press.

Pope, W., & Danigelis, N. (1981). Sociology's one law. *Social Forces, 60,* 495–516.

Schwab, R., & Petersen, K.U. (1990). Religiousness: Its relation to loneliness, neuroticism and subjective well-being. *Journal for the Scientific Study of Religion, 29,* 335–345.

Spendlove, D.C., West, D.W., & Stanish, W.M. (1984). Risk factors in the prevalence of depression in Mormon women. *Social Science and Medicine, 18,* 491–495.

Stack, S. (1980). Religion and suicide: A reanalysis. *Social Psychiatry, 15,* 65–70.

Stack, S. (1981). Suicide and religion: A comparative analysis. *Sociological Focus, 14,* 207–220.

Stack, S. (1982). Suicide: A decade review of the sociological literature. *Deviant Behavior, 4,* 41–66.

Stack, S. (1983a). The effect of the decline in institutionalized religion on suicide, 1954–1978. *Journal for the Scientific Study of Religion, 22,* 239–252.

Stack, S. (1983b). The effect of religious commitment on suicide: A cross-national analysis. *Journal of Health and Social Behavior, 24,* 362–374.

Stack, S. (1983c). Comment on Breault and Barkey. *Sociological Quarterly, 24,* 625–627.

Stack, S. (1985a). The effect of domestic/religious individualism on suicide, 1954–1978. *Journal of Marriage and the Family, 47,* 431–447.

Stack, S. (1985b). Religion and anomia: Regional vs national specifications. *Journal of Social Psychology, 125,* 133–134.

Stack, S. (1989). The impact of divorce on suicide in Norway. *Journal of Marriage and the Family, 51,* 229–238.

Stack, S. (1990). The effect of divorce on suicide in Denmark. *Sociological Quarterly, 31,* 359–370.

Stark, R., & Bainbridge, W.S. (1980). Toward a theory of religion: Religious commitment. *Journal for the Scientific Study of Religion, 19,* 114–128.

Stark, R., Doyle, D.P., & Rushing, L. (1983). Beyond Durkheim: Religion and suicide. *Journal for the Scientific Study of Religion, 22,* 120–131.

Steinitz, L. (1980). Religiosity, well-being, and weltanschauung among the elderly. *Journal for the Scientific Study of Religion, 19,* 60–67

Tittle, C., & Welch, M. (1983). Religiosity and deviance. *Social Forces, 61,* 653–682.

Wuthnow, R. (1977). A longitudinal cross-national indicator of societal religious commitment. *Journal for the Scientific Study of Religion, 16,* 87–99.

6

Religion, Anxiety, and Fear of Death

Peter Pressman, John S. Lyons,
David B. Larson, and John Gartner

Anxiety is a common affective experience. Everyone experiences transient episodes of anxiety during normal daily living. In its extreme, however, anxiety also represents a major etiologic factor in the development of serious psychopathology. Understanding the cognitive, developmental, and environmental factors that exacerbate and ameliorate anxiety thus informs our understanding of both normal and abnormal human behavior.

Anxiety is not only a focal issue in normal personality development (Call, 1979; Horney, 1937, 1950; Sullivan, 1953) but also a central feature of psychiatric illness (Kaplan & Sadock, 1981). An often cited review (Lader & Marks, 1971) summarized 22 studies of anxiety prevalence, with figures ranging from 2 percent to 4.7 percent for the total population, and between 6 percent and 27 percent for psychiatric populations. More recently, the Epidemiological Catchment Area study has estimated that more than 10 percent of all American citizens will experience a diagnosable anxiety disorder during their lifetime (Robins et al., 1984). Cadoret and King (1983) cite one study estimating persistent anxiety signs and symptoms in 10 percent to 30 percent of patients seen by primary care physicians.

As a universal human experience, anxiety is described as an apprehensive uneasiness of mind, or even dread, over an anticipated but unidentified or uncertain danger (Tyrer, 1982). Feelings of isolation and helplessness along with certain somatic symptoms (Lacey, Bateman, & van Lehn, 1953) are additional correlates of anxiety. In psychoanalytic thinking, anxiety may be a response to feelings of disapproval from a significant adult, or, alternately, it may evolve from a forbidden instinctual drive that is about to escape from control (Freud, 1926).

Bowlby (1973) differed from Freud, and regarded anxiety as primarily a consequence of loss or incomplete attachment behavior in childhood. It is also notable that Bowlby (1960) regards anxiety and depression as part of the same process. In fact, Noyes et al. (1990) have reported that depression is the most common comorbid condition within anxiety disorders. The most recent edition of the American Psychiatric Association's Diagnostic and Statistical Manual of Mental Disorders (DSM-III-R, 1987) lists anxiety among associated features (noncriterion symptoms) of depression.

Religion and Anxiety

God treated me severely to rebuke me; frightening me with His mock sternness
to double my delight in His real and everlasting kindness.

RADWAN HUSAINI, from
Midaq Alley, by Naguib Mafouz

Husaini sees life as tough and capricious, but with an underlying if invisible sanity
orchestrated by an omnipresent God who will reward one's anxious struggle with
infinite peace and love. Mafouz, the Egyptian Nobel laureate, wrote prolifically of
the colliding systems of Islamic belief and behavior and those of cultural and
national chauvinism. In *Midaq Alley,* Mafouz (1947) shows that Husaini's interpretation of Islam serves his immediate needs but also may ultimately be maladaptive, both for Husaini himself and for the nation. Thus, we begin to see that religion
has the potential either to increase or to decrease anxiety, depending on various
sociocultural, situational, or individual factors. Direction and level of analysis must
be specified in this sort of discussion.

Addressing the Christian tradition, Melinsky (1970) postulated that the cry of
anxiety-driven loneliness could be ameliorated by the Old and New Testament God
who is near and cares. Mathers (1970) echoes this thinking (as do psychoanalytic
theorists), characterizing Jesus as someone who cares for people by "sharing their
anxieties as a parent" (p. 22). The metaphor does not constitute an unreasonable
leap in light of the biblical story of Genesis, in which God paternally fashions
human beings in his own image and makes them his delegates.

Mathers (1970) extends the metaphor by linking repentance with a "working
through" of anxiety. Repentance is seen as a change of mind (metanoia) in the
direction of reconciliation with God and brethren. Repentance begins with anxiety,
but this intrapersonal angst has pertinent interpersonal implications; communion
with fellow humans is restored and intensified, anxiety is reduced. The beginning
of this process is indicated in Psalm 51:1

Have mercy upon me, Oh God, according to Your loving kindness: according unto
the multitude of Your tender mercies, blot out my sin.

On the other hand, Bowers (1969) points out that there are idiosyncracies of
religious conviction that are carriers of pathologic ideation; for example, the distortion of the God-idea with fierce superego demand and expectations of punishment. Bowers links the success of psychotherapy with religious personnel to the
therapist's acumen in discovering individual distortions of religious doctrine. Freud
himself hypothesized that one's understanding of religious experience is very
strongly influenced by developmental psychological experience. In his case, this
view seems to have led to an understanding of religion as an obsessive-compulsive
response to anxieties about certain aspects of his own life (Meissner, 1984).

A representative example of a developmental factor confounding a salutary
effect of religion is the case of severe anxiety in a grade-school-age child who was
awaiting minor surgery. She had been told on the occasion of her grandfather's
death (in the hospital) that angels had come in his sleep to take him to heaven. As

a result, she became quite distressed that the same vague but frightening fate awaited her with the sleep of anesthesia (Coppolillo, 1980).

Moreover, in the absence of developmental or situational forces, culture itself colors the impact of religion. Lambert, Triandis, and Wolf (1959) demonstrated that societies with aggressive deities tend to be less nurturant of infants and to have elevated levels of anxiety in the child. The reverse situation was found in groups with more benevolent deities. Even in mainstream Western religion, there appears to be an affiliation-specific contribution to lowering anxiety. Egbert (1986) presented data suggesting that Catholic patients were more likely (75 percent) to voice that their religion had helped them through the stress of having an operation than were Protestants (46 percent) or Jews (23 percent). Various religiously structured groups may tap different aspects and proportions of religion, culture, and social support in recovering from illness and surgery.

In a broad sociological frame, it is important to note that the perspectives of Western religion are neither universal nor inevitable (Broom & Selznick, 1973). In comparison with the ideas of Hinduism and Buddhism, Hebraic tradition celebrates a more person-centered approach with a clear duality of man and nature. The Eastern systems emphasize extinction of selfhood and renunciation of individual aspiration, while promoting unity with a cosmic consciousness encompassing all of nature (i.e., it is difficult to fail in the eyes of a metaphoric parent, and it is impossible to be disconnected and alone).

Diametrically opposed to Eastern thinking lies a hallmark of Western culture, namely the Protestant Ethic. In 1904, Weber argued that Protestant doctrine shaped the personalities of the emerging class of entrepreneurs. Initiative, acquisition, individualism and hard work were prized. Only God was to be a confidant as other people could not be so readily trusted. Furthermore, because of uncertainty about who were among the elect, there was much anxiety (Tawney, 1947/1926; Gerth & Mills, 1953; Broom & Selznick, 1973). Relief from religious anxiety was found in disciplined effort. One may speculate about tradeoffs of mental health for industrial productivity.

Writing just prior to Weber, Durkheim (1897) blended psychoanalytic theory with sociological analysis in his classic treatise, *Suicide.* Durkheim hypothesized about the comparative immunity of Catholics to suicide and ascribed it to the manner in which the individual was integrated into the Catholic group. This group thrived on mechanisms that made all sins expiable, established a system of father-substitutes, and painted a poetic image of the mother. In contrast, Protestant groups had higher suicide rates, and this was attributed to the Protestant emphasis on individualism, individual conscience, and attendant guilt, which had no comparable outlet through confession.

Below is an excerpt from the diary of Moritz Thomsen (1965), a farmer and Peace Corps volunteer. It represents a most dramatic example of the interaction of sociocultural and religious variables impinging upon a religion-anxiety equation.

> The statistics, of course, I knew—that in the country areas [in Ecuador] 3 out of 5 babies die before their third year. And I was also aware of the Catholic philosophy which makes these deaths bearable to the country people. They hold the profound belief that when a baby dies, it dies in a state of grace and flies directly to heaven.

> Within this framework then, the death of a child is something to celebrate; he has been released from a life of suffering and poverty to become one of God's angels. But, knowing all this, I still could not accept it. . . . What I was going to do in that unrewarding spot for 18 more months . . . sent me reeling into a depression.

Thomsen says he *could not accept it,* even though he acknowledges the reality of these people and their effective use of religion. His own cognitive dissonance produces an anxiety that is nearly overwhelming. And then there is anger about the ready acceptance, followed by fear and the prospect of isolation, eventuating in anxiety for him in this upside-down world.

One need look no further than Thomsen's example to keenly appreciate the mandate for specifying direction and level of analysis when exploring the relationships between religion and anxiety. In this one vignette, the same basic religious tradition was transduced very differently by each sociocultural milieu represented. On an individual level Thomsen may be attributing the maintenance of a negative, anxiety-provoking situation to the status quo effects of religion, echoing the Marxian "opiate of the people" position. Religion, however, as a philosophical system is not intended to maintain a destructive or medieval status quo (James, 1961/1902; Larson, Pattison, Blazer, Omran, & Kaplan, 1986). Vibrant examples of religion as popular activism are summarized by Whiteside (1991), who notes Gustavo Guttierez, the Peruvian priest who affirms "liberation theology" and promotes church-supported social justice for Latin Americans. Other examples include Martin Luther King's *Letter from Birmingham Jail,* and texts by Lao Tze and Gandhi. Whiteside also notes sociologist Robert Bellah's investigation of the way in which Abraham Lincoln "found in biblical language a way to express the most profound moral vision in 19th century America" (p. 19). Indeed, as will be illustrated below, much of the psychological research that we have found has documented the frequently beneficial role of religious commitment on clinical, psychiatric, and physical status.

Recent Research

Within the latter half of the 1980s, psychology and psychiatry have intensified the scientific scrutiny and practice of research on religious variables in general (Larson et al., 1986; Levin & Vanderpool, 1987; Schiller & Levin, 1988; Levin & Schiller, 1987; Gartner, Larson, & Allen, 1991; Jarvis & Northcott, 1987; Craigie, Liu, Larson, & Lyons, 1988; Craigie, Larson, & Liu, 1990; Larson & Sherrill, 1988; Payne, Bergin, Bielema, & Jenkins, 1991; Larson et al., 1988; Pressman, Lyons, Larson, & Strain, 1990; Larson et al., 1989; Williams, Larson, Buckler, Heckmann, & Pyle, 1991).

Findings on the causal relationship between religion and anxiety are difficult to evaluate since most studies are cross-sectional. Research is obviously needed to clarify causal directionality in the relationships observed. It seems self-evident that sociocultural and psychological factors may be either cause *or* consequence of religious beliefs or behavior.

Sanua (1969) reported that the research literature indicates that the "religious person" may alternately show greater and less anxiety than one who is not religious. Bergin (1983) also found confusing results in studies of manifest anxiety. In the most recent review, Gartner et al. (1991) found four studies reporting that religious subjects were *more* anxious (Gupta, 1983; Hassan & Khalique, 1981; Spellman, Baskett, & Byrne, 1971; Wilson & Miller, 1968), three studies that found *lower* anxiety in religious subjects (Hertsgaard & Light, 1984; Williams & Cole, 1968) or *less* anxious after participation in religious pilgrimage (Morris, 1982), and three studies that found *no* relationship between anxiety and religiosity (Brown, 1962; Epstein, Tamir, & Natan, 1985; Heitzelman & Fehr, 1976).

A possible explanation for the discrepancy in findings is the form of religiousness under study. DeFigueirdo & Lemkan (1978) found that somatic manifestations of anxiety were negatively associated with public religious participation, but positively associated with private religiosity. Age may also constitute an impinging variable, with its mediating value increasing with years lived (Koenig, Smiley, & Gonzales, 1988; Gutmann, 1989). In a study of elderly patients with broken hips, Pressman et al. (1990) found both religious beliefs and practices to be significantly associated with lower levels of depressive symptoms and better ambulation status following discharge from the hospital.

Bergin, Masters, and Richards (1987) addressed styles of religious commitment. They found "intrinsic" religiousness (Allport & Ross, 1967), a style valuing religion for intrapersonal enhancement, to be correlated with lower anxiety. In contrast is "extrinsic" religiousness, a style that values religion for its interpersonal benefits (i.e., social status, acceptance), which was associated with higher levels of anxiety.

In their study of the impact of religion on men's blood pressure, Larson et al. (1989) found significantly lower diastolic blood pressures in subjects who attended church frequently and those who held their religion as very important. This finding was in contrast with higher blood pressure for those with low church attendance, and those who attached little importance to religion. The difference persisted after adjusting for age, socioeconomic status, smoking, and weight-height ratio. High blood pressure then, may be taken as a proxy for psychosocial factors, including anxiety, which have been linked by abundant evidence to cardiovascular status (Levin & Vanderpool, 1989).

Religion and Death Anxiety

> I can hardly remember a dying patient who was afraid of death.
>
> SIR WILLIAM OSLER

Fear of death and anxiety are generally thought of as consubstantial. Fear is usually associated with a very specific threat, whereas anxiety is often nonspecific. Cassell (1979) points out that the "fear of death" first appears in children 4 or 5 years old who have simply not yet developed the cognitive framework to *fear* any of the specific *external* dangers (i.e., pain, nausea, thirst, weakness). The predominant distress associated with fear of death is one with an *internal* source or *anxiety* about the unknown and separation from or disappearance of the parent (see also Bowlby,

1969, 1973). Thus, the fear of death is not, strictly speaking, a fear. Rather it is a ubiquitous anxiety state that points to an existential fact-of-life. Freud himself consistently held the position that (nonspecific) anxiety was distinct from (specific) fear (Bowlby, 1961).

In their review of psychological problems in the surgical patient, Modell and Guerra (1980) describe one study in which 75 percent of patients reported "fearing death" when directly asked. Garner (1980) also addressed concerns in the perioperative period. He specifically cautioned that caregivers must respect religious beliefs that represent ways of coping with illness, treatment, and death. If a physician implies that he or she is at all antagonized by these beliefs, there is a risk of precluding the expression of anxiety, and this may have detrimental clinical effects.

In a recent case review of older men undergoing treatment for advanced head and neck cancer, we found evidence suggesting that belief in God played a more important role in mediating anxiety than did coping abilities (Pressman, Larson, Lyons, & Humes, in press).

That so much of the world's religious tradition both explicitly and implicitly addresses death and dying is abundant testimony to the salience of our concerns about these issues (Werkman, 1981). Historically, religion and medicine were fused in response to illness and death. Shamans, medicine men, witch doctors, and priest-physicians embodied the effort to confront death. Images of reincarnation, nirvana, immortality, eternal sleep, and Heaven (all states ostensibly free from anxiety) evolved to meet the urgent need for explanation, meaning, and comfort (Morris, 1964). More recently, the church played a major role in the building and staffing of early hospitals. Even today a large number of medical centers have specific religious affiliations.

The empirical research on the relationship of religious beliefs to death anxiety reveals mixed results (Thorsen & Powell, 1989; Chaggaris & Lester, 1989). It appears that religious beliefs may be related to specific aspects of death anxiety, but not to the total construct as it is generally defined. That is, the dimension of death anxiety sometimes referred to as "fear of the unknown" has been related to religious motivation (Thorsen & Powell, 1989). This dimension involves concerns about what might happen after death. Some research suggests a cross-cultural difference in the strength of association between religious beliefs and fear of death (Long & Elghanemi, 1987).

Gartner et al. (1991) also reviewed the literature concerning the relationship between religious commitment and death anxiety. Six studies found *less* fear of death in religiously committed subjects (Aday, 1984; Richardson, Berman, & Piwowarski, 1983; Smith, Nehemkis, & Charter, 1983; Tobacyk, 1983; Westman & Canter, 1985; Young & Daniels, 1980). Three studies found *more* fear of death in religiously committed groups (Beg & Zilli, 1982; Dodd & Mills, 1985; Florian, Kravetz, & Frankel, 1984). Five studies found no relationship between religious commitment and death anxiety (Dahawn & Sripat, 1986; Kunzendorff, 1985; Mahabeer & Bhana, 1984; Muchnik & Rosenheim, 1982; Rosenheim & Muchnik, 1984). As a possible explanation, two studies found a curvilinear relationship between religious commitment and death anxiety, such that the moderately religious were the most anxious and the very religious and nonreligious were the least anxious (Downey, 1984; McMordie, 1981). Finally, two studies found that the religiously committed were more anxious about some aspects of death but less anxious about others (Florian & Kravetz, 1983; Hoelter, 1979).

Again, there are apparent inconsistencies and frank divergence in the few research studies in this area. A number of investigators have called into question the appropriateness of various study populations (Bergin, 1983; Gartner et al., 1991), as well as the actual measures used (Baker & Gorsuch, 1982). Also, some have noted methodological difficulties in psychological tests that may be value-biased in the context of religious research (Gartner, 1983; Watson, Hood, Morris, & Hall, 1985).

Guidelines for Future Research

In any text on mental health research, the prospects for *prevention* must be addressed. In this chapter, there is the broad question, *can religion help to diminish or even prevent anxiety?* The reply, to paraphrase Schiller & Levin (1988), is an unqualified, "It depends . . ."

If the question of prevention here is to be more fully answered, it should be evident by now that religion must be viewed as one of Geertz's "multiplicity of complex structures . . . superimposed upon or knotted into one another" (1973, p. 10). Geertz suggests that the investigation of complex psychosocial/cultural structures (such as religion) requires what amounts to ethnographic technique (i.e., an interpretative anthropology). An immersion in direct contact with subjects is requisite to rapport and meaningful interview and observation.

Paraphrasing Geertz (1973, p. 16), it is not only against thinned descriptions or a body of data that is apparently too difficult or too easy to interpret that we must measure the cogency of our explications, but against the power of the scientific imagination to bring us in touch with the lives of strangers.

In advancing religious research, we must be more precise and rigorous in formulating and responding to the important questions. Additionally, we could profit from more full-bodied designs which contain ethnographic complements to assist in the selection and interpretation, and perhaps the further construction of our psychometric armamentarium.

As noted in previous research and research reviews, further investigations are needed to allow for a more complete understanding of the role of religion in health and mental health. There is substantial evidence that religion can play a beneficial role in clinical status. This appears to be true for anxiety as well as for other mental health outcomes. However, "religion" in the clinical domain remains, as Geertz (1973) observed, a complex, multidimensional phenomenon. Empirical evidence from both psychiatry and primary care medicine indicates that ritual and support dimensions of religious practice are almost invariably associated with benefit (Craigie et al., 1990; Larson, Sherrill, Lyons, Craigie, & Thielman, in press). Research that measured aspects of religious meaning (e.g., beliefs) report far more equivocal results with evidence of both benefit and potential harm. Therefore, the behavioral sciences demand that future research consider the multiple dimensions on which religious beliefs and practices must be measured. Failure to do so will likely result in a continued absence of clarity of findings.

In conjunction with ethnographic (naturalistic) observation, properly informed psychological research will constitute a powerful heuristic in the development of research. One recent study of the impact of religious belief on recovery from a fractured femur resulted from the incidental observation of spontaneous discussions of the personal importance of religious beliefs (Pressman, Lyons, Larson, & Strain, 1990). The study was actually an assessment of the cost-effectiveness of a psychiatric intervention where religion was not initially being considered as part of the research hypothesis. When a hypothesis that included religious belief was studied, however, religiousness emerged as an important, previously overlooked, dimension. Such flexibility in modifying research protocols based on serendipitous findings is a vital aspect of research development. Research should look for the opportunities to include religious variables in other ongoing protocols. We believe that research has gone through a paradigm shift. In the past religious commitment would have been considered something of a bizarre variable to study, but today scientists are open and even quite interested in better understanding this institution that has been with us since the beginning.

References

Aday, R.H. (1984). Belief in afterlife and death anxiety: Correlates and comparisons. *Omega Journal of Death and Dying, 15,* 67–75.

Allport, G., & Ross, J.M. (1967). Personal religious orientation and prejudice. *Journal of Personality and Social Psychology, 5,* 432–443.

Baker, M., & Gorsuch, R. (1982). Trait anxiety and intrinsic-extrinsic religiousness. *Journal for the Scientific Study of Religion, 21,* 119–122.

Beg, M.A., & Zilli, A.S. (1982). A study of the relationship of death anxiety and religious faith to age differentials. *Psychologia, 25,* 121–125.

Bergin, A.E. (1983). Religiosity and mental health: A critical reevaluation and meta-analysis. *Professional Psychology, 14,* 170–184.

Bergin, A., Masters, K.S., & Richards, P.S. (1987). Religiousness and mental health reconsidered: A study of an intrinsically religious sample. *Journal of Counseling Psychology, 34,* 197–204.

Bowers, M.K. (1969). Psychotherapy of religious conflict. In E.M. Pattison (Ed.), *Clinical psychiatry and religion* (pp. 233–242). Boston: Little Brown.

Bowlby, J. (1960). Separation anxiety. *International Journal of Psychoanalysis, 41,* 89–113.

Bowlby, J. (1961). Separation anxiety: A critical review of the literature. *Journal of Child Psychology and Psychiatry, 1,* 251–269.

Bowlby, J. (1969). *Attachment and loss: Vol. 1. Attachment.* New York: Basic Books.

Bowlby, J. (1973). *Separation, anxiety, and anger.* London: Hogarth.

Broom, L., & Selznick, P. (1973). *Sociology: A text with adapted readings,* ed. 5. New York: Harper & Row.

Brown, L.B. (1962). A study of religious belief. *British Journal of Psychology, 53,* 259–272.

Cadoret, R.J., & King, L.J. (1983). *Psychiatry in primary care.* St. Louis: C.V. Mosby.

Call, J.D. (1979). Introduction: Current status of psychoanalytic developmental psychology. In J.D. Noshpitz (Ed.), *Basic handbook of child psychiatry* (vol. 1, p. 8). New York: Basic Books.

Cassell, E.J. (1979). The physician and the dying patient. In G. Usdin & J.M. Lewis (Eds.), *Psychiatry in general medical practice* (pp. 729–731). New York: McGraw-Hill.

Chaggaris, M., & Lester, D. (1989). Fear of death and religious belief. *Psychological Reports, 64,* 274.

Coppolillo, H.P. (1980). Management of the child in the perioperative period. In F. Guerra & J.A. Aldrete (Eds.), *Emotional and psychological responses to anesthesia and surgery.* New York: Grune & Stratton.

Craigie, F.C., Larson, D.B., & Liu, I.Y. (1990). References to religion in the Journal of Family Practice: Dimensions and valence of spirituality. *Journal of Family Practice, 30,* 477–480.

Craigie, F.C., Liu, I.Y., Larson, D.B., & Lyons, J.S. (1988). A systematic analysis of religious variables in the Journal of Family Practice, 1976–1986. *Journal of Family Practice, 27,* 509–513.

Dahawn, N., & Sripat, K. (1986). Fear of death and religiosity as related to need for affiliation. *Psychological Studies, 31,* 35–38.

DeFigueirdo, J.M., & Lemkan, P.V. (1978). The prevalence of psychosomatic symptoms in a rapidly changing bilingual culture: An exploratory study. *Social Psychiatry, 13,* 125–133.

Diagnostic and statistical manual of mental disorders (1987). Rev., ed. 3. Washington, DC: American Psychiatric Association.

Dodd, D.K., & Mills, L.L. (1985). FADIS: A measure of the fear of accidental death and injury. *The Psychological Record, 35,* 269–275.

Downey, A.M. (1984). Relationship of religiosity to death anxiety of middle-aged males. *Psychological Reports, 54,* 811–822.

Durkheim, E. (1897). *Suicide.* New York: The Free Press.

Egbert, L.D. (1986). Preoperative anxiety: The adult patient. In B.J. Hindman (Ed.), *Neurological and psychological complications of surgery and anesthesia.* Boston: Little Brown.

Epstein, L., Tamir, A., & Natan, T. (1985). Emotional health state of adolescents. *International Journal of Adolescent Medicine and Health, 1,* 13–22.

Florian, V., & Kravetz, S. (1983). Fear of personal death: Attribution, structure, and relation to religious belief. *Journal of Personality and Social Psychology, 44,* 600–607.

Florian, V., Kravetz, S., & Frankel, J. (1984). Aspects of fear of personal death, levels of awareness, and religious commitment. *Journal of Research in Personality, 18,* 289–304.

Freud, S. (1926). Inhibitions, symptoms and anxiety. In *Standard edition* (vol. 20). London: Hogarth Press.

Garner, V.M.T. (1980). Specific ethnocultural considerations in the perioperative period. In F.Guerra & J.A. Aldrete (Eds.), *Emotional and psychological responses to anesthesia and surgery.* New York: Grune & Stratton.

Gartner, J. (1983). Self-esteem tests: Assumptions and values. In C. Ellison (Ed.), *Your better self: Psychology, Christianity and self-esteem.* New York: Harper & Row.

Gartner, J., Larson, D.B., Allen, G.D. (1991). Religious commitment and mental health: A review of the empirical literature. *Journal of Psychology and Theology, 19,* 6–25.

Geertz, C. (1973). *Thick description.* New York: Basic Books.

Gerth, H., & Mills, C.W. (1953). *Character and social structure.* New York: Harcourt, Brace & Jovanovich.

Gupta, A. (1983). Mental health and religion. *Asian Journal of Psychology Education, 11,* 8–13.

Gutmann, D. (1989). *Reclaimed powers: Toward a new psychology of men and women in later life.* New York: Basic Books.

Hassan, M.K., & Khalique, A. (1981). Religiosity and its correlates in college students. *Journal of Psychological Research, 25,* 129–136.

Heitzelman, M.E., & Fehr, L.A. (1976). Relationship between religious orthodoxy and three personality variables. *Psychological Reports, 38,* 756–758.

Hertsgaard, D., & Light, H. (1984). Anxiety, depression, and hostility in rural women. *Psychological Reports, 55,* 673–674.

Hoelter, J. (1979). Religiosity, fear of death and suicide acceptability. *Suicide and Life Threatening Behavior, 9,* 163–172.

Horney, K. (1937). *Neurotic personality of our times.* New York: Norton.

Horney, K. (1950). *Neurosis and human growth.* New York: Norton.

James, W. (1961). *The varieties of religious experience: A study of human nature.* London: Collier-Macmillan. (Original work published 1902.)

Jarvis, G.K., & Northcott, H.C. (1987). Religion and differences in morbidity and mortality. *Social Science and Medicine, 25,* 813–824.

Kaplan, H.I., & Sadock, B.J. (1981). *Modern synopsis of comprehensive textbook of psychiatry III.* Baltimore: Williams & Wilkins.

Koenig, H.G., Smiley, M., & Gonzales, J.A.P. (1988). *Religion, health, and aging: A review and theoretical integration.* Westport, CT: Greenwood Press.

Kunzendorff, R. (1985). Repressed fear of inexistence and its hypnotic recovery in religious students. *Omega Journal of Death and Dying, 16,* 23–33.

Lacey, J.I., Bateman, D.E., & van Lehn, R. (1953). Autonomic response specificity: An experimental study. *Psychosomatic Medicine, 15,* 8–21.

Lader, M., & Marks, I. (1971). *Clinical anxiety.* London: Heinemann.

Lambert, W.W., Triandis, L.M., & Wolf, M. (1959). Some correlates of beliefs in the malevolence and benevolence of supernatural beings: A cross-sectional study. *Journal of Abnormal and Social Psychology, 58,* 162–169.

Larson, D.B., Hohmann, A., Kessler, L.G., Meador, K.G., Boyd, J.H., & McSherry, E. (1988). The couch and the cloth: The need for linkage. *Hospital and Community Psychiatry, 39,* 1064–1069.

Larson, D.B., Koenig, B.H., Kaplan, B., Greenberg, R.S., Logue, E., & Tyroler, H.A. (1989). The impact of religion on men's blood pressure. *Journal of Religion and Health, 28,* 265–278.

Larson, D.B., Pattison, E.M., Blazer, D., Omran, A., & Kaplan, B. (1986). Research on religious variables in four major psychiatric journals. *American Journal of Psychiatry, 143,* 329–334.

Larson, D.B., & Sherrill, K.A. (1988). Adult burn patients: The role of religion in recovery. *Southern Medical Journal, 81,* 821–825.

Larson, D.B., Sherrill, K.A., Lyons, J.S., Craigie, F.C., & Thielman, S.B. (in press). Dimensions and valence measures of religious commitment in the American Journal of Psychiatry and Archives of General Psychiatry 1978–1989. *American Journal of Psychiatry.*

Levin, J.S., & Schiller, P.L. (1987). Is there a religious factor in health? *Journal of Religion and Health, 26,* 9–36.

Levin, J.S., & Vanderpool, H.Y. (1987). Is frequent religious attendance really conducive to better health?: Toward an epidemiology of religion. *Social Science and Medicine, 24,* 589–600.

Levin, J.S., & Vanderpool, H.Y. (1989). Is religion therapeutically significant for hypertension? *Social Science and Medicine, 29,* 69–78.

Long, D.D., & Elghanemi, S. (1987). Religious correlates of fear of death among Saudi Arabians. *Death Studies, 11,* 89–97.

Mafouz, N. (1947). *Midaq alley.* Beirut: Khagat.

Mahabeer, M., & Bhana, K. (1984). The relationship between religion, religiosity and death anxiety among Indian adolescents. *South African Journal of Psychology, 14,* 7–9.

Mathers, J. (1970). The concept of anxiety. In A.H. Melinsky (Ed.), *Religion and medicine.* London: SCM Press.

McMordie, W.R. (1981). Religiosity and fear of death: Strength of belief system. *Psychological Reports, 49,* 921–922.

Meissner, W.W. (1984). *Psychoanalysis and religious experience.* New Haven, CT: Yale University Press.

Melinsky, H. (1970). Clinical theology: A survey. In A.H. Melinsky (Ed.), *Religion and medicine.* London: SCM Press.

Modell, J.G., & Guerra, F. (1980). Psychological problems in the surgical patient. In F. Guerra & J.A. Aldrete (Eds.), *Emotional and psychological responses to anesthesia and surgery.* New York: Grune & Stratton.

Morris, I. (1964). *The world of the shining prince: Court life in ancient Japan.* New York: Knopf.

Morris, P.A. (1982). The effect of pilgrimage on anxiety, depression and religious attitude. *Psychological Medicine, 12,* 291–294.

Muchnik, B., & Rosenheim, E. (1982). Fear of death, defense style, and religiosity among Israeli Jews. *Israeli Journal of Psychiatry and Related Sciences, 19,* 157–164.

Noyes, R., Reich, J., Christiansen, S., Suelzer, M., Pfohl, B., & Coryell, W.A. (1990). Outcome of panic disorder: Relationship to diagnostic subtypes and comorbidity. *Archives of General Psychiatry, 47,* 809–818.

Payne, R., Bergin, A., Bielema, K.A., & Jenkins, P.H. (1991). Review of religion and mental health: Prevention and enhancement of psychosocial functioning. *Prevention in Human Services, 9,* 11–40.

Pressman, P., Larson, D.B., Lyons, J.S., & Humes, D.L. (in press). Religious belief, coping strategies, and psychological distress in 7 eldery males with head and neck cancer. Manuscript submitted for publication.

Pressman, P., Lyons, J.S., Larson, D.B., & Strain, J.J. (1990). Religious belief, depression, and ambulation status in elderly women with broken hips. *American Journal of Psychiatry, 147,* 758–760.

Richardson, V., Berman, S., & Piwowarski, M. (1983). Projective assessment of the relationships between the salience of death, religion, and age among adults in America. *Journal of General Psychology, 109,* 149–156.

Robins, L.N., Helzer, J.E., Weissman, M.W., Orvaschel, H., Gruenberg, E., Burke, J., & Regier, D.A. (1984). Lifetime prevalence of specific psychiatric disorders in 3 sites. *Archives of General Psychiatry, 41,* 949–958.

Rosenheim, E., & Muchnik, B. (1984). Death concerns in differential levels of consciousness as functions of defense strategy and religious belief. *Omega Journal of Death and Dying, 15,* 15–24.

Sanua, V.D. (1969). Religion, mental health, and personality: A review of empirical studies. *American Journal of Psychiatry, 125,* 1203–1213.

Schiller, P.L., & Levin, J.S. (1988). Is there a religious factor in health care utilization?: A review. *Social Science and Medicine, 27,* 1369–1379.

Smith, D.K., Nehemkis, A.M., & Charter, R.A. (1983). Fear of death, death attitudes, and religious conviction in the terminally ill. *International Journal of Psychiatry in Medicine, 13,* 221–232.

Spellman, C.M., Baskett, G.D., & Byrne, D. (1971). Manifest anxiety as a contributing factor in religious conversion. *Journal of Consulting and Clinical Psychology, 36,* 245–247.

Sullivan, H.S. (1953). *The interpersonal theory of psychiatry.* New York: Norton.

Tawney, R.H. (1947). *Religion and the rise of capitalism.* New York: Penguin. (Original work published 1926.)

Thomsen, M. (1965). The culture shock of quiet death. *San Francisco Chronicle* (This World, April 25, 1965, p. 26).

Thorsen, J.A., & Powell, F.C. (1989). Death anxiety and religion in an older male sample. *Psychological Reports, 64,* 985–986.

Tobacyk, J. (1983). Death threat, death concerns, and paranormal belief. *Death Education, 7,* 115–124.

Tyrer, P.J. (1982). Anxiety states. In E.S. Paykel (Ed.), *Handbook of affective disorders* (pp. 59–69). New York: Guilford Press.

Watson, P.J., Hood, R.W., Jr., Morris, R.J., & Hall, J.R. (1985). Religiosity, sin and self-esteem. *Journal of Psychology and Theology, 13,* 116–128.

Werkman, S.L. (1981). Death and dying: Historical and religious perspectives. In R.C. Simons & H. Pardes (Eds.), *Understanding human behavior in health and illness* (pp. 472–476). Baltimore: Williams & Wilkins.

Westman, A.S., & Canter, F.M. (1985). Fear of death and the concept of extended self. *Psychological Reports, 56,* 419–425.

Whiteside, W. (1991). To pray or not to pray. *Bowdoin, 63,* 16–19.

Williams, D.R., Larson, D.B., Buckler, R.E., Heckmann, R.C., & Pyle, C.M. (1991). Religion and psychological distress in a community sample. *Social Science and Medicine, 32,* 1257–1262.

Williams, R.L., & Cole, S. (1968). Religiosity, generalized anxiety, and apprehension concerning death. *Journal of Social Psychology, 75,* 111–117.

Wilson, W., & Miller, H.L. (1968). Fear, anxiety, and religiousness. *Journal for the Scientific Study of Religion, 7,* 111.

Young, M., & Daniels, S. (1980). Born again status as a factor in death anxiety. *Psychological Reports, 47,* 367–370.

7

Sin and Guilt in Faith Traditions: Issues for Self-Esteem

Ralph W. Hood, Jr.

The antipathy of contemporary psychology to religion is well established in the empirical literature (for reviews, see Spilka, Hood, & Gorsuch, 1985; Wulff, 1991). While the reasons for this antipathy are complex, one distinct factor that appears in the empirical literature is the decidedly different evaluations psychologists and religionists are likely to make with respect to guilt and related constructs such as shame and sin.

Perhaps not many psychologists would agree with Ellis's extreme assertion that "... the concept of sin is the direct and indirect cause of virtually all neurotic disturbances" (1962, p. 146). But few people, except for psychological apologists within more fundamentalist Christian faith traditions, would accept the validity of such concepts as "original sin." The focus of empirical psychology has been upon *feelings* of guilt and related constructs, not upon the ontology of guilt. Buber criticized psychology for this, noting that "this omission has not been presented and methodologically grounded as such. It has been treated as a limitation that follows as a matter of course from the nature of psychology" (1971, p. 86). While a debate of this claim is beyond the scope of this chapter, it will be seen that it is not irrelevant to an evaluation of empirical literature. For now we can simply note how readily most psychologists would probably subscribe to Branden's assertion that, "... if a man feels guilt, it is not because he is guilty by nature; sin is not 'original,' it is *originated*" (1969, p. 161).

How guilt is originated has been the dominant focus of theoretically grounded psychologies of guilt, especially psychoanalytic ones, and these account in no small measure for their confrontations with faith traditions. Perhaps the most frequently debated empirical hypothesis is that faith traditions in general (and, in particular, more fundamentalist Christian faith traditions) foster lower self-esteem through mechanisms of guilt, shame, and sin.

The Empirical Literature

Religion and Self-Esteem

Gartner (1983) was able to identify eighteen studies relating religion and self-esteem. A simple comparison of results across all studies indicated no clear pattern. Of the eighteen studies, eight found no relationship between religion and self-esteem, six found a positive relationship, and four found a negative relationship. The studies vary widely in quality and in operational indices of self-esteem and religiosity. Furthermore, eight are unpublished dissertations, and several are in obscure journals. In a recent follow-up survey Gartner, Larson, and Allen (1991) cited four additional studies relating religion and self-esteem. Two of these studies (both unpublished dissertations) found no relationship between religion and self-esteem, one study reported a negative relationship, and one found a positive relationship. Thus, at the simple empirical level, no consistent pattern of relationship between religion and self-esteem emerges.

Many studies have admittedly used crude indices of religiosity and self-esteem (Bahr & Martin, 1983). This is even the case with some studies published in methodologically demanding journals. But some investigators are beginning to employ more sophisticated measurement instruments. Furthermore, a more adequate empirical question has been raised: "How are different *forms* of religion related to self-esteem and the constructs of guilt, sin, and shame?" Some of this research has made use of Allport's distinction between intrinsic and extrinsic forms of religious commitment.

Intrinsic/Extrinsic Religion and Self-Esteem

The dominant empirical paradigm in the American psychology of religion has centered on Gordon Allport's distinction between intrinsic and extrinsic religion (for reviews, see Donahue, 1985; Gorsuch, 1988; Kirpatrick & Hood, 1990). Whether conceived as forms (i.e., "types") of religious commitment (intrinsic versus extrinsic) or used as dimensions of religiosity (intrinsicness/extrinsicness), a clear pattern of relationship between religiosity and self-esteem emerges when Allport's conceptualizations are employed. For instance, Wickstrom and Fleck (1983) found negative self-esteem only among "consensual" (extrinsic) religiosity, and not "committed" (intrinsic) religiosity. Likewise, Baker & Gorsuch (1982) found that Cattel's IPAT Anxiety Battery correlated significantly with extrinsic religiosity but not with intrinsic religiosity. Furthermore, this pattern was also seen on several subscales of the IPAT. Extrinsic religion correlated positively with lack of self-sentiment, ego weakness, and paranoid-type insecurity, while intrinsic religion was negatively correlated with these subscales. Curiously, neither form of religiosity correlated with guilt.

As a general rule, people committed to the dominant Western faith traditions hold predominantly positive images of God (Gorsuch, 1968). Furthermore, conceiving God as loving and kind is more typical of intrinsic religious types, while conceiving God as vindictive and punishing is more typical of extrinsic religious types (Hunt & King, 1971). This suggests that concepts of God partially mediate self-esteem, possibly as the result of their relationship to intrinsic and extrinsic religiosity. Yet, image of God has effects independent of its relationship to intrinsic and extrinsic religiosity. For instance, Benson and Spilka (1973) found positive self-esteem among those who subscribed to loving images of God and negative self-esteem among those who held punitive images of God.

These findings support the one consistent thread throughout the empirical literature (at least with Western faith traditions), namely that both intrinsic religiosity and positive conceptions of God are associated with positive self-esteem, while both extrinsic religiosity and a punitive conception of God are associated with negative self-esteem. Furthermore, intrinsic religion is likely to relate to a positive, loving concept of God, and extrinsic religion with a negative, punitive concept of God. At the present time, these are the generalizations that can be made on the basis of quantitative research. They have been reported with considerable consistency by independent investigators using various indices of self-esteem and different techniques for assessing concepts of God (for a review, see Spilka et al., 1985). Yet even this simple set of generalizations is not without its critics, especially with respect to findings associated with intrinsic religiosity (e.g., Batson & Ventis, 1982).

Guilt and Related Constructs

The relationships between self-esteem and different forms of religious commitment seem reasonably clear. However, less certainty surrounds the roles of guilt and related constructs that might mediate a relationship to self-esteem within faith traditions. The most logical hypothesis is that extrinsic people, with their punitive and vindictive God constructs, are susceptible to guilt, while their intrinsic counterparts, with their loving and forgiving God constructs, are unlikely to feel guilt. Yet this hypothesis has no consistent support in the empirical literature. Part of the problem is that reliable quantitative measures of guilt, shame, and sin are not available (Harder & Lewis, 1987; Harder & Zalma, 1990; Watson, Morris, & Hood, 1987). Another problem is that, despite important conceptual distinctions between shame and guilt (to be discussed in detail later in this chapter), empirical indices of shame and guilt correlate positively with each other (Wright, O'Leary, & Balkin, 1989). Additionally, shame and guilt scales tend to correlate equally with indices of depression (Harder & Zalma, 1990).

These facts, combined with the typically low magnitude of correlations between indices of religiosity, self-esteem, and guilt (despite statistical significance), cloud easy assessments of the interrelationships between these closely aligned constructs (for a review, see Watson, Morris, & Hood, 1989). Even so, some advancement has been made in the form of more conceptually precise research interrelating guilt, self-esteem, and other variables within intrinsic and extrinsic forms of faith commitment. Certain conclusions are now possible as a result of such research.

For example, it is abundantly evident that indices of depression, sin, and shame, whether religiously interpreted or not, are unable to differentiate the diagnosed mentally ill from others. For instance, Kroll and Sheehan (1989) showed that, among psychiatric inpatients in Minnesota, the percentage who reported sinning (during the previous week) was approximately equal to the percentage who said they had not sinned. Also, those who reported sinning had significantly higher scores on a standardized measure of depression than those who reported they had not sinned. Gender was the only significant discriminator between the two sin groups, and depression added no predictive value. While psychiatric patients from diverse diagnostic categories subscribe to the belief that sinful thoughts or actions can cause illness, such beliefs are always reported by a minority of patients. This can be seen with nonhospitalized populations (with, of course, the exception of some specific faith traditions such as Christian Scientist).

Sheehan and Kroll (1990) also found that depressed patients in a hospitalized Minnesota sample reported fewer sin-related items than other diagnostic categories, such as schizophrenia or personality disorders. These researchers noted that no depressed patient endorsed the statement "I am in the hospital now because I have sinned" (p. 112). While depression and sin may be related sometimes, clinically depressed patients in general (and even those with faith commitments) apparently are not preoccupied with issues of sin and guilt. Moreover, their religious beliefs, practices, and experiences parallel those of nonhospitalized populations (Kroll & Sheehan, 1989). These findings hold under the limiting conditions that religious variables are only nominally identified and not theory driven, as with intrinsic and extrinsic religiosity.

Watson and his colleagues have tried to tease out some of the complex relationships between religion (as conceptualized within the Allport intrinsic/extrinsic tradition) and the constructs of sin, guilt, and grace. Despite the measurement problems already noted, several recurrent empirical patterns have emerged across numerous independent samples of college students. Of particular importance is the consistent finding that extrinsic, rather than intrinsic, religiosity tends to correlate negatively with sin and guilt measures (Watson, Hood, & Morris, 1985; Watson, Hood, Foster, & Morris, 1988; Watson, Morris, & Hood, 1987, 1988a,b,c, 1989). Additionally, measures of guilt (otherwise related to low self-esteem) are reversed when corrected by a sin/grace measure. This is the case even among people with an intrinsic religious orientation. The concept of grace permits forgiveness of sins, even essential ones, by a personal and forgiving God.

The sin/grace survey used in these studies includes items such as "I am a hopeless sinner, but I am worthy in the sight of God" and "Forgiveness will follow if we confess our sins" (Watson, et al., 1987, p. 539). It was found that sin/grace, but not guilt, correlates with lower depression. Thus, while sin, guilt, and a variety of low self-esteem and poor adjustment measures do share overlapping variance, guilt (in the context of sin/grace) can form a matrix within faith commitments to allow a religious definition of health. This includes positive self-esteem from within a faith tradition perspective. The later point is paradoxical outside of faith traditions, and may appear exactly the opposite. For instance, Vitz (1977) argued that high self-esteem can be viewed negatively as sin (e.g., pride) in some faith traditions. Watson, Morris and Hood (1990) introduced an "ideological surround" procedure designed to allow empirical measures to be related in ways that account for differing interpretations of the religious meaning of constructs. In this sense, correlations between sin and self-esteem, corrected for meaning within a faith tradition, become interpretable as healthy. This parallels well-known claims that, at least from a sociological perspective, functioning groups are "normal" by definition (Hood, 1983; Spilka et al., 1985).

Thus, the more conceptually guided research on religion, self-esteem, guilt, and related constructs has been helpful in affirming at least two considerations. First, form of faith commitment, and not simply religion conceived globally, must be considered while interrelating measures of self-esteem, depression, guilt, and sin. Second, empirical measures of such value-laden constructs must consider their differential meaning within various traditions, both secular and religious (Deconchy, 1991). Accounting for these differences in meaning or "ideological surround" alters the patterns of complex correlational matrices. To date, the conceptual arguments exceed the small amount of empirical support, as gauged by the actual percent variance explained for any given set of related measures. However, future research cannot hope to be more successful without such conceptual and theoretical guidance, especially when using Allport's intrinsic and extrinsic measures. (For contrasting views, see Gorsuch, 1984; Kirpatrick & Hood, 1990.)

Psychoanalytic and Phenomenological Perspectives

If the empirical literature, largely correlational and positivistic in orientation, has made some progress in clarifying the complex interrelations between guilt, sin, and self-esteem, so too has another tradition. As Stern (1985) argued with respect to developmental psychology and Wulff (1991) with respect to the psychology of religion, psychoanalytic and positivistic psychologies can both benefit from closer interchange. This is certainly the case with the empirical issues that have concerned us so far in this chapter. Much of the conceptual meaningfulness of the empirical studies already discussed have parallels in the psychoanalytic literature, particularly that which is informed by phenomenology. It must be emphasized that these traditions are also properly empirical, and that no contemporary psychology of religion can afford to ignore them (for a review, see Wulff, 1991).

Guilt and Religion in Psychoanalytic Theory

The centrality of guilt and related constructs to psychoanalytic perspectives on religion is rooted in the more sociological of Freud's writings, including *Totem and Taboo* (1950/1913), *Civilization and Its Discontents* (1961/1930), and *Moses and Monotheism* (1967/1939). Few contemporary investigators support Freud's claim to an inherited collective mind containing the phylogenetic memory of a monotraumatic primal murder. Nevertheless, Badcock (1980) proposed a *polytraumatic* modification of Freud's speculation, compatible with contemporary empirical evidence and with the evolutionary principles of sociobiology. Some might dispute Badcock's (1980) claim that Freud's theory of the origin of culture is the most plausible social scientific interpretation of the available empirical data. Regardless, his theory does set the backdrop for interpretations of the centrality of guilt in the context of culture, especially when reality in its ultimate form is viewed as personal.

In this vein, Freud (1961/1930) aims "to represent the sense of guilt as the most important problem in the development of civilization and to show that the price we pay for our advance in civilization is a loss of happiness through the heightening of the sense of guilt" (p. 81). Of course, this applies only to people held within the boundaries of parentally-rooted object choices (e.g., religion) rather than in object choices dictated by a sense-perceived reality (e.g., science). Herein lies the root of Freud's insistence that religion, even as a social form, is at best neurotic. He went beyond his controversial cultural origins theory in asserting that religion becomes not simply illusion and neurosis (Freud, 1927) but delusion as well (Freud, 1961/ 1930).

For Freud, culture's origin is in a primal act of murder, either carried out in reality (leading to remorse), or carried out in fantasy (leading to guilt). The latter view is what Alston (1964) referred to as the "more sober version" (p. 71) of the primal murder scenario, one requiring only an ontogenetically based assumption of a universal unconscious hatred of fathers. In either case, classic Freudian theory and fundamental Christian traditions share curiously similar views about the necessary role of guilt or remorse in both phylogenetic (i.e., cultural) and ontogenetic (i.e., individual) development due to a primal act of "father murder" (see also Reik, 1957). Of course, the concept of "murder," whether literal or symbolic, separates Freud and Freudian psychoanalysis from other than the most liberal faith traditions, at least within Western religion.

This controversial theoretical model contextualizes current discussions of the hypothetical role of guilt, whether in terms of faith traditions or not. Within faith-committed samples, more fundamental religions (articulating a punitive and vindictive God) are often deemed more "pathological" insofar as such theologies articulate a "return of the repressed" in explicit conscious theologies. Here the *content* of beliefs about God, largely expressed in superego language, corresponds to unconscious projections of God *images* or what Rizutto (1979) has called the "living God." Empirically oriented investigators, influenced by Freud's theory, have employed phenomenological and positivistic research techniques to explore the nature of guilt and shame within various hypothetical superego structures. Most provocative of these efforts has been the work of Lewis (1971, 1986).

Superego Functions

Lewis (1971) begins with the established critiques of Freud's initial formation of the superego construct wherein Freud described the punitive nature of the superego. As the "heir of the Oedipus complex," especially among males, the superego functions via identification with authority (typically the father) to ward off threats of punishment. Thus, conformity as submission to authority is rooted in a primary fear of the loss of love, and repressed aggression forms the basis of a punitive conscience. In this sense, the individual ontogenetically completes a socialization process similar to the phylogenetic pattern noted above. Yet, in so doing, the capacity for neuroses parallels the capacity to be civilized. Historically conditioned faith traditions maintain this developmental neuroses, even beyond its necessity (see Badcock, 1980; Freud, 1950/1913; 1961/1930).

On the other hand, Lewis (1971) details the theoretical basis for a differentiation that was inadequately developed by Freud. This involves identification with a threatening parent (internalized threat), which produces guilt, but also identification with an idealized parent (ego ideal), which leads to the possibility of shame. In shame, "a shadow of the imago" (Lewis, 1971, p. 23) falls on the self and one can either be prideful or shameful depending on the evaluative basis of the self so perceived. Furthermore, if the ideal is maximized as a god, the capacity for shame (or pride) is enhanced precisely to the extent of that aggrandizement. Thus, implicit in Lewis's clarification of two superego functions (shame due to ego ideal; guilt due to internalized threat) is the crucial role of faith traditions. For those committed to an explicit personalized God concept, there is an enhanced probability of both shame and guilt, precisely because God as punisher or ideal transcends anyone merely human.

The Phenomenology of Shame and Guilt

Lewis's phenomenological analysis of shame and guilt helps us to understand better the empirical research literature. As Lewis (1971, 1986) has pointed out, there is a "doubling" of the self in shame as the self takes itself as an object. More specifically, both shame and pride entail an awareness of self through the eyes of a superior other that can serve to either diminish or inflate the self. Negatively evaluating the self relative to this ideal other leads to shame. According to Laing (1960), shame is an "implosion of the self" (p. 47). In shame, I become depressed (or "compressed"!). In Freudian language, in shame I am seen as small and diminished with respect to an ego ideal; in pride I am inflated, seen as being one with my ego ideal. What matters in shame or pride is the other's evaluation of me insofar as I take the perspective of the other. Faith traditions with a personal God allow maximum possibility of both shame and pride. In addition, both shame and pride require sharp self boundaries. In shame or pride the self is clearly localized; the entire self stands suddenly revealed (Lynd, 1958).

Guilt reveals a related but differentiated phenomenology. It entails awareness of the self in relation to some act, thought, or deed. Guilt remains self-contained, and demands punishment. It is also more cognitive since it entails an obsession with the idea of violation, one that can remain long after the affect dissipates. In guilt, the self demands punishment for its perception of the violation of an objective order. The self, being aware of its violation, experiences guilt. It is Nietzschean in that it both experiences guilt and can pride itself in demanding its own punishment. In Freudian terms, the thought is one with the deed. The thought itself produces guilt whether or not acted out. When acted out, guilt becomes remorse. Thus, there is a hidden pride and hence suppressed shame is experienced in the discovery that one is either guilty or remorseful.

Empirical Studies

Lewis's phenomenological studies stand upon their own merit as well as being valuable clarifications of classic Freudian superego theory. In addition, they shed new light on the interrelationships between self-esteem, shame, guilt, and sin within faith traditions as those constructs are identified positivistically in empirical research.

Shame involves a more focused awareness of self, with the self split while observing itself through the eyes of an idealized other (ego ideal). Thus, the self should function less effectively, absorbed as it is with itself. Guilt, on the other hand, permits more effective self-functioning since, despite the obsession with normative standards of conduct, the self remains largely in the background. In a provocative study, Witkin, Lewis, and Weil (1968) selected patients for field dependence or field independence. Then one field dependent and one field independent patient were assigned identical therapists. Complete transcripts of therapy sessions were analyzed using the Gottschalk and Gleser (1969) procedure for assessing affect in verbal expressions. As predicted, field dependent patients made significantly more reference to shame and shame-related feelings than to guilt. By contrast, field independent patients made significantly more reference to guilt and guilt-related feelings than to shame.

These data provide empirical support for Lewis's careful phenomenological analysis of shame and guilt, despite the fact that shame and guilt tend to correlate with measures of depression (Wright et al., 1989). This is not sufficient evidence to collapse these two constructs as one. In addition, much of the problem of the low reliability of guilt and shame scales is probably due to the failure to construct scales based upon their necessary phenomenologial distinctions. It has long been established that such distinctions are difficult for naive subjects to make in terms of self-reports of various emotions (Polivy 1981), and this could contribute to the difficulty of constructing reliable shame and guilt scales.

Empirical Research in View of Hermeneutical Studies of Augustine's *Confessions*

If shame and guilt are intimately related, each can mask the other. Efforts to separate these effects within the empirical literature have proved to be quite complex, as noted earlier. This is also the case with hermeneutically based studies, as Capps (1990) has demonstrated with respect to studies of St. Augustine. A brief consideration of Capps's thesis will serve to illuminate the diverse literature already discussed.

Ferrari (1990) made a strong case for the fact that Augustine's childhood beatings were developmentally significant in creating the man history knows as St. Augustine. It is widely accepted that, by his own admission, Augustine came to view his childhood beatings as originating from God. Yet, as Capps (1990) persuasively argued, as a youth Augustine was less disturbed by the beatings at the hand of his schoolmaster than at the mockery and laughter of his parents when he reported such beatings. This response, Capps correctly observed, is one of shame, and not guilt. Capps asserted that it is the shamed Augustine who later seeks to hide his shame in the guilt, with the guilt becoming the motif for typical interpretations of his *Confessions*.

Capps also noted that Augustine's *Confessions* can be read as a justification of shaming, hidden by guilt which was attributed to a reproachful, scourging God. In fact, this became the hallmark of Augustinian theology. Augustine's youthful shaming at the hands of his parents, as well as his own shaming of his son later in life, completes the circle of the shame that is central to Augustine's *Confessions*. In Capps's (1990) insightful conclusion, the *Confessions* actually legitimized the shaming of children for which no self-reproach in the form of guilt is excessive.

Empirical studies offer some support for Capps's conjectures. For instance, Nunn (1964) found that children raised by parents who argue that "God will punish you" as a means of controlling their children (by an implicit coalition with God), produce children who report self-reproach and blame. This puzzled Nunn as he had assumed that parents who appeal to a personal punishing God would simply produce children who would seek compliance, and not the internalization of authority necessary for a conscience that could generate self-reproach.

Nelson and Kroliczak (1984) clarified Nunn's findings by showing that self-reproach stemming from the "God will punish you" method of control only appears in faith traditions where God is perceived as *personally* involved. These data are congruent with Capps's analysis of some aspects of the psychohistorical roots of Augustinian theology. A personal God who demands obedience leads to guilt or a self that seeks its own punishment when viewing itself as disobedient through the eyes of that God. This guilt can also mask a more fundamental shame and can be sought precisely for that reason.

These data further suggest that much of the research by Watson and colleagues makes conceptual sense when the complex interrelationships between guilt, depression, and self-esteem are considered in view of the phenomenology of shame and guilt. Guilt, as internalized aggression toward the self, leads to a strong conscience insofar as it demands punishment for wrongdoing. Its root, as the fear of loss of love, is deeply buried in childhood antecedents, if not phylogenetic ones. Within faith traditions which articulate a personal, punitive God concept, such guilt gains added force, especially when supported by parents and other authorities who form a "coalition" with this God against the child. This will function most effectively if the child in turn holds a punitive view of a personal God. All these combine to produce lower self-esteem in such people, mediated by feelings of guilt and/or shame. Yet the possibility exists that this God also conforms to an ego ideal capable of granting forgiveness and grace, and therefore relief from guilt. But, paradoxically, this can produce shame or its obverse, pride. A balance between superego functions of internalized aggression and ego ideal permit a relief of guilt and shame paradoxically produced by the same conditions. One could speculate that this happens within faith traditions among intrinsically committed people.

Nelson and Kroliczak (1984) accurately noted the predominance of an angry and punitive God within fundamentalist traditions, but they missed the presence of an equally forgiving and compassionate God within those traditions (see Hood, 1983). This paradox permits the Nietzschean twist already noted whereby despising one's self stimulates pride precisely because, in the process, one is paradoxically identified with God. This is in a context of faith commitment supported by tradition. Hence, there is the understandable finding that religion can produce a complex pattern of interrelationships between depression, guilt, shame, sin, and measures of self-esteem. Yet, when appropriately interpreted, these interrelationships can be functional within a given faith tradition, as noted in the empirical research cited above. The same is true regarding the psychoanalytic, phenomenological, and hermeneutical studies.

We have made progress on several fronts in unraveling this complex process and its empirical correlates, at least within varieties of the Christian faith tradition. The studies of Watson and his colleagues mesh well with a simple empirical documentation of the paradoxical effect in which guilt is stimulated by a punitive God only to be forgiven in turn (especially in more fundamentalist Christian traditions). Yet, for people who internalize such traditions, test items such as "I am a hopeless sinner, but I am worthy in the sight of God" evoke what would *otherwise* be merely inappropriate guilt ("I am a sinner") and equally inappropriate pride ("I am worthy in the sight of God"). This faith tradition can be critiqued as incorporating a subtle and refined patriarchical authority in the form of community, thus masking inequalities and special privileges (Hodges, 1971; van Herik, 1982).

Certainly, other forms of faith tradition have been established in other dynamics. Yet, unfortunately, such traditions have been studied little by American psychologists. A strong case can be made that faith traditions in which the role of a god is minimized or absent create conditions where self-esteem is less rooted in evaluations of a superior other. It could also be argued that guilt, as internalized aggression, is less common in such traditions. Such may be the case in Buddhism and less personalized forms of the Christian faith tradition (de Silva, 1979). Yet, until such traditions have been studied by social scientists who are familiar with their content, we are forced to evaluate the psychodynamics and empirical consequences of Christian faith traditions as the most common object of scientific investigation.

References

Alston, W.P. (1964). Psychoanalytic theory and theistic belief. In J. Hick (Ed.), *Faith and the philosophers* (pp. 63–102). New York: St. Martin's Press.

Badcock, C.R. (1980). *The psychoanalysis of culture.* Oxford: Basil Blackwell.

Bahr, H.M., & Martin, T.K. (1983). "And thy neighbor as thyself": Self-esteem and faith in people as correlates of religiosity and family solidarity among Middletown High School students. *Journal for the Scientific Study of Religion, 22,* 132–144.

Baker, M., & Gorsuch, R. (1982). Trait anxiety and intrinsic-extrinsic religiousness. *Journal for the Scientific Study of Religion, 21,* 119–122.

Batson, C.D., & Ventis, W.L. (1982). *The religious experience.* New York: Oxford University Press.

Benson, P.L., & Spilka, B.P. (1973). God image as a function of self-esteem and locus of control. *Journal for the Scientific Study of Religion, 13,* 297–310.

Branden, N. (1969). *The psychology of self-esteem.* New York: Bantam.

Buber, M. (1971). Existential guilt. In R.W. Smith (Ed.), *Guilt, man, and society* (pp. 85–116). New York: Anchor Books.

Capps, D. (1990). The scourge of shame and the silencing of Adeodatus. In D. Capps & J.E. Dittes (Eds.), *The hunger of the heart: Reflections on the confessions of St. Augustine* (pp.

69–92). West Lafayette, IN: Society for the Scientific Study of Religion, Monograph Series, No. 8.

Deconchy, J.P. (1991). Religious belief systems: Their ideological representations and ractical constraints. *The International Journal for the Psychology of Religion, 1,* 5–21.

de Silva, L.A. (1979). *The problem of the self in Buddhism and Christianity.* New York: Barnes & Noble.

Donahue, M.J. (1985). Intrinsic and extrinsic religiousness: Review and meta-analysis. *Journal of Personality and Social Psychology, 48,* 400–419.

Ellis, A. (1962). *Reason and emotion in psychotherapy.* New Jersey: Lyle Stuart.

Ferrari, L.C. (1990). The boyhood beatings of Augustine. In D. Capps & J.E. Dittes (Eds.), *The hunger of the heart: Reflections on the confessions of St. Augustine* (pp. 55–67, Monograph Series No. 8). West Lafayette, IN: Society for the Scientific Study of Religion.

Freud, S. (1927). *The future of an illusion* (J. Strachey, Trans.). New York: W.W. Norton.

Freud, S. (1950). *Totem and taboo* (J. Strachey, Trans.). New York: W.W. Norton. (Original work published 1913.)

Freud, S. (1961). *Civilization and its discontents* (J. Strachey, Trans.). New York: W.W. Norton. (Original work published 1930.)

Freud, S. (1967). *Moses and monotheism* (K. Jones, Trans.). New York: Bantam Books. (Original work published 1939.)

Gartner, J. (1983). Self-esteem tests: Assumptions and values. In C. Ellison (Ed.), *Your better self: Psychology, Christianity and self-esteem* (pp. 98–110). New York: Harper & Row.

Gartner, J., Larson, D.B., & Allen, G.D. (1991). Religious commitment and mental health: A review of the empirical literature. *Journal of Psychology and Theology, 19,* 6–25.

Gorsuch, R.L. (1968). The conceptualization of God as seen in adjective ratings. *Journal for the Scientific Study of Religion, 7,* 56–64.

Gorsuch, R.L. (1984). Measurement: The boon and bane of investigating religion. *American Psychologist, 39,* 228–236.

Gorsuch, R.L. (1988). Psychology of religion. *Annual Review of Psychology, 39,* 201–221.

Gottschalk, L., & Gleser, G. (1969). *The measurement of psychological states through content analysis of verbal behavior.* Berkeley: University of California Press.

Harder, D.H., & Lewis, S.J. (1987). The assessment of shame and guilt. In J.N. Butcher & C.D. Spielberger (Eds.), *Advances in personality assessment* (Vol. 6, pp. 89–114). Hillsdale, NJ: Lawrence Earlbaum Associates.

Harder, D.H., Zalma, A. (1990). Two promising shame and guilt scales: A construct validation comparison. *Journal of Personality Assessment, 55,* 729–745.

Hodges, D.C. (1971). Fratricide and fraternity. In R.W. Smith (Ed.), *Guilt, man, and society* (pp. 198–216). New York: Anchor Books.

Hood, R.W., Jr. (1983). Social psychology and religious fundamentalism. In A.W. Childs & G.B. Melton (Eds.), *Rural psychology* (pp. 169–198). New York: Plenum.

Hunt, R.A., & King, M.B. (1971). The intrinsic-extrinsic concept: A review and evaluation. *Journal for the Scientific Study of Religion, 10,* 339–356.

Kirpatrick, L.A., & Hood, R.W., Jr. (1990). Intrinsic-extrinsic religious orientation: The boon or bane of the psychology of religion. *Journal for the Scientific Study of Religion, 29,* 442–462.

Kroll, J., & Sheehan, W. (1989). Religious beliefs and practices among 52 psychiatric inpatients in Minnesota. *American Journal of Psychiatry, 146,* 67–72.

Laing, R.D. (1960). *The divided self.* Chicago: Quadrangle Books.

Lewis, H.B. (1971). *Shame and guilt in neuroses.* New York: International Universities Press.

Lewis, H.B. (1986). The role of shame in depression. In M. Rutter, C.E. Izard, & P.B. Read (Eds.), *Depression in young people* (pp. 325–339). New York: Guilford.

Lynd, H.M. (1958). *On shame and the search for identity.* New York: Harcourt, Brace, & Co.

Nelson, H.M., & Kroliczak, A. (1984). Parental use of the threat "God will punish": Replication and extension. *Journal for the Scientific Study of Religion, 23,* 267–277.

Nunn, C.Z. (1964). Child control through a "coalition with God." *Child Development, 35,* 417–432.

Polivy, J. (1981). On the induction of emotions in the laboratory: Discrete moods or multiple affect states? *Journal of Personality and Social Psychology, 41,* 803–817.

Reik, T. (1957). *Myth and guilt.* New York: Grosset & Dunlap.

Rizutto, A.M. (1979). *The birth of the living God.* Chicago: University of Chicago Press.

Sheehan, W., & Kroll, J. (1990). Psychiatric patients' belief in general health factors and sin as causes of illness. *American Journal of Psychiatry, 147,* 112–113.

Spilka, B., Hood, R.W., Jr., & Gorsuch, R.L. (1985). *The psychology of religion: An empirical approach.* Englewood Cliffs, NJ: Prentice-Hall.

Stern, D. (1985). *The interpersonal world of the infant: A view from psychoanalysis and developmental psychology.* New York: Basic Books.

van Herik, J. (1982). *Freud on femininity and faith.* Berkeley: University of California Press.

Vitz, P. (1977). *Psychology as religion: The cult of self-worship.* Grand Rapids, MI: Erdmans.

Watson, P.J., Hood, R.W., Jr., Foster, S.G., & Morris, R.J. (1988). Sin, depression, and narcissism. *Review of Religious Research, 29,* 295–305.

Watson, P.J., Hood, R.W., Jr., & Morris, R.J. (1985). Religiosity, sin, and self-esteem. *Journal of Psychology and Theology, 13,* 116–128.

Watson, P.J., Morris, R.J., & Hood, R.W., Jr. (1987). Antireligious humanistic values, guilt, and self-esteem. *Journal for the Scientific Study of Religion, 26,* 535–546.

Watson, P.J., Morris, R.J., & Hood, R.W., Jr. (1988a). Sin and self-functioning, part 1: Grace, guilt, and self-consciousness. *Journal of Psychology and Theology, 16,* 254–269.

Watson, P.J., Morris, R.J., & Hood, R.W., Jr. (1988b). Sin and self-functioning, part 2: Grace, guilt, and psychological adjustment. *Journal of Psychology and Theology, 16,* 270–281.

Watson, P.J., Morris, R.J., & Hood, R.W., Jr. (1988c). Sin and self-functioning, part 3: The psychology of ideology and irrational beliefs. *Journal of Psychology and Theology, 16,* 348–361.

Watson, P.J., Morris, R.J., & Hood, R.W., Jr. (1989). Sin and self-functioning, part 4: Depression, assertiveness, and religious commitment. *Journal of Psychology and Theology, 17,* 44–58.

Watson, P.J., Morris, R.J., & Hood, R.W., Jr. (1990). Intrinsicness, self-actualization, and the ideological surround. *Journal of Psychology and Theology, 18,* 40–53.

Wickstrom, D.L., & Fleck, J.R. (1983). Missionary children: Correlates of self-esteem and dependency. *Journal of Psychology and Theology, 11,* 226–235.

Witkin, H.A., Lewis, H.B., & Weil, E. (1968). Affective reactions and patient-therapist interaction among more differentiated and less differentiated patients early in therapy. *Journal of Nervous and Mental Diseases, 146,* 193–208.

Wright, F., O'Leary, J.O., & Balkin, J. (1989). Shame, guilt, narcissism, and depression: Correlates and sex differences. *Journal of Motivation and Emotion, 7,* 25–39.

Wulff, D.M. (1991). *Psychology of religion: Classic and contemporary views.* New York: John Wiley & Sons.

8

Religion and Rationality

James E. Alcock

The recent conflict in the Persian Gulf exploited many products of modern scientific research and technology—computers, laser beams, ballistic missiles, "night vision" devices and satellites—for the waging of war. At the same time, leaders in Iraq, the United States, Great Britain, and other countries urged their peoples to appeal to a supernatural Being, to pray for victory and for peace. The computer and the chapel, the missile and the mosque: modern science and ancient theology employed together to the same end.

Religion in its various manifestations has been the preeminent belief system of humankind: none other has ever come even close in terms of either social impact or longevity. No political figure, no philosopher, no warrior, no explorer, no scientist has ever had such pervasive and profound influence on the lives and thoughts of humankind as have had such figures as Christ, Buddha, and Mohammed. While science and technology yield quantum mechanics, organ transplants, genetic engineering, and moon walks—mighty products indeed—it is religion that reaches into the hearts of people. It moves hundreds of millions of people every day to offer up prayers, and to guide themselves by what they take to be the wishes of their gods.

Religion has begotten both the sublime and the ghastly in the realm of human behavior. Because of religious faith, countless individuals have selflessly dedicated their lives to the well-being of others while eschewing the pleasures of the secular world. Others have painted masterpieces, written magnificent music, and erected glorious edifices in expression of their devotion. Yet, religious faith has also provoked intolerance and persecution, inquisitions and holy wars. Is such behavior, whether productive or destructive, ever *rational?*

Functions of Religion

Scientists and philosophers have often viewed religious belief as little more than magical thinking employed in the pathetic attempt to understand nature and to influence natural forces that are otherwise beyond our control. Because of this view, it was believed by nineteenth-century positivist philosophers that religion would wither away as scientific thought advanced, but such was not to be. Partly because of its durability, sociologists and anthropologists earlier in this century rejected the idea that religion is simply an expression of ignorance and superstition, and came to the view that it speaks to deep existential needs within the human psyche that cannot be quelled by deductive logic or materialistic science. Because it serves such needs, religious belief is resistant to attempts to uproot it: three generations of suppression in the Soviet Union failed to expunge it.

Led by curiosity or pushed by anxiety, humans have forced nature to give up many of its secrets. These same motives provoke us to seek some ultimate meaning to our lives. However, we are no further ahead than the ancients in understanding why or even how ("Big Bang" or not) the universe came to exist in the first place, and whether there is any purpose behind it. Can life have meaning if our personalities are extinguished at death? We may readily accept that leeks and lettuce and lemmings and lizards are nothing but biological configurations of atoms and molecules, and thus undeserving of any postmortem existence. Yet, when we consider ourselves, it is upsetting to many people to contemplate the possibility that our lives carry no more significance, and endure but little longer, than those of the flora and fauna with which we share this planet. For some, these questions about the meaning of life and death are unanswerable, and such people tolerate living with ambiguity about such matters. Many others seek some kind of certainty. As Albert Ellis (1977) has written:

> People in search for certainty invent gods and devils that supposedly govern our lives; ideas of universal harmony and the oneness of all existing things; spirits and deathless souls; these provide a false sense of security, a "logical" explanation of the way things are, and they hold on to them mightily, even though they cannot confirm or deny their existence. This need for certainty explains why virtually all peoples in all times have created and tend to dogmatically believe in gods and religions. (p. 39)

Thus, religion provides a framework of meaning and purpose. It is the framework, more than the particular content, that is so vital. It does not seem to matter much whether one believes in a god who sent his only begotten son to provide salvation from the burden of sin, or in an all but endless cycle of birth-death-rebirth, or in the necessity of clearing unwanted engrams from one's psyche. Moreover, whether through reincarnation or everlasting life, virtually all religions offer some escape from the finality of death. Therefore, so long as one can believe, both life and death "make sense." In this regard, Malinowski (1954) wrote:

> Man's conviction of continued life is one of the supreme gifts of religion, which judges and selects the better of the two alternatives suggested by self-preservation— the hope of continued life and the fear of annihilation. The belief in spirits is the result of the belief in immortality. The substance of which the spirits are made is the full-blooded passion and desire for life, rather than the shadowy stuff which haunts his dreams and illusions. . . ." (p. 51)

Not only does religion reduce existential anxiety, it is also a powerful agent for reducing anxiety in general, be it based in illness, uncertainty, or threats to oneself or one's loved ones. By praying for divine intervention, by accepting that "someone up there" is looking after us, anxiety is reduced. Religion undoubtedly offers other positive benefits to the believer as well, although it is not exclusive in this regard. It can counter feelings of powerlessness and normlessness, enhance social integration, provide a moral code that promotes interpersonal harmony and social responsibility, and produce greater optimism and a better acceptance of pain, disability, and misfortune (Spilka, Hood, & Gorsuch, 1985).

Religion and Rationality

Yet religion is not without cost. While religious faith helps many to face their daily struggles, to wrestle with their fears, and to accept their misfortunes, it would appear to the nonbeliever that the believer relies on fantasy rather than rationality to confront problems and allay fears. Indeed, in the late nineteenth and early twentieth centuries, religion was seen by some (e.g., Freud and Marx) to be not just superstitious fantasy, but a pernicious delusion that produces in its adherents a distortion of reality that diverts them from critical thinking and jeopardizes their ability to act rationally.

But what does it mean to act rationally? Rationality is a very complex concept, which involves many criteria, techniques, and procedures. By its very nature, it cannot be precisely defined (James, 1982). However, in general terms, the rationality involved in holding a belief depends on whether the belief can be tested, and whether the believer will abandon the belief if the test refutes it (Alcock, 1981). What is rational is relative to various things, such as the knowledge base at the time and the conceptual apparatus (formal logic, mathematics) available. What is rational in one era, relative to the current knowledge base, may appear quite irrational in a subsequent era imbued with greater understanding of nature. Thus, while we would consider it irrational to give ailing human patients transfusions of cow's milk, this was not irrational a century ago when little was known about blood chemistry. Milk transfusions were used across North America as an experimental treatment for cholera during the 1870s (Oberman, 1969).

It could be argued that if one's belief system is rooted in the axiom that a God exists who demands our allegiance and who will punish our transgressions, then it would be rational to behave accordingly. However, that axiom cannot be empirically tested, and therefore it makes little sense to inquire about its rationality or irrationality. Rather, it is more appropriate to view such beliefs as *non*rational.

In any case, people rarely, if ever, come to religious conviction as a consequence of rational examination. Deductive logic is little guide to choosing between Hinduism, Buddhism, or Christianity. For the most part, such axiomatic belief in a god or gods is inculcated in childhood, when the individual has not yet mastered critical thinking. The child is taught about the miraculous nature of the deity. In North America, many children are also told about Santa Claus, the Easter Bunny, and the Tooth Fairy. However, these latter claims sooner or later run into difficulty because the adult world does not believe the very myths it disseminates to children. In addition, as children's intellectual abilities develop, they begin to question such beliefs on the basis of their inconsistency with other more directly verifiable knowledge.

How can Santa's reindeer fly? How could one rabbit manage to deliver eggs to children everywhere on the same day?

While Easter Bunny claims are easily falsified, religious claims are generally unfalsifiable, and therefore, resistant to the challenge of experience. It may seem unusual that God can apparently hear the prayers of millions of people simultaneously, but then God is not subject to human constraints. If one's prayer goes unanswered, that does not necessarily indicate that God is not there. Instead, the deity may simply have chosen not to answer the prayer. And unlike Santa Claus, the Easter Rabbit, and the Tooth Fairy, deities do not usually provide clear, specific evidence (e.g., gifts, chocolate eggs, money) which might cry out for alternative physicalist explanations.

However, does the willingness to accept a religious axiom, or the beliefs that derive from it, interfere with the ability to apply rationality in other areas? In other words, is religious belief antithetical to rationality in general? Such belief has certainly been seen to promote behaviors and beliefs that appear irrational or incomprehensible to those not of the faith: nonmaterial beings, sacred cows, injunctions against the use of condoms in the midst of a worldwide AIDS epidemic, a million dollar bounty on the head of a blasphemous author, and claims that the earth, consistent with the story of Adam and Eve, is only a few thousand years old. To the believer, such behaviors and beliefs are rarely questioned since they are sustained by faith and dogmatic authority.

Yet, many scientists have made significant contributions to our understanding of nature while all the while holding profound religious beliefs. Scientists who are religious do not generally allow their religious beliefs to intrude into their laboratories. Like most people, they partition their world so that rational thinking is applied in some domains, while faith reigns in others. It is important to note that none of us are rational all the time. No matter how much we might try to be, our behavior and thinking undoubtedly include pockets of irrationality which belie our more rational approach to the world: buying lottery tickets in the face of daunting odds, consuming vitamins in abnormal quantities to head off colds, making investments in the stock market based on a rumor carried by a friend of a friend.

How can rationality and irrationality or nonrationality come to coexist with such apparent ease? In fact, they "grow up" together. We are not born to rationality. Instead, logic and reason must be acquired by the child. Magical thinking comes to us much more naturally, and even when we come to espouse the virtues of reason, the magical mode of thinking continues to lurk not far below the surface. Such thinking makes us amenable to accepting the miraculousness of religion. As we grow, we gradually learn to depend more and more on logic and rationality because our experience teaches us that they serve us well in most domains of our daily lives. However, we can never really divest ourselves of the tendency toward magical thought, no more than we can rid ourselves of fear, awe, or other emotional reactions. As adults, we may have long ago rejected theism, yet when in grave danger we find to our surprise that we are appealing to a god whose existence we normally disavow.

The dichotomy between rationality and magical thought is reflected in the development of two essentially separate belief systems within each individual. We encourage this dichotomy when we teach children to reason, and also tell them stories of gods or ghosts or goblins. Frank (1977) refers to these two systems as the scientific-humanist and the transcendental. In the scientific-humanist system, it is assumed that there is one and only one reality that is perceived in the ordinary waking state, and that is subject to deterministic laws. The transcendental belief system, on the other hand, is based on the notion that there exist one or more realities which are not directly tied to the material world. Moreover, while the scientific-humanist system relies on information that conforms to some kind of rules of evidence, transcendental beliefs are held on the basis of dogma, faith, and personal subjective experience and "intuition."

Religious beliefs, especially those that are familiar because they were acquired in our childhood, may carry considerable intuitive appeal. Reed (1984) examined the impact of logical versus intuitive thought and argued that the latter often seems more compelling than the former because we are unable to see the process by which we arrive at intuitive "conclusions." Logical reasoning is open to us, and we can see each step of the process. We are thus "in control" of logical thought, while we merely receive the outcomes of intuitive thought. While one might reason that it is unlikely that God exists, or that it is unlikely that God has heard our prayers, the *feeling* that God has answered our prayers may be more compelling precisely because we cannot see the process by which that feeling came about, and therefore we cannot examine whether that conclusion "makes sense." It just *feels right.*

Dysfunctional Aspects of Religious Belief

If we accept that religion serves an important purpose for many people, and if we accept as well that many people are able to confine the influence of religion to areas of their lives where there is little or no conflict with rationality, then we should not be too concerned about individual religiosity, whether we are disdainful of the basic beliefs or not. However, religious belief often goes beyond helping people to find meaning and escape from anxiety. It can often produce consequences, such as those discussed below, that not only can be inimical to personal well-being, but that also are destructive of the ability to think or act rationally.

Dogmatic Belief

Many religions enjoin their adherents not to question the "received" interpretation of reality. The fundamentalist Christian who opposes AIDS research because AIDS is God's punishment of homosexuality; the Christian Scientist who accepts that disease is a problem for faith, not medicine; or the New Age adherent who believes that wishing, not chemotherapy, is the best way to attack cancer—all these people have been led away from free thinking and rational inquiry because they dare not or will not question the faith or challenge the dogma. Even worse, some religions, and this applies to many modern cults, are so controlling that the individual adherent becomes dependent upon the leader for his or her own self-esteem. Moreover, such a person comes to accept dogmatic authority rather than rational inquiry as the basis for much of his or her belief and action.

Guilt and Worthlessness

Many religions emphasize the importance of *sin*. Sin is something to be avoided, or if committed, to feel very guilty about. The more orthodox one is in one's religion, the greater the tendency both to experience guilt and to attribute guilt to others for deviations from traditional values and norms (Thyer, Kramer, Walker, & Papsdorf, 1981). Examples include sex outside of marriage or sex for pleasure rather than procreation, the exposure of a woman's face to the public, drinking from the same tap as an Untouchable, eating pork, eating beef, consuming alcohol, working on the Sabbath, cursing, and so forth. These and other transgressions could lead, in the name of religion, to fear of eternal damnation or even to danger of being stoned or executed. An obsession with avoiding sin and with conforming to religious dictates constrains one's thinking and makes free intellectual inquiry and self-understanding more difficult to achieve (Meadow & Kahoe, 1984). Even questioning one's faith can produce guilt, which discourages further questioning.

Some religions go beyond sin, stressing the essential worthlessness of human beings. Followers of authoritarian religions often see themselves as insignificant creatures in the eyes of the Divine: all goodness flows from God and all flesh is corrupt. Such belief diminishes self-esteem and can lead to feelings of impotence with regard to finding realistic solutions to one's problems (Meadow & Kahoe, 1984).

Prejudice and Intolerance

Religions often promote contradictory sets of beliefs. Most religions encourage the faithful to love one another and all humanity, and yet many also promote the idea that only their adherents possess God's truth, thus promoting a sense of self-righteousness and a belief that those not of the faith are in error and in need of conversion. Intolerance of nonbelief and deviance is thereby fostered: if scripture proscribes homosexuality, then homosexuals should be treated as sinners. Only a small minority of religious people seem to adopt the concept of a bond of love and tolerance that unifies all peoples, while the majority internalize the more divisive message of uniqueness and specialness (Allport, 1954). Indeed, Allport found that churchgoers in the 1950s harbored *more* ethnic prejudice than nonchurchgoers, although those churchgoers who attended because of intrinsic motives (e.g., belief in a duty to God) were significantly less prejudiced than those who attended for reasons of extrinsic reward (e.g., entry to Heaven, approbation of others) (Allport & Ross, 1967). Studies of religious values generally indicate that orthodox religious beliefs are accompanied by greater intolerance, emotionality, and conservatism (Robertson & Shaver, 1973).

Some religions continue to promote social inequality, racism, and especially sexism. For if religions are not the work of gods, they are surely the works of men, and throughout history, men have distinguished themselves by their sexist attitudes. Most religions are patriarchal, and their scriptures often relegate women to an inferior status, which encourages subservience to men.

Inadequacy and Psychopathology

Does religion foster psychopathology? From the beginning, the study of religion has revealed some connection between religiosity and emotional problems. William James (1902) noted that leaders of religious groups:

> often have led a discordant inner life, and had melancholy during a part of their career. They have . . . been liable to obsessions and fixed ideas; and frequently they have fallen into trances, heard voices, seen visions, and presented all sorts of peculiarities which are ordinarily classed as pathological. Often, moreover, these pathological features in their career have helped to give them their religious authority and influence. (p. 8)

Religion can allow the expression of otherwise deviant behavior, and conversely, it can sometimes suppress or control pathological behavior and thought. Some mystical experiences may reflect a psychotic process that is interpreted in a religious vein, while scrupulosity, which involves agonizing about sin and guilt and the careful observance of religious law, may reflect an obsessive-compulsive disorder (Spilka, Hood, & Gorsuch, 1985).

As well as providing expression for emotional pathology, intense religiosity may actually produce it. Religion itself can be a stressor, as individuals try to live up to the strict exhortations of their faith. The guilt and feelings of unworthiness discussed earlier can contribute powerfully to feelings of low self-esteem, which are maladaptive to the individual's well-being.

Ellis (1988) wisely argues that not all religiosity is associated with emotional pathology. He distinguishes between mild and absolutist religiosity, and contends that it is the latter that is antithetical to emotional health. He argues that those who are imbued with intense religiosity are emotionally disturbed (usually neurotic, but sometimes psychotic). Specifically, these people put service to their hypothesized gods above all else. While becoming dependent on their god and their religion, they sacrifice intimate interpersonal relationships in order to concentrate on their love of god. They also accept the rules of their religion as right for all, and thus they become intolerant of others who do not share their beliefs. Perhaps most importantly, they shy away from healthy tolerance of ambiguity and uncertainty in favor of religious certainty, and such dogmatism interferes with flexible thinking.

New Religions and Parapsychology

In primitive times, humans huddled together against the metaphysical darkness and created magical and religious beliefs in the attempt to shield themselves both from nature's more brutal side and from their fears of death and the unknown. Today, we have developed our knowledge of the universe to the point that most people no longer explain its workings in terms of animism or natural magic. For large numbers of people in the West, even traditional theistic beliefs have been eroded or destroyed as science probes ever further outward into the cosmos and inward into the basic structure of matter itself. The Great Religions of the world are based in myth and legend dating back millennia, and such mythology lacks credibility to many people in this scientific age.

To the extent that modern science and philosophy have taken away the religious shield that people have always used to ward off existential anxiety, little has been offered to replace it. It is more perplexing to try to find meaning in life if one does not believe in heavenly immortality. It can be difficult to find the motivation to carry on in the face of personal crisis if one believes that the personality is extinguished at bodily death, and that even the universe will ultimately vanish when it eventually collapses unto itself. Many are seduced by what Kurtz (1986) calls the "transcendental temptation." For some, this "temptation" takes the form of Eastern religions with their esotericism and exoticism. For others, the authority structure offered by various cultic organizations provides the sense of meaningfulness, belongingness, and immortality that conventional religion has always bestowed upon its faithful. There can be little doubt that the recent proliferation of New Age religion and the associated "channeling" craze (Alcock, 1989; Reed, 1989) reflect the need felt by many people to fill a spiritual void, and to assuage their anxieties both about their own existence and about the meaning of life.

Unfortunately, New Age religion actively encourages delusions of grandeur (we are all gods; we create our own reality; we possess limitless wisdom and power) and discourages critical thinking. Why bother to try to understand and find rational solutions for problems if one can wish them away with god-like omnipotence, especially since rational inquiry involves effort and sometimes produces disquieting conclusions? Wish it and it will be so: this is nothing but a full-blown surrender to magical thinking.

What about parapsychology? Modern parapsychology was born from the hope that science might be able to put the existence of the soul on an empirical basis (Alcock, 1985). To this day, a fundamental motivation behind the research of most parapsychologists is to establish that the human personality is not tied to flesh and blood, that there is an aspect of our existence that transcends the physical realm (Alcock, 1987a, 1987b).

Formal parapsychology has made considerable effort to bring the methods of science to bear on the question of the nature of human existence. For many, it provides the ideal bridge between science and religion, allowing its adherents to employ scientific principles while pursuing quasi-religious goals (e.g., establishing the nonphysicality of our "essence" and survival of the personality after death).

Is the parapsychological quest irrational? One might question the wisdom of continuing to research supposed phenomena that have yielded no persuasive evidence of their existence in over a century of formal inquiry. But so long as parapsychologists are willing to submit their hypotheses to empirical test, and so long as they are prepared to surrender their beliefs in the face of compelling counter evidence, then one could argue that their pursuit can well be accommodated within the definition of rationality given at the beginning of this chapter. However, putative psychic phenomena, in the way that they are approached by many within para-psychology, are no more subject to falsification than are many religious claims. To assign scientific status to beliefs that can be neither confirmed nor falsified is pseudoscientific.

In Conclusion

We live in troubling times. Science and technology have changed our world so rapidly that it is often difficult for individuals and societies to find their bearings, to chart their course. While religion provides solace for many, it is reason that can save us from internecine destruction and that will best help us to fight social injustice, conquer disease, and harness nature. Religion, whether ancient or modern, has shown itself to be of little help in this regard.

It has been argued that religion encourages the transfer of responsibility for solutions to our problems to some deity whose existence is questionable, that critical thinking is constrained by dogmatic belief or authoritarian religious leaders, that the believer is led into guilt, feelings of unworthiness, or intolerance of others. To the extent that this is true, religion is inimical to individual and societal well-being and destructive of rationality. However, while we should discourage any system of belief that enslaves intellect to the dictates of dogma, we must be careful not to tar all religious belief by the same brush. Existential questions are rarely amenable to reason and scientific inquiry, and yet many people yearn for answers to them. We must avoid dogmatic rejection of religious beliefs that offer meaning and hope to people, so long as they do not throw rationality into jeopardy. Fundamentalist dogma, fanatical adherence to any system of belief (religious or political), absolutist religiosity—these are the real enemies of reason. We ignore them at our peril.

References

Alcock, J.E. (1981). *Parapsychology: Science or magic?* Oxford: Pergamon.
Alcock, J.E. (1985). Parapsychology as a "spiritual" science. In P. Kurtz (Ed.), *A skeptic's handbook of parapsychology.* Buffalo: Prometheus Books.
Alcock, J.E. (1987a). Parapsychology: Science of the anomalous or search for the soul? *Behavioral and Brain Sciences, 10,* 553–643.
Alcock, J.E. (1987b). A to-do about dualism or a duel about data? *Behavioral and Brain Sciences, 10,* 627–634.
Alcock, J.E. (1989). Channeling: Brief history and contemporary context. *Skeptical Inquirer, 13,* 380–384.
Allport, G. (1954). *The nature of prejudice.* New York: Addison-Wesley.
Allport, G., & Ross, J.M. (1967). Personal religious orientation and prejudice. *Journal of Personality and Social Psychology, 5,* 432–443.
Ellis, A. (1977). Religious belief in the United States today. *The Humanist, 37,* 38–41.
Ellis, A. (1988). Is religiosity pathological? *Free Inquiry, 8,* 27–32.
Frank, J.T. (1977). Nature and function of belief systems. *American Psychologist, 32,* 555–559.

James, E.W. (1982). On dismissing astrology and other irrationalities. In P. Grim (Ed.), *Philosophy of science and the occult* (pp. 24–32). Albany, NY: State University of New York Press.

James, W. (1902). *The varieties of religious experience.* New York: Modern Library.

Kurtz, P. (1986). *The transcendental temptation.* Buffalo: Prometheus Books.

Malinowski, B. (1954). *Magic, science and religion.* New York: Doubleday.

Meadow, M.J., & Kahoe, R.D. (1984). *Psychology of religion.* New York: Harper & Row.

Oberman, H.A. (1969). Early history of blood substitutes: Transfusions of milk. *Transfusion, 9,* 74–77.

Reed, G. (1984, August). Superstitious beliefs and cognitive processes. Paper presented at Symposium on *Anomalistic Psychology,* conducted at the annual meeting of the American Psychological Association, Toronto.

Reed, G. (1989). The psychology of channeling. *Skeptical Inquirer, 13,* 385–390.

Robertson, J.P., & Shaver, P.D. (1973). *Measures of social psychological attitudes* (revised ed.). Ann Arbor, MI: Institute for Social Research.

Spilka, B., Hood, R.W., Jr., & Gorsuch, B.L. (1985). *The psychology of religion: An empirical approach.* Englewood Cliffs, NJ: Prentice-Hall.

Thyer, B.A., Kramer, M.K., Walker, J., & Papsdorf, J.D. (1981). Religious orthodoxy and rational thinking. *Psychological Reports, 49,* 802.

9

Religion and Self-Actualization

Joseph B. Tamney

Since the 1960s self-actualization has been a popular symbol for people critical of established culture. The works of Abraham Maslow remain readily available, and it is these books more than anything else that has shaped the understanding of self-actualization. Given the countercultural context for the championing of this personal ideal, it is not surprising that researchers have tended to assume that established religion is inimical to self-actualization.

In this chapter the following topics are considered: (1) Maslow's model of self-actualization; (2) religion, personality, and self-actualization; and (3) society and self-actualization.

Maslow's Model of Self-Actualization

Maslow's psychology expresses a positive, optimistic attitude. The goal of living is not survival or adjustment but perfection of one's biologically based inner nature.

> This inner nature, as much as we know of it so far, seems not to be intrinsically or primarily or necessarily evil. The basic needs (for life, for safety and security, for belongingness and affection, for respect and self-respect, and for self-actualization), the basic human emotions and the basic human capacities are on their face either neutral, pre-moral or positively "good." Destructiveness, sadism, cruelty, malice, etc., seem so far to be not intrinsic but rather they seem to be violent reactions against frustration of our intrinsic needs, emotions, and capacities. (Maslow, 1972, p. 3)

Since human nature is not bad, according to self-actualization theory, cultural values and structural arrangements should not work to suppress nature but to allow its flowering. Ideally, action is spontaneous, impulsive, instinctive, and unrestrained (Maslow, 1968). Likewise, the purpose of therapy is to help "the patient hear his drowned-out inner voices, the weak commands of his own nature on the Spinozistic principle that true freedom consists of accepting and loving the inevitable, the nature of reality" (Maslow, 1972, p. 124).

Aware of his critics, Maslow regretted that self-actualization had been interpreted to mean selfishness:

> Self-actualizing people are without one single exception, involved in a cause outside their skin, in something outside of themselves. They are devoted, working at something, something which is very precious to them—some calling or vocation in the old sense, the priestly sense. (Maslow, 1972, p. 43)

In Maslow's view, personal growth involves discipline, deprivation, frustration, pain, and tragedy. Such experiences contribute to the development of healthy self-esteem. We must believe we are capable of controlling our impulses, so that we can be unafraid of them. But, the emphasis in his writings was not on discipline and pain; rather, the telling words that kept reappearing included creativity, love, and play.

During the 1960s, Maslow grew sensitive to the need for a humanistic psychology of evil. His revisions of *Toward a Psychology of Being,* which originally appeared in 1962, reflected his acute awareness that there are few actualized people and that they are often treated badly. A psychology of evil would study such things as the inability to turn anger into productive activities and the "fear of maturity and the godlikeness that comes with maturity" (Maslow, 1968, iv).

Maslow's later writings show an Eastern influence, as he expanded his ideology to incorporate the goal of transcendence. To transcend is to directly experience others, nature, the cosmos, and feel a unity with them. Maslow presented what he called "Theory Z," a formulation that claimed that, while self-actualization and transcendence are separable phenomena, the ideal life embodied both conditions. Those who experienced only self-actualization were type Y, and they were called "merely healthy people" (Maslow, 1972, p. 282). Maslow noted many ways in which type Z differed from type Y. The former people pursue and have peak experiences, use the language of poets and mystics, perceive reality intuitively, are more responsive to beauty, are more innovative, and have an understanding that is more godlike or "from above" (Maslow, 1972, pp. 283–294). The appeal of type Z is that it represents the full development of the self; the Z person actualizes all levels of consciousness and satisfies all biologically based needs and values.

In Maslow's model, the healthy person is priestlike, mysticlike, and godlike. Maslow's ideal person is not anti-spiritual. However, Maslow (1968) did believe that religions tend to affirm asceticism, self-denial, and the deliberate rejection of the needs of the organism, and that such a perspective would prevent self-actualization. Moreover, the description of the healthy person as godlike suggests the difficulty of reconciling Maslow's philosophy and any religion based on belief in a transcendent deity.

Religion and Self-Actualization

In their review of the literature, Gartner, Larson, and Allen (1991) reported that religiosity had been negatively related to self-actualization in all fifteen studies they found. All of these research projects used the Personal Orientation Inventory (POI) as the measure of self-actualization. Like others, I focus on the Inner Support Scale, which included 127 of the 150 items in the inventory. This scale supposedly measures the "tendency to be guided by one's own principles and motives independent of external social constraints, yet not simply out of rebelliousness" (Hood, 1977, p. 266). It is logical that such a personality trait would be a necessary, if not sufficient, condition for self-actualization to occur.

A variety of religiosity measures have been found to be negatively related to scores on the Inner Support Scale. However, the attributes of religion that supposedly prevent self-actualization were never measured directly in these studies. For example, Hjelle (1975) theorized that religion reinforces deference to authorities, but he measured only frequency of participation in church activities, which was negatively related to Inner Support Scale scores.

Stewart and Webster (1970) conducted one of the few studies that was done outside the United States, and in which the subjects were not college students. They found that, among a small sample of Baptist ministers, the more theologically conservative had lower Inner Support Scale scores, as well as higher scores on a measure of dogmatism. This study is noteworthy because it linked lower Inner Support Scale scores to a specific theological tradition, and because the results are suggestive that a key aspect of the religious institution from the point of view of self-actualization is the cultivation of dogmatism among the adherents.

Studies based on small samples of charismatics have produced inconsistent results. Using a sample of U.S. students at a Catholic college, Niesz and Kronenberger (1978) found that students who participated in a neo-Pentecostal group had higher score on the Inner Support Scale than students not in such groups. Using a South African sample of white students, Stones (1980) found evidence that participation in a Jesus People group resulted in lowered scores on the Inner Support Scale. The author noted methodological problems, but he also suggested that, after joining the Jesus group, members were socialized into accepting the need for conformity. In interpreting the American study, it might be important to consider that the neo-Pentecostals at a Catholic college were probably a deviant group in that context.

Recent studies have tended to use as a measure of religiosity Allport and Ross's (1967) Intrinsic Religiosity Scale. This scale has been found to be unrelated to Inner Support Scale scores (Watson, Hood, and Morris, 1984) and to be negatively related to the Inner Support Scale (Watson, Morris, and Hood, 1987). In the 1987 study, twenty of the items composing the Inner Support Scale were individually related to the Intrinsic Scale. Factor analyzing these items, three "clearly interpretable factors," as Watson et al. described them, emerged that explained 83 percent of the variance. The researchers' labeling of these factors suggests that self-actualizers (assuming the validity of the Inner Support Scale) who tend not to be intrinsically religious are people who are not always honest, lack emotional control, and are anti-religious. An alternative description of these people using the same data could be: not morally compulsive, spontaneous, and not orthodoxly religious. In any case, it might be true that intrinsic religiosity, as measured by the Allport and Ross scale, is incompatible with aspects of personality appropriate for self-actualization.

Using a 15-statement Short Index of Self-Actualization (SISA), based on Shostrum's (1974) Personal Orientation Inventory, Watson, Morris, and Hood (1990) failed to find any anti-religious elements in the SISA (i.e., any statements subjects judged to be against their religious beliefs). Moreover, they found a positive relationship between scores on the SISA and those on the Intrinsic Religiosity Scale. In all, research about the relationship between intrinsic religiosity and self-actualization has not produced consistent results.

An obvious problem with these studies is that they have not measured directly those attributes of Christianity identified as being incongruent with self-actualization. Maslow did not claim that self-actualizers were anti-religious. Consistent with his analysis, students with high scores on the Inner Support Scale also had high scores on a Mysticism Scale (Hood, 1977). There is also some evidence that participation in a transcendental meditation program results in higher scores on the Inner Support Scale (Seeman, Nidich, and Banta, 1972; Nidich, Seeman, and Dreskin, 1973). More attention needs to be paid to the religious traditions accepted by people. It is not enough to know whether a person is religious.

Society and Self-Actualization

Inglehart (1990) has proposed a theory of cultural change for advanced industrial societies. He emphasizes that economic development has meant the satisfaction of sustenance needs for an increasingly large proportion of the populations in industrial societies. As a consequence, people in such societies are giving more attention to their needs for belonging, esteem, and self-realization. Inglehart labeled such people "postmaterialists." Based on numerous survey studies, Inglehart found that Western countries are shifting toward postmaterialism. Moreover, at least in Western Europe, postmaterialists, less often than materialists, said God is important in their lives, or described themselves as religious. Inglehart (1990) concluded that postmaterialists are estranged from conventional religion, but not anti-religious. Inglehart's theory was based on Maslow's hierarchy of needs. Regrettably, his measure of postmaterialism is not clearly related to Maslow's actual concept of self-actualization.

Yankelovitch (1981) described a cultural revolution quite similar to Inglehart's cultural shift. He found that most Americans to some degree valued self-fulfillment. However, it was the younger and more educated Americans who were more likely to report that they are concerned with self-fulfillment, that they work at self-improvement, and that they spend a great deal of time thinking about themselves. People with such values also tended to be religiously unaffiliated.

Following up on Yankelovitch's study, Tamney and Johnson (1988) hypothesized that having fundamentalist convictions would be negatively related to valuing self-actualization. It was suggested that the dominant message heard by fundamentalists would be the evilness of the current "cult of self-worship" (Vitz, 1977), so that they would tend not to value self-actualization as often as other Americans. However, Tamney and Johnson found no relationship between fundamentalism and self-actualization. But, among white Protestant fundamentalists, Christian Rightists tended not to accept self-actualization.[1] The authors concluded that it is only the Christian Rightists who reject outright the goal of self-actualization, although among other fundamentalists the meaning of fulfilling the self may not be the same as among nonfundamentalists; perhaps among the latter only, self-actualization means placing the individual above received cultural traditions.

In sum, studies suggest that, in modern societies, valuing self-actualization is more common among those not committed to conventional religion and is least often found among the religious right. Inglehart's theory suggests that religion could indirectly affect self-actualization by influencing public policies that concern people's quality of life. This topic needs to be considered in any complete assessment of the relation between religion and self-actualization.[2]

Conclusion

Self-actualization is a lifestyle. Whether a person follows this way of living depends on personality and structural and cultural factors. At this time research suggests that being religious is not conducive to having a personality suitable for pursuing self-actualization. But studies need to differentiate among religious traditions, which would allow for analysis of how different forms of religiosity affect self-actualization. Holifield (1983) has described how self-actualization has become an important idea within liberal and moderate Protestantism. Thus, it should be expected that those influenced by these traditions would more often be self-actualizers than those accepting conservative Protestantism. However, regarding this matter, conservative Protestantism is not unified (Hunter, 1987; Carter, 1988). What is needed are precise analyses of possible inconsistencies between specific religious traditions and Maslow's self-actualization model. The relation between religiosity and self-actualization will, no doubt, vary by religious tradition. Future studies might also assume that the ideal is not Maslow's (1972) type Y, but rather type Z.

Moreover, little attention has been given to how religion influences self-actualization by shaping structural and cultural conditions. Research suggests that people not affiliated with established religions are more likely to value self-actualization. But, religion can also have an important indirect effect on self-actualization by creating societies in which feelings of security are widespread. This indirect role needs to be studied.

Notes

1. Christian Rightism meant preferring a religious political party, wanting clergy to support political candidates, believing that the United States is God's instrument in the fight against communism, and accepting that America is God's chosen nation.

2. Several studies have found that social class, assumed to be an indicator of economic security, is positively related to priority being given to self-actualization (see studies cited in Agnew, 1983). However, feelings of security do not universally result in valuing self-actualization. Maslow's model is culture-bound (Blunt and Jones, 1986; Inglehart, 1990). The aforementioned relationship seems to occur among people whose culture gives primacy to individualism. Thus, religion can indirectly affect self-actualization by shaping the cultural importance of individualism.

References

Agnew, R.S. (1983). Social class and success goals: An examination of relative and absolute aspirations. *Sociological Quarterly, 24,* 435–452.

Allport, G., & Ross, J.M. (1967). Personal religious orientation and prejudice. *Journal of Personality and Social Psychology, 5,* 432–443.

Blunt, P., & Jones, M. (1986). Management motivation in Kenya and Malawi: A cross-cultural comparison. *Journal of Modern African Studies, 24,* 165–175.

Carter, J.D. (1988). Maturity. In D.G. Benner (Ed.), *Psychology and religion* (pp. 165–176). Grand Rapids, Michigan: Baker Book House.

Gartner, J., Larson, D.B., & Allen, G.D. (1991). Religious commitment and mental health: A review of the empirical literature. *Journal of Psychology and Theology, 19,* 6–25.

Hjelle, L.A. (1975). Relationship of a measure of self-actualization to religious participation. *Journal of Psychology, 89,* 179–182.

Holifield, E.B. (1983). *A history of pastoral care in America.* Nashville, TN: Abingdon Press.

Hood, R.W., Jr., (1977). Differential triggering of mystical experience as a function of self-actualization. *Review of Religious Research, 18,* 264–270.

Hunter, J.D. (1987). *Evangelicalism.* Chicago: University of Chicago Press.

Inglehart, R. (1990). *Culture shift in advanced industrial society.* Princeton, NJ: Princeton University Press.

Maslow, A.H. (1968). *Toward a psychology of being* (2nd ed.). New York: Van Nostrand.

Maslow, A.H. (1972). *The farther reaches of human nature.* New York: Viking Press.

Nidich, S., Seeman, W., & Dreskin, T. (1973). Influence of transcendental meditation: A replication. *Journal of Counseling Psychology, 20,* 565–566.

Niesz, N.L., & Kronenberger, E.J. (1978). Self-actualization in glossolalic and non-glossolatic Pentecostals. *Sociological Analysis, 39,* 250–256.

Seeman, W., Nidich, S., & Banta, T. (1972). Influence of transcendental meditation on a measure of self-actualization. *Journal of Counseling Psychology, 19,* 184–187.

Shostrum, E.L. (1974). *Manual for the Personal Orientation Inventory.* San Diego: Educational and Industrial Testing Service.

Stewart, T.A., & Webster, A.C. (1970). Scale for theological conservatism and its personality correlates. *Perceptual and Motor Skills, 30,* 867–870.

Stones, C.R. (1980). A Jesus community in South Africa: Self-actualization or need for security. *Psychological Reports, 46,* 287–290.

Tamney, J.B., & Johnson, S.D. (1988). Fundamentalism and self-actualization. *Review of Religious Research, 30,* 276–286.

Vitz, P.C. (1977). *Psychology as religion: The cult of self worship.* Grand Rapids, MI: William B. Eerdmans.

Watson, P.J., Hood, R.W., Jr., & Morris, R.J. (1984). Religious orientation, humanistic values, and narcissism. *Review of Religious Research, 25,* 257–264.

Watson, P.J., Morris, R.J., & Hood, R.W., Jr. (1987). Antireligious humanistic values, guilt, and self-esteem. *Journal for the Scientific Study of Religion, 26,* 535–546.

Watson, P.J., Morris, R.J., & Hood, R.W., Jr. (1990). Intrinsicness, self-actualization, and the ideological surround. *Journal of Psychology and Theology, 18,* 40–53.

Yankelovitch, D. (1981). New rules in American life: Searching for self-fulfillment in a world turned upside down. *Psychology Today, 15,* 35–91.

10

Religiosity, Meaning in Life, and Psychological Well-Being

Kerry Chamberlain and Sheryl Zika

Religion has frequently been considered to have a significant influence on mental health and psychological well-being, although the direction of this influence has often been debated (Bergin, Masters, & Richards, 1987; Bergin, Stinchfield, Gaskin, Masters, & Sullivan, 1988). Most recent research and reviews of the evidence suggest, however, that religiosity has a positive association with well-being and mental health.

In an initial review, Lea (1982) concluded that religiosity was positively associated with personal adjustment in the adult population, and was more strongly so for the elderly. Witter, Stock, Okun, and Haring (1985) undertook a meta-analysis of 28 studies that provided 56 effect sizes of the relationship between religion and subjective well-being. Effect sizes ranged from $-.01$ to $+.58$, and Witter et al. concluded that "religion is positively associated with perceptions of well-being" (p. 335). Measures of religion were classified as either religious activity (church attendance or rated participation) or religiosity (interest in religion or religious-mindedness), and effect sizes were found to be slightly larger for religious activity than for religiosity. Well-being measures were also classified as assessing life satisfaction, morale, quality of life, well-being, or happiness, but no differences in effect size were found between these.

Bergin (1983) reported a meta-analysis of 24 studies that examined the relation between religiosity and psychopathology. Effect sizes here ranged from $-.32$ to $+.82$. A small number (23 percent) involved a negative relationship between religiosity and mental health, whereas almost half (47 percent) exhibited a positive relationship. However, most effects were small and nonsignificant. Bergin concluded that previous claims of religious belief exerting negative effects on mental health could not be sustained but noted the difficulties of assessing the relationship clearly, given the diversity of measures of religion and of mental health involved.

Donahue (1985) reviewed a wide range of studies examining extrinsic and intrinsic religiousness. Although not directly concerned with mental health and well-being issues, Donahue reported that several relevant constructs were differentially related to these religiosity dimensions. Extrinsicness was found to be positively correlated with prejudice and dogmatism, whereas intrinsicness was uncorrelated with these traits. Extrinsicness was positively correlated with anxiety, whereas intrinsicness was negatively correlated with anxiety.

Peterson and Roy (1985) concluded from their review that religiosity facilitates psychological well-being. Bergin et al. (1987) found an intrinsic religious orientation to be negatively correlated with anxiety and positively correlated with self-control and personal adjustment. They suggested that "significant religious involvement can be a positive correlate of normal personal functioning" (p. 200), and not necessarily related to poorer mental health. Bergin et al. (1988), in a qualitative study with religious participants, found no evidence for religiosity to correlate negatively with mental health, and found better adjustment for those participants whose religion was integrated positively into their lifestyle. Willits and Crider (1988) reported that religiosity in a middle-aged sample was positively correlated with overall psychological well-being. Pollner (1989) found that symbolic relations with a "divine other" were a significant correlate of subjective well-being.

Together, the weight of evidence suggests that religion has a small but positive relationship with mental health and psychological well-being. However, the findings are frequently mixed and appear to depend upon how both religiosity and well-being are measured. Several of the researchers in this field have noted these effects, suggesting that religion could have both enhancing and pathogenic aspects (e.g., Bergin et al., 1988; Willits & Crider, 1988). The relationship has also been found to vary depending on which other variables are involved and controlled for (e.g., Lea, 1982; Peterson & Roy, 1985).

The mechanisms through which religion might exert effects on well-being have not been explored extensively, although some hypotheses have been advanced. Pollner (1989) proposed three processes through which religiosity could influence mental health and well-being. First, religion could provide a resource for explaining and resolving problematic situations. Second, religion may operate to enhance a sense of self as empowered or efficacious. Third, religion may provide the basis for a sense of meaning, direction, and personal identity, and invest potentially alienating events with meaning. Similar arguments were advanced by Peterson and Roy (1985), who suggested in particular that religion could provide an overarching interpretive scheme that allows an individual to make sense of existence. Thus, religion may not contribute directly to a person's well-being, but rather it may influence well-being indirectly by giving a sense of meaning and purposeful direction in life.

Regardless of where meaning arises, whether from a religious source or not, there is a clear link between people's search for (and attainment of) meaning and their emotional health. This view has been supported both theoretically and empirically. Frankl (1959, 1967) believed that the will to meaning was an essential human motive, and that when a person's search for meaning was blocked, existential frustration occurred, leading to the pathological condition he called "noogenic neurosis." Maddi (1967) described an analogous condition, existential neurosis, which was "characterised by the belief that one's life is meaningless, by the affective tone of apathy and boredom, and by the absence of selectivity in actions" (p. 313). Similarly, Reker and Wong (1988) proposed that the attainment of personal meaning provides a person with an interpretation of life experiences, worthwhile and purposeful goals, and feelings of satisfaction and fulfillment.

Research also supports the general conclusion that the attainment of meaning is associated with positive mental health outcomes, whereas a lack of meaning is associated with pathological outcomes (Coleman, Kaplan, & Downing, 1986; Ganellen & Blaney, 1984; Harlow, Newcomb, & Bentler, 1986; Yalom, 1980; Zika & Chamberlain, 1987). The search for meaning and its attainment appears to be fundamental to successful living (Lacocque, 1982; Yalom, 1980).

In addition to being closely related to psychological well-being, meaning is also conceptually linked with religion. Yalom (1980) distinguished between two broad classes of meaning; cosmic meaning, which ". . . implies some design existing outside of and superior to the person and invariably refers to some magical or spiritual ordering of the universe" (p. 423), and terrestrial meaning, which is personal and has entirely secular foundations. Yalom argued that it would be possible to have terrestrial meaning without cosmic meaning, but that the reverse was unlikely. People with cosmic meaning would experience personal meaning fulfilled in harmony with that cosmic meaning. The existence of a sense of cosmic meaning would provide a clear link between religiosity and meaning systems.

The notion that religion provides a framework that gives meaning and purpose to life has been supported by several empirical investigations. Meaning in life has been found to be higher for the intrinsically than for the extrinsically religious (Bolt, 1975; Crandall & Rasmussen, 1975; Soderstrom & Wright, 1977), for those with a committed rather than an uncommitted religious viewpoint (Soderstrom & Wright, 1977), for those who are conservatively religious rather than nonreligious (Dufton & Perlman, 1986), and for those recently experiencing religious conversion (Paloutzian, 1981). Yalom (1980) reported that a positive sense of meaning in life was associated with both self-transcendent values and deeply held religious beliefs.

However, the place of meaning in the context of religiosity has been ambiguous. Researchers proposing dimensions of religiosity have suggested that meaning is one such dimension (King & Hunt, 1975; Hilty, Morgan, & Burns, 1984). Other researchers have located meaning as a part of psychological well-being (e.g., Peterson & Roy, 1985). Still others have treated meaning as a separate construct (Reker & Wong, 1988), with some noting its strong relevance to religion and spirituality (e.g., Yalom, 1980; Paloutzian, 1981).

Clearly, meaning can be derived from a variety of sources, and religion may be only one of a number that are accessible. Battista and Almond (1973) suggested several different models for identifying meaning in life, with meaning stemming from God (religious), from being (existential), from humanity (humanistic), or from life (self-transcendent). They found that people were frequently committed to two or more systems of belief, with meaning derived from a combination of sources. DeVogler-Ebersole and Ebersole (1985) found that meaning could be classified into eight different sources, with individuals typically reporting about four as relevant to themselves. Reker and Wong (1988) proposed thirteen important sources of meaning, including religious beliefs and activities. Reker and Guppy (1988) found age changes in sources, with religion becoming an increasingly important source with age. Chamberlain and Zika (1988), in a factor analytic study of meaning measures, concluded that meaning was multidimensional. They suggested that meaning may have several origins, through goal achievement or fulfillment, through an enthusiastic orientation that views life as interesting and exciting, through having a clear philosophy or framework, or through contentedness and satisfaction with what one has in life. Thus, meaning can have a variety of different sources, including religion. Although religion may promote meaning, it is unlikely to be the sole source of meaning, and it appears inappropriate to constrain meaning to a dimension of religiosity.

Our own research has examined the relationships between religiosity, meaning in life, and psychological well-being. Below are the details of two such studies. As noted, meaning can derive from several sources other than religion, and thus we wanted to assess the association between religiosity and well-being when meaning was taken into account. A further reason for including meaning was because it has strong links with both religion and well-being, and therefore we considered it to be a critical control variable.

Recent research has suggested that well-being is composed of at least three major dimensions: life satisfaction, positive affect, and negative affect (Chamberlain, 1988; Diener, 1984). Life satisfaction is considered to be a cognitively based (rational) evaluation of well-being, in contrast to positive and negative affect, which provide affectively based (emotional) evaluations. It seemed appropriate to include all three dimensions of well-being because empirical evidence indicates that they have different correlates (Chamberlain, 1988). Because of the mixed results from previous research linking religiosity and well-being, we considered it important to examine whether religiosity would relate differently to each of these well-being dimensions.

Study 1

This study[1] involved two different groups from the community who were participating in a general study of personality and well-being, and who have been suggested to be "at risk" in terms of having lower well-being. These groups were mothers at home caring for young children, and elderly people. Individuals in these groups have been considered to be "at risk" because they tend to be somewhat isolated, do not have paid employment, frequently have limited financial resources, and often have a degree of dependence on others. Additionally, mothers have the demands and responsibilities of child care, and elderly people commonly face health problems.

Mothers were included in the study if they were not in paid employment and had the care of at least one child under five years of age. Of the 188 mothers in the group, almost all were married (95 percent) and few lived alone (5 percent). To be included in the elderly sample, participants had to be aged 60 years or more. In contrast to the mothers, a much smaller proportion (54 percent) of the 137 elderly subjects was married, and a much larger proportion (43 percent) lived alone. Both groups of respondents completed a questionnaire that contained measures of psychological well-being, religiosity, and purpose in life.

Psychological well-being was assessed with two different measures. The affective dimensions of well-being, positive and negative affect, were determined with the Affectometer (Kammann & Flett, 1983). The other well-being component, life satisfaction, was assessed with Andrews and Withey's (1976) global measure, Life-3. Meaning in life was assessed with the Purpose in Life Test (Crumbaugh & Maholick, 1964). Religiosity was measured with two of the King and Hunt (1975) scales, Orientation to Growth and Striving, and Salience: Cognition. These scales were noted by King and Hunt (1975) to cover the intrinsic dimension of religiosity, and were chosen as the most relevant to examine in the context of life-meaning. A correlational analysis of the items from these scales led us to combine them into a single measure of religiosity for our analyses.

When we examined the relationships between the measures, meaning was substantially correlated with all well-being measures for both groups. Religiosity had a small correlation only with life satisfaction for the mothers, and a moderate correlation with life satisfaction and positive affect for the elderly. Negative affect was uncorrelated with religiosity in either group. These associations, where significant, were higher for the elderly than for the mothers, in agreement with previous findings on age differences (Lea, 1982; Witter et al., 1985). The relationship between meaning and religiosity was also higher for the elderly than for the mothers, confirming Reker and Guppy's (1988) findings. These effects may be a function of religion becoming more salient with age, or they could reflect age cohort differences in the salience of religion.

The lack of any significant association between religiosity and negative affect also supports Bergin's conclusions (Bergin et al., 1987, 1988) that religiosity is associated with normal functioning and should not be considered a limitation to sound mental health.

The next step was to examine the relation between religiosity and well-being while controlling for meaning.[2] When we did this, we found the same pattern in every case, for both groups and for all three well-being measures. Meaning explained substantial unique variance in well-being, but religiosity contributed almost nothing. These results demonstrate that the significant correlations between religiosity and well-being, where they occur, are substantially attenuated if meaning in life is controlled for. In contrast, life meaning remains a consistent predictor of well-being after effects due to religiosity are partialled out. It appears that the relation between religiosity and well-being is mediated by meaning.

One limitation of this study was the use of a single religiosity measure. We chose an intrinsic measure in line with previous research that had shown intrinsicness to be more strongly associated with meaning (Bolt, 1975; Crandall & Rasmussen, 1975; Soderstrom & Wright, 1977). However, the association between religiosity and well-being may vary with different components of religiosity as well as with different components of well-being. We decided to examine this in a second study using a multidimensional measure of religiosity.

The size of the effects found in this study were lower than expected, particularly after meaning was controlled for. One reason for this may have been that the samples were from the general population, and religion may have had limited relevance for some of them. Religious groups, in contrast, should provide a source of participants for whom religion is salient and also relevant as a source of meaning. In the second study, therefore, we involved two religious groups, Pentecostals and Roman

Catholics. Pentecostalism emphasizes the experiential element of being religious (McGaw, 1980), and Hood (1973) suggests that Pentecostals tend to live for their religion, and thus should have a strong intrinsic orientation. Catholicism, in contrast, places an emphasis on ritual and tradition, and Catholics tend to spend less time on religious activities and to have fewer church responsibilities (McClure & Loden, 1982). Catholics, therefore, could be expected to be less intrinsic than Pentecostals.

Study 2

This study[3] continued to examine the association between religion and well-being in the context of meaning, using religious samples and a multidimensional measure of religiosity. Two groups of religious respondents were recruited through their local congregation Bible study groups, 99 Roman Catholics and 112 members of a Pentecostal congregation. Each respondent completed a written questionnaire that included measures of religiosity, meaning in life, and psychological well-being.

The affective dimensions of well-being were again assessed with the Affectometer. Life satisfaction was measured with the Satisfaction with Life Scale (Diener, Emmons, Larsen, & Griffin, 1985). Meaning in life was once more evaluated with the Purpose in Life Test. To assess religiosity in more detail, we used the revised King and Hunt scales proposed by Hilty et al. (1984). Two scales were omitted: Life Purpose, which we measured with the Purpose in Life Test, and Intolerance of Ambiguity, which contained culturally inappropriate items for our samples. The Social Conscience scale was also modified by removing references to blacks.

We first compared the Catholics and Pentecostals for differences in religiosity, life meaning, and well-being. There were no differences between the groups in well-being except for positive affect, where Pentecostals had a slightly higher level than Catholics. There were also no differences in life meaning, but substantial differences emerged in religiosity.

Pentecostals scored higher on personal faith, which assesses the importance of religion in an individual's private life, and is a measure of intrinsic religiosity. Given the Pentecostal emphasis on personal spirituality and commitment, this result confirmed expectations for Pentecostals to be more intrinsic. Pentecostals also scored higher on church involvement, which assesses the financial and social involvement within the church setting, and reflects an extrinsic orientation. Again, the Pentecostal emphasis on personal participation within church meetings, coupled with strong expectations to support the church and engage in evangelism, would predict this result. These findings suggest that Pentecostals fit Hood's (1978) category of the indiscriminately proreligious.

Pentecostals also scored higher on orthodoxy, a measure of acceptance of traditional beliefs and doctrines. This reflects the Pentecostal emphasis on fundamental beliefs and literal interpretation of the Bible (McGaw, 1980). Catholics scored higher on social conscience, suggesting that they see themselves and their church as having a stronger role in society and social issues than do Pentecostals. There were no differences on the religious knowledge dimension, probably because Bible study groups were the source of participants from both churches.

Next we examined the associations between the dimensions of religiosity, and included life meaning because Hilty et al. (1984) considered it among their dimensions. For both groups, three religiosity dimensions (personal faith, church involvement, and orthodoxy) were intercorrelated at moderate levels, and all three correlated moderately with purpose in life. The other two religiosity dimensions differed between groups. For Pentecostals, social conscience and religious knowledge were uncorrelated with other dimensions and with each other. In the Catholic group, these two dimensions were correlated with some other dimensions. Purpose in life was uncorrelated with both these dimensions. These results are generally similar to the Hilty et al. (1984) findings, with a few exceptions. Here, religious knowledge did not correlate negatively with other dimensions in either group, and social conscience had higher correlations for Catholics.

Finally, we examined the relationships between religiosity, meaning, and well-being for both groups. For Catholics, the three intercorrelated religiosity dimensions, personal faith, church involvement and orthodoxy, were all correlated at moderate to low levels with life satisfaction and positive affect, but were uncorrelated with negative affect. For Pentecostals, these three religiosity dimensions were correlated at moderate levels with all three measures of well-being. The other two religiosity dimensions, social conscience and religious knowledge, were uncorrelated with well-being, except for a small negative association between religious knowledge and negative affect in the Pentecostal group. As expected, purpose in life was correlated moderately with all dimensions of well-being in both groups.

These results suggest that, where religiosity is significantly associated with well-being, it could account for between 5 percent and 23 percent of the variance in well-being, depending on which dimensions of religiosity and well-being are involved. These findings parallel earlier results involving direct correlations between components of religiosity and measures of well-being and mental health (Bergin, 1983; Witter et al., 1985).

Our major interest was to examine how these associations between religiosity and well-being would persist when life meaning was taken into account. Because there were differences in religiosity between groups, separate analyses were run for each group.[4] However, controlling for meaning produced the same result in the two groups, in spite of the religiosity differences. The analyses revealed that each dimension of religiosity accounted for negligible amounts of variance in any dimension of well-being once meaning in life was partialled out. In the best case, religiosity explained only one-half of one percent of variance in well-being. As in Study 1, controlling for the effects of meaning effectively removed any association between religiosity and well-being suggested by the simple (first-order) correlations. In contrast, life meaning with religiosity partialled out was a substantial predictor of every well-being dimension, explaining between 20 percent and 30 percent of the variance in well-being.

Discussion and Conclusions

Relations obtained in these studies confirm previous research findings of modest positive associations between religiosity and psychological well-being (Bergin,

1983; Lea, 1982; Witter et al., 1985). However, as previous researchers have noted, the strength of the relationship can depend on how well-being is measured, how religiosity is measured, and the nature of the group involved.

Although it is difficult to compare findings from Study 1 and Study 2 directly, a comparison can be made across groups for the intrinsic religiosity measure in Study 1 and the intrinsic measure, personal faith, in Study 2. This comparison suggests that the salience of religion for the group influences the strength and scope of the association. Mothers have a small positive correlation with life satisfaction only. But the elderly, for whom religion has increased salience, have moderate positive correlations with both life satisfaction and positive affect. Catholics show a pattern similar to that of the elderly, while Pentecostals, with their more intrinsic orientation, have stronger relationships with all three measures of well-being.

Findings from Study 2 demonstrate clearly that different religiosity dimensions relate differently to well-being. Three of the religiosity variables showed consistent associations with well-being, whereas two did not. The three dimensions that relate (personal faith, church involvement, and orthodoxy) are concerned with personal religious belief, commitment, and involvement, and it may be that only religiosity dimensions of this kind are relevant to achieving psychological well-being. The other two dimensions (social conscience and religious knowledge) do not provide a measure of personal religiosity in the same sense. In fact, it would be possible to be nonreligious and still have high levels of religious knowledge and positive attitudes toward church involvement in social issues. This raises concerns as to what exactly is meant by religiosity and what its scope should be. Previously we have argued that meaning in life, although highly relevant to mature religious belief, can be attained in nonreligious ways and is broader than a dimension of religiosity. These conceptual issues require clarification.

There may also be a need to clarify the construct of well-being used in studies investigating religiosity. A number of researchers (Ellison, 1983; Moberg, 1984; Moberg & Brusek, 1978; Paloutzian & Ellison, 1982) have argued strongly for the need to include aspects of spiritual well-being in such studies. However, these notions raise a number of consequent concerns. There is considerable diversity of view as to what constitutes spiritual well-being. Moberg (1971) proposed two major dimensions, one relating to a sense of well-being in relation to God, and the other relating to a sense of life satisfaction and purpose. In a later publication, Moberg (1984) suggested that spiritual well-being "is a multidimensional phenomenon with possibly hundreds of components" (p. 352). Paloutzian and Ellison proposed that spiritual well-being could be divided into religious well-being and existential well-being (Ellison, 1983). Research in this area will progress more rapidly once a clearer conception of spiritual well-being is formulated, and once its relationship with secular aspects of well-being is established.

Furthermore, our understanding of the relation between religiosity and well-being or mental health may be better advanced if the constructs are separated as clearly as possible. This could be achieved by keeping the focus on nonspiritual aspects of well-being and mental health, and was the rationale for the approach taken in the present research. However, this focus should not preclude investigations into spiritual well-being in its own right. Given greater conceptual clarity of the spiritual well-being construct, interesting questions could be addressed concerning its determinants and relation to nonspiritual well-being.

The above discussion suggests the need to consider the context in which links between religiosity and well-being are examined. Our own research indicates that relations between religiosity and well-being can be mediated by meaning. Although religion may provide an important source of meaning, for most people meaning is likely to be derived from a combination of sources (Battista & Almond, 1973). Our findings suggest that meaning in life is strongly associated with psychological well-being, and that any relation between religiosity and well-being may have its route through meaning.

Religion, however, does appear to have an important role in the development of meaning systems. Within the literature on life meaning, there is debate about whether meaning is discovered or created. Baird (1985) argued that meaning is a product of creation rather than discovery. Individuals must find and construct their own sense of order and meaning out of their achievements, commitments, and relationships. Reker and Wong (1988) maintained that meaning is created through making choices, taking actions, and entering relationships, but that meaning is also discovered from the givens such as the existence of the universe and life. Religion, as Yalom (1980) has commented, provides a potential framework that could exist as a given for many people. One reason why religious people tend to have higher levels of life meaning may be that there is something "out there" for them to discover. This issue could be usefully explored in future research.

We have not attempted to distinguish between cosmic and terrestrial meaning systems. Cosmic meaning, relating to notions of spiritual order in the universe (Yalom, 1980), is directly relevant to religious belief. Yalom argued that a comprehensive meaning schema, in this sense, has been provided by the Judeo-Christian tradition within the Western world. Although we have argued that religion is only one of several available sources of meaning, it should have a significant role in the development of cosmic meaning. Therefore, it may be fruitful to explore the distinction between cosmic and terrestrial meaning in future research examining the association between religiosity and well-being, and in particular to compare religious and nonreligious groups on these issues.

Notes

1. Some material from this study has been published previously in *Journal for the Scientific Study of Religion*, volume 27.

2. This was done by regressing each well-being variable in turn on the life meaning and religiosity variables, both entered on a single step in a standard multiple regression. The squared semi-partial correlations were used to estimate the amount of unique variance explained in well-being by each variable, providing a test of the association between each variable and well-being with the other variable partialled out.

3. We acknowledge the assistance of Thenmoliee Joe in the collection of data for this study.

4. These were the same analyses as those run for Study 1, except that here each religiosity variable was entered into a separate regression with life meaning predicting to each well-being variable in turn.

References

Andrews, F.M., & Withey, S.B. (1976). *Social indicators of wellbeing.* New York: Plenum.

Baird, R.M. (1985). Meaning in life: Discovered or created? *Journal of Religion and Health, 24,* 117–124.

Battista, J., & Almond, R. (1973). The development of meaning in life. *Psychiatry, 36,* 409–427.

Bergin, A.E. (1983). Religiosity and mental health: A critical reevaluation and meta-analysis. *Professional Psychology: Research and Practice, 14,* 170–184.

Bergin, A.E., Masters, K.S., & Richards, P.S. (1987). Religiousness and mental health reconsidered: A study of an intrinsically religious sample. *Journal of Counseling Psychology, 34,* 197–204.

Bergin, A.E., Stinchfield, R.D., Gaskin, T.A., Masters, K.S., & Sullivan, C.E. (1988). Religious life-styles and mental health: An exploratory study. *Journal of Counseling Psychology, 35,* 91–98.

Bolt, M. (1975). Purpose in life and religious orientation. *Journal of Psychology and Theology, 3,* 116–118.

Chamberlain, K. (1988). On the structure of subjective well-being. *Social Indicators Research, 20,* 581–604.

Chamberlain, K., & Zika, S. (1988). Measuring meaning in life: An examination of three scales. *Personality and Individual Differences, 9,* 589–596.

Coleman, S., Kaplan, J., & Downing, R. (1986). Life cycle and loss—the spiritual vacuum of heroin addiction. *Family Process, 25,* 5–23.

Crandall, J.E., & Rasmussen, R.D. (1975). Purpose in life as related to specific values. *Journal of Clinical Psychology, 31,* 483–485.

Crumbaugh, J.C., & Maholick, L.T. (1964). An experimental study in existentialism: The psychometric approach to Frankl's concept of noogenic neurosis. *Journal of Clinical Psychology, 20,* 200–207.

DeVogler-Ebersole, K.L., & Ebersole, P. (1985). Depth of meaning in life. *Psychological Reports, 56,* 303–310.

Diener, E. (1984). Subjective well-being. *Psychological Bulletin, 95,* 542–575.

Diener, E., Emmons, R.A., Larsen, R.J., & Griffin, S. (1985). The Satisfaction with Life Scale. *Journal of Personality Assessment, 49,* 71–75.

Donahue, M.J. (1985). Intrinsic and extrinsic religiousness: Review and meta-analysis. *Journal of Personality and Social Psychology, 48,* 400–419.

Dufton, B.D., & Perlman, D. (1986). The association between religiosity and the Purpose in Life Test: Does it reflect purpose or satisfaction? *Journal of Psychology and Theology, 14,* 42–48.

Ellison, C.W. (1983). Spiritual well-being: Conceptualization and measurement. *Journal of Psychology and Theology, 11,* 330–340.

Frankl, V. (1959). *Man's search for meaning.* London: Hodder & Stoughton.

Frankl, V. (1967). *Psychotherapy and existentialism.* New York: Simon & Schuster.

Ganellen, R.J., & Blaney, P.H. (1984). Hardiness and social support as moderators of the effects of life stress. *Journal of Personality and Social Psychology, 47,* 156–163.

Harlow, L.L., Newcomb, M.D., & Bentler, P.M. (1986). Depression, self-derogation, substance use, and suicide ideation: Lack of purpose in life as a mediational factor. *Journal of Clinical Psychology, 42,* 5–21.

Hilty, D.M., Morgan, R.L., & Burns, J.E. (1984). King and Hunt revisited: Dimensions of religious involvement. *Journal for the Scientific Study of Religion, 23,* 252–266.

Hood, R.W. (1973). Forms of religious commitment and intense religious experience. *Review of Religious Research, 15,* 29–36.

Hood, R.W. (1978). The usefulness of indiscriminately pro and anti categories of religious orientation. *Journal for the Scientific Study of Religion, 17,* 419–431.

Kammann, R., & Flett, R. (1983). Affectometer 2: A scale to measure current level of general happiness. *Australian Journal of Psychology, 35,* 257–265.

King, M.B., & Hunt, R.A. (1975). Measuring the religious variable: National replication. *Journal for the Scientific Study of Religion, 14,* 13–22.

Lacocque, P.E. (1982). On the search for meaning. *Journal of Religion and Health, 21,* 219–227.

Lea, G. (1982). Religion, mental health, and clinical issues. *Journal of Religion and Health, 21,* 336–351.

McClure, R.F., & Loden, M. (1982). Religious activity, denomination membership and life satisfaction. *Psychology: A Quarterly Journal of Human Behavior, 19,* 12–17.

McGaw, D.B. (1980). Meaning and belonging in a charismatic congregation: An investigation into sources of neo-Pentecostal success. *Review of Religious Research, 21,* 284–301.

Maddi, S.R. (1967). The existential neurosis. *Journal of Abnormal Psychology, 72,* 311–325.

Moberg, D.O. (1971). *Spiritual well-being: Background and issues.* Washington, DC: White House Conference on Aging.

Moberg, D.O. (1984). Subjective measures of spiritual well-being. *Review of Religious Research, 25,* 351–364.

Moberg, D.O., & Brusek, P.M. (1978). Spiritual well-being: A neglected subject in quality of life research. *Social Indicators Research, 5,* 303–323.

Paloutzian, R.F. (1981). Purpose in life and value changes following conversion. *Journal of Personality and Social Psychology, 41,* 1153–1160.

Paloutzian R.F., & Ellison, C.W. (1982). Loneliness, spiritual well-being, and quality of life. In L.A. Peplau & D. Perlman (Eds.), *Loneliness: A sourcebook of current theory, research, and therapy.* New York: Wiley.

Peterson, L.R., & Roy, A. (1985). Religiosity, anxiety, and meaning and purpose: Religion's consequences for psychological well-being. *Review of Religious Research, 27,* 49–62.

Pollner, M. (1989). Divine relations, social relations, and well-being. *Journal of Health and Social Behavior, 30,* 92–104.

Reker, G.T., & Guppy, B. (1988, October). *Sources of personal meaning among young, middle-aged, and older adults.* Paper presented at the Annual Meeting of the Canadian Association on Gerontology, Halifax, Nova Scotia.

Reker, G.T., & Wong, P.T. (1988). Aging as an individual process: Toward a theory of personal meaning. In J.E. Birren & B.L. Bengtson (Eds.), *Emergent theories of aging* (pp. 214–246). New York: Springer.

Soderstrom, D., & Wright, E.W. (1977). Religious orientation and meaning in life. *Journal of Clinical Psychology, 33,* 65–68.

Willits, F.K., & Crider, D.M. (1988). Religion and well-being: Men and women in the middle years. *Review of Religious Research, 29,* 281–294.

Witter, R.A., Stock, W.A., Okun, M.A., & Haring, M.J. (1985). Religion and subjective well-being in adulthood: A quantitative synthesis. *Review of Religious Research, 26,* 332–342.

Yalom, I.D. (1980). *Existential psychotherapy.* New York: Basic Books.

Zika, S., & Chamberlain, K. (1987). Relation of hassles and personality to subjective well-being. *Journal of Personality and Social Psychology, 53,* 155–162.

11

Religion, Neuroticism, and Psychoticism

Leslie J. Francis

Attempts to synthesize the findings of research concerned with the relationship between religion and mental health confront three fundamental problems. Two of these problems involve definition of the central constructs "religion" and "mental health." The third is concerned with the methodology of demonstrating a relationship between such constructs. Concluding their review of the area, Spilka and Werme (1971) argued that studies locating mental health within a dimensional model of personality might offer a new and potentially fruitful approach to the question. Two decades later their suggestion still remains inadequately explored. Therefore, the present chapter explores, from theoretical and empirical perspectives, a possible reconceptualization of both mental illness and religiosity as continuous (rather than discrete) variables. Such a reconceptualization places the question about the relationship between religion and mental illness within the context of a psychometric equation, amenable to analysis by means of multiple correlational techniques, analogous to other psychometric equations.

A Dimensional Approach

The two main approaches to defining mental disorders derive either from a dimensional theory of personality or a discrete categorization model. The traditional medically based model argues that there is discontinuity rather than continuity between the characteristics of a normal personality and a mentally ill personality. Assignment to the category of the mentally ill depends upon the judgment of the clinician. Historically, some studies have claimed high agreement among clinicians (Kreitman, 1961) while others have disputed this (Spitzer & Fleiss, 1974).

Recently, however, several independent lines of research have suggested mental disorders are associated with characteristics that are continuous with a normal personality. Such characteristics can be observed in normal people and are thought to help define the predisposing features of mental disorders. On this account, psychiatric disorders, even in their most severe forms, are not "brain diseases" in the generally accepted sense, but rather abnormal manifestations of temperamental and

149

personality characteristics present to a greater or lesser extent in everybody (Claridge, 1985).

Hans Eysenck and his associates have refined a dimensional theory of personality which locates mental disorders on a finite set of personality continua (Eysenck & Eysenck, 1976). Eysenck argues that neurotic disorders lie at the extreme of one dimension of (normal) personality, and that psychotic disorders lie at the extreme of another dimension of (normal) personality. Accordingly, it is both desirable and possible to define and operationalize the continua of neuroticism and psychoticism so that they appear to be orthogonal and independent of each other.

Eysenck's measures of neuroticism have evolved through a long process of empirical development, including the Maudsley Medical Questionnaire (Eysenck, 1947), the Maudsley Personality Inventory (Eysenck, 1959), and the Eysenck Personality Inventory (Eysenck & Eysenck, 1964). Eysenck's measures of psychoticism have had a somewhat shorter history of development. Psychoticism appeared alongside neuroticism for the first time in the "PEN" (Psychoticism, Extraversion, and Neuroticism) Inventory (Eysenck & Eysenck, 1969) and was further refined in the Eysenck Personality Questionnaire (Eysenck & Eysenck, 1975) and the Revised Eysenck Personality Questionnaire (Eysenck, Eysenck, & Barrett, 1985).

Alongside these adult measures, a junior form of the neuroticism scale was published in the Junior Eysenck Personality Inventory (Eysenck, 1965). Junior forms of both the neuroticism and psychoticism scales were published in the Junior Eysenck Personality Questionnaire (Eysenck & Eysenck, 1975) and the Revised Junior Eysenck Personality Questionnaire (Corulla, 1990).

Although Eysenck's theories and scales were originally developed and refined on British data, a considerable body of international research has now confirmed the presence and stability of the underlying personality constructs of neuroticism and psychoticism across cultures (Eysenck & Eysenck, 1982; Barrett & Eysenck, 1984).

In recent years, a growing number of studies has explored the relationships between Eysenck's dimensional model of personality and religiosity. While agreeing on a common definition and operationalization of personality constructs, these studies have employed different definitions and measures of religion. As a consequence, the lack of agreement on what is being measured by these different indices of religiosity still makes the integration and interpretation of the findings of such studies problematic. This chapter includes a discussion of the somewhat more systematic attempt by Leslie Francis and his colleagues to construct a coherent view of the relationship between Eysenck's dimensions of personality and religiosity. Several studies are mentioned in this regard, all of which employed the Francis scale of attitude toward Christianity as a continuous measure of religiosity, either in its junior form (Francis, 1978, 1989) or adult form (Francis & Stubbs, 1987).

Neuroticism and Religion

Eysenck and Gudjonsson (1989) recently characterized the neurotic person as anxious, depressed, tense, irrational, shy, moody, emotional, and suffering from guilt feelings and low self-esteem. In a more extended description of the characteristics that constitute the neuroticism scale, Eysenck and Eysenck (1975) defined the high scorers as being anxious, worrying, moody, and frequently depressed individuals who are likely to sleep badly and to suffer from various psychosomatic disorders. The high scorers are seen as overly emotional, reacting too strongly to all sorts of stimuli, and finding it difficult to get back on an even keel after emotionally arousing experiences. Strong reactions interfere with their proper adjustment, making them react in irrational, sometimes rigid ways. The highly neurotic individual is a worrier whose main characteristic is a constant preoccupation with things that might go wrong, and a strong anxiety reaction to these thoughts.

Eysenck's own discussion of the personality dimension measured by his neuroticism scales contains no explicit theoretical link between neuroticism and religiosity. Within the psychology of religion, however, there is a large theoretical literature on the relationship between religion and aspects of emotional stability, which may help to formulate clear hypotheses about the link between religion and the Eysenckian construct of neuroticism (Batson & Ventis, 1982; Spilka, Hood, & Gorsuch, 1985; Brown, 1987).

Two basic and conflicting psychological accounts emerge from this literature. The first one suggests that religion either fosters, or is an expression of, instability (Freud, 1950; Ellis, 1962; Vine, 1978) and predicts a positive correlation between religiosity and neuroticism. The second account suggests that religion fosters stability (Jung, 1938; Allport, 1950; Mowrer, 1960) and predicts a negative correlation between religiosity and neuroticism.

Empirical studies, using a variety of indices of emotional stability, self-concept, and anxiety, which are themselves known to correlate with neuroticism, seem to offer support to both the contradictory hypotheses. For example, Brown and Lowe (1951), Bender (1958), Stanley (1964), Sturgeon and Hamley (1979), McClain (1978), Ness and Wintrob (1980), and Paloutzian and Ellison (1982) reported that religiosity is associated with greater personal stability, emotional adjustment, and psychological well-being. In contrast, Cowen (1954), Roberts (1965), Keene (1967), Wilson and Miller (1968), Graff and Ladd (1971), and Balswick and Balkwell (1978) found that some aspects of religiosity are associated with lower self-esteem, less self-acceptance, greater anxiety, higher neuroticism, and emotional immaturity. Meanwhile, a third group of studies reported no significant correlation in either direction (Brown, 1962; Hanawalt, 1963; Heintzelman & Fehr, 1976; Fehr & Heintzelman, 1977; Westman & Brackney, 1990). Baker and Gorsuch (1982) found significant correlations in both directions with different indices of religiosity.

A confusing theoretical picture is consequently compounded by conflicting empirical findings. Eysenck's theory would argue that the lack of agreement among the empirical studies might, at least in part, be a consequence of reliance on the observed correlation with measures of primary or lower order personality traits, rather than with a measure of the higher order personality dimension of neuroticism itself. To test this theory, Francis, Pearson, Carter, and Kay (1981a) administered the Junior Eysenck Personality Inventory alongside the Francis scale of attitude towards Christianity to a sample of 1,088 fifteen- and sixteen-year-olds within state-maintained schools. The initial study was based on this age group because it was possible to sample the whole range of ability and social class.

Preliminary analysis revealed a significant positive correlation between neuroticism and religiosity. More sophisticated analysis of the data, however, revealed two other important significant relationships. To begin with, the females in the sample obtained higher scores than the males on the index of religiosity. This finding is consistent with much research concerned with sex differences in religiosity (Ekehammar & Sidanius, 1982). At the same time, the females also recorded higher scores on the index of neuroticism. This, too, is consistent with much research concerned with sex differences in neuroticism (Jorm, 1987). When sex differences were partialled out, the apparent significant correlation between neuroticism and religiosity disappeared, indicating that the observed relationship was entirely an artifact of sex differences. This result emphasizes the importance of controlling for sex differences in the psychometric exploration of relationships between dimensions of personality and religion, and it may help to account for some of the discrepant findings in earlier studies.

Francis, Pearson, and Kay (1983a) employed a different edition of the Eysenck neuroticism scale and set out to check this finding over a wider age range. The Junior Eysenck Personality Questionnaire was completed, together with the Francis scale of attitude towards Christianity, by a sample of 1,715 eleven- to seventeen-year-olds. Once again these data demonstrated that, after taking sex differences into account, neuroticism and religiosity are unrelated factors.

More recently Francis and Pearson (1991) explored the comparability of six different indices of neuroticism in relationship to the Francis scale of attitude towards Christianity among a sample of 177 fifteen- and sixteen-year-olds. The neuroticism scales employed were from the Junior Eysenck Personality Inventory, the Junior Eysenck Personality Questionnaire, the Eysenck Personality Questionnaire, and the short form of the Revised Eysenck Personality Questionnaire, together with the 24-item gender-related neuroticism scale and the 21-item gender-free neuroticism scale identified by Francis (1992). According to all six measures, neuroticism and religiosity remain unrelated factors.

The lack of any significant relationship between neuroticism and religion is further confirmed in relationship to the Francis scale of attitude towards Christianity among eleven-year-olds, using the short form of the Junior Eysenck Personality Questionnaire (Francis, Lankshear, & Pearson, 1989); among eleven- to sixteen-year-old girls, using the abbreviated Junior Eysenck Personality Questionnaire (Francis & Montgomery, 1992), among fifteen- and sixteen-year-olds using both the Eysenck Personality Questionnaire and the short form of the Revised Eysenck Personality Questionnaire (Francis & Pearson, 1988b); and among adult drug misusers, using the Eysenck Personality Questionnaire (Francis & Bennett, in press). It is also consistent with the findings of studies that used other indices of religiosity among eleven- and twelve-year-olds (Nias, 1973b), thirteen- and fourteen-year-olds (Pearson & Sheffield, 1976), 8–15-year-olds (Powell & Stewart, 1978), sixteen-year-olds (Egan, 1989), first-year undergraduates (Caird, 1987), psychology students (Robinson, 1990), student teachers (Wilson & Brazendale, 1973), 23–40-year-old graduates (Chlewinski, 1981), and the general population (Nias, 1973a). In contrast, Pearson, and Stubbs (1985) reported a positive relationship between neuroticism and religious attitudes among low-ability pupils in residential special schools. Biegel and Lester (1990) reported a positive relationship among undergraduates, while Francis (1991) found a negative relationship among adult churchgoers.

Heaven (1990) reported no relationship between religiosity and neuroticism among women, but a positive relationship was found among men. While Johnson et al. (1989) found no relationship in their Missouri sample, they reported both a significant positive correlation between neuroticism and extrinsic religiosity and a significant negative correlation between neuroticism and intrinsic religiosity in their Hawaii sample. Watson, Morris, Foster, and Hood (1986) reported no relationship between neuroticism and end religiosity, but significant positive correlations between neuroticism and quest and means religiosity.

The overall weight of evidence from the above studies suggests that there is neither a positive nor a negative relationship between the Eysenckian construct of neuroticism and religion.

Psychoticism and Religion

Eysenck claims that, although there are very real differences between different psychotic disorders of the functional variety, there is an important unity underlying these differences. He concludes that evidence favors a general factor of psychoticism, rather than sharply segregated schizophrenic and manic-depressive illnesses.

In their description of the characteristics that constitute the psychoticism scale, Eysenck and Eysenck (1976) define the high scorer as being cold, impersonal, hostile, lacking in sympathy, unfriendly, untrustful, odd, unemotional, unhelpful, lacking in insight, and strange, with paranoid ideas that people were against him or her. Elsewhere they also use the following descriptors: egocentric, self-centered, impersonal, lacking in empathy, solitary, troublesome, cruel, glacial, inhumane, insensitive, sensation-seeking, aggressive, foolhardy, making fools of others, and liking odd and unusual things. Eysenck and Eysenck (1975) also maintained that emotions such as empathy and guilt are characteristically absent in people who score high on measures of psychoticism.

Unlike the situation regarding the relationship between neuroticism and religiosity, Eysenck's theory generates a specific hypothesis regarding the link between psychoticism and religiosity. This hypothesis hinges on Eysenck's discussion of the relationship between conditioning and social attitudes, the role of personality in conditionability, and the location of religion within the domain of "tenderminded" social attitudes.

In *The Psychology of Politics,* Eysenck (1954) postulated a relationship between personality and social attitudes in terms of a theory of social learning or socialization. He argued that aggressive and sexual impulses are socialized through conditioning. This process of socialization is reflected in tenderminded social attitudes (Eysenck, 1961). According to Eysenck, toughminded social attitudes are concerned with immediate satisfaction of aggressive and sexual impulses, while tenderminded social attitudes are concerned with ethical and religious ideas, which act as barriers to such satisfaction. This theory clearly locates religion among tenderminded social attitudes and links religiosity to conditionability. A number of studies concerned with the structure of social attitudes provided empirical support to this location (Eysenck, 1975, 1976; Bruni & Eysenck, 1976).

According to Eysenck's earlier model of personality, which summarized individual differences in terms of the two constructs of neuroticism and extraversion, empirical studies consistently demonstrated that introverts conditioned more readily than extraverts (Eysenck, 1967). Siegman (1963) recognized in this finding a clear basis for hypothesizing a negative relationship between extraversion and religiosity. Attempts to test this hypothesis produced conflicting evidence. Wilson and Brazendale (1973), Chlewinsky (1981), Francis, Pearson, Carter, and Kay (1981b) and Francis, Pearson, and Kay (1983b) confirmed the hypothesized negative relationship. However, Powell and Stewart (1978) found a positive relationship and Pearson and Sheffield (1976) and Biegel and Lester (1990) found no significant relationship in one direction or another. In Siegman's (1963) own set of three studies, the first found a significant correlation in the direction opposite to that hypothesized; the second found that, although the relationships between extraversion and two measures of religiosity were in the expected direction, only one was significant; and the third found that the direction of the relationship varied according to both sex and denominational background.

This apparently simple hypothesized link between introversion and religiosity is made more complex by the recognition that extraversion itself embraces two main components, namely sociability and impulsivity (Eysenck & Eysenck, 1963; Sparrow & Ross, 1964). Additionally, Eysenck and Levey (1972) and Frcka and Martin (1987) demonstrated that the impulsivity component alone is responsible for the correlation between extraversion and conditionability.

Eysenck's more recent model of personality summarizes individual differences in terms of the three constructs of neuroticism, extraversion, and psychoticism. According to this model, impulsivity has become associated with the dimension of psychoticism rather than with extraversion (Eysenck & Eysenck, 1976), leaving newer editions of the extraversion scale defined largely in terms of sociability (Rocklin & Revelle, 1981). Consistent with this shift in the construct of extraversion, most recent studies have failed to report a significant relationship between introversion and religiosity. These include studies using the Eysenck Personality Questionnaire (Francis & Pearson, 1985b; Watson et al., 1986; Caird, 1987; Egan, 1989; Robinson, 1990; Francis & Bennett, in press), the Revised Eysenck Personality Questionnaire (Johnson et al., 1989), and the short form of the Revised Eysenck Personality Questionnaire (Francis & Pearson, 1988b; Heaven, 1990; Francis, 1991).

In Eysenck's more recent model of personality, impulsivity is associated with psychoticism rather than with extraversion. Consequently, conditionability has been found to switch its allegiance (Beyts, Frcka, Martin, & Levey, 1983). Accordingly, Eysenck and Wilson (1978) argued that, in their new conceptualization, psychoticism rather than extraversion is fundamental to toughmindedness. This argument provides a very clear theory for hypothesizing a negative relationship between psychoticism and religiosity on the grounds that religion belongs to the domain of tenderminded social attitudes. Such a hypothesis fits well with the fact that Eysenck's description of the psychotic personality emerges as the mirror image of Becker's (1971) description of the mature religious personality.

Empirical evidence, however, of the relationship between psychoticism and toughminded social attitudes is not as clear as the theory would predict. For example, Eaves and Eysenck (1974) reported that psychoticism correlates positively with toughmindedness, whereas no such relationship was found by McKelvie (1983). More specifically in the area of religiosity, Nias (1973b) reported a significant negative correlation between religion and psychoticism among eleven- and twelve-year-old boys and girls, while Powell and Stewart (1978) discovered a similar relationship for both boys and girls, and for both 8–10-year-olds and 11–15-year-olds. In contrast, Kay (1981) reported a different finding. Computing correlations for both boys and girls within the first, second, third, and fourth years of the secondary school separately, Kay found a significant negative correlation for boys in each of the four year groups, but no significant correlation for girls in any of the four year groups.

Kay explored a range of hypotheses to account for these differences, but regarded the most satisfactory explanation to be concerned with cultural norms and stereotypes. This was linked with Eysenck's notion that the biological basis of psychoticism could be partly sought in hormonal differences, particularly with respect to the sex hormones (Eysenck & Eysenck, 1976). Kay's findings could also be explained by the theory that the junior psychoticism scale (used in Kay's study) fails to operationalize psychoticism in a way equally appropriate for both sexes (Powell, 1977). At the same time the junior scale suffers from a severe distribution problem, which impairs the suitability of the scale for correlational analysis alongside other continuous variables. The adult version of the psychoticism scale is not thought to be so contaminated in these ways.

Francis and Pearson (1985a) sought to determine whether the same relationships existed between religiosity and different versions of the psychoticism scale. They administered the psychoticism scales from both the Junior Eysenck Personality Questionnaire and the Adult Eysenck Personality Questionnaire, alongside the Francis scale of attitude towards Christianity, to 132 fifteen-year-olds. It was thought that they represented a critical overlap age group for whom both the adult and the junior scales were appropriate (Pearson & Francis, 1984). Before taking sex differences into account, there was a significant negative correlation between attitude toward religion and psychoticism as measured on both the junior scale and the adult scale. After taking into account sex differences by means of multiple regression analysis, a significant negative relationship between psychoticism and attitude toward religion still existed in relationship to the adult scale, but this was no longer the case with the junior scale. Francis and Pearson (1985a) assumed that the adult scale was the more adequate operationalization of the construct of psychoticism. On that basis, they concluded that these data supported the hypothesis derived from Eysenck's theory relating personality to social attitudes; namely that there is a significant negative correlation between psychoticism for both male and female adolescents.

To test the generalizability of these discrepant findings in relation to the junior and adult versions of the psychoticism scale, Francis (in press) administered both scales, together with the Francis scale of attitude towards Christianity, to a larger sample of 1,347 fifteen- and sixteen-year-olds. Francis found a clear negative relationship between psychoticism and religiosity according to both the junior scale and the adult scale for both male and female subjects.

The significant negative relationship between psychoticism and religion was further confirmed in relation to the Francis scale of attitude toward Christianity using the short form of the Junior Eysenck Personality Questionnaire among eleven-year-olds (Francis et al., 1989), and fifteen- and sixteen-year-olds (Francis & Pearson, 1988a). A similar finding was reported by Francis and Montgomery (1992), using the abbreviated Junior Eysenck Personality Inventory with 11–16-year-old girls, while Francis and Bennett (in press) used the Eysenck Personality Questionnaire and found a negative relationship with a sample of female drug misusers. Additionally, Francis (1991) employed the short form of the Revised Eysenck Personality Questionnaire and found a negative relationship between religion and psychoticism among adult churchgoers. In contrast, other recent studies employing various forms of the Eysenckian psychoticism scale in conjunction with different indices of religiosity have failed to find a consistent negative correlation between religion and psychoticism (Nias, 1973a; Watson et al., 1986; Caird, 1987; Egan, 1989; Johnson et al., 1989; Chau et al., 1990; Heaven, 1990; Robinson, 1990).

While the theory clearly predicts that religious people should record lower scores on the Eysenckian scale of psychoticism, the empirical data still seem to remain somewhat equivocal. The theory now needs more consistent testing with the recent improved measures of psychoticism incorporated into the Revised Eysenck Personality Questionnaire and the Junior Revised Eysenck Personality Questionnaire.

Conclusion

Working within Eysenck's dimensional model of personality, the findings of this review suggest that there is no relationship between neuroticism and religiosity, but that a significant negative relationship exists between psychoticism and religiosity. According to these criteria, there is no evidence to suggest that religious people experience lower levels of mental health, and some clear evidence to suggest that they enjoy higher levels of mental health. The theoretical framework employed from Eysenck's personality theory has suggested that personality represents the prior variables, and the empirical evidence is not inconsistent with this theory. Correlational studies, however, could equally be interpreted to support causality in the opposite direction. Longitudinal studies employing Eysenck's measures in the psychological exploration of the relationship between religion and mental health are now needed to throw additional light on this longstanding and perplexing puzzle.

References

Allport, G.W. (1950). *The individual and his religion.* New York: Macmillan.
Baker, M., & Gorsuch, R. (1982). Trait anxiety and intrinsic-extrinsic religiousness. *Journal for the Scientific Study of Religion, 21,* 119–122.
Balswick, J.O., & Balkwell, J.W. (1978). Religious orthodoxy and emotionality. *Review of Religious Research, 19,* 308–319.

Barrett, P., & Eysenck, S.B.G. (1984). The assessment of personality factors across twenty-five countries. *Personality and Individual Differences, 5,* 615–632.

Batson, C.D., & Ventis, W.L. (1982). *The religious experience: A social-psychological perspective.* Oxford: Oxford University Press.

Becker, R.J. (1971). Religion and psychological health. In M.P. Strommen (Ed.), *Research on religious development: A comprehensive handbook* (pp. 391–421). New York: Hawthorn Books.

Bender, I.E. (1958). Changes in religious interest: A retest after 15 years. *Journal of Abnormal and Social Psychology, 57,* 41–46.

Beyts, J., Frcka, G., Martin, I., & Levey, A.B. (1983). The influence of psychoticism and extraversion on classical eyelid conditioning using a paraorbital shock UCS. *Personality and Individual Differences, 4,* 275–283.

Biegel, K., & Lester, D. (1990). Religiosity and psychological disturbance. *Psychological Reports, 67,* 874.

Brown, D.G., & Lowe, W.L. (1951). Religious beliefs and personality characteristics of college students. *Journal of Social Psychology, 33,* 103–129.

Brown, L.B. (1962). A study of religious belief. *British Journal of Psycholgy, 53,* 259–272.

Brown, L.B. (1987). *The psychology of religious belief.* London: Academic Press.

Bruni, P., & Eysenck, H.J. (1976). Structure of attitudes: An Italian sample. *Psychological Reports, 38,* 956–958.

Caird, D. (1987). Religiosity and personality: Are mystics introverted, neurotic, or psychotic? *British Journal of Social Psychology, 26,* 345–346.

Chau, L.L., Johnson, R.C., Bowers, J.K., Darvill, T.J., & Danko, G.P. (1990). Intrinsic and extrinsic religiosity as related to conscience, adjustment, and altruism. *Personality and Individual Differences, 11,* 397–400.

Chlewinski, Z. (1981). Personality and attitude towards religion in Poland. *Personality and Individual Differences, 2,* 243–245.

Claridge, G. (1985). *Origins of mental illness.* Oxford: Basil Blackwell.

Corulla, W.J. (1990). A revised version of the psychoticism scale for children. *Personality and Individual Differences, 11,* 65–76.

Cowen, E.L. (1954). The negative concept as a personality measure. *Journal of Consulting Psychology, 18,* 138–142.

Eaves, L.J., & Eysenck, H.J. (1974). Genetics and the development of social attitudes. *Nature, 249,* 288–289.

Egan, V. (1989). Links between personality, ability and attitudes in a low-IQ sample. *Personality and Individual Differences, 10,* 997–1001.

Ekehammar, B., & Sidanius, J. (1982). Sex differences in sociopolitical attitudes: A replication and extension. *British Journal of Social Psychology, 21,* 249–257.

Ellis, A. (1962). *The case against religion.* New York: Institute for Rational Living.

Eysenck, H J. (1947). *Dimensions of personality.* London: Routledge and Kegan Paul.

Eysenck, H.J. (1954). *The psychology of politics.* London: Routledge and Kegan Paul.

Eysenck, H.J. (1959). *Manual for the Maudsley Personality Inventory.* London: University of London Press.

Eysenck, H.J. (1961). Personality and social attitudes. *Journal of Social Psychology, 53,* 243–248.

Eysenck, H.J. (1967). *The biological basis of personality.* Springfield, IL: Charles C. Thomas.

Eysenck, H.J. (1975). The structure of social attitudes. *British Journal of Social and Clinical Psychology, 14,* 323–331.

Eysenck, H.J. (1976). Structure of social attitudes. *Psychological Reports, 39,* 463–466.

Eysenck, H.J., & Eysenck, S.B.G. (1964). *Manual of the Eysenck Personality Inventory.* London: University of London Press.

Eysenck, H.J., & Eysenck, S.B.G. (1975). *Manual of the Eysenck Personality Questionnaire.* London: Hodder and Stoughton.

Eysenck, H.J., & Eysenck, S.B.G. (1976). *Psychoticism as a dimension of personality.* London: Hodder and Stoughton.

Eysenck, H.J., & Eysenck, S.B.G. (1982). Recent advances in the cross-cultural study of personality. In C.D. Spielberger & J.N. Butcher (Eds.), *Advances in personality assessment* (pp. 41–69). Hillsdale, NY: Erlbaum.

Eysenck, H.J., & Gudjonsson, G. (1989). *Causes and cures of criminality.* New York: Plenum Press.

Eysenck, H.J., & Levey, A. (1972). Conditioning, introversion-extraversion and the strength of the nervous system. In V.D. Neblitzyn & J.A. Gray (Eds.), *Biological bases of individual behaviour* (pp. 206–220). New York: Academic Press.

Eysenck, H.J., & Wilson, G.D. (1978). *The psychological basis of ideology.* Lancaster: Medical and Technical Publishers.

Eysenck, S.B.G. (1965). *Manual of the Junior Eysenck Personality Inventory.* London: University of London Press.

Eysenck, S.B.G., & Eysenck, H.J. (1963). On the dual nature of extraversion. *British Journal of Social and Clinical Psychology, 2,* 46–55.

Eysenck, S.B.G., & Eysenck, H.J. (1969). Scores on three personality variables as a function of age, sex and social class. *British Journal of Social and Clinical Psychology, 8,* 69–76.

Eysenck, S.B.G., Eysenck, H.J., & Barrett, P. (1985). A revised version of the psychoticism scale. *Personality and Individual Differences, 6,* 21–29.

Fehr, L.A., & Heintzelman, M.E. (1977). Personality and attitude correlates of religiosity: Source of controversy. *Journal of Psychology, 95,* 63–66.

Francis, L.J. (1978). Attitude and longitude: A study in measurement. *Character Potential, 8,* 119–130.

Francis, L.J. (1989). Measuring attitude towards Christianity during childhood and adolescence. *Personality and Individual Differences, 10,* 695–698.

Francis, L.J. (1991). Personality and attitude towards religion among adult churchgoers in England. *Psychological Reports, 69,* 791–794.

Francis, L.J. (1992). The dual nature of the Eysenckian neuroticism scales: A question of sex differences? Manuscript submitted for publication.

Francis, L.J. (in press). Is psychoticism really the dimension of personality fundamental to religiosity? *Personality and Individual Differences.*

Francis, L.J., & Bennett, G.A. (in press). The relationship between personality and religion among female drug misusers. *Drug and Alcohol Dependence.*

Francis, L.J., Lankshear, D.W., & Pearson, P.R. (1989). The relationship between religiosity and the short form JEPQ (JEPQ-S) indices of E, N, L and P among eleven year olds. *Personality and Individual Differences, 10,* 763–769.

Francis, L.J., & Montgomery, A. (1992). Personality and attitudes towards religion among 11–16 year old girls in a single sex Catholic school. *British Journal of Religious Education, 14,* 114–119.

Francis, L.J., & Pearson, P.R. (1985a). Psychoticism and religiosity among 15 year olds. *Personality and Individual Differences, 6,* 397–398.

Francis, L.J., & Pearson, P.R. (1985b). Extraversion and religiosity. *Journal of Social Psychology, 125,* 269–270.

Francis, L.J., & Pearson, P.R. (1988a). The development of a short form of the JEPQ (JEPQ-S): Its use in measuring personality and religion. *Personality and Individual Differences, 9,* 911–916.

Francis, L.J., & Pearson, P.R. (1988b). Religiosity and the short-scale EPQ-R indices or E, N and L, compared with the JEPI, JEPQ and EPQ. *Personality and Individual Differences, 9,* 653–657.

Francis, L.J., & Pearson, P.R. (1991). Religiosity, gender and the two faces of neuroticism. *Irish Journal of Psychology, 12,* 60–67.

Francis, L.J., Pearson, P.R., Carter, M., & Kay, W.K. (1981a). The relationship between neuroticism and religiosity among English 15- and 16-year olds. *Journal of Social Psychology, 114,* 99–102.

Francis, L.J., Pearson, P.R., Carter, M., & Kay, W.K. (1981b). Are introverts more religious? *British Journal of Social Psychology, 20,* 101–104.

Francis, L.J., Pearson, P.R., & Kay, W.K. (1983a). Neuroticism and religiosity among English school children. *Journal of Social Psychology, 121,* 149–150.

Francis, L.J., Pearson, P.R., & Kay, W.K. (1983b). Are introverts still more religious? *Personality and Individual Differences, 4,* 211–212.

Francis, L.J., Pearson, P.R., & Stubbs, M.T. (1985). Personality and religion among low ability children in residential special schools. *British Journal of Mental Subnormality, 31,* 41–45.

Francis, L.J., & Stubbs, M.T. (1987). Measuring attitudes towards Christianity: From childhood to adulthood. *Personality and Individual Differences, 8,* 741–743.

Frcka, G., & Martin, I. (1987). Is there or is there not an influence of impulsiveness on classical eyelid conditioning? *Personality and Individual Differences, 8,* 241–252.

Freud, S. (1950). *The future of an illusion.* New Haven, CT: Yale University Press.

Graff, R.W., & Ladd, C.E. (1971). POI correlates of a religious commitment inventory. *Journal of Clinical Psychology, 27,* 502–504.

Hanawalt, N.G. (1963). Feelings of security and self-esteem in relation to religious belief. *Journal of Social Psychology, 59,* 347–353.

Heaven, P.C.L. (1990). Attitudinal and personality correlates of achievement motivation among high school students. *Personality and Individual Differences, 11,* 705–710.

Heintzelman, M.E., & Fehr, L.A. (1976). Relationship between religious orthodoxy and three personality variables. *Psychological Reports, 38,* 756–758.

Johnson, R.C., Danko, G.P., Darvill, T.J., Bochner, S., Bowers, J.K., Huang, Y-H., Park, J.Y., Pecjak, V., Rahim, A.R.A., & Pennington, D. (1989). Cross-cultural assessment of altruism and its correlates. *Personality and Individual Differences, 10,* 855–868.

Jorm, A.F. (1987). Sex differences in neuroticism: A quantitative synthesis of published research. *Australian and New Zealand Journal of Psychiatry, 21,* 501–506.

Jung, C.G. (1938). *Psychology and religion.* New Haven: Yale University Press.

Kay, W.K. (1981). Psychoticism and attitude to religion. *Personality and Individual Differences, 2,* 249–252.

Keene, J.J. (1967). Religious behaviour and neuroticism, spontaneity and worldmindedness. *Sociometry, 30,* 137–157.

Kreitman, N. (1961). The reliability of psychiatric diagnosis. *Journal of Mental Science, 107,* 876–886.

McClain, E.W. (1978). Personality differences between intrinsically religious and non-religious students: Factor analytic study. *Journal of Personality Assessment, 42,* 159–166.

McKelvie, S.J. (1983). Personality and belief in capital punishment: A replication and extension. *Personality and Individual Differences, 4,* 217–218.

Mowrer, O.H. (1960). Some constructive features of the concept of sin. *Journal of Counselling Psychology, 7,* 185–188.

Ness, R.C., & Wintrob, R.M. (1980). The emotional impact of fundamentalist religious participation: An empirical study of intragroup variation. *American Journal of Orthopsychiatry, 50,* 302–315.

Nias, D.K.B. (1973a). Attitudes to the Common Market: A case study in conservatism. In G.D. Wilson (Ed.), *The psychology of conservatism* (pp. 239-255). London: Academic Press.

Nias, D.K.B. (1973b). Measurement and structure of children's attitudes. In G.D. Wilson (Ed.), *The psychology of conservatism* (pp. 93-113). London: Academic Press.

Paloutzian, R.F., & Ellison, C.W. (1982). Loneliness, spiritual well-being, and the quality of life. In L.A. Peplau & D. Perlman (Eds.), *Loneliness: A source book of current theory, research and therapy* (pp. 224-237). New York: Wiley-Interscience.

Pearson, P.R., & Francis, L.J. (1984). The comparability of the JEPI, JEPQ and EPQ among 15- to 16-year olds. *Personality and Individual Differences, 5,* 743-745.

Pearson, P.R., & Sheffield, B.F. (1976). Is personality related to social attitudes? An attempt at replication. *Social Behaviour and Personality, 4,* 109-111.

Powell, G.E. (1977). Psychoticism and social deviancy in children. *Advances in Behaviour Research and Therapy, 1,* 27-56.

Powell, G.E., & Stewart, R.A. (1978). The relationship of age, sex and personality to social attitudes in children aged 8-15 years. *British Journal of Social and Clinical Psychology, 17,* 307-317.

Roberts, F.J. (1965). Some psychological factors in religious conversion. *British Journal of Social and Clinical Psychology, 4,* 185-187.

Robinson, T.N. (1990). Eysenck personality measures and religious orientation. *Personality and Individual Differences, 11,* 915-921.

Rocklin, T., & Revelle, W. (1981). The measurement of extraversion: A comparison of the Eysenck Personality Inventory and the Eysenck Personality Questionnaire. *British Journal of Social Psychology, 20,* 279-284.

Siegman, A.W. (1963). A cross-cultural investigation of the relationship between introversion, social attitudes and social behaviour. *British Journal of Social and Clinical Psychology, 2,* 196-208.

Sparrow, N.H., & Ross, J. (1964). The dual nature of extraversion: A replication. *Australian Journal of Psychology, 16,* 214-218.

Spilka, B., Hood, R.W., & Gorsuch, R.L. (1985). *The psychology of religion: An empirical approach.* Englewood Cliffs, NJ: Prentice-Hall.

Spilka, B., & Werme, P.H. (1971). Religion and mental disorder: A research perspective. In M.P. Strommen (Ed.), *Research on religious development: A comprehensive handbook* (pp. 461-481). New York: Hawthorn Books.

Spitzer, R.L., & Fleiss, J.L. (1974). A re-analysis of the reliability of psychometric diagnosis. *British Journal of Psychiatry, 125,* 341-347.

Stanley, G. (1964). Personality and attitude correlates of religious conversion. *Journal for the Scientific Study of Religion, 4,* 60-63.

Sturgeon, R.S., & Hamley, R.W. (1979). Religiosity and anxiety. *Journal of Social Psychology, 108,* 137-138.

Vine, I. (1978). Facts and values in the psychology of religion. *Bulletin British Psychological Society, 31,* 414-417.

Watson, P.J., Morris, R.J., Foster, J.E., & Hood, R.W. (1986). Religiosity and social desirability. *Journal for the Scientific Study of Religion, 25,* 215-232.

Westman, A.S., & Brackney, B.E. (1990). Relationships between indices of neuroticism, attitudes towards and concepts of death, and religiosity. *Psychological Reports, 66,* 1039-1043.

Wilson, G.D., & Brazendale, A.H. (1973). Social attitude correlates of Eysenck's personality dimensions. *Social Behaviour and Personality, 1,* 115-118.

Wilson, W., & Miller, H.L. (1968). Fear, anxiety and religiousness. *Journal for the Scientific Study of Religion, 7,* 111.

III

PSYCHOSOCIAL DIMENSIONS

12

Religion and Mental Health in Early Life

Edward P. Shafranske

Religion is both a personal enterprise and a cultural institution through which people are initiated into a sense of purpose and place within the social and ontological
universes. Religion provides a language that captures, within the limits of discourse,
an individual's apprehension of the meaningfulness and, at times, the anomie that
existence presents. As Erikson (1962/1958) noted, religion "elaborates on what
feels profoundly true even though it is not demonstrable: it translates into significant words, images, and codes the exceeding darkness which surrounds man's existence, and the light which pervades it beyond all discrete comprehension" (p. 21).
Religion informs the individual of the moral values, and prescribed behaviors
which will sustain fruitful participation within family, neighborhood, and society.
Religion holds an integral role in the fabric of the culture and in the individual life
of the person. Religion provides a cultural "binding," as its etymology suggests, to
the realm of personal meaning and human relations. Embedded within the weave
of culture, religion appears for some as a predominant strand, and, for others, as a
nearly unnoticeable thread in the course of their life. Religion, as a preeminent
institutional force, shaping fundamental beliefs and behaviors, whether explicitly
or implicitly, has import as a factor in the psychological functioning of the individual. In light of this observation, it is suggested that religion plays a significant role
in mental health. This chapter examines the role of religion in mental health with
an eye toward its seminal influence within the early life of the person. It presents a
theoretical model through which the religious life of children may be apprehended
as relevant to their development in toto, and as a staging arena upon which mature
faith takes root. We will examine those processes, falling within the rubric of "religious," which contain the potential to affirm and to support the mental health of
children.

Overview

The task of making sense out of existence and finding a place within the human
order commences within childhood. Formal religious instruction and personal
notions of spirituality, however conveyed, provide the bedrock upon which essen-

tial existential questions (e.g., Where did I come from? What happened to grandfather when he died?) are answered and through which the transmission of culturally sanctioned beliefs, attributions, and behaviors is accomplished. The religious
faith of the child may be understood as a synthesis of three interrelated domains of
experience. The child appropriates a religious sensitivity through conscious and
unconscious God representations, attributions and beliefs, and institutional affiliations.

These avenues not only instill religious sentiments but they also foster relationships, attitudes, and behaviors that contribute positively or negatively to the mental
health of the young person. For example, one might consider the positive benefits
for a young Tennessee girl, who related to Robert Coles (1990), her picturing of
"God who is in heaven [and] is in my mind, too . . . a companion who will not
leave" (p. 128). Supported by a faith community that reinforces this belief, she may
be encouraged to develop a deep trust in her God and communion with other
believers. Her faith, nourished through her participation in a religious congregation, may contribute to a positive sense of self and may assist her in the many decisions that she will make and tribulations she will face throughout the course of her
life. She is but one of a majority of children who possess religious faith, who are
raised within a family of believers in the existence of God, and who communicate
a personal, religious perspective (Gallup, 1978; Gallup & Castelli, 1989).

Most individuals possess some form of religious faith. Gallup and Castelli
(1989) reported, for example, that 90 percent of all Americans say that they have
never doubted the existence of God and 85 percent consider religion important in
their lives. Further, 82 percent of all Americans reported having received religious
instructions as children, and 90 percent of those parents with children age 4–18 say
they want religious training for their children (Gallup & Castelli, 1989). The findings of these recent polls suggest that religion is perceived to be an influential and
integral aspect of human life. As such, it may be concluded that religious institutions and personal religiousness play vital roles in mental health.

We turn now to the influence of religion within the early life of the child, mindful of Allport's comment: "since religion, whatever else it may be, involves meaning
and integration at every step, we must concede at the outset that the religion of
childhood is of a special order, having little in common with the religion of adulthood" (1961/1950, p. 27). We will consider the unique constituents of the religious
experience of children, those representations, beliefs, attributions, and affiliations
that contribute to the child's developing sense of self, others, and purpose, and
which have the potential to enhance or impede mental health.

Representational Aspects of Religion

The particular vitality expressed in the religious life of the young child is found in
the developmental capacity to comfortably play within what Winnicott (1971)
referred to as the transitional space. In his work, he focused attention on the child's
propensity to occupy an intermediate area of experience in which distinctions
between external reality and inner fantasy are blurred. Drawing upon these obser-

vations, Pruyser (1983, 1985) suggested that it is within the "illusionistic world" that the stories found within all religious traditions come to life and become real within the personal history of the child. An emphasis is placed on the child's exercise of imagination in which the allegory is not merely heard but rather is *experienced* in the depths of the psyche. The characters and the events of the stories exist not as mere fiction but rather as experienced narratives. One need only hear a child speaking about an encounter with an imaginary friend, or see a child distressed by a ghoulish fairy tale "that was real!" to realize the psychic potency of the transitional realm. Religious narratives hold equal stead with other stories and personal memories in their evocative power within the domain of transitional phenomena. It is within its character as a set of transitional phenomena that religion, as Meissner (1984) concluded, "achieves its psychological reality and its psychic vitality in the potential space of illusory experience" (pp. 177–178).

Representations of God, understood within the context of transitional phenomena, are viewed not simply as abstract religious conceptions. Rather, they are seen as psychologically complex, meaningful embodiments of interpersonal experience and internalized narratives. Rizzuto (1974, 1976, 1979, 1986, 1989) and others (Jones, 1991; McDargh, 1983; Meissner, 1978, 1984, 1987; Potvin, 1977; Shafranske, in press; Spero, 1990) suggest that God representations are psychological gestalts of conscious and unconscious processes culled out of all life experience. They are conceived to be amalgams of internalized parental imagos, fantasy, compensatory operations, and acculturation that serve a dynamic role in the representational world of the individual. These representations play a sustaining role, not only during childhood, but throughout the adult's religious experience.

Rizzuto's understanding goes beyond Freud's projection hypothesis in asserting that the God representation is "a *new* original representation which, because it is new, may have the varied components that serve to soothe and comfort, provide inspiration and courage—or terror and dread—far beyond that inspired by the actual parents" (1979, p. 46). Parens (1970) noted that such representations preserve a sense of "inner sustainment" and may serve a soothing function for the person. Through its creation by means of memorial, fantasy, and conceptual abilities, the God representation comes to exist as a virtual object for the believer.

From the perspective of psychoanalytic object relations theory, God representations are not ideas about God but rather are objects that the child encounters within the transitional realm. It is by virtue of such encounters that the mental health of the child may be affected. In the circumstance in which the child has experienced a benevolent, trusting relationship with the parents (in consort with other positive fantasies and beliefs about God), the resultant God representation might resonate a positive, loving quality. Such a representation may be always at hand, available as the transitional object of the teddy bear or special blanket, to sustain and comfort the child in private moments of hardship and suffering. The obverse holds true as well. Individuals raised in hostile, critical homes and bereft of positive images of God may find their gods to be equally rejecting and punishing. These brief examples are inadequate to convey the complexity of the psychological nature of God representational processes. It is important to keep in mind that God representations are not static, intellectual concepts or simply projections of parental imagos.

Rather, they are dynamic personal objects that are influenced by history, stories, and fantasies.

The salience of the representational aspects of religious faith may be illustrated in the dynamics of prayer. When individual children kneel in prayer, they do not pray to an idea of the sacred, but to the person of God. Within the transitional space, the child meets the God representation in a direct and unmediated way. The following excerpt from Robert Coles's (1990) discussions may illustrate the point.

> Anne remarked, "Jesus answers our prayers, if we keep praying and we deserve it. I'm not boasting. Maybe he's not happy with me a lot of the time! But if I do pray and He does answer—then it's *Him,* He's the one I'm seeing, and He's the one I'm hearing. . . . I'm sure grateful when I hear Jesus speaking. It's real helpful. I can remember what he's said later, when I need to remember. I can be calm then, and not goof up!" (pp. 85–86)

Such a young person, in appropriating faith in a mythic-literal manner (Fowler & Keen, 1978; Fowler, 1981), may enter the transitional space time and time again to encounter God representations in a highly personal and evocative way. Meissner (1978) reflects:

> In this activity, the believer immerses himself in the religious experience in a more direct, immediate, and personal way than in any other aspect of his religious involvement. . . . It is here that the qualities of the God-representation and their relationship to the believer's self-representation become immediate. The God he prays to is not ultimately the God of the theologian or of the philosophers, nor is this God likely to be in any sense reconcilable with the God of Scripture. Rather, the individual believer prays to a God who is represented by the highly personalized transitional object representation in his inner, private, personally idiosyncratic belief system. . . . One might say that in prayer the individual figuratively enters the transitional space where he meets his God-representation. Prayer can become a channel for expressing what is most unique, profound, and personal in individual psychology. (p. 182)

The representational dimension includes what William James (1985/1902) alluded to as the *hither side,* or the subconscious aspects of religious experience. God representations and other religious figures, seen as transitional phenomena, play a vital role in the religious lives of children. Further, encounters with God in the transitional realm may provide a psychologically potent relationship that sustains the child in times of crisis, comforts in times of distress, hearkens in times of moral doubt, and is simply there in moments of communion and isolation. As McDargh (1983) observed, these conscious and unconscious configurations of affect, imagery, and memory, which form around the complex symbol of God, offer a potentially rich source of relationship that may significantly contribute to the mental health of the child.

Beliefs and Attributions

Beliefs are the features that are most commonly associated with religious involvement. In keeping with Wilfred Cantwell Smith's (1979) critique, the holding of particular beliefs is integral to a religious faith that challenges people "to see, to feel, [and] to act in terms of, a transcendent dimension" (p. 12). Beliefs are personally held statements that reflect a particular understanding of the nature of the self within existence. In this view, religious beliefs may be seen to contribute primarily to a person's identity rather than solely to an intellectual construction of the nature of ontology. Beliefs inform the self of its ontological underpinning for the purpose of defining and encouraging its relationship within the totality of existence. Beliefs are essential aspects of an individual's evolving sense of self, identity, and relationship. As Niebuhr (1941) commented: "the participating self cannot escape the necessity of looking for pattern and meaning in its life and relations" (p. 72). The child's beliefs reflect important thoughts about who he or she is, and they provide rudimentary conceptions which organize the experience of living. With the development of language, the child's capacity to organize experience and to elaborate meaning is greatly enhanced.

The language of religious belief provides a narrative out of which experience is organized and understood. Coles (1990) provides another example in the form of a recorded conversation with an Islamic child. This young person spoke with great resolve about his belief in Allah's direct involvement in his life and his call to surrender to Allah's will. This example portrays the organizational ability of deeply embedded religious frames of reference.

> He can breathe his power into you! He can make you feel that the world will listen to you, it'll obey you. Sometimes, you can feel everything isn't working. My mother told us of someone who had a car, and nothing [in the car] worked, until the man [the owner] said his prayers, and he kept saying them, and he got up and went to the car, and he could run it, he could laugh at the car and *dare* it to give him more trouble, and it didn't. (p. 229)

This illustrates the power of beliefs to orient one's personal identity within a religious system. The mother's story suggests that a transcendent force operates not only in grievous issues of ontology. Through faith, it also influences mundane matters such as automobiles and the like. Religious beliefs are eminently practical in their manner of bringing coherence and meaning to the child's world of experience. Religious narratives contribute directly to the child's developing sense of identity.

Religious belief systems present guidelines for social behavior and morality as well as models for identity. An inspection of the research findings regarding adults' religious attitudes may provide a context for understanding the influence religion serves, vis-à-vis the family, in instilling moral behavior in children. The majority of American adults reported that their religious beliefs and traditions had an impact upon their personal behavior. Sixty percent said that "as a moral and ethical teacher," Jesus had a great impact on their lives, while 26 percent reported that Jesus had "some influence" as a teacher (Gallup & Castelli, 1989, p. 65). Three-quarters of respondents claimed that they made "at least some effort" to follow the example of Jesus. These survey data, taken with the previously stated finding that 90 percent of parents wish their children to receive religious instruction, suggest the significant role religion plays in acculturation and in the psychological, social, and moral development of children. Caplan (as cited in Payne, Bergin, Bielema, & Jenkins, 1991, p. 12) observed that "next to families, religious institutions are the most universal of all groups that provide support" to positive mental health and psychosocial functioning. Religious beliefs convey models of selfhood and prescribe codes of right and wrong behavior which may contribute to a child's mental health.

Religious beliefs hold the potential to instill a positive sense of self and to provide the foundation upon which the fabric of society develops. Moreover, it has been pointed out that "moral and ethical value systems have proven themselves to be of great value in helping persons evolve a pattern of social existence which enables them to live more adequately with themselves, their families, and their neighbors" (Joint Commission on the Mental Health of Children, 1973, p. 448). The influence of religion on how a child lives his or her life is not simply a matter of following a code of behavior. At a more fundamental level, it involves an apprehension of the moral quality inherent in a specific decision or personal act. Religious belief systems provide the frameworks by which the definitions of situations are constructed. From the perspective of symbolic interaction, it is "the definition of the situation that is the salient factor for human behavior" (Caldwell, 1971, p. 39), and the nexus where religion asserts its influence. In keeping with the application of attribution theory to religion, it is through the attachment of cognitive labels to a given immediate situation that religious beliefs make their mark in human affairs (Spilka, Shaver, & Kirkpatrick, 1985).

A religion's moral imperative is of personal consequence only to the extent that it has fostered an appreciation of events as embodiments of moral situations. The sacralization of cultural norms of behavior enhances the adoption of prosocial behavior based on religious beliefs (Roberts, 1991). The elevation of certain behaviors to the realm of the moral consequence may prompt the child to achieve a more sophisticated cognitive appraisal of the situations and behaviors. For example, the Christian parable of the Good Samaritan speaks directly about the dignity of an individual, regardless of the social group or caste to which the person belongs. Further, the story depicts a behavioral response of providing assistance to the downtrodden in keeping with such a moral appraisal. The possibility exists that through exposure to such stories (which are found within all religious traditions), children are encouraged to perceive life events within the context of a personally meaningful, transcendent dimension. If we allow the possibility that religious ideals and virtues reflect sound principles for mental health, then religion offers an important resource for the psychosocial well-being of children (Clinebell, 1970; Maton & Pargament, 1987; Pargament, 1980; Pargament, Maton, & Hess, 1991). Therefore, it is suggested that religion may have a significant influence in both the formation of identity and the encouragement of prosocial behavior.

Religious beliefs may also offer a resource by which the child can face life's difficulties and confusions within a meaningful frame of reference. Research on coping behavior suggests that attributions play a significant role in the manner in which individuals experience and respond to psychologically challenging situations. (Lazarus & Folkman, 1984). Religious beliefs may provide a unique context through which appraisals of life events lead to effective coping. This may particularly be the case in facing situations that involve limit experiences. Limit experiences are those circumstances that exist at or beyond the limit of one's ordinary comprehension of the nature of existence. Personal catastrophies, tragedies born of death, and loss and change in status may present considerable emotional distress and tax a person's ability to make sense of the situation. Hathaway and Pargament (1991) discuss the role that religious beliefs may play in coping with such limit experiences:

> Individuals make a variety of attributions about situations from a religious frame-work. For instance, differing views of God can lead to different appraisals of situations. Life events can be viewed as a reward from a loving God, punishment from an angry God, unintended by a kind, non-intervening God, as the will of a mysterious God, and as an opportunity for growth. (pp. 74–75)

Considerable research conducted with adults demonstrates the coping function religious beliefs may provide (for a comprehensive review, see Hathaway & Pargament, 1991; Park & Cohen, in press). Religious beliefs may be all the more timely for children facing devastating life events in that their knowledge and experience of the world is limited. The child, as with the adult, struggles to find meaning and order in those life circumstances that confront him or her with experiences of helplessness and anomie. Coles (1990) discussed such an event with a boy grappling with the accidental death of his older sister:

> Where is Sally? [I had asked him where he thought she is.] That's where she is, with God, I guess. I mean maybe He did overlook her that day [the day that she was killed]. But He must take His people home, after they die like Sally [did]. He can't just let her be there [in the grave], and that's the end of it. . . . Sally is there, in heaven, and that's where you'd want your sister to be, if she can't be with you! . . . Sally did her best to be good, and she prayed to Him, and she must be there with Him. I believe she is! That's what God taught, that He'll look after us, and He's a teacher whose word is good! (pp. 218–219)

This illustrates the child's use of religious belief in forging a faith that makes sense out of the limit experience of his sister's death. Such faith is both a manifestation of a history of religious involvement and an outcome of the crisis. This second point alludes to the fact that, out of the process of grappling with limit experiences, new constructions of faith and belief (or doubt and nihilism) are formed (Pargament, 1988).

Religious faith is involved in ongoing coping as well as in making sense of past traumatic events. Religious belief and affiliation have been shown to be associated, for example, in coping with terminal illness (Balk, 1983; Hipol, 1978; Jenkins & Pargament, 1988; Peteet, 1985; Spilka, Zwartjes, Zwartjes, Heidman, & Cilli, 1987; Tebbi, Mallon, Richards, Bigler, 1987). In this regard, Orr, Hoffmans, and Bennetts (1984) reported that two of nine adolescents with cancer in their study stated that they had become more religious following the diagnosis of their illness and that church attendance was beneficial. It was found that "they also thought that they had influenced others to become more religious by serving as role models of sick kids who are still able to make it to church" (Orr et al., 1984, p. 56). Religious beliefs may serve children in making sense of the challenges that confront them. Fervently held beliefs (e.g., God's omnipotent control and benevolence) may provide a sturdy anchor for a sense of hope and may reduce the child's anxiety in the face of the limits of personal control. Hathaway and Pargament (1991) suggest that cognitive stress inoculation training (Meichenbaum & Jaremko, 1983) could be introduced through religious education programs in presenting multiple ways of understanding life situations. Constructing appraisals of life situations within a transcendent framework may contribute to enhanced coping.

Religious beliefs provide seminal statements about the nature of the child's relationships with the transcendent (within the Judeo-Christian tradition as God), the self, and others. These beliefs provide a context for the appraisal of their behaviors and for constructing meaning for limit experiences. Religious beliefs, together with God representations, contribute significantly to a child's sense of identity, discernment of appropriate behavior, and coping with the challenges of life. This is especially true for those events that test the limits of the child's rational understanding. We now turn to the role of religious affiliation in the life of the child.

Affiliation in Religious Faith Communities

Religious conceptions and representations are predominantly shaped by the child's immediate family and social environment. On this subject, Berger (1963) wrote:

> The [child] derives his world view [including religious faith and beliefs], in very much the same way that he derives his roles and identity. In other words, his emotions and his self-interpretation like his actions are predefined for him by society, and so is his cognitive approach to the universe that surrounds him. . . . Society predefines for us that fundamental symbolic apparatus [as expressed in part through religious language] with which we grasp the world, order our experience and interpret our own existence. (p. 117)

Hunsberger and Brown (1984) and others (e.g., Hoge, Petrillo, & Smith, 1982) have found that children are likely to adopt the religious perspectives of their parents. In their review of the literature, Batson and Ventis (1982) concluded "that what may seem to be a freely chosen and highly personal religious stance is in large measure a product of social influence" (p. 27). Even more to the point, they asserted that "you are free to choose only the religious stance that your particular social background dictates" (p. 27). This is particularly the case for the child for whom religious beliefs are presented within the authority of the family and the community setting of organized religious affiliation. Religious affiliation is a primary influence in the development and maintenance of religious beliefs and practices. Beliefs almost attain the quality of fact through the consensus faith communities convey. The social influence of religious affiliation provides a basis for the child's faithfully held beliefs.

The child's internal God representations, as well as beliefs, are influenced by the reactions of those significant others to whom the child looks for validation. The child's observation of his or her parents kneeling in prayer to a transcendent God provides not only modeling of religious practices but, more importantly, it validates the child's personal experience of God. The practice of religious observances and rituals within a community of adults and peers supplies meanigful social support for the child's God representations and nascent faith convictions. Society also encourages religiousness through the acceptance of representational, ritual, and belief dimensions. God representations are a class of transitional phenomena that are embraced and well integrated into the fabric of many cultures. This cultural sanction encourages people throughout their life spans to express their religious beliefs and sentiments within the transitional realm of experience.

Religious institutions help to make sense of personal events and developments through particular practices and rituals. Bar/Bat mitzvah, confirmation, marriage, christening, and services for the ill and the dead are powerful rituals that provide an orientation to these significant moments of transition. These rituals initiate children into a faith community in which personal representations, communal images, and shared beliefs coalesce within an environment of social support. In the process, a transcendent orientation is ascribed to specific events and developmental transitions. For example, rituals for the dead have an implicit eschatology that addresses the child's need to make sense of living and dying, and they provide a ritual vehicle for mourning and working through of a specific event. Bar/Bat mitzvah, both symbolically and within the context of the religious support community, demarks an important transition in identity and responsibility. The continuity that religion provides may serve in assisting the individual in navigating the events and the developmental transitions in life. This may be particularly the case in the transitions from childhood to adolescence and adolescence to adulthood.

Religious affiliation has also been posited to play a significant role in the encouragement of psychosocial functioning and in the proscription of certain attitudes and behaviors. Erikson (1962/1958) wrote that religions "formulate obligations and privileges, restraints and freedoms, in such a way that man can submit to law and order with a minimum of doubt and with little loss of face" (p. 254). Clearly, religions present, implicitly and explicitly, models and codes for ethical behavior. Participation in religious faith communities has been shown to correlate positively with inhibition of premarital sexual behavior, nonusage or moderate usage of alcohol, decreased use of the drugs, and prohibitions against suicide (for a recent review of the literature, see Payne et al., 1991). For example, studies of adolescents suggest that, through the development of close ties within the church community, youth are discouraged through social control from using alcohol (Benson, Wood, Johnson, Elkin, & Mills, 1983; Cochran, Beeghley, & Beck, 1988; Linden, 1977). These studies suggest that social influence, in consort with the attributional role of beliefs, plays a significant role in mediating alcohol use and other behaviors.

Research on the development of prosocial behaviors, such as helping others, however, has yielded only tentative observations. Batson and Ventis (1982) conclude that religious affiliation in itself does not predict prosocial attitudes and behaviors. Rather, specific religious orientations (i.e., extrinsic-means, intrinsic-ends, and quest) are differentially related to measures of prosocial behavior. Although a comprehensive review is beyond the scope of this chapter, an inspection of the literature indicates that *how* a person is religious is more relevant than to what extent a person affiliates with religion (for a comprehensive review, see Wulff, 1991).

Religious affiliation may be based on an internalized, personally meaningful construction of faith, or on the holding of beliefs out of social convention, or on extrinsic motivations. Research that takes these differences into account suggests that intrinsic religious affiliation is associated with positive mental health variables. In families whose religiosity is intrinsically derived, religion more likely serves as a positive factor in child development. The question then is not *if* religion contributes to the mental health of children, but rather *how* affiliation and belief is constructed within the family.

Recent research has suggested that affiliation in religion, specifically intrinsically derived religious participation, contributes to mental health (Bergin, 1983; Payne et al., 1991). In a comprehensive study of religious lifestyles and mental health, Bergin, Stinchfield, Gaskin, Masters, and Sullivan (1988) found that continuous religious development was associated with better functioning. They concluded: "for those individuals whose religion was positively integrated into their family life and their own emerging lifestyles, it seemed to provide a source of stability that in turn was related to better adjustment" (p. 96). Longitudinal studies of Mormon college students indicated that religion plays a beneficial role in reinforcing positive aspects of family life and contributes to healthy adjustment (Bergin et al., 1990).

Religious affiliation has been found to correlate with positive marital and family factors. Personal well-being and marital satisfaction were reported to be positively related to religious attitudes and beliefs (Payne et al., 1991). This may suggest one particular feature of religion that contributes to the healthy development of the child as the research previously cited indicated. Further, it was reported that, during the child-raising years, religious families perceived themselves as having lower stress than nonreligious families (Olson et al., 1983). It is assumed that religion's contribution to harmonious relations between parents, as well as reduced stress, is beneficial to the child. Strayhorn, Weidman, and Larson (1990), in a study of low-income predominantly black families, found that "more religious parents reported more favorable parenting practices, lower self-reported hostility, and greater social support from friends" (p. 41). It may be posited, therefore, that religion, particularly if intrinsically held, may serve a beneficial role in the promotion of mental health of children and adolescents.

Religious affiliation contributes to the formation and maintenance of religious representations and beliefs. It has been shown to be a factor of social influence that shapes a child's behaviors and attitudes. Participation in a religious institution may provide a system of attributions and support that contributes to the enhancement of psychosocial functioning.

A Caveat: Religion as a Counterforce to Mental Health

Our discussion, to this point, has concerned the potentially beneficial contributions of religion to the mental health of children. It has been shown that religious representations, beliefs, attributions, and affiliations offer powerful agents in the child's developing sense of self and others, norms of behavior, and coping resources. Such a potent force as religion, which leaves its indelible mark on the foundation of a child's sense of self and the world, holds the potential to serve a damaging role as well as the affirming one that has been presented in this chapter. Vergote (1988) reminds us that "religion is no more immune to decadence than other forms of life" (p. 29).

God representations derived in part from critical, sadistic parental imagos may serve not to salve, but rather to inflict more injury on the child's abused self. Beliefs that are culled to disparage the nature of humaneness, or that offer no tolerance for the vicissitudes of childhood existence, distort and condemn the child to self-doubt and self-recrimination. These negative features, if given credence by a religious body and enforced through social influence, hold the potential to act as a counter-force to mental health. Extrinsic orientations to religious affiliation and practice have been shown to correlate with variables that are contrary to factors related to mental health (Batson & Ventis, 1982). It appears, in keeping with the conclusions of others (Payne et al., 1991; Batson & Ventis, 1982; Vergote, 1988), that some ways of being religious are healthier than others. In light of its potential for both positive and negative influence, religion is considered an important subject for continued investigation.

Conclusion

The religiousness of a child may be viewed as a complex, multidimensional experience that includes religious representations, beliefs, attributions, affiliations, and practices. Representations are artifacts of dynamic intrapsychic processes in which parental imagos, mythic characters transmitted within religious texts and oral traditions, and fantasies form a personal sense of the sacred and relationship with God. Beliefs and attributions organize the young person's understanding of events and relationships within both the interpersonal and physical world. Affiliations and practices support the child's nascent religiousness and expand religious experience from the exclusively private, familial setting to the public context of the faith community. These interrelated features contribute to a child's sense of self and others and to a code of prescribed and proscribed behaviors. Further, attributions and systems of social support may promote coping and adaptation to the developmental transitions and life challenges that children face.

Religion is an integral experience in the lives of the majority of children. The results of empirical research studies suggest that how one is religious, rather than simply whether one is religious, may have important consequences for coping with life's fortunes and misfortunes. Although further research and scholarship is required before a definitive assessment of religion's specific impact on mental health can be provided, it may be concluded that religion is an influential force in the lives of children.

References

Allport, G.W. (1961). *The individual and his religion.* New York: Macmillan. (Original work published 1950.)

Balk, D. (1983). How teenagers cope with sibling death: Some implications for school counselors. *School Counselor, 31,* 150–158.

Batson, C.D., & Ventis, W.L. (1982). *The religious experience.* New York: Oxford University Press.

Benson, P.L., Wood, P.K., Johnson, A.L., Elkin, C.H., & Mills, J.E. (1983). *Report on 1983 Minnesota Survey on Drug Use and Drug-related Activities.* Minneapolis: Search Institute.

Berger, P.L. (1963). *Invitation to sociology: A humanistic perspective.* Garden City, NY: Anchor Books.

Bergin, A.E. (1983). Religiosity and mental health: A critical re-evaluation and meta-analysis. *Professional Psychology: Research and Practice, 14,* 170–184.

Bergin, A.E., Stinchfield, R.D., Gaskin, T.A., Masters, K.S., & Sullivan, C.E. (1988). Religious life-styles and mental health: An exploratory study. *Journal of Counseling Psychology, 35,* 91–98.

Bergin, A.E., Masters, K.S., Stinchfield, R.D., Gaskin, T.A., Sullivan, C.E., Reynolds, E.M., & Greaves, D.W. (1990). Religious life-styles and mental health. In L.B. Brown & H.N. Malony (Eds.), *Religion, personality, and mental health.* New York: Springer.

Cardwell, J.D. (1971). *Social psychology: A symbolic interaction perspective.* Philadelphia: F.A. Davis Company.

Clinebell, H.J. (1970). The local church's contributions to positive mental health. In H.J. Clinebell (Ed.), *Community mental health: The role of church and temple* (pp. 46–56). Nashville, TN: Abingdon Press.

Cochran, J.K., Beeghley, L., & Bock, E.W. (1988). Religiosity and alcohol behavior: An exploration of reference group theory. *Sociological Forum, 3,* 256–276.

Coles, R. (1990). *The spiritual life of children.* Boston: Houghton Mifflin.

Erikson, E.H. (1962). *Young man Luther.* New York: W.W. Norton. (Original work published 1958).

Fowler, J.W. (1981). *Stages of faith: The psychology of human development and the quest for meaning.* San Francisco: Harper & Row.

Fowler, J.W., & Keen, S. (1978). *Life maps: Conversations on the journey of faith.* Waco, TX: Word Books.

Gallup, G.H. (1978). *Gallup Youth Survey, 1978.* Princeton, NJ: Gallup Associates.

Gallup, G., Jr., & Castelli, J. (1989). *The people's religion.* New York: Macmillan.

Hathaway, W.I., & Pargament, K.I. (1991). The religious dimension of coping: Implications for prevention and promotion. In K.I. Pargament, K.I. Maton, & R.E. Hess (Eds.), *Religion and prevention in mental health: Conceptual and empirical foundations* (pp. 65–92). New York: Haworth Press.

Hipol, C. (1978). Anxiety and coping mechanisms of terminally ill children and their mothers. *Philippine Journal of Psychology, 11,* 40–54.

Hoge, D.R., Petrillo, G.H., & Smith, E.I. (1982). Transmission of religious and social values from parents to teenage children. *Journal of Marriage and the Family, 44,* 569–580.

Hunsberger, B., & Brown, L.B. (1984). Religious socialization, apostasy, and the impact of family background. *Journal for the Scientific Study of Religion, 23,* 239–251.

James, W. (1985). *The principles of psychology.* New York: Holt, Rinehart & Winston. (Original work published 1902).

Jenkins, R.I., & Pargament, K.I. (1988). Cognitive appraisals in cancer patients. *Social Science in Medicine, 26,* 625–633.

Joint Commission on Mental Health and Children. (1973). *Mental health from infancy through adolescence. Reports of Task Forces I, II, III and the Committees on Education and Religion by the Joint Commission on Mental Health and Children.* New York: Harper & Row.

Jones, J.W. (1991). *Contemporary psychoanalysis and religion.* New Haven, CT: Yale University Press.

Lazarus, R., & Folkman, S. (1984). *Stress, appraisal, and coping.* New York: Springer.

Linden, R. (1977). Religiosity and drug use: A test of social control theory. *Canadian Journal of Criminology and Corrections, 19,* 346–355.

Maton, K.I., & Pargament, K.I. (1987). The roles of religion in prevention and promotion. *Prevention in Human Services, 5,* 161–205.

McDargh, J. (1983). *Psychoanalytic Object Relations Theory and the study of religion.* New York: University Press of America.

Meichenbaum, D., & Jaremko, M.E. (1983). *Stress reduction and prevention.* New York: Plenum.

Meissner, W.W. (1978). Psychoanalytic aspects of religious experience. *Annual of Psychoanalysis, 6,* 103–142.

Meissner, W.W. (1984). *Psychoanalysis and religion.* New Haven, CT: Yale Univeristy Press.

Meissner, W.W. (1987). *Life and faith: Psychological perspectives on religious experience.* Washington, DC: Georgetown University Press.

Niebuhr, H.R. (1941). *The meaning of revelation.* New York: Macmillan.

Olson, D.H., McCubbin, H.I.H., Barnes, H., Larsen, A., Muxen, M., & Wilson, M. (1983). *Families: What makes them work.* Beverly Hills: Sage.

Orr, D.P., Hoffmans, M.A., & Bennetts, G. (1984). Adolescents with cancer report their psychosocial needs. *Journal of Psychosocial Oncology, 2,* 47–59.

Parens, H. (1970). Inner sustainment: Metapsychological considerations. *Psychoanalytic Quarterly, 39,* 223–239.

Pargament, K.I. (1980). The interface among religion, religious support systems, and mental health. In D.E. Biegel & A.J. Naparstek (Eds.), *Community support systems and mental health* (pp. 161–174). New York: Springer.

Pargament, K.I. (1988). God help me. Towards a theoretical framework of coping for the psychology of religion. *Psychologists Interested in Religious Issues Newletter, 13,* 1–6.

Pargament, K.I., Maton, K.I., & Hess, R.E. (Eds.). (1991). *Religion and prevention in mental health: Conceptual and empirical foundations.* New York: Haworth Press.

Park, C., & Cohen, L.H. (in press). Religious beliefs and practices and the coping process. In B. Carpenter (Ed.), *Personal coping: Theory, research, and application.* New York: Praeger.

Payne, I.R., Bergin, A.E., Bielema, K.A., & Jenkins, P.H. (1991). Review of religion and mental health: Prevention and the enhancement of psychosocial functioning. In K.I. Pargament, K.I. Maton, & R.E. Hess (Eds.), *Religion and prevention in mental health: Conceptual and empirical foundations* (pp. 11–40). New York: Haworth Press.

Peteet, J.R. (1985). Religious issues presented by cancer patients seen in psychiatric consultation. *Journal of Psychosocial Oncology, 3,* 53–66.

Potvin, R.H. (1977). Adolescent God images. *Review of Religious Research, 19,* 43–53.

Pruyser, P.W. (1983). *The play of the imagination: Toward a psychoanalysis of culture.* New York: International Universities Press.

Pruyser, P.W. (1985). Forms and function of imagination in religion. *Bulletin of the Menninger Clinic, 49,* 353–370.

Rizzuto, A-M. (1974). Object relation and the formation of the image of God. *British Journal of Medical Psychology, 47,* 83–99.

Rizzuto, A-M. (1976). Freud, God, the Devil and the theory of object representation. *International Review of Psycho-Analysis, 31,* 165.

Rizzuto, A.-M. (1979). *The birth of the living God.* Chicago: University of Chicago Press.

Rizzuto, A.-M. (1986). *Religious experience and psychoanalysis.* Unpublished paper presented at William James Lecture, The Divinity School, Harvard University, Cambridge, Massachusetts.

Rizzuto, A.-M. (1989, June). Interview with Edward P. Shafranske, ed. *APA Division, 36 Newsletter,* pp. 1, 4.

Roberts, K.A. (1991). A sociological overview: Mental health implications of religio-cultural megatrends in the United States. In K.I. Pargament, K.I. Maton, & R.E. Hess (Eds.), *Religion and prevention in mental health: Conceptual and empirical foundations* (pp. 113–135). New York: Haworth Press.

Shafranske, E.P. (1992). God representation as the transformational object. In M. Finn & J. Gartner (Eds.), *Religion and Object Relations Theory.* New York: Praeger.

Smith, W.C. (1979). *Faith and belief.* Princeton, NJ: Princeton University Press.

Spero, M.H. (1990). Parallel dimensions of experience in psychoanalytic psychotherapy of the religious patient. *Psychotherapy, 27,* 53–71.

Spilka, B., Shaver, P., & Kirkpatrick, L. (1985). A general attribution theory for the psychology of religion. *Journal for the Scientific Study of Religion, 24,* 1–20.

Spilka, B., Zwartjes, W.J., Zwartjes, G.M., Heidman, D., & Cilli, K.A. (1987). *The role of religion in coping with cancer.* Unpublished manuscript, Unviersity of Denver.

Strayhorn, J.M., Weidman, C.S., & Larson, D. (1990). A measure of religiousness, and its relation to parent and child mental health variables. *Journal of Community Psychology, 18,* 34–43.

Tebbi, C., Mallon, J., Richards, M., & Bigler, L. (1987). Religiosity and locus of control of adolescent cancer patients. *Psychological Reports, 61,* 683–696.

Vergote. A. (1988). *Guilt and desire.* Translated by M.H. Wood. New Haven, CT: Yale University Press.

Winnicott, D.W. (1971). *Playing and reality.* New York: Basic Books.

Wulff, D.M. (1991). *Psychology of religion: Classic and contemporary views.* New York: John Wiley & Sons.

13

Religion and Mental Health in Later Life

Harold G. Koenig

Surveys by the Gallup organization (Princeton Religion Research Center, 1982) and other investigators (Koenig, Moberg, & Kvale, 1988) report a wide prevalence of religious beliefs and activities among Americans, particularly the elderly. In this country, involvement in churches or synagogues is the most common form of voluntary group activity for older adults. In fact, more elders are members of religious organizations than all other voluntary social groups combined (Payne, 1972; Cutler, 1976). Half of all persons age 65 or over attend church at least once weekly. There is some evidence to suggest that the amount of social support provided by church members to many elders may even rival that provided by family. One study found that over half of older adults reported 80 percent or more of their closest friends were from their church congregation (Koenig, Moberg, & Kvale, 1988). While church attendance and other group religious activity has been shown to decline after the age of 70 (due to physical illness and disability), private religious behaviors such as prayer increase in frequency and have greater meaning. Belief in God, prayer, and reading of religious literature appear to be very common in this age group (Koenig, Smiley, & Gonzales, 1988).

Of particular interest here is that religious beliefs and behaviors are utilized by a significant proportion of elders to *cope* with environmental, interpersonal, and physical health stresses. Several studies have reported that, when elderly persons are asked in an open-ended question how they deal with ill health or what factor keeps them afloat during difficult life circumstances, between 20 percent and 30 percent spontaneously and without prompting offer a religious response (Rosen, 1982; Koenig, George, & Siegler, 1988). When asked a direct question about the helpfulness of religion in coping, almost 90 percent of adults age 60 or over answer affirmatively (Americana Healthcare Corporation, 1980–1981).

Definition of Religion

In beginning the discussion of religion and mental health in later life, my first task is to define "religion" as it is used in this chapter. In formulating research questions and then designing studies to answer them, the investigator must carefully delineate the specific dependent and independent variables under consideration. *Religion* is a difficult word to define since its meaning may vary by the context of use. For this reason and a desire to be all-inclusive, religion is typically defined in vague terms that are difficult to operationalize, such as "the state of being ultimately concerned or being grasped by an ultimate concern" (Tillich, 1957) or as "the quality of one's relation to that which he conceives to be ultimate reality" (Maves, 1960). While these definitions suffice for theoretical purposes, they are inadequate for the intentions of research. In contrast, the Concise Oxford Dictionary provides a specific definition of religion that is relevant to older Americans and is suitably narrow for research purposes: "the human recognition of superhuman controlling power and especially of a personal God entitled to obedience, and the effect of such recognition on conduct and mental attitude."

While this definition may be criticized as too narrow or subservient to a particular religious tradition (i.e., Judeo-Christian), there is a rationale behind this bias. Given the research data thus far collected and the type of population under study, this is practically the only definition possible. First, most of the systematically collected population data on this subject comes from English-speaking countries whose populace is primarily Judeo-Christian. Second, this is the religious background of over 95 percent of older adults in the United States, the country in which most of the research has been conducted.

Hence, unless otherwise specified, I will restrict my definition of religion to beliefs and behaviors based in the Judeo-Christian tradition. Because of this restriction, my conclusions on the relationship between religion and mental health in this chapter can only be generalized to religious beliefs and behaviors in that tradition.

Mental Health and Aging in the Judeo-Christian Tradition

Returning now to the relationship between Judeo-Christian religion and mental health in later life, let us ask what we know and where this information comes from? Freud, Albert Ellis, and other pioneers in the fields of psychiatry and psychology held the view that religion was equivalent to neurosis and involved distorted thinking (Freud, 1927; Ellis, 1980). Due to a repression of natural drives and perfectionistic thinking, the devoutly religious person was felt to be at high risk for emotional disturbance. The emotionally healthy person is portrayed as flexible, open, tolerant, and changing—features uncharacteristic of the religious person who is pictured as inflexible, closed, intolerant, and unchanging. Freud (at the age of 70) wrote in *Future of an Illusion* that, as the human being continued to evolve, religious beliefs would be replaced by "the rational operation of the intellect" (Freud, 1927).

Recent years have seen great advances in technology and education, yet there is no evidence that interest or involvement in religion has declined significantly in the past fifty years (Princeton Religion Research Center, 1985). A recent study presented at the American Academy of Religion by sociologists Wade Clark Roof and David Roozen found that, as the "baby-boomers" have grown older, many are returning to religion in order to train their children and to answer questions about meaning for themselves. America is not the only country in which such trend-reversals may be occurring. One of Mikhail Gorbachev's first political moves in initiating *Glasnost* (opening) and *Peristroika* (restructuring) was to allow Russian people religious expression.

Religion and Gerontology: Research and Education

Despite the prevalence of belief and practice, the topic of religion today receives very little attention in gerontology research and higher education. The great struggle by those in the fields of science and medicine to free themselves from control by religious institutions during the third through eighteenth centuries has provided much impetus to maintain the separation of religion and science. In today's world, where modern science and technology have clearly established themselves, there should be less reluctance to examine religion carefully as a resource for older adults. Nevertheless, research focusing specifically on the role of religious attitudes and behaviors in the lives of older adults is decidingly rare in comparison to the attention paid to other social forces. An exception has been the American Society on Aging (ASA), which since 1987 has set aside a full day during its annual meeting to address issues related to religion and aging. This action represents a major advance toward the recognition by professionals of the vital role of religion in the social, psychological, and physical health of older Americans. No other national gerontological organization has been as farsighted as the ASA in this regard.

Religion and Mental Health in Later Life

Evidence is accumulating to support the view that devout and mature commitment to religious beliefs and activities based in the Judeo-Christian tradition is related to greater well-being and lower levels of depression and anxiety (Koenig, 1990). Religion is most appropriately operationalized in terms of (1) organizational religious activity (church attendance, other group religious behaviors), (2) nonorganizational religious activity (prayer, scripture reading, religious TV or radio), (3) religious ritual (sacraments, dietary laws, dress), and (4) religious belief, intrinsic religiosity, and strength of religious commitment. Religious coping, as noted earlier, is the use of any or all of these forms of religious expression to help deal with psychological stress. A number of studies have examined the relationship between these religious constructs and mental health in later life.

Church attendance has been consistently related to personal adjustment (Moberg, 1953; Lloyd, 1955; Scott, 1955; Argyle & Beit-Hallami, 1975; Blazer & Palmore, 1976), happiness or life satisfaction (O'Reilly, 1957; Shanas, 1962; Edwards & Klemmack, 1973; Guy, 1982; Hunsberger, 1985), well-being (Koenig, Kvale, & Ferrel, 1988), lower suicide rates (Argyle & Beit-Hallami, 1975; Nelson, 1977), fewer depressive symptoms (Brown & Prudo, 1981; Goldberg, van Natta, & Comstock, 1985; Idler, 1987), lower death anxiety (Swenson, 1961; Feifel & Nagy, 1981; Koenig, 1988), and better adjustment to bereavement (Yates, Chalmber, St. James,

Follansbee, & McKegney, 1981; Berardo, 1970) both in community-dwelling and institutionalized elderly.

Involvement in the religious community provides companionship and friends of similar age and interest, a supportive environment to buffer stressful life changes, an atmosphere of acceptance, hope, and forgiveness, a source of practical assistance when needed, and a common world view and philosophy of life. A valid concern with these studies, however, is that church attendance may be highly confounded by health status. In other words, those elderly who attend church frequently may be a select group of older people who possess particularly good physical health that enables them to get out of the house and go to church. Because there is a very strong relationship between good physical health and psychological well-being, church attendance may relate to well-being only because of its relationship with physical health (Levin & Markides, 1986). Church attendance may simply serve as a marker of physical health, and *by itself* may have little to do with mental health. Nevertheless, even when physical health status has been controlled in most studies, the relationship between church attendance and well-being has tended to persist (Idler, 1987; Koenig, Kvale, & Ferrel, 1988). Furthermore, involvement in church-related activities is more likely to be associated with mental health and well-being than participation in social activity without a religious orientation (Pihlblad & Adams, 1972; Edwards & Klemmack, 1973; Cutler, 1976).

Nonorganizational religious activities such as prayer and Bible reading have also been related to life satisfaction and well-being in later life, though not as strongly as religious community activity. Prayer was ranked seventh in effectiveness among a field of 25 possible coping behaviors mediating between life-events and depression in a sample of 176 patients attending a general practice clinic (Parker & Brown, 1982). Stark (1968) showed that a private devotionalism (frequency and importance of prayer) increased greatly with age, particularly among conservative Protestants. In a study of 836 older adults in the mid-western United States, non-organizational religious activity (prayer, Bible reading, and religious TV/radio) was significantly related to well-being (Koenig, Kvale, & Ferrel, 1988).

Markides Levin, and Ray (1987), who conducted an eight-year longitudinal study of religion, aging, and life satisfaction among older Mexican Americans and Anglos in Texas, found that the positive correlation between prayer and life satisfaction declined over time, suggesting an increase in prayer among those elders in poorer physical or psychological health. The increase in frequency and salience of private prayer among the old and sick elderly is consistent with our findings in mid-America (Koenig et al., 1988) and with Biblical teachings in this regard: "Is anyone among you suffering? Let him pray" (James 5:13, New American Standard). Thus, turning to religion and prayer in times of distress (religious coping) may partly neutralize whatever positive cross-section correlation exists between this activity and mental health. This point will be developed further later in the chapter.

Belief, attitude, and intrinsic commitment largely reflect cognitive rather than behavioral aspects of religious expression. One significant advantage is that they are less confounded by health than are activities such as church attendance. The results are similar, however, in that the studies among older persons generally indicate a positive relationship between religious belief and personal adjustment (Moberg,

1953, 1958; Hunsberger, 1985; Gass, 1987). Blazer and Palmore (1976), in a report from the eighteen-year First Duke Longitudinal Study of Aging, found religious attitudes positively related to adjustment. Furthermore, the strength of the relationship increased as people aged. Among the elderly, intrinsic religiosity is inversely related to anger and hostility (Acklin, Brown, & Mauger, 1983) and positively related to an internal locus of control. A positive correlation also exists in elderly samples between intrinsic religiosity and the maintenance of an ideal self-concept (Kivett, 1979), lower levels of prejudice and higher levels of education (Allport & Ross, 1967; Strickland & Shaffer, 1971), and greater well-being (Koenig, Kvale, & Ferrel, 1988).

Religious coping, typically operationalized as a global measure of the use of religious activities or beliefs in dealing with stress, has also been linked to better adjustment among the elderly (Rosen, 1982; Manfredi & Pickett, 1987; Conway, 1985; Koenig, Siegler, & George, 1989). In the only study that has thus far examined the relationship between religious coping and *personality* in later life, no evidence was found to support earlier findings among college students and young adults that suggested a pathological influence of religion on personality formation (Koenig, Siegler, Meador, & George, 1990). Instead, religious copers scored lower on aggression and hostile traits, and tended to be more responsible and conscientious. Among women in the longitudinal portion of the study, there was less tension and greater relaxation, and more tranquillity and composure *with aging* among religious copers than with nonreligious copers.

Factors Affecting the Religion-Mental Health Relationship in the Elderly

Despite the consensus that religious attitudes and behaviors are related to better mental health, the correlations between religious and mental health variables in population studies are typically much lower than one would expect, given the widespread testimonials by older adults themselves of the vital role that religion plays in enabling them to cope (Koenig, Smiley, & Gonzales, 1988). There are four major factors affecting the relationship between religion and mental health among the elderly. Let us examine each of these.

Changing Nature of Religious Feelings and Emotional State

Neither emotional well-being nor religious yearnings are static phenomena. Instead, they are constantly changing and fluctuating, often interacting, in a dynamic fashion. Many older people may "turn to" religion at a time of physical or mental distress, as noted earlier. Even if religion were quite effective in alleviating worry or depression, it might actually appear to be "associated" with mental distress in studies that address this question at a single point in time (cross-sectional research). A similar situation is encountered when one compares the well-being of individuals taking antidepressant medication with the well-being of individuals not requiring such therapy. Indeed, those taking antidepressants would probably have more depressive symptoms than those who are mentally healthy and not taking antidepressants. Would we thus conclude that antidepressants cause unhappiness or depression? Of course not. The situation may be similar for religion.

The "low" correlations between religious behaviors and mental health typically reported in cross-sectional epidemiological studies, then, may simply represent a "net effect" of (a) religion's helpfulness in the long run in buffering against emotional distress and (b) the short-term increased emotional distress that prompts some individuals to turn to religion for help, but in whom it has not yet had time to be effective. Unfortunately, few well-designed longitudinal studies have examined the impact of religion on mental health over time, while controlling for this effect.

Measurement of Religious Attitudes and Behaviors

A second reason for the low correlations observed is the variability introduced by inaccurate measurement of religious attitudes and behaviors. As we have seen, even defining what attitudes and behaviors can be considered "religious" is a challenging task. Researchers typically measure religion by denomination or church attendance.

Categorization of individuals by religious denomination is totally inadequate, since religious affiliation and religious experience or commitment may vary tremendously. Niebuhr (1929) divided religious behavior into three types: (1) Primary religious behavior, which is a creative personal experience of considerable intensity and awareness during which the individual experiences ecstasy, vision, and insight. This is the intense type of religious experience, termed "nuclear" by Fichter (1954), that often occurs at and following conversion. (2) Secondary or "modal" (Fichter, 1954) religious behavior occurs among people who at one time had an intense religious experience, but whose behavior has dropped into a level of routine or habit. (3) Tertiary or "dormant" (Fichter, 1954) religious behavior is imitative or conventional religious behavior, often simply involving compliance with social influence, such as family tradition or class patterns. In religious denominations that have been in existence for several generations, about 50 percent of people claiming affiliation are "dormant," 40 percent are "modal," and 10 percent are "nuclear." Consequently, the majority of inactive members tend to dilute the effect of a committed religious faith—as manifested at a primary or nuclear level—on mental health.

As in the case of membership or denominational affiliation, church attendance is a poor indicator of "religiosity." Many people attend church for reasons other than religious ones. For instance, some go to avoid social isolation, to please their parents or others, or to mark themselves as a member of a "superior" group. Furthermore, as noted previously, church attendance is strongly influenced by health and the physical ability of getting to church. Given the strong relationship between physical health and well-being, any positive correlation between church attendance and well-being must be suspect, unless health status is controlled for. This does not mean that church attendance or involvement in group religious activity is not an important factor in maintaining mental health in later life. It simply means that, for research purposes, church attendance is affected by many factors other than religiosity.

Religious commitment or strength of adherence to an internal belief system may be a better measure of religiosity or religiousness. Scales available for this purpose typically address religiosity based in the Judeo-Christian tradition and measure religious cognitions, attitudes, and beliefs (Hoge, 1972). These factors are not as easily influenced by physical health status. In general, any comprehensive study that seeks to measure religiosity in later life should (ideally) seek to capture all important dimensions. These include organizational as well as nonorganizational religious activity, religious ritual, and the cognitive aspects of religion such as strength of belief, commitment, or intrinsic religiosity. Because our research at Duke University focuses on the interaction between religion and mental health, we have sought to assess the extent to which individuals rely on these different dimensions of religious behavior in order to cope with stress.

Once the investigator has decided on which dimensions of religion to measure, problems may be encountered during the interview process itself. Some elderly people are unwilling or unable to express their religiosity in terms that are easily abstractable for statistical analysis. Religion is a sensitive and very private part of life, and some people are reluctant to divulge valid information on this topic to a stranger.

Likewise, the accurate measurement of mental health constructs such as well-being, life satisfaction, coping, and "adjustment" is not an easy task, particularly when employing cross-sectional research methods. Many people deny feelings of life dissatisfaction, unhappiness, or depression. Additionally, people from different cultures may express themselves more dramatically than those from other cultures (e.g., Jewish vs. Irish). Moods may also fluctuate from day to day, from moment to moment. Therefore, inaccurate measurement of both religion and mental health adds considerable variability to correlations and weakens their strength.

Genetic, Developmental, and Socioeconomic Considerations

It is well known that depression and anxiety are more common among the lower classes, the poor, and the uneducated (Hollingshead & Redlich, 1958; Catalano & Dooley, 1977; Frerichs, Aneshensel, & Clark, 1981). The reasons for this phenomenon are probably related to genetic loading and developmental factors (i.e., "downward drift"), as well as fewer social, economic, and health resources to help buffer stresses when they occur. Because religion is also more prevalent in the lower classes, it may appear (like poor socioeconomic status) to be associated with mental distress. For this reason, large research studies that contain a mixture of subjects from different classes, economic, and educational levels should carefully measure and control for socioeconomic factors and prior family or personal psychiatric illness.

Religion, if an effective buffer against stress in later life, should increase the well-being of older people, regardless of mental health status. For instance, a maladjusted individual with poor genetic loading and/or inadequate nurturing in early life may, with a solid, mature religious faith, have higher well-being than if he or she did not have such faith. Likewise, even a well-adjusted and generally contented individual may weather difficult times and experience greater fulfillment with a strong religious faith than without one. However, the more educated, wealthy, and socially gifted person may have less need for religion than the troubled individual who has fewer alternative resources. Hence, well-adjusted individuals, who "naturally" possess high well-being for genetic or developmental reasons, may have lower measured religiosity than maladjusted or genetically and environmentally disabled people with lower levels of well-being. The latter individuals may be happier with religion than without it, but not as happy as the well-adjusted individual who has no need for religion. Consequently, the association between well-being and religiosity will appear weak.

Neurotic Expression of Religion

Not all religious belief systems and practices are beneficial to mental health. Religion may be expressed or used either maturely or neurotically (Runions, 1974; Pruyser, 1977). Deciding on which beliefs are neurotic, however, is a tricky issue heavily influenced by personal bias. But basic principles of mental health can help some in making this distinction. First, there is the mature, integrated religious faith that leads to greater tolerance, greater capacity to deal with stress, and greater emotional stability.

On the other hand, in its immature or neurotic expression, religion may be employed as a primitive psychological defense. Religion may be used to deny or carefully conceal aggression and anger. It may be used to regressively meet dependency needs, such as in the excessive dependency on a designated authority or intolerance of any dissenter. Such a neurotic use of religion leads to inflexibility, insensitivity to the needs of or background of the individual, and a focus on rules, rather than love, compassion, and understanding. This form of religion may be associated with, or lead to, mental disturbance at any age.

Another expression of religion is in psychosis. Because of its pervasiveness in human culture and world view, religion may become intertwined in the presenting symptoms of serious mental illness in later life. An example is the older adult with manic-depressive illness or late-onset schizophrenia who expresses religious delusions, such as voices from God or the Devil commanding them to discontinue medications, hurt themselves, or hurt others. Hence, given the many complex, interacting factors noted above, it is not surprising that correlations between religious behaviors or cognitions and mental health are so meager. In fact, it is remarkable that they are generally positive and as strong as they have been.

Studies of Religious Coping and Depression

Recent studies at Duke University with hospitalized medically ill patients have attempted to examine both the cross-sectional and longitudinal relationship between mental health and religion among older and younger men, while controlling for some of the factors discussed above. As a result, we have found that religious coping behaviors (such as church attendance, prayer, reading of various religious literature, and attitudes of trust or faith in God) appear to buffer against the stresses of hospitalization and medical illness (Koenig et al., 1990). Both depressive symptoms and major depressive disorder were significantly less common among religious copers, who were also less likely to become depressed over time. As one would predict, this buffering effect of religious coping is particularly strong among men who are severely ill or disabled. While these studies were conducted in North Carolina, an area traditionally known as part of the "Bible Belt" of the South, similar results have been reported from several other American locations (Conway, 1985; Idler, 1987; Koenig, Kvale, & Ferrel, 1988; Kroll & Sheehan, 1989; O'Brien, 1981, 1982; Pressman, Lyons, Larson, & Strain, 1990; Swanson & Harter, 1971).

Ease of, and Need for, Research

Although some elderly do not talk about their religion, we have found that most elderly are very willing to talk about this subject to sympathetic listeners; that is, people who do not condemn, criticize, or preach to them. In surveying over a thousand men at the Duke Veterans Administration medical center, many of whom were very ill and not really wanting to talk with anyone, virtually no one took offense at the questions we asked. In fact, many people were appreciative of the chance to talk about their beliefs. Listening to the beliefs and attitudes of older people who have acquired experience in successful (and some in not so successful) living is an enriching experience and contributes to the understanding and personal maturity of those doing the research.

Clinical Implications

Because of the prevalence of religious behaviors and cognitions in later life, professionals working with older adults should be aware of the importance and function of religion as a world view and coping strategy. More often than not, religious beliefs and activities successfully act to buffer against the stress of adverse life changes that elders face. Among these are sudden or chronic medical illness, bereavement or illness of loved ones, anxieties surrounding death, loss of social roles, and declining social and financial resources. Consequently, clinicians might consider altering their approach in counseling or psychotherapy of religious elders to take advantage of this often hidden resource and personality strength. This is particularly true for patients with reactive or situational depression or anxiety that occurs in the setting of physical illness. Propst (1987) has integrated religious principles into a cognitive and behavioral therapy framework that may be particularly helpful for therapists wishing to pursue this approach. Nurses, physicians, and mental health professionals should be prepared to address religious issues as they arise in their older patients, especially during times of severe medical illness or near death. Appropriate behaviors in this setting may include simple listening, support of the patient's beliefs, prayer, scripture reading, or referral to a religious professional (Koenig, Bearon, & Dayringer, 1989). All of these warrant further investigation.

References

Acklin, M.W., Brown, E.C., & Mauger, P.A. (1983). The role of religious values in coping with cancer. *Journal of Religion and Health, 22,* 322–333.

Allport, G.W., & Ross, J.M. (1967). Personal religious orientation and prejudice. *Journal of Personality and Social Psychology, 5,* 432–443.

Americana Healthcare Corporation (1980–1981). *Aging in America: Trials and triumphs.* Westport, CT: US-Research and Forecasts Survey Sampling Corporation.

Argyle, M., & Beit-Hallami, B. (1975). *The social psychology of religion.* Boston: Routledge and Kegan Paul.

Berardo, F.M. (1970). Survivorship and social isolation. *Family Coordinator, 19,* 11–25.

Blazer, D.G., & Palmore, E. (1976). Religion and aging in a longitudinal panel. *The Gerontologist, 16,* 82–85.

Brown, G.W., & Prudo, R. (1981). Psychiatric disorder in a rural and an urban population. *Psychological Medicine, 11,* 581–599.

Catalano, R., & Dooley, D. (1977). Economic predictors of depressed mood and stressful life events in a metropolitan community. *Journal of Health and Social Behavior, 18,* 292–307.

Conway, K. (1985). Coping with the stress of medical problems among black and white elderly. *International Journal of Aging and Human Development, 21,* 39–48.

Cutler, S.J. (1976). Membership in different types of voluntary associations and psychological well-being. *The Gerontologist, 16,* 335–339.

Edwards, J.N., & Klemmack, D.L. (1973). Correlates of life satisfaction: A reexamination. *Journal of Gerontology, 28,* 497–502.

Ellis, A. (1980). Psychotherapy and atheistic values: A response to A.E. Bergin's "Psychotherapy and religious values." *Journal of Consulting and Clinical Psychology, 48,* 642–645.

Feifel, H., & Nagy, V.T. (1981). Another look at fear of death. *Journal of Consulting and Clinical Psychology, 49,* 278–286.

Fichter, J.H. (1954). *Social relations in the urban parish.* Chicago: Univeristy of Chicago Press.

Frerichs, R.R., Aneshensel, C.S., & Clark, V.A. (1981). Prevalence of depression in Los Angeles County. *American Journal of Epidemiology, 113,* 691–699.

Freud, S. (1927). *The future of an illusion.* (London: The Hogarth Press, 1962 edition, J. Strachey, Ed.)

Gass, K.A. (1987). The health of conjugally bereaved older widows: The role of appraisal, coping, and resources. *Research in Nursing and Health, 10,* 39–47.

Goldberg, E.L., van Natta, P., & Comstock, G.W. (1985). Depressive symptoms, social networks and social support of elderly women. *American Journal of Epidemiology, 121,* 448–456.

Guy, R.F. (1982). Religion, physical disabilities and life satisfaction in older age cohorts. *International Journal of Aging and Human Development, 15,* 225–232.

Hoge, D.R. (1972). A validated intrinsic religious motivation scale. *Journal for the Scientific Study of Religion, 11,* 369–376.

Hollingshead, A., & Redlich, F. (1958). *Social class and mental illness: A community study.* New York: John Wiley.

Hunsberger, B. (1985). Religion, age, life satisfaction, and perceived sources of religiousness: A study of older persons. *Journal of Gerontology, 40,* 615–620.

Idler, E.L. (1987). Religious involvement and health of the elderly: Some hypotheses and an initial test. *Social Forces, 66,* 226–238.

Kivett, V.R. (1979). Religious motivation in middle age: Correlates and implications. *Journal of Gerontology, 34,* 106–115.

Koenig, H.G. (1988). Religion and death anxiety in later life. *Hospice Journal, 4*(1), 3–24.

Koenig, H.G. (1990). Research on religion and mental health in later life: A review and commentary. *Journal of Geriatric Psychiatry, 23,* 23–53.

Koenig, H.G., Bearon, L.B., & Dayringer, R. (1989). Physician perspectives on the role of religion in the physician-older patient relationship. *Journal of Family Practice, 28,* 441–448.

Koenig, H.G., George, L.K., & Siegler, I.C. (1988). The use of religion and other emotion-regulating coping strategies among older adults. *The Gerontologist, 28,* 303–310.

Koenig, H.G., Kvale, J.N., & Ferrel, C. (1988). Religion and well-being in later life. *The Gerontologist, 28,* 18–28.

Koenig, H.G., Cohen, H.J., Blazer, D.G., Piper, C., Shelp, F., Goli, V., & DiPasquale, R. (1992). Religious coping and depression in hospitalized medically ill men. *American Journal of Psychiatry,* in submission.

Koenig, H.G., Moberg, D.O., & Kvale, J.N. (1988). Religious activities and attitudes of older adults in a geriatric assessment clinic. *Journal of the American Geriatrics Society, 36,* 362–374.

Koenig, H.G., Siegler, I.C., & George, L.K. (1989). Religious and non-religious coping: Impact on adaptation in later life. *Journal of Religion and Aging, 5*(4), 73–94.

Koenig, H.G., Siegler, I.C., Meador, K.G., & George, L.K. (1990). Religious coping and personality in later life. *International Journal of Geriatric Psychiatry, 5,* 123–131.

Koenig, H.G., Smiley, M., & Gonzales, J.P. (1988). *Religion, health, and aging: A review and theoretical integration.* Westport, CT: Greenwood Press.

Kroll, J., & Sheehan, W. (1989). Religious beliefs and practices among 52 psychiatric inpatients in Minnesota. *American Journal of Psychiatry, 146,* 67–72.

Levin, J.S., & Markides, K.S. (1986). Religious attendance and subjective health. *Journal for the Scientific Study of Religion, 25,* 31–40.

Lloyd, R.G. (1955). Social and personal adjustment of retired persons. *Sociology and Social Research, 39,* 312–316.

Manfredi, C., & Pickett, M. (1987). Perceived stressful situations and coping strategies utilized by the elderly. *Journal of Community Health Nursing, 4,* 99–110.

Markides, K.S., Levin, J.S., & Ray, L.A. (1987). Religion, aging, and life satisfaction: An eight-year three-wave longitudinal study. *The Gerontologist, 27,* 660–665.

Maves, P.B. (1960). Aging, religion, and the church. In C. Tibbitts (Ed.), *Handbook of social gerontology* (p. 706). Chicago: University of Chicago Press.

Moberg, D.O. (1953). Church membership and personal adjustment in old age. *Journal of Gerontology, 8,* 207–211.

Moberg, D.O. (1958). Christian beliefs and personal adjustment in old age. *Journal of American Science Affiliates, 10,* 8–12.

Nelson, F.L. (1977). Religiosity and self-destructive crises in the institutionalized elderly. *Suicide and Life-Threatening Behavior, 7,* 67–73.

Niebuhr, H.R. (1929). *The social sources of denominationalism.* New York: Henry Holt and Company.

O'Brien, M.E. (1981). Effective social environment and hemodialysis adaptation—a panel analysis. *Journal of Health and Social Behavior, 21,* 360–370.

O'Brien, M.E. (1982). Religious faith and adjustment to long-term hemodialysis. *Journal of Religion and Health, 21,* 68–80.

O'Reilly, C.T. (1957). Religious practice and personal adjustments of older people. *Sociology and Social Research, 43,* 119–121.

Parker, G.B., & Brown, L.B. (1982). Coping behaviors that mediate between life events and depression. *Archives of General Psychiatry, 39,* 1386–1391.

Payne, B.P. (1972). Social background and role determinants of individual participation in organized voluntary action. *Voluntary Action Research.* Boston: D.C. Heath.

Pihlblad, C.T., & Adams, D.L. (1972). Widowhood, social participation and life satisfaction. *International Journal of Aging and Human Development, 3,* 323–330.

Pressman, P., Lyons, J.S., Larson, D.B., & Strain, J.J. (1990). Religious belief, depression, and ambulation status in elderly women with broken hips. *American Journal of Psychiatry, 147,* 758–760.

Princeton Religion Research Center (1982). *Religion in America.* Princeton, NJ: The Gallup Poll.

Princeton Religion Research Center (1985). *Religion in America.* Princeton, NJ: The Gallup Poll.

Propst, L.R. (1987). *Psychotherapy in a religious framework.* New York: Human Sciences Press.

Pruyser, P.W. (1977). The seamy side of current religious beliefs. *Bulletin of the Menninger Clinic, 41,* 329–348.

Rosen, C.C. (1982). Ethnic differences among impoverished rural elderly in the use of religion as a coping mechanism. *Journal of Rural Community Psychology, 3,* 27–34.

Runions, J.E. (1974). Religion and psychiatric practice. *Canadian Psychiatric Association, 19,* 79–85.

Scott, F.G. (1955). Factors in the personal adjustment of institutionalized aged. *American Sociological Review, 20,* 530–540.

Shanas, E. (1962). The personal adjustment of recipients of old age assistance. In R.M. Gray & D.O. Moberg (Eds.), *The church and the older person.* Grand Rapids, MI: Erdmans.

Stark, R. (1968). Age and faith: A changing outlook at an old process. *Sociological Analysis, 29,* 1–10.

Strickland, B.R., & Shaffer, S. (1971). Intrinsic-extrinsic, I-E, and F. *Journal for the Scientific Study of Religion, 10,* 366–369.

Swanson, W.C., & Harter, C.L. (1971). How do elderly blacks cope in New Orleans? *International Journal of Aging and Human Development, 2,* 210–216.

Swenson, W.M. (1961). Attitudes toward death in aged population. *Journal of Gerontology, 16,* 49–52.

Tillich, P. (1957). *Systematic theology: Existence and the Christ, Vol. 2.* Chicago: University of Chicago Press.

Yates, J.W., Chalmber, B.J., St. James, P., Follansbee, M., & McKegney, F.P. (1981). Religion in patients with advanced cancer. *Medical and Pediatric Oncology, 9,* 121–128.

14

Religion and Marital Adjustment

Gary L. Hansen

Marital adjustment, which is used almost synonymously with satisfaction, happiness, and quality, has been one of the major research foci of family social science for more than half a century (Adams, 1988).[1] In the process, religion has consistently been identified as a factor associated with adjustment. This chapter reviews the research in this area and outlines possible explanations for the observed trends.

The Secularization Hypothesis

The very idea that a strong link between the institutions of religion and family exists in modern society may seem implausible to those who accept the secularization hypothesis without question. Secularization is considered by some to be an accomplished fact in Western societies (Berger, 1967; Wilson, 1982). It refers to the process by which sectors of culture and society are removed from the domination of religious institutions and results in individuals who look upon both the world and their own lives without the benefit of religious interpretations.

While some have referred to secularization, in general, as a myth (Bahr & Chadwick, 1985; Greeley, 1972), there is particular reason to question it in the specific area of marital and family life. As Berger (1967) pointed out, both religion and family have been relegated to the private sphere. Therefore, the connection between religion and family may well have remained stronger than religion's connection with either the political or the economic realm, both of which are found in the public sphere.

Support for this position comes from a study by Heaton and Cornwall (1989) which used Canadian census data from 1971 and 1981. They found that religious group differences in the economic behavior of women had declined during that decade but that changes in the variability of family behavior across groups were less dramatic. This has been interpreted as indicating that religion influences economic behavior less than it does family behavior (Thomas & Cornwall, 1990a). Further evidence comes from Bahr and Chadwick's (1985) study using data from a 50-year replication of the classic community study of the midwestern U.S. city, "Middletown." They found both familism and religiosity to be just as strong as 50 years ago

189

and concluded that there is little doubt that the two institutions are intertwined. Similarly, Thornton (1985, 1989) has documented an intricate web of reciprocal interrelationships between religious institutions and values and family structure and behavior, suggesting that trends in family attitudes parallel trends in religion.

Given this strong evidence that secularization has not dramatically weakened the general link between religion and family, we can now consider the specific nature of the relationship between religion and marital adjustment. Let us begin by examining why and how religion may affect adjustment, and then look at the two areas that have received the most research attention—religiosity and religious homogamy.

Conceptualizing the Religion/Adjustment Link

According to Berger (1967), whatever else it may be, religion, from a sociological perspective, is a humanly constructed universe of meaning. As such, it is a normative system that includes specific ideals about the structure of marriage and marital interaction. When accepted and internalized by an individual, this normative system provides a set of expectations for both husbands and wives that sets the standard by which they evaluate the marital relationship. In addition, religion may influence marital adjustment because it provides a context for much human behavior and many significant events centered on marital relationships (Thomas & Cornwall, 1990b). For example, events like the marriage ceremony and the birth of a child may carry an added, or at least a different, significance when religious meaning is attached to them.

D'Antonio, Newman, and Wright (1982) contended that religious and family institutions reinforce one another in two different modes—social control and social support. With social control, religion constrains and sanctions deviant attitudes and behaviors perceived as threatening to culturally valued family patterns. Social support, on the other hand, encompasses how religion provides norms for familial love, family solidarity, self-esteem, marital stability, marital satisfaction, and family values and meanings. Clearly, the primary link between religion and marital adjustment is through the social support aspects of religion. Interestingly, social support has been the focus of far less social science research than the social control function of religion (D'Antonio et al., 1982).

Religiosity and Marital Adjustment

Two distinct questions have been addressed in the research on religiosity and adjustment. The first question is whether religiosity is associated with marital adjustment. The second is whether different factors are associated with adjustment for those high and low on religiosity.

Studies focusing on the first question have produced one of the most consistent findings in family social science: Highly religious people report higher levels of marital adjustment than those who are less religious (Thomas and Cornwall, 1990b).

In fact, most studies find the religiosity/adjustment relationship to be a relatively strong one. For example, Filsinger and Wilson (1984) examined the predictive effects of religiosity, socioeconomic rewards, and family development characteristics and found that religiosity is the best predictor of adjustment. In addition, a later study by the same two researchers (Wilson & Filsinger, 1986) looked at various dimensions of both religiosity (e.g., belief, ritualism) and adjustment (e.g., commitment, cohesion) and found a "broad-based relationship" across multiple dimensions of both variables.

A recent study by Hansen and Gage (1990) used data from the National Survey of Families and Households to look at the effect of one dimension of religiosity, namely fundamentalism, on marital interaction. Fundamentalism was measured using three items: "the Bible is God's word and everything happened or will happen exactly as it says," "the Bible is the answer to all important human problems," and "I regard myself as a religious fundamentalist." Results indicated that high fundamentalism is associated with marital happiness, positive perceptions of the spousal relationship, and perceptions of relationship fairness. High fundamentalism spouses reported fewer disagreements and, when disagreements did occur, they were more likely to calmly discuss the situation and less likely to argue heatedly or shout than were those low on fundamentalism. In addition, those scoring high on fundamentalism were less likely than those scoring low to report that their marriage is in trouble and divorce is likely.

There is some indication that the religiosity/adjustment relationship may differ for men and women. Women attend church more frequently, express stronger beliefs in traditional religious tenets, and are more likely to report having felt the presence of something otherworldly (de Vaus & McAllister, 1987). They are also more likely to align themselves with a particular religious body (Caplow, Bahr, & Chadwick, 1983). Despite these indications of women's greater religiosity, Heaton and Pratt (1990) used national survey data and found that men's religiosity is more consequential than women's religiosity to the satisfaction and stability of marriages. They explain this finding by noting that American men are socialized to suppress emotion (Madsen, 1979) and that women are expected to be more sensitive (Harris, 1979). If this is true, the fact that one purpose of organized religion is to help people overcome selfish tendencies and to be sensitive to the needs of others may mean that religion has a greater socializing influence on men than on women.

Prior to the 1980s, social scientists either simply ignored the positive relationship between religiosity and adjustment or explained it in terms of marital conventionalization or social desirability (e.g., Edmonds, Withers, & Dibatista, 1972). Marital adjustment measures were believed to be severely contaminated by social desirability, and it was assumed that highly religious individuals were more likely than others to give conventional or socially desirable answers to adjustment questions (i.e., answers indicating high adjustment). A series of studies began to challenge this explanation in the early 1980s. Hansen (1981) reexamined the entire marital adjustment and conventionalization issue and found a significant relationship between self-reported influence of religion on one's life and marital adjustment, even after controlling for marital conventionalization. Other studies that have controlled for conventionality reported similar positive relationships between religiosity and adjustment (Filsinger & Wilson, 1984; Schumm, Bollman, & Jurich, 1982).

While these studies call the conventionalization explanation into question, new explanations for the religiosity/adjustment relationship have been slow to develop, and few have gained widespread acceptance. However, Filsinger and Wilson (1984) offered a couple of reasons worthy of consideration. First, since choice involves difficulty (Chavez, 1980), religion may simply make life easier by providing a set of norms by which to live. Their second explanation builds upon Burr's (1973) use of Wallin and Clark's (1964) notion of "compensatoriness." Simply stated, the argument holds that religion tends to compensate for lack of satisfaction in other areas. Filsinger and Wilson (1984) acknowledged that this sounds like religion as "the opiate of the people," but argued that it is not a negative phenomenon:

> Part of adjustment at the individual level refers to changing oneself (e.g., goals, expectations) to be more in line with what is real. This is the process of accommodation. Religion may facilitate accommodation, thereby making life, or a marriage, more acceptable and the spouses more satisfied. (p. 668)

A related explanation, which will be discussed in more detail below, argues that religion performs a buffering or insulating function rather than a strictly compensatory one. Religion is believed to insulate marital functioning from the effects of a variety of factors commonly associated with decreased adjustment or happiness (Hansen, 1991; Hansen & Gage, 1990).

Works by Wallin (1957) and Wallin and Clark (1964) were among the first to suggest that religiosity may influence the strength of the relationship between adjustment and other factors. Wallin (1957) argued that the positive relationship between sexual gratification and spouses' satisfaction with their relationship would occur to a lesser degree for people with a religious orientation than for the more secular minded. He suggested that this may be the case because organizations concerned with religious training and activity foster and sustain an otherworldly outlook that deprecates the pleasures of the world in general, and physical gratification in particular. This was found to be the case for women, but not men, in both the early (Wallin, 1957) and middle (Wallin & Clark, 1964) years of marriage. Wallin and Clark (1964) offered an explanation for the finding that a religious orientation is effective with women, but not with men, in countering the impact of low sexual gratification on marital satisfaction. Specifically, they suggested that differential cultural conditioning results in the lack of sexual gratification in marriage being regarded as less of a deprivation by women than by men (Wallin & Clark, 1964). If this is true, it follows that religiosity must counteract a more potent dissatisfaction in men who are sexually ungratified than in sexually ungratified women.

Subsequent research has continued to demonstrate that religiosity affects the factors associated with marital adjustment. Social psychologists have made increasing use of social exchange principles to explain the satisfaction or adjustment of partners in intimate relationships. For example, Hansen (1987) addressed the issue of whether religiosity affects the relationship between exchange variables (i.e., rewards received, equality, equity) and perceptions of marital adjustment. Both men and women were divided into high and low religiosity groups. Results for men indicated that religiosity did not affect the relationship between the exchange variables and adjustment. Among women, however, religiosity had a dramatic effect, with the exchange variables explaining 65.4 percent of the variance in the low religiosity group's marital adjustment, but only 21.0 percent of the variance for the high religiosity group.

Hansen (1987) noted that high religiosity is associated with traditional gender-role attitudes (Brinkerhoff & MacKie, 1985) in his explanation for the differential effect of religiosity on men and women. Religious women may internalize such attributes as compassion, self-sacrifice, obedience, and humility as being both feminine and religiously appropriate during the socialization process. If high religiosity women actually evidence these characteristics more than low religiosity women, it is not surprising that what one personally receives from the marital relationship would have less of an impact on adjustment for them than for low religiosity women. Wives who feel it is their "duty" to sacrifice, be obedient, etc., are less likely than others to emphasize what they receive from marriage when evaluating it. In other words, they are less likely to develop an exchange orientation toward marriage.

A subsequent study by Hansen (1991) continued the same line of inquiry. Rather than examining overall level of rewards received, it looked at rewards received in seven specific areas. In so doing, it also sought to determine whether factors other than exchange variables (e.g., length of marriage, trust, presence of children) also explain less of the variance in marital adjustment for those high in religiosity. In general, religiosity diminished the impact of a variety of factors on marital adjustment, ones that were not limited to exchange variables. Furthermore, its effect was much more pronounced for women than for men. Hansen (1991) explained this finding in terms of religion performing an insulator or buffering function. Religion may insulate marital functioning from, or at least reduce the impact of, a variety of factors commonly associated with adjustment. This insulator function was graphically demonstrated by the finding that marital happiness (which is usually considered to be either a component of adjustment or highly related to it) explained 52.5 percent of the variance in adjustment for high religiosity women, but only 11.8 percent of the variance for their low religiosity counterparts.

This same study also found that four reward areas (love, information, sexual satisfaction, status) were significantly better predictors of adjustment for low than high religiosity women and that three factors (money, services, goods) were not. Hansen (1991) noted that various aspects of the four rewards that are better predictors (e.g., emotional support, intellectual stimulation, feelings of esteem and respect) are important characteristics of modern "companionate" marriage. Also, it was suggested that the mutual-development and person-centered norms of companionate marriage may not characterize the marriages of high religiosity women. While high religiosity women reported receiving the rewards at the same levels as low religiosity women, variations in those levels appeared to have less of an impact on their marital functioning.

The explanations given both by Wallin and Clark (1964) and by Hansen (1991) for their respective findings make a number of points similar to those outlined by D'Antonio (1980). He contrasted a traditional family model with a modern family model in his attempt to summarize the work of Miner (1939) and Lenski (1963) on Protestant/Catholic family differences. In the traditional model, the meaning of interpersonal relationships is found in ties extending well beyond the married couple, to extended families, to the community, and especially to the norms, values, and beliefs set by the church. Duty to family and to church comes ahead of personal pleasures. With the modern model, however, primacy of the relationship is at the level of individual happiness. One's family is of secondary consideration to one's ability to get ahead and to satisfy personal desires. Marriage is a type of interpersonal relationship in which the partners themselves control the meaning of interaction. Thus, the relationship may have little meaning beyond what they give to it. While the traditional model was originally seen as being exemplified by the Catholic farm family and the modern model by Protestants, D'Antonio's (1980) summary of follow-up studies to Lenski's work emphasized Catholic/Protestant convergence in a variety of areas. It seems reasonable to assume, however, that the two models represent opposite ends of a continuum with those high in religiosity tending toward the "traditional" end and those low in religiosity toward the "modern" end.

Religious Homogamy and Marital Adjustment

Most research on religious homogamy versus heterogamy has been conducted in the United States and has compared interfaith marriages among various combinations of Catholics, Protestants, and Jews with same-faith marriages.[2] In general, studies have found that individuals married to same-faith spouses have higher levels of marital adjustment than individuals in interfaith marriages (Glenn, 1982; Heaton, 1984; Heaton & Pratt, 1990; Ortega, Whitt, & Williams, 1988) and lower likelihood of divorce (Bahr, 1981; Bumpass & Sweet, 1972; Heaton, Albrecht, & Martin, 1985). Some studies suggested that these findings may not hold for all religious groups, however. For example, Shehan, Bock, and Lee (1990) did not find a negative relationship between heterogamy and marital satisfaction among Catholics.

Glenn (1982) found that the negative effect of religious heterogamy on happiness existed for white males but not for white females. This difference was explained in terms of a greater ability of wives than of husbands to control the religious socialization of children. This interpretation also proposed that the religious identification of children tends to be a major source of strain in heterogamous marriages. Heaton (1984) tested this explanation by controlling for the presence of children and found that the homogamy effect remained significant. This indicated that conflict over appropriate religious values for children does not account for lower adjustment in heterogamous marriages.

Several other explanations exist for the positive association between religious homogamy and both marital adjustment and stability. First, there is a positive relationship between homogamy, in general, and marital adjustment. Since homogamy implies consensus, there is a lower probability of conflict in homogamous marriages. In the specific area of religion, religious similarity is associated with value consensus (Albrecht, Bahr, & Goodman, 1983). Since decisions about many aspects of marital activities and interaction (e.g., childrearing, leisure activities) are influenced by those religious values, it is not surprising that same-faith couples would report higher adjustment. In addition, the value differences that exist for interfaith couples are likely to be reinforced by the couple's significant others, including family (Bumpass & Sweet, 1972). As Heaton and Pratt (1990) pointed out, common religious orientations may also create a more integrated social network of relatives, friends, and religious advisors. They speculated that this social network and value consensus combine to increase marital satisfaction and stability.

Another explanation draws upon the positive association between religiosity and adjustment discussed above. Homogamous marriages may be characterized by greater religious activity. If so, religious involvement, rather than homogamy, may account for higher levels of adjustment. Religious involvement may be higher in homogamous marriages for a couple of reasons. First, highly religious individuals seem to be relatively unlikely to marry someone of another religious faith (Peterson, 1986). Second, interfaith marriages may have a secularizing influence and thereby weaken the religious commitment of the individuals who form them. The rationale for why this may occur is outlined in Berger's (1967, 1969) plausibility structure thesis. According to Berger, participation in networks of people who share one's views of reality serves to validate or reinforce those views. Such validation ensures that an individual's beliefs remain personally plausible and that they will influence his or her behavior.

Heaton (1984) provided the most explicit test of the hypothesis that greater religiosity explains the positive association between religious homogamy and adjustment. Using national survey data, he found homogamous marriages to be more satisfying. When frequency of religious attendance was taken into account, however, the homogamy effect became nonsignificant. Thus, Heaton (1984) wrote that "patterns of religious involvement apparently underlie the higher level of satisfaction expressed in religiously homogamous marriages" (p. 732).

Conclusion

Despite the trend toward secularization in modern society, the research evidence reviewed in this chapter suggests that religion continues to influence marital and family life in general, and marital adjustment in particular. Religiosity is associated with higher levels of adjustment and appears to influence the strength of the relationship between adjustment and other factors. Higher religiosity levels also appear to explain the fact that individuals in same-faith marriages generally report higher adjustment than those in interfaith marriages. Research also shows that religion has a significant impact on social psychological processes in families. This has a number of implications for family scholars and practitioners. Most important, family professionals need to develop theoretical models and intervention strategies that incorporate the impact of religion on family processes. If they do not, their ability to understand family phenomena and assist family members may be significantly less for families whose members are religious than for others.

Notes

1. The marital adjustment/satisfaction/happiness/quality literature has been characterized by considerable conceptual confusion and disagreement about measurement. While conceptual and measurement issues are not particularly relevant to the purposes of this chapter, interested readers should see Glenn (1990) for a recent discussion of the most pertinent ones.

2. While most marriages are still religiously homogamous, interfaith marriage is increasingly common (Glenn, 1982, 1984). At least in the United States, no strong barriers to religious outmarriage exist for most religious groups. The relatively high degree of homogamy in current religious preference is achieved to a large extent by people changing their religious preferences to agree with those of their spouses either after or in anticipation of marriage.

References

Adams, B.N. (1988). Fifty years of family research: What does it all mean? *Journal of Marriage and the Family, 50,* 5–17.

Albrecht, S.L., Bahr, H.M., & Goodman, K.L. (1983). *Divorce and remarriage.* Westport, CT: Greenwood.

Bahr, H.M. (1981). Religious intermarriage and divorce in Utah and the mountain states. *Journal for the Scientific Study of Religion, 20,* 251–261.

Bahr, H.M., & Chadwick, B.A. (1985). Religion and family in Middletown, USA. *Journal of Marriage and the Family, 47,* 404–414.

Berger, P. (1967). *The sacred canopy: Elements of a sociological theory of religion.* Garden City, NY: Doubleday & Co.

Berger, P. (1969). *A rumor of angels.* Garden City, NY: Anchor Books.

Brinkerhoff, M.B., & MacKie, M. (1985). Religion and gender: A comparison of Canadian and American student attitudes. *Journal of Marriage and the Family, 47,* 415–429.

Bumpass, L.L., & Sweet, J.A. (1972). Differentials in marital instability. *American Sociological Review, 37,* 754–766.

Burr, W.R. (1973). *Theory construction and the sociology of the family.* New York: Wiley.

Chavez, J.S. (1980). Conflict resolution in marriage. *Journal of Social Issues, 1,* 397–421.

Caplow, T., Bahr, H.M., & Chadwick, B.A. (1983). *All faithful people: Change and continuity in Middletown's religion.* Minneapolis: University of Minnesota Press.

D'Antonio, W.V. (1980). The family and religion: Exploring a changing relationship. *Journal for the Scientific Study of Religion, 19,* 89–104.

D'Antonio, W.V., Newman, W.M., & Wright, S.A. (1982). Religion and family life: How social scientists view the relationship. *Journal for the Scientific Study of Religion, 21,* 218–225.

de Vaus, D., & McAllister, I. (1987). Gender differences in religion: A test of the structural location theory. *American Sociological Review, 52,* 472–481.

Edmonds, V.H., Withers, G., & Dibatista, B. (1972). Adjustment, conservatism, and marital conventionalization. *Journal of Marriage and the Family, 29,* 681–688.

Filsinger, E.F., & Wilson, M.R. (1984). Religiosity, socioeconomic rewards, and family development: Predictors of marital adjustment. *Journal of Marriage and the Family, 46,* 663–670.

Glenn, N.D. (1982). Interreligious marriage in the United States: Patterns and recent trends. *Journal of Marriage and the Family, 44,* 555–566.

Glenn, N.D. (1984). A note on estimating the strength of influences for religious endogamy. *Journal of Marriage and the Family, 46,* 725–727.

Glenn, N.D. (1990). Quantitative research on marital quality in the 1980s: A critical review. *Journal of Marriage and the Family, 52,* 818–831.

Greeley, A. (1972). *Unsecular man: The persistence of religion.* New York: Schocken Books.

Hansen, G.L. (1981). Marital adjustment and conventionalization: A reexamination. *Journal of Marriage and the Family, 43,* 855–863.

Hansen, G.L. (1987). The effect of religiosity on factors predicting marital adjustment. *Social Psychology Quarterly, 50* 264–269.

Hansen, G.L. (1991). Religiosity and the marital adjustment process. *Family Perspective, 25,* 7–17.

Hansen, G.L., & Gage, B. (1990, November). *Fundamentalism and marital interaction.* Presented at the National Council on Family Relations annual meetings, Seattle, WA.

Harris, D.V. (1979). Physical sex differences. In E.C. Snyder (Ed.), *The study of women: Enlarging perspectives of social reality* (pp. 184–206). New York: Harper & Row.

Heaton, T.B. (1984). Religious homogamy and marital satisfaction reconsidered. *Journal of Marriage and the Family, 46,* 729–733.

Heaton, T.B., Albrecht, S. L., & Martin, T.K. (1985). The timing of divorce. *Journal of Marriage and the Family, 47,* 631–639.

Heaton, T.B., & Cornwall, M. (1989). Religious group variation in the socioeconomic status and family behavior of women. *Journal for the Scientific Study of Religion, 28,* 283–299.

Heaton, T.B., & Pratt, E.L. (1990). The effects of religious homogamy on marital satisfaction and stability. *Journal of Family Issues, 11,* 191–207.

Lenski, G. (1963). *The religious factor.* Garden City, NY: Doubleday & Co.

Madsen, J. (1979). Women and children's literature. In E.C. Snyder (Ed.), *The study of women: Enlarging perspectives of social reality* (pp. 207–227). New York: Harper & Row.

Miner, H. (1939). *St. Denis, a French-Canadian parish.* Chicago: The University of Chicago Press.

Ortega, S.T., Whitt, H.P., & Williams, J.A., Jr. (1988). Religious homogamy and marital happiness. *Journal of Family Issues, 9,* 224–239.

Peterson, L.R. (1986). Interfaith marriage and religious commitment among Catholics. *Journal of Marriage and the Family, 48,* 725–735.

Schumm, W.R., Bollman, S.R., & Jurich, A.P. (1982). The "marital conventionalization" argument: Implications for the study of religiosity and marital satisfaction. *Journal of Psychology and Theology, 10,* 236–241.

Shehan, C.L., Bock, W., & Lee, G.R. (1990). Religious heterogamy, religiosity, and marital happiness: The case of Catholics. *Journal of Marriage and the Family, 52,* 73–79.

Thomas, D., & Cornwall, M. (1990a). Religion and family in the 1980s: Discovery and development. *Journal of Marriage and the Family, 52,* 983–992.

Thomas, D., & Cornwall, M. (1990b, July). *The religion and family interface: Theoretical and empirical explorations.* Presented at the International Sociological Association annual meetings, Madrid, Spain.

Thornton, A. (1985). Reciprocal influences of family and religion in a changing world. *Journal of Marriage and the Family, 47,* 381–391.

Thornton, A. (1989). Changing attitudes toward family issues in the United States. *Journal of Marriage and the Family, 51,* 873–893.

Wallin, P. (1957). Religiosity, sexual gratification, and marital satisfaction. *American Sociological Review, 22,* 300–305.

Wallin, P., & Clark, A. (1964). Religiosity, sexual gratification and marital satisfaction in the middle years of marriage. *Social Forces, 42,* 303–309.

Wilson, B. (1982). *Religion in sociological perspective.* Oxford, England: Oxford University Press.

Wilson, M.R., & Filsinger, E.E. (1986). Religiosity and marital adjustment: Multidimensional relationships. *Journal of Marriage and the Family, 48,* 147–151.

15

Crime, Delinquency, and Religion

William Sims Bainbridge

Crime and Juvenile Delinquency

Scholars debate the origins of the word *religion*, but it seems to have derived from the Latin *religare*, to bind or to tie back, from which we also get our word *rely*. Religion binds the individual to the society, subordinating personal wishes to collective demands. In *King John*, Shakespeare said, "It is religion that doth make vows kept," implying we can rely upon the word of a religious person. Sociologists connect *religion* with *regulation*, suggesting that a chief function of the church is to control the thoughts and actions of its members. Through sermons, parables, and the example of religious leaders, a person is socialized to the norms and values of the society. Therefore, religion should be especially potent in preventing juvenile delinquency and adult crime.

The majority of clergy and lay members of churches probably agree with this scholarly opinion, and no one would be surprised to learn that religious youth were less delinquent, and religious adults less criminal, than their irreligious peers. However, several major research studies have failed to find evidence in support of these assumptions, and the consensus among social scientists today is probably that religion lacks any distinctive power to make people obey society's rules. Much evidence contradicts the notion that religion's commandments are important shapers of human behavior, and sociological theories that place stress on the concepts of values and norms are thus in as deep trouble as religious faith itself.

In recent years, however, sociological research has deepened our understanding of the possible role religion may play in deterring delinquency and crime. While new questions have been raised by the research, and the old ones have not been fully answered, we are in a far better position than formerly to address this important topic.

The Contradictory Evidence on Delinquency

Early in this century, Hartshorne and May (1928) discovered that children who attended Sunday school were no less likely to become delinquent than children who

199

avoided this experience of religious indoctrination. Occasional other research done over the decades has also placed religion's capacity to deter deviant behavior in doubt. Clearly the most influential study was "Hellfire and Delinquency" by criminologist Travis Hirschi and sociologist of religion Rodney Stark (Hirschi & Stark, 1969). Employing the best survey dataset then available in a theoretically sophisticated analysis, this study showed that young people who believed in the supernatural sanctions represented by the Devil and life after death were just as likely to commit delinquent acts as were nonbelievers. Furthermore, church attendance did not show the negative association with delinquency that ministers and many traditional social theorists might have wished. Widely cited and reprinted, this study was taken by many nonreligious social scientists as proof for what they had always "known"—that religion was moribund and irrelevant in the modern world. The Hirschi and Stark research was performed in California, and a subsequent survey conducted in the Pacific Northwest also failed to find a religion effect on larceny among young people (Burkett & White, 1974).

In the 1970s, however, other studies appeared, based on survey data collected outside the Pacific region of the United States, showing that religion did appear to deter delinquency (Rhodes & Reiss, 1970; Higgins & Albrecht, 1977; Albrecht, Chadwick, & Alcorn, 1977; Elifson, Petersen, & Hadaway, 1983; Peek, Curry, & Chalfant, 1985). While not identical, these research projects followed very similar approaches, and respected scholars had worked on both sides of the debate. Therefore, the disagreement between them was difficult to explain.

A partial resolution of the mystery was achieved by Stark, who was able to show that the deterrent power of religion depended upon the social context (Stark, Kent, & Doyle, 1982; Tittle & Welch, 1983). The primary negative results had come from the Pacific region, where rates of church membership are low. Employing a national survey of youth, Stark was able to show that a strong negative correlation between religion and delinquency exists in communities where the majority are religious. But where only a minority are religious, religion has no power to deter delinquency among individually religious young people.

I shall call this phenomenon, which Stark discovered and which he has endeavored to explain, the *Stark effect*. It poses a great challenge to sociological theory, and a complete explanation is not yet at hand. Supported by several independent datasets, the effect is consistent but complex. Research on larceny-like delinquency has consistently found no relationship between religiousness and delinquency at the individual level in communities where organized religion is weak (e.g., as measured by the church member rate). But, equally consistently, studies performed where organized religion is relatively strong have shown that church-going and believing individuals were far less likely to steal than were their irreligious peers. Here, obviously, is a case where human behavior cannot be understood purely in terms of the individual. A person's religious faith apparently is powerless to affect his actions, unless the community somehow makes a connection between beliefs and behavior.

The Stark effect was an unexpected discovery of great importance, but in retrospect we should not have been so surprised when Stark announced it. For years, a debate has raged within social psychology over the extent to which one could predict a person's behavior on the basis of his attitudes (Liska, 1974; Schuman & Johnson, 1976; Hill, 1981; Bainbridge, in press). Put simply, words and deeds are not necessarily congruent, and often people perform actions logically at variance with their verbally expressed values, beliefs and attitudes. Thus, the pious words of religion could have no power to restrain vile deeds. In recent years, the emphasis in the attitude–behavior literature has been on understanding the mental processes and situational factors that intervene between attitudes and behavior. Social support has been found to be a powerful and complex determinant of the degree to which words are in harmony with deeds.

Stark's own explanation of the effect stresses the influence of friends in determining whether young people will commit acts of deviance or not. Religious beliefs are not automatically salient for behavior, in Stark's theory, but must be made salient through some social process (see Stark & Bainbridge, 1985, pp. 325–345). While a few families may be so involved in extreme religious groups that religion is salient for all aspects of their lives, the typical teenager from a moderately religious family will not be constantly reminded of religious commandments, especially in those settings far from parental influence, where most delinquency occurs. Thus, the crucial factor is whether religion is brought into the private lives of teenagers by the youth themselves. If a majority of a juvenile's friends are religious, then religion will become a part of their shared experience and deter delinquency. But if a majority are not religious, then the personal beliefs of the individual will not be rendered salient, and religious individuals will be as likely as others to commit delinquent acts (Stark, 1984).

The most interesting complication, not specifically examined by Stark, is the fact that religion does appear to deter certain forms of deviance, even in areas where the churches are weak: illegal drug use, heavy alcohol drinking, promiscuous sexuality, and other "hedonistic" or "anti-ascetic" acts (Middleton & Putney, 1962; Burkett & White, 1974; Wuthnow, 1978; Hadaway, Elifson, & Petersen, 1984).

For example, in previously unpublished data I collected through a questionnaire survey of 1,465 college students at the University of Washington in Seattle, the failure of religion to deter larceny in a low-religion city was fully replicated, yet individual religiousness was significantly negatively correlated with drugs, alcohol, and premarital sex. Within the margins of statistical reliability, religious youth were just as likely as irreligious youth to have stolen things of value, destroyed property, broken into a building, or been arrested by the police. However, as Table 1 shows, there were substantial differences for the hedonistic variables.

Table 15.1 divides respondents into six groups by frequency of church attendance, from 303 who participate in religious services at least once a week, to 231 who never do. It also separates the 643 men from the 795 women, because sexes generally show somewhat different patterns of deviance, and because too few women sold illegal drugs to permit calculating reliable percentages for them. While drinking alcohol more than once a week and having experienced sexual intercourse were hardly illegal, they reflected a hedonistic lifestyle for these young respondents. Driving an automobile while under the influence of alcohol was illegal, as was the use of marijuana and cocaine.

On average, as the row of figures for all respondents near the bottom shows,

Table 15.1. Church Attendance and Hedonism—Percent Admitting the Behavior

	How Often the Person Attends Religious Services					
	Once a Week or More	2 or 3 Times Month	Once a Month	Only Holidays	Hardly Ever	Never
643 males						
Driven under influence (%)	39	43	60	66	62	58
Drinks more than once a week (%)	12	15	40	39	33	40
Sold illegal drugs (%)	5	13	10	17	18	24
Used cocaine (%)	11	23	21	27	33	33
Used marijuana (%)	44	56	61	70	72	66
Sexual intercourse (%)	34	65	55	57	70	68
795 females						
Driven under influence (%)	21	37	43	43	51	42
Drinks more than once a week (%)	9	22	22	20	23	23
Used cocaine (%)	7	11	22	23	29	30
Used marijuana (%)	33	59	61	64	72	64
Sexual intercourse (%)	27	37	58	67	58	69
All respondents Average of eleven preceding rows (%)	22	35	41	45	47	47
Number in column	303	156	140	258	354	231

those who never attended church were more than twice as likely as weekly attenders to engage in these hedonistic acts. Use of cocaine is three times as common in the group untouched by religion as among the most frequent church-goers. And it should be recalled that these same respondents showed no effect of church to deter larceny and similar acts of delinquency. Thus, hedonistic acts (including some that are illegal) fail to exhibit the Stark effect, unless we wish to conceptualize it in a more complicated manner.

For those who like simple explanations of human behavior, this complication is quite undesirable. However, it suggests that one possible criticism of Stark's findings is false. It might be claimed that in religious areas individual irreligiousness is simply one more kind of deviance, thus correlating with other kinds of deviance, while in areas of weak organized religion, it is not deviant at all and thus should not correlate with deviance. But it is difficult to square the idea that irreligiousness is merely a contingent marker for general deviance with the consistent finding that some religion–deviance correlations survive in areas of low church membership, despite the collapse of others.

In his most recent formulation, Stark states the effect as follows: "Religious individuals will be less likely than others to break the norms, but only in communities where the majority of people are actively religious" (Stark, 1989, p. 96). We have seen, however, that the effect is more complex than this, and might be stated thus: *to deter larceny and similar crimes, individual religiousness must be immersed in a religious community, while it can deter hedonistic deviance even in communities where religion is weak.*

An approach toward understanding the Stark effect is to compare the two categories of delinquency, the larceny-type with the hedonistic. One distinction is that the former are crimes with victims, while the latter are victimless crimes. It may be that religion has the power to deter people from committing acts that would be to their obvious individual advantage (e.g., by instilling a strict moral code or humane sympathy for the feelings of potential victims), but only when religion spreads its message powerfully through influential social networks. This power would collapse when the church member rate was low.

Religion may also have an *advisory function,* in helping an individual decide what to do in ambiguous circumstances, where each available course seems to have advantages and disadvantages. Thus, even when not sustained by a social majority, religious teachings may convincingly warn young people that they themselves will be hurt if they indulge in drugs, excessive alcohol, and uncontrolled sex. This analysis is based on a utilitarian theory (Stark & Bainbridge, 1987), which derives religion from the human need to gain rewards and avoid costs, and which views religious beliefs as guides for personal decision making about dangerous and ambiguous matters.

One may also begin an analysis with the different social bases of the two types of deviance. Whereas larceny may be performed by either individuals or gangs, and the degree to which larceny is a collective crime has long been debated, the hedonistic acts are clearly social. Young deviants take drugs supplied through an elaborate social network (Ritter, 1988); they drink alcohol typically obtained and imbibed in groups (Rabow, Neuman, & Hernandez, 1987), and the social nature of sexual intercourse in undeniable. Thus, in areas where organized religion is weak, congregations may function as subcultures in competition with the subcultures of drugs, alcohol, and sex. By the principles of differential association (Sutherland & Cressey, 1974), individuals will be pulled more toward one subculture or another, and a negative correlation between religion and deviant hedonism will result. Alternatively, those who become members of hedonistic subcultures may feel themselves estranged from religion, and they may be rejected in turn by religion. This is because their collective brand of deviant behavior is difficult to hide, while occasional larcenies will go unnoticed by the church.

Two studies that found a deterrence effect on hedonism but not on larceny, published before the Stark effect had been discovered, noted that religion and secular culture were in agreement that larceny was wrong, but differed with respect to hedonism (Middleton & Putney, 1962; Burkett & White, 1974). The authors felt that if religion added merely a supernatural assent to secular norms, it could be responsible for little variation in behavior. This explanation is weakened by the evidence that religion is negatively associated with larceny in communities with medium or high church member rates, and its flaw is the failure to recognize that the salience of religious prohibitions depends upon the structure of social relationships in which the individual is embedded.

Limited Evidence on Adult Crime

Rodney Stark (1989) was able to find some evidence concerning the connection between religion and crime in previously conducted national polls of about 3,000 American adults. One of the items in these surveys asked whether the respondent had been "picked up by the police" for something other than a minor traffic offense. This is a valid if crude measure of criminal activity. Another item asked how frequently the respondent attended church. Of those adults who attended church at least every week, just 5.9 percent had been picked up by the police, compared with 10.5 percent of those who attended monthly, 12.9 percent of those who attended about yearly, and fully 22.0 percent of those who attended even less frequently. Thus, the proportion picked up by police is about 3.7 times as high among those who hardly ever attend church as it is among the most frequent church-goers.

Other data on individual adults' religion and criminal behavior is very hard to find. While major polls regularly inquire whether respondents have been victims of crimes, surveys almost never ask adults whether they have committed crimes. A general lack of interest in religion on the part of criminologists has often meant that no religion question was included in the few surveys of adult crime. Also, while juvenile offenses are both common and lightly punished, the adult offenses of interest to criminologists are both rare and severely sanctioned. This has meant that few adult respondents may have been guilty of particular crimes, and few of those who were would have been willing to admit it.

Some obscure datasets allow comparison of religious affiliation of imprisoned convicts with that of the general public, for example, the century-old censuses of the Australian state of Queensland. However, once a person has been arrested and convicted of crimes, the person lives under conditions that are hardly comparable with the status of free citizen. Religion may be imposed by prison officials, and convicts may simulate religiousness to curry favor with authorities. Or, a census enumerator may simply read irreligiousness into the criminal's deviant history.

One approach that has been followed by several research studies is to compare features of large social units—typically cities or states—rather than of lone individuals. Forty years ago, Austin Porterfield (1952) examined the effect of secularization on homicide and other serious crimes, using data on American states. Results were somewhat confusing because three different measures of religion produced different correlations with the crime rates. High rates of homicide and other serious crimes tended to be found in states with many church congregations but few people belonging to them, while the number of ministers did not matter at all.

Subsequent research tended to concentrate on rates of church membership, and to ignore the number of formal church organizations and the number of ministers, because church membership measures the direct participation of the general public in religion. It is from their ranks that criminals come. For example, Stark, Doyle, and Kent (1980) found a substantial negative correlation (r = −0.44) between the 1971 rate of church membership and the official 1972 crime rate reported by the Federal Bureau of Investigation for 193 metropolitan areas in the United States. This indicates that crime rates are low where many people belong to churches, and crime rates are high where few people are church members. It is strong evidence in favor of the theory that religion deters crime.

However, different crimes appear influenced in very different degrees by religion. Stark, Doyle, and Kent divided crimes into two categories; property crimes (burglary, larceny, and auto theft) and violent crimes (homicide, rape, robbery, and assault). Violent crimes achieved a much weaker negative correlation with church membership than did property crimes, −0.20 compared with −0.45. And within each category of crime there were offenses that behaved differently from the others of their category. Despite being a property crime, auto theft had only a weak correlation with church membership (−0.18). Rape would appear to be a violent crime, but it has a strong correlation with church membership (−0.41). Parallel research done with data from the 1920s revealed a similar range of associations between church membership and particular crimes, with forgery achieving the strongest negative correlation at −0.56 (Stark, Bainbridge, Crutchfield, Doyle, & Finke, 1983).

Stark's (1989) explanation was that religion is better at deterring consciously committed crimes that belong to sustained periods of deviant behavior, and worse at deterring impulsively violent acts like murder and assault. This explanation requires him to argue that rape is an intentional crime, committed by repeat offenders who know very well what they are doing, while auto theft rates mainly reflect sudden impulsive acts of juveniles. Robbery is difficult to categorize, because it has affinities with both property and violent crime. Like larceny, it involves stealing something, but like assault it involves a direct attack against another person. Clearly, Stark's interpretations of robbery and rape are open to criticism, but his analysis offers some important clues toward understanding the apparently variable power of religion to deter crime.

In my own view, the rates of auto theft are probably not very good indicators of the social conditions in particular cities. That is because professional auto thieves find their most rewarding work in places near large markets for hot cars and auto parts. In the American Northeast, it is a short drive from one city to another, to escape detection and arrest, and autos stolen in Boston can easily be chopped up or sold whole in New York. Thus, correlations for auto theft are probably meaningless and suffer from the statistical flaw known as Galton's problem (Ember, 1971), a lack of independence among the cases. Interpretation of correlations achieved by the other crimes should be done in the context of appropriate control variables.

Recent research using data on 75 large American metropolitan areas examined religion's power to deter six crimes: murder, rape, assault, robbery, burglary, and larceny (Bainbridge, 1989). But religion cannot be the only variable affecting crime, and some of the others may affect church membership. For example, evidence abounds that there is a robust negative correlation between church membership and the rate of geographic mobility. That is, where people tend to move often from one home to another, church membership is low. And where the population is stable in residence, church membership is high. Furthermore, population instability is also associated with larceny and several other kinds of deviance. Thus, the correlation between church membership and larceny may be spurious, an illusion produced by the fact that both these variables correlate highly with geographic mobility.

Other variables may show a similar pattern. Divorce is a different kind of social instability. Both crime and church membership may be affected by poverty and social discrimination. Therefore, the research not only examined the simple correlations between the rate of church members and the rates of six crimes but also looked at the same correlations after controlling for other variables: percent who moved homes in the past five years, percent of families in poverty, percent black, and percent divorced. The statistical method used was multiple regression, with standardized betas taking the place of ordinary correlation coefficients. Table 15.2 shows the results.

The first column of figures in Table 15.2 gives the correlations before statistical controls were introduced. The pattern is irregular, but similar to that found by Stark and his associates. Larceny has the strongest negative association with church membership, and burglary, another property crime, in second place. But rape is in third place with a respectable -0.38, and robbery (which has -0.01) does not fit with the property crimes where we might want to place it.

Controlling for the four other variables produces a far clearer picture, as shown in the second column of figures in Table 15.2. Murder (which includes non-negligent homicide) fails to achieve a negative correlation. In fact, its insignificant coefficient is positive, and thus Stark's explanation that it is an impulsive crime of passion undeterrable by religion gains support. The -0.11 correlation between church membership and rape is on the minus side but statistically insignificant, and thus it is compatible with the commonsensical proposition that rape is also a crime of passion. But the four other crimes all have solid negative correlations with church

Table 15.2. Church Membership and Crime Rates, American Metropolitan Areas, 1980

Crime	Correlation with Church Membership	Correlation with Church Membership, Controlling for Other Variables*
Murder	0.03	0.06
Rape	-0.38	-0.11
Assault	-0.23	-0.26
Robbery	-0.01	-0.23
Burglary	-0.44	-0.22
Larceny	-0.63	-0.39

*Four measures of social instability and economic deprivation: percent who moved homes in the past five years, percent of families in poverty, percent black, and percent divorced.

membership, good evidence that religion deters assault, robbery, burglary, and larceny.

The robust negative correlation between church membership and assault, -0.23 initially and -0.26 after controlling for the four variables, brings Stark's categorization of crimes into question. Clearly, assault is not simply a lesser form of murder or attacks that just missed becoming homicides. I cannot guess what percentage of assaults were committed during the performance of robberies. But every armed robbery implies the possibility that the robber will physically harm his victim if the victim does not quickly comply with his demands. In any case, after the statistical controls, the correlations linking religion to assault, robbery, and burglary are so close to each other as to count as identical.

Larceny stands out, with a substantially bigger negative correlation with church membership than achieved by the other crimes, both before and after introduction of the four control variables. In the delinquency studies, as we noted, larceny stood out as well. The Stark effect directly implies that there will be a strong negative correlation between rates of religion and larceny. In religious areas, church membership greatly reduces larceny for church members. But in irreligious areas, church membership does not limit larceny by anybody. This implies a big difference in the larceny rates between religious and irreligious areas.

Thus, the data on adult crime, limited as they are, harmonize with findings from the more extensive questionnaire studies of juvenile delinquency. Religion is an important factor in determining crime rates, but it is not an overwhelming factor, and it cannot be understood without attention to other variables as well.

Moral Communities

Since the pioneering theories of Emile Durkheim (1897, 1915), sociologists have postulated that religion contributed significantly to the strength of moral communities. A moral community is a group that functions as a moral unit, inspiring most members to conform to shared norms, and thus it is inimical to crime and delinquency. To the extent that a particular city or neighborhood is a moral community, its rates of crime and delinquency will be low. To the extent that an individual is a member of such a community, he will be neither a juvenile delinquent nor an adult criminal.

Writing a generation before Durkheim, the American sociologist John Humphrey Noyes (1870) argued that moral communities have two dimensions: shared religious beliefs and strong social bonds between individuals. In modern sociology, these two aspects of moral community are called moral integration and social integration. Stark (1989) defined social integration as "the degree to which persons in a group have many strong attachments to one another," while moral integration is "the degree to which members of a group are united by shared beliefs" (p. 202). Angell (1949) has defined moral integration as "the degree to which the life of the group proceeds in terms of shared ends and values" (p. 248). This "involves a mutually consistent set of norms derived from common values, norms which members of the group, community, or society have internalized as guides to their behavior"

(Angell, 1974, p. 610). Thus, moral integration does not necessarily depend on a shared religious faith, and a society could conceivably be a moral community without being religious.

The concept of *community* has not been as fully explicated in these writings as it deserves. For example, one might conjecture that social units far smaller than an entire city might constitute the effective communities of some individuals. Hoge and de Zulueta (1985) have argued that family life and sexuality are among the very few areas in which religion influences values directly, and for some people a close-knit family may constitute a sufficient moral community, regardless of the nature of the surrounding society. Similarly, an ethnic area of a city or a neighborhood may possess a set of shared values, even if the city in which it is set does not.

Close examination of the Hirschi-Stark data reveals evidence that religion may deter delinquency, if very weakly, even in the irreligious Pacific region. Among the boys who attend church at least once a week, 19 percent admit two or more delinquent acts, compared with 22 percent of the boys who attend less frequently. Among girls, the corresponding figures are 6 percent and 9 percent. The two other Pacific region datasets I have inspected show the same pattern. There are weak relationships that fall just short of statistical significance but hint at some residual capacity of religion to limit delinquency. This is quite reasonable. Some people, even in very irreligious cities, live in somewhat closed, homogeneous neighborhoods, and a few of these neighborhoods may be religious and function locally as moral communities.

While the analysis of church membership and crime rates shows that certain crimes are deterred by religion, it does not exactly prove that irreligious people are the ones committing crimes. The delinquency data, of course, suggest a more complex pattern. In particular, they show that religious individuals in irreligious communities also contribute to the crime rate. And it is possible that individually irreligious people imbedded in moral communities are deterred to some extent by the religion of the people with whom they may have strong social attachments.

Many questions remain to be resolved about the nature of the moral community that can give religion the power to deter juvenile delinquency and adult crime, but there is little doubt that the process is a social one. Religion is not merely a psychological variable, conferring a particular kind of personality pattern on an individual. True, evidence is fairly strong that religiosity in our culture inhibits hedonism, including some acts that are contrary to law. But religious beliefs have the power to deter some very important delinquent and criminal acts only when supported by social bonds. And other severely harmful acts, such as murder, may not be controlled by religion at all.

References

Albrecht, S.L., Chadwick, B.A., & Alcorn, D.S. (1977). Religiosity and deviance: Application of an attitude–behavior contingent consistency model. *Journal for the Scientific Study of Religion, 16,* 263–274.

Angell, R.C. (1949). Moral integration and interpersonal integration in American cities. *American Sociological Review, 14,* 245–251.

Angell, R.C. (1974). Moral integration of American cities. *American Journal of Sociology, 80,* 607–629.

Bainbridge, W.S. (1989). The religious ecology of deviance. *American Sociological Review, 54,* 288–295.

Bainbridge, W.S. (in press). Attitudes and behavior. In *Encyclopedia of Language and Linguistics.* Aberdeen, Scotland: Aberdeen University Press.

Burkett, S.R., & White, M. (1974). Hellfire and delinquency: Another look. *Journal for the Scientific Study of Religion, 13,* 455–462.

Durkheim, E. (1897). *Suicide.* New York: Free Press.

Durkheim, E. (1915). *Elementary forms of religious life.* London: Allen and Unwin.

Elifson, K.W., Petersen, D.M., & Hadaway, C.K. (1983). Religiosity and delinquency. *Crim-*

Ember, M. (1971). An empirical test of Galton's problem. *Ethnology, 10,* 98–106.

Hadaway, C.K., Elifson, K.W., & Petersen, D.M. (1984). Religious involvement and drug use among urban adolescents. *Journal for the Scientific Study of Religion, 23,* 109–128.

Hartshorne, H., & May, M.A. (1928). *Studies in deceit.* New York: Macmillan.

Higgins, P.C., & Albrecht, G.L. (1977). Hellfire and delinquency revisited. *Social Forces, 55,* 952–958.

Hill, R.J. (1981). Attitudes and behavior. In M. Rosenberg & R.H. Turner (Eds.), *Social psychology* (pp. 347–377). New York: Basic Books.

Hirschi, T., & Stark, R. (1969). Hellfire and delinquency. *Social Problems, 17,* 202–213.

Hoge, D.R., & de Zulueta, E. (1985). Salience as a condition for various social consequences of religious commitment. *Journal for the Scientific Study of Religion, 24,* 21–38

Liska, A.E. (1974). Emergent issues in the attitude–behavior consistency controversy. *American Sociological Review, 39,* 261–272.

Middleton, R., & Putney, S. (1962). Religion, normative standards, and behavior. *Sociometry, 25,* 141–152.

Noyes, J.H. (1870). *History of American socialisms.* Philadelphia: Lippincott.

Peek, C.W., Curry, E.W., & Chalfant, H.P. (1985). Religiosity and delinquency over time. *Social Science Quarterly, 66,* 120–131.

Porterfield, A.L. (1952). Suicide and crime in folk and in secular society. *American Journal of Sociology, 57,* 331–338.

Rabow, J., Neuman, C.A., & Hernandez, A.C.R. (1987). Contingent consistency in attitudes, social support and the consumption of alcohol. *Social Psychology Quarterly, 50,* 56–63.

Rhodes, A.L., & Reiss, A.J. (1970). The "religious factor" and delinquent behavior. *Journal of Research in Crime and Delinquency, 7,* 83–98.

Ritter, C. (1988). Resources, behavior intentions, and drug use. *Social Psychology Quarterly, 51,* 250–264.

Schuman, H., & Johnson, M.P. (1976). Attitudes and behavior. *Annual Review of Sociology, 2,* 161–207.

Stark, R. (1984). Religion and conformity: Reaffirming a *sociology* of religion. *Sociological Analysis, 45,* 273–282.

Stark, R. (1989). *Sociology.* Third Edition. Belmont, California: Wadsworth.

Stark, R., & Bainbridge, W.S. (1985). *The future of religion.* Berkeley: University of California Press.

Stark, R., & Bainbridge, W.S. (1987). *A theory of religion.* New York: Peter Lang.

Stark, R., Bainbridge, W.S., Crutchfield, R.D., Doyle, D.P., & Finke, R. (1983). Crime and delinquency in the roaring twenties. *Journal of Research in Crime and Delinquency, 20,* 4–23.

Stark, R., Doyle, D.P., & Kent, L. (1980). Rediscovering moral communities: Church membership and crime. In T. Hirschi & M. Gottfredson (Eds.), *Understanding crime* (pp. 43–52). Beverly Hills, California: Sage.

Stark, R., Kent, L., & Doyle, D.P. (1982). Religion and delinquency: The ecology of a "lost" relationship. *Journal of Research in Crime and Delinquency, 19,* 4–24.

Sutherland, E.H., & Cressey, D.R. (1974). *Principles of criminology.* Philadelphia: Lippincott.

Tittle, C.R., & Welch, M.R. (1983). Religiosity and deviance: Toward a contingency theory of constraining effects. *Social Forces, 61,* 653–682.

Wuthnow, R. (1978). *Experimentation in American religion.* Berkeley: University of California Press.

16

Religion and Substance Use

Peter L. Benson

A considerable body of literature on the relationship between personal religiousness and substance use has emerged since the mid 1970s, when Gorsuch and Butler (1976) briefly reviewed this area of inquiry. This more recent research has added depth to explaining how and when religion functions to inhibit substance use, with additional efforts aimed at disentangling the effect of religiousness from its demographic, social, and psychological correlates.

As is the case in many areas of social psychological research, samples are largely comprised of students attending high school or college. This skews our knowledge about the connection between religiousness and substance use in a significant way. The literature tells us more about the role of religion in preventing onset of use than it does about the role of religion in preventing problem use (e.g., addiction).

This review focuses on empirical studies investigating the connection between personal religiousness and measures of substance use. Substance use includes a range of chemicals, including alcohol, tobacco, and illicit drugs used for nonmedical purposes (e.g., cocaine, heroin, amphetamines, barbiturates, and psychedelics). Emphasis is given to studies published since 1975. Two related areas of research are not included in this review: pursuit of religious experience through the use of drugs (see Argyle & Beit-Hallahmi, 1975, for a review of this research) and the role of religious sentiment and activity in treatment.

The Basic Relationship and Its Generalizability

Gorsuch and Butler (1976) concluded that the dominant theme in research published through the mid 1970s was the negative association between religiousness and substance use. This basic relationship also prevails in research conducted since their review. With only a few exceptions (to be cited below), the negative association between the two domains holds true in multiple demographic subgroups and across multiple measures of religion and substance use.

211

Demographics

Though this basic relationship has been reported most frequently on samples of high school adolescents (Benson & Donahue, 1989; Benson, Wood, Johnson, Eklin, & Mills, 1983; Burkett & White, 1974; Donahue, 1987; Schlegel & Sanborn, 1979), it has also been established among junior high youth (Benson, Williams, & Johnson, 1987; Jessor, Jessor, & Finney, 1973), college students (Brook, White-man, Gordon, & Brook, 1984; Dudley, Mutch, & Cruise, 1987; Gergen, Gergen, & Morse, 1972; Perkins, 1985, 1987; Rohrbaugh & Jessor, 1975; Steffenhagen, McAree, & Nixon, 1972), and adults (Bock, Cochran, & Beeghley, 1987; Cochran, Beeghley, & Bock, 1988; Gottlieb & Green, 1984; Perkins, 1987; Wuthnow, 1978).

Negative correlations between religiousness and substance use have been consistently reported among both males and females (Adlaf & Smart, 1985; Benson & Donahue, 1989; Donahue, 1987; Gottlieb & Green, 1984; Hundleby, 1987; Jessor et al., 1973; Rohrbaugh & Jessor, 1975). Though the vast majority of studies do not report findings by race or ethnicity, three replicate the basic relationship in studies of African Americans (Benson & Donahue, 1989; Donahue, 1987; McIntosh, Fitch, Wilson, & Nyberg, 1981). The McIntosh et al. (1981) study also extends the finding to Hispanics.

Donahue (1987) reported significant negative relationships between church attendance and religious importance and a series of substance use measures within each of the four United States census regions (Northeast, Northcentral, South, and West). Though most studies surveyed in this review use samples from the United States, the same negative association between religiousness and substance use has been reported in Canada (Adlaf & Smart, 1985; Hundleby, 1987; Whitehead, 1970).

Measures of Religion

The inverse relationship between religiousness and chemical use has been documented on a wide variety of religion measures. The three most commonly employed measures are affiliated versus nonaffiliated (Bock et al., 1987; Gergen et al., 1972; Jensen & Erickson, 1979; Mauss, 1969; Nelsen & Rooney, 1982; Perkins, 1987; Weinstein, 1976; Whitehead, 1970), church attendance (Benson et al., 1983; Burkett & White, 1974; Brook et al., 1984; Fors & Rojek, 1983; Lorch & Hughes, 1985; McIntosh et al., 1981; Margulies, Kessler, & Kandel, 1977), and religious salience or importance (Adlaf & Smart, 1985; Benson et al., 1987; Donahue, 1987; Hadaway, Elifson, & Petersen, 1984; McIntosh et al., 1981; Middleton & Putney, 1962; Perkins, 1985).

The same pattern of findings extends to a number of other measures of religion. Apparently, the rule seems to be that any measure of religious sentiment or activity will be inversely related to substance use, including parent religiousness (Brook et al., 1984; Coombs, Wellisch, & Fawzy, 1985; Hadaway et al., 1984), orthodoxy (Benson, Yeager, Wood, Guerra, & Manno, 1986; Globetti & Windham, 1967; Hadaway et al., 1984; Vener, Zaenglein, & Stewart, 1977), participation in church-based youth programs (Benson, 1990; Benson et al., 1983); frequency of devotional behaviors such as prayer or Bible-reading (Dudley et al., 1987) and belief in life after death (Cochran et al., 1988).

Rohrbaugh and Jessor (1975) reported a negative relationship using an adaptation of Glock and Stark's (1965) dimensions of religiosity. Benson and his colleagues (1986) extended the negative relationship to a series of religious orientations, including vertical religion (the degree of emphasis given in a religious belief system to establishing a personal relationship with God), horizontal religion (the degree of emphasis given to action on behalf of others, through interpersonal helping or involvement in promoting peace and justice), and comforting religion (the degree to which one's religious sentiments provide comfort and solace).

It has been suggested that the important constructs of intrinsic and extrinsic religion should be linked to substance use (Donahue, 1985). Surprisingly, this prediction has rarely been tested. In one study known to pursue this line of inquiry, intrinsic religion was negatively related to alcohol and marijuana use among high school students (Benson et al., 1986).

Because religion measures tend to be highly intercorrelated, it is unclear whether multiple measures of religion can provide independent effects on substance use. In a recent reanalysis of 47,000 public school students, Benson (1990) found main effects for both church attendance and religious importance on multiple measures of substance use.

Measures of Substance Use

The most commonly investigated relationships are to alcohol and/or marijuana use. Of the 38 covered in this review, 29 report a negative relationship with alcohol, and 26 with marijuana. Though investigations of tobacco use (Benson & Donahue, 1989; Benson et al., 1983; Dudley et al., 1987; Gottlieb & Green, 1984; Hundleby, 1987; Lorch & Hughes, 1985; Vener et al., 1977) and illicit drug use other than marijuana (Benson et al., 1983; Donahue, 1987; Hadaway et al., 1984; Nelsen & Rooney, 1982; Whitehead, 1970) are less common, reported relationships with religion are invariably negative.

Exceptions to the Rule

Exceptions to the basic rule are extremely rare. In two cases, nonsignificant results may be due in part to low substance use rates (see Jessor et al., 1973, for marijuana use among junior high males, and Jessor & Jessor, 1977, for "times drunk" among high school students). Additionally, Burkett (1977) reported a weak connection between parents' church attendance and substance use, and Mookherjee (1985) found that a religious fundamentalism–liberalism scale did not differentiate between alcoholics and nonalcoholics. Two other studies reported positive connections between religion measures and substance use, but in both cases the measures tap what might be considered negative forms of religiousness. One of these employed a measure of restricting religion, defined as the degree to which one views religion as rule-based, authoritarian, and demanding of obedience (Benson et al.,

1987). The other documented weak but positive relationships between religious doubt and both alcohol and marijuana use (Benson et al., 1986).

Finally, Wuthnow (1978) compared rates for being "high on drugs" for five religious orientations. Consistent with most research, the nonreligious reported higher rates than those with conservative, liberal, or nominal religious orientations, with the nominals higher than the conservatives and liberals. However, those with an "experimental" orientation, in which acceptance of nonconventional religious ideas (e.g., Eastern religions, the occult) replaces traditional beliefs, reported higher use rates than the nonreligious.

Summary

Overall, there is a persistent tendency for religion to be inversely related to substance use. This point is elegantly reinforced in Donahue's (1987) reanalysis of data from *Monitoring the Future*, an annual, large sample, cross-sectional survey of high school seniors conducted by the Institute for Social Research at the University of Michigan. Examining the relationship of church attendance and religious importance to 25 measures of substance use (e.g., alcohol, marijuana, cocaine, amphetamines, barbiturates, tranquilizers) for multiple subgroups (gender, race, region) within each year from 1976 to 1985, he calculated 2200 correlations. A negative correlation between religiousness and substance use was found in all but 14 cases.

The Strength of the Relationship

Zero-Order Correlations

Though the relationship between religiousness and substance use is highly persistent, it tends also to be rather modest. Across a number of studies, the correlation between religion and alcohol use tends to be in the range of $-.10/-.15$ (Hundleby, 1987; Lorch & Hughes, 1985) to $-.20/-.25$ (Benson et al., 1983; Benson, 1990; Dudley et al., 1987; Donahue, 1987; Vener et al., 1977). With marijuana, religious measures correlate in the range of $-.15/-.20$ (Benson et al., 1986; Hundleby, 1987; McIntosh et al., 1981) to $-.25/-.30$ (Benson et al., 1983; Brook et al., 1984; Donahue, 1987; Rohrbaugh & Jessor, 1975). In a sample of Seventh-day Adventist youth in which the percentage of marijuana uses was very small (Dudley et al., 1987), church attendance correlated $-.07$ with marijuana use. Correlations with tobacco use are in the same range of about $-.15$ (Dudley et al., 1987; Hundleby, 1987) to about $-.30$ (Vener et al., 1977).

Across a number of studies, the average correlation with alcohol, tobacco, and marijuana use is about $-.20$. The correlations with other illicit drugs (cocaine, heroin, LSD, amphetamines, barbiturates) tend to be lower (Donahue, 1987). This may be due to relatively low use rates.

Hadaway et al. (1984) argued that zero-order correlations with religion should be greater for marijuana than for alcohol, because religious institutions speak more clearly against the use of the former than the latter. However, findings are somewhat equivocal. In addition to their findings, Donahue (1987) and Vener et al. (1977) also reported slightly higher correlations with marijuana. However, a number of other studies reported similar correlations for alcohol and marijuana (Benson et al., 1986; Benson, 1990; Lorch & Hughes, 1985). And one study (Dudley et al., 1987) found a much lower correlation with marijuana than with alcohol, though this may reflect the extremely low marijuana use rate (3%) in a Seventh-day Adventist sample.

Some studies looked at the relationship of a number of social and psychological variables in addition to religious variables. All of these studies use secondary school or college samples. Overall, religion predicts substance use better than some variables, and not as well as others. Church attendance and/or salience of religious belief predicts alcohol and other drug use better than does self-esteem (Benson, 1990; Benson et al., 1986; Rohrbaugh & Jessor, 1975; Jessor & Jessor, 1977), internal-external control (Benson et al., 1986; Rohrbaugh & Jessor, 1975; Jessor & Jessor, 1977), self-reported school ability or grade point average (Benson et al., 1986), and student participation in co-curricular activities at school or in the community (Benson, 1990; Benson et al., 1983).

On the other hand, religious variables tend not to predict as well as academic aspirations or achievement motivation (Benson, 1990; Jessor & Jessor, 1977), frequency of socializing with peers (Benson et al., 1983; Hundleby, 1987), frequency of marijuana use by one's peers (Hadaway et al., 1984), tolerance of deviance (Brook et al., 1984; Jessor & Jessor, 1977), and parental standard and rules against substance use (Benson et al., 1983).

It appears that religious variables tend to predict better than personality constructs (e.g., self-esteem, locus of control, purpose in life) and not as well as mechanisms of constraint (parental standards) or encouragement (peer use, tolerance of deviance) present in one's social environment. More research is needed to clarify these relationships.

There is some evidence that religious variables tend to predict substance use better than other forms of "deviance." Burkett and White (1974) predicted this pattern, arguing that religiousness has a more profound inhibiting effect on "victimless" crimes than on those that involve crimes against people (e.g., theft, vandalism, aggression). Burkett and White's (1974) data supported this reasoning, as did the findings of Jessor and Jessor (1977). These two studies, along with a series of others (see Hadaway et al., 1984, for a review), document that religion functions to inhibit multiple forms of "deviance," in contradiction of Hirschi and Stark's (1969) influential claim that religion is "irrelevant to delinquency."

Controls for Covariates

Religiousness tends to be correlated with a range of demographic (age, gender, region, education) and social-psychological (family dynamics, characteristics of parents, peer relationships) variables. A number of studies, using multivariate statistical techniques such as discriminant function analysis and regression analysis, have investigated whether religiousness has an effect on substance use independent of these covariates.

Three studies found that independent effects remain for church attendance and/or religious salience after controlling for these sets of demographic influences: age and gender (Lorch & Hughes, 1985); age, gender, race, region, education and income (Cochran et al., 1988); region, high school type, gender, race, community size, father presence–absence, parental education, and maternal employment (Benson & Donahue, 1989). In a fourth such study, an independent effect for religiousness was found only among conservative Protestants (Bock et al., 1987).

Additionally, several studies reported independent religious effects after controlling for these combinations of social and environmental factors: peer marijuana use, relationship with parents, and school performance (Hadaway et al., 1984); school performance, peer drug use, and communication with parents (Fors & Rojeck, 1983); and attitudes of friends and parents toward alcohol (Perkins, 1985). Each of these three studies also included demographic variables in the model tested. Finally, one study found conflicting results following statistical controls, with an independent effect for church attendance found for marijuana but not for alcohol (Kandel, Treiman, Faust, & Single, 1976).

Explanations

In recent years, particularly since 1974, considerable research has been guided by attempts to explain how and why religiousness suppresses substance use. Nearly all of these efforts appeal to the social control function of religion, in which religious institutions and traditions maintain the social order by discouraging deviance, delinquency, and self-destructive behavior. Religion, then, prevents use through a system of norms and values that favor personal restraint. Consistent with this, some authors postulate that the greater the religiousness, the greater the internalization of values and standards discouraging use (Jessor & Jessor, 1977; Rohrbaugh & Jessor, 1975).

Burkett and White (1974) tested this reasoning more directly, showing that a particular set of personal beliefs (e.g., supernatural sanctions—"alcohol and drug use is a sin"), is inversely related to alcohol and marijuana use (also see, Burkett, 1980).

A significant body of literature has tested the controlling function of religion by investigating how variability in denominational norms relates to substance use. The appeal here is to reference group theory and the notion that individual inhibitions to use chemicals are tied to the clarity with which religious groups speak against substance use. In this vein, some studies categorized conservative Protestants as high on norms discouraging use, Catholics as low, and liberal Protestants falling in between. Consistent with this reasoning, conservative Protestants are found to have the lowest alcohol use rates, Catholics the highest, and liberal Protestants between these two extremes (Cahalan, 1976; Cahalan & Cisin, 1968). The two studies reported this patterning for both rates of heavy alcohol use and alcohol abuse. Other research also found a Catholic–Protestant difference (Burkett, 1980; Knupfer & Room, 1967; Schlegel & Sanborn, 1979; Zucker & Harford, 1983). One important study tested reference group theory by showing that the independent, explanatory power of religion is strongest among conservative Protestant denominations in which norms against alcohol use are particularly clear (Bock et al., 1987).

A parallel series of studies placed Judaism at the conservative end of the spectrum (with strong norms against misuse) and found, consistent with predictions, that alcohol use was highest for Catholic students, lowest for Jewish students, with Protestants in between these two groups (Perkins, 1985). However, the author also noted that the lower use by Jewish students evaporates as they become increasingly acculturated to more lenient norms on a college campus. Some scholars have noted that the traditional role of Judaism in preventing use and/or misuse may be changing as Jews become increasingly socialized to mainstream American values (Spilka, Hood, & Gorsuch, 1985). Consequently, some research now shows that Jewish alcohol use rates are not too dissimilar from those found among Catholics (Zucker & Harford, 1983). However, the weight of the evidence suggests that heavy or problem use, including alcoholism, tends to be relatively low among Jews (Cochran et al., 1988; Wechsler, Demone, Thum, & Kasey, 1970).

In an important refinement of reference group theory, some scholars have argued that the role of religious norms against use is informed by the degree to which those religious norms stand over and against cultural norms. That is, religion will have its strongest inhibiting effect when there is social dissensus about use, and its least influence when religion is but one voice working in concert with other social control mechanisms to discourage use (Hadaway et al., 1984; Nelsen & Rooney, 1982). Accordingly, Hadaway et al. (1984) found that religiousness had more constraint on the use of alcohol (because religious traditions discourage use in a climate of social dissensus) than on marijuana (because religious traditions are but one voice in a climate of social consensus).

Conclusions

Significant strides in understanding the connection between religiousness and substance use have been made in the last decade. Still, there are several issues that deserve more thoughtful inquiry. Most research fails to address the role of religion in the various stages of substance use. These stages include onset of use, regular use, and problem use. The vast majority of studies have investigated the role of religion in preventing the onset of use. Less clear is the role of religion in preventing movement from onset (or experimental use) to regular use, or from regular use to problem use (e.g., addiction). Particularly useful here would be longitudinal research, in which changes in religiousness are related to changes in substance use patterns.

Efforts to explain why religion inhibits use depend almost exclusively on religion as a social control mechanism. This work needs to be augmented with efforts to understand how religion promotes the kinds of personal and social resources that then function to prevent use. It is now widely documented that both social resources (e.g., family harmony, parent–child communication, parental support, support from nonparent adults) and personal resources (e.g., academic achievement, prosocial values, social competence) inhibit among adolescents a wide-range of health-compromising choices, including alcohol, tobacco, and illicit drug use

(Benson, 1990). Institutional religious involvement may well increase access to or development of these resources. Consequently, the role of religion inhibits use not only by its direct pronouncements against use but also by its indirect role in promoting environmental and psychological assets that constrain risk-taking.

Both of these approaches (religion as social control and religion as promoter of positive environmental and psychological assets) tend to view personal religiousness within an institutional context. Our understanding of the role of religion in substance use must also take into account that spiritual development and growth also can occur outside institutional boundaries. Theoretical and empirical work is needed to understand how such spiritual development influences life style and behavioral choices, including substance use.

Though there is now an impressive body of literature documenting the role of religion in preventing substance use, one would not know it by looking at the mainstream literature on prevention. For example, three recent reviews of the prevention literature, each of which surveys social, demographic, and personal correlates of use, fail to discuss or reference the literature covered in this review (Bratter & Forrest, 1985: Burchard & Burchard, 1987; Galizio & Maisto, 1985). As happens too often, the empirical study of religion remains known only to a small circle of scholars, with the consequence that this significant literature is not brought to bear on social policy, community planning, or program development. Research is needed to better understand how knowledge about the religious dimension of life can be successfully and usefully transferred to these spheres of activity.

References

Adlaf, E.M., & Smart, R.G. (1985). Drug use and religious affiliation, feelings, and behavior. *British Journal of Addiction, 80*, 163–171.

Argyle, M., & Beit-Hallahmi, B. (1975). *The social psychology of religion.* London: Routledge & Kegan Paul.

Benson, P.L. (1990). *The troubled journey: A portrait of 6th-12th grade youth.* Minneapolis: Lutheran Brotherhood.

Benson, P.L., & Donahue, M.J. (1989). Ten year trends in at-risk behavior: A national study of black adolescents. *Journal of Adolescent Research, 4*(2), 125–139.

Benson, P.L., Williams, D.L., & Johnson, A.L. (1987). *The quicksilver years: The hopes and fears of early adolescence.* San Francisco: Harper & Row.

Benson, P.L., Wood P.K., Johnson, A.L., Eklin, C.H., & Mills, J.E. (1983). *Report on 1983 Minnesota survey of drug use and drug-related attitudes.* Minneapolis: Search Institute.

Benson, P.L., Yeager, R.J., Wood, P.K., Guerra, M.J., & Manno, B.V. (1986). *Catholic high schools: Their impact on low-income students.* Washington, DC: National Catholic Educational Association.

Bock, E.W., Cochran, J.K., & Beeghley, L. (1987). Moral messages: The relative influence of denomination on the religiosity-alcohol relationship. *The Sociological Quarterly, 28*(1), 89–103.

Bratter, T.E., & Forrest, G.G. (1985). *Alcoholism and substance abuse: Strategies for clinical intervention.* New York: The Free Press.

Brook, J.S., Whiteman, M., Gordon, A.S., & Brook, D.W. (1984). Paternal determinants of female adolescents' marijuana use. *Developmental Psychology, 20*(6), 1032–1043.

Burchard, J.D., & Burchard, S.N. (Eds.) (1987). *Prevention of delinquent behavior.* Newbury Park, CA: Sage Publications.

Burkett, S.R. (1977). Religion, parental influences, and adolescent alcohol and marijuana use. *Journal of Drug Issues, 7*(3), 263–273.

Burkett, S.R. (1980). Religiosity, beliefs, normative standards, and adolescent drinking. *Journal of Studies on Alcohol, 41*(7), 662–671.

Burkett, S.R., & White, M. (1974). Hellfire and delinquency: Another look. *Journal for the Scientific Study of Religion, 13,* 455–462.

Cahalan, D. (1976). *Problem drinkers.* San Francisco: Jossey-Bass.

Cahalan, D., & Cisin, I.H. (1968). American drinking practices: Summary of findings from a national probability sample. *Quarterly Journal of Studies on Alcohol, 29,* 130–151.

Cochran, J.K., Beeghley, L., & Bock, E.W. (1988). Religiosity and alcohol behavior: An exploration of reference group theory. *Sociological Forum, 3*(2), 256–276.

Coombs, R.H., Wellisch, D.K., & Fawzy, F.I. (1985). Drinking patterns and problems among female children and adolescents: A comparison of abstainers, past users, and current users. *American Journal of Drug and Alcohol Abuse, 11,* 315–348.

Donahue, M.J. (1985). Intrinsic and extrinsic religiousness: Review and meta-analysis. *Journal of Personality and Social Psychology, 48*(2), 400–419.

Donahue, M.J. (1987). *Religion and drug use: 1976–1985.* Paper presented at the annual meeting of the Society for the Scientific Study of Religion, Louisville, Kentucky.

Dudley, R.L., Mutch, P.B., & Cruise, R.J. (1987). Religious factors and drug usage among Seventh-day Adventist youth in North America. *Journal for the Scientific Study of Religion, 26*(2), 218–233.

Fors, S.W., & Rojek, D.G. (1983). The social and demographic correlates of adolescent drug use patterns. *Journal of Drug Education, 13*(3), 205–222.

Galizio, M., & Maisto, S.A. (Eds.) (1985). *Determinants of substance abuse: Biological, psychological, & environmental factors.* New York: Plenum Press.

Gergen, M.K., Gergen, K.J., & Morse, S.J. (1972). Correlates of marijuana use among college students. *Journal of Applied Social Psychology, 2*(1), 1–16.

Globetti, G., & Windham, G.O. (1967). The social adjustment of high school students and the use of beverage alcohol. *Journal of Applied Social Psychology, 2,* 1–16.

Glock, C., & Stark, R. (1965). *Religion and society in tension.* Chicago: Rand McNally.

Gorsuch, R.L., & Butler, M.C. (1976). Initial drug abuse: A review of predisposing social psychological factors. *Psychological Bulletin, 83*(1), 120–137.

Gottlieb, N.H., & Green, L.W. (1984). Life events, social network, life-style, and health: An analysis of the 1979 national survey of personal health practices and consequences. *Health Education Quarterly, 11*(1), 91–105.

Hadaway, C.K., Elifson, K.W., & Petersen, D.M. (1984). Religious involvement and drug use among urban adolescents. *Journal for the Scientific Study of Religion, 23*(2), 109–128.

Higgins, P.C., & Albrecht, G.L. (1977). Hellfire and delinquency revisited. *Social Forces, 55,* 952–958.

Hirschi, T., & Stark, R. (1969). Hellfire and delinquency. *Social Problems, 17,* 202–213.

Hundleby, J.D. (1987). Adolescent drug use in a behavioral matrix: A confirmation and comparison of the sexes. *Addictive Behaviors, 12,* 103–112.

Jensen, G.F., & Erickson, M.L. (1979). The religious factor and delinquency: Another look at the hellfire hypothesis. In R. Wuthnow (Ed.), *The religious dimension: New direction in quantitative research* (pp. 155–177). New York: Academic Press.

Jessor, R., Jessor, S.L. (1977). *Problem behavior and psychosocial development: A longitudinal study of youth.* New York: Academic Press.

Jessor, R., Jessor, S.L., & Finney, J. (1973). A social psychology of marijuana use: Longitudinal studies of high school and college youth. *Journal of Personality and Social Psychology, 26*(1), 1–15.

Kandel, D.B., Trieman, D., Faust, R., & Single, E. (1976). Adolescent involvement in legal and illegal drug use: A multiple classification analysis. *Social Forces, 55*(2), 438–458.

Knupfer, G., & Room, R. (1967). Drinking patterns and attitudes of Irish, Jewish, and white Protestant men. *Quarterly Journal of Studies on Alcohol, 28,* 676–699.

Lorch, B.R., & Hughes, R.H. (1985). Religion and youth substance use. *Journal of Religion and Health, 24*(3), 197–208.

Margulies, R.Z., Kessler, R.C., & Kandel, D.B. (1977). A longitudinal study of onset of drinking among high-school students. *Journal of Studies on Alcohol, 38*(5), 1977.

Mauss, A.L. (1969). Anticipatory socialization toward college as a factor in adolescent marijuana use. *Social Problems, 76,* 357–364.

McIntosh, W.A., Fitch, S.D., Wilson, J.B., & Nyberg, K.L. (1981). The effects of mainstream religious social controls on adolescent drug use in rural areas. *Review of Religious Research, 23*(1), 54–75.

Middleton, R., & Putney, S. (1962). Religion, normative standards, and behavior. *Sociometry, 25,* 145–152.

Mookherjee, H.N. (1985). Comparison of some personality characteristics of male problem dinkers in rural Tennessee. *Journal of Alcohol and Drug Education, 33,* 23–28.

Nelsen, H.M., & Rooney, J.F. (1982). Fire and brimstone, lager and pot: Religious involvement and substance use. *Sociological Analysis, 43*(3), 247–256.

Nicholi, A.M. (1985). Characteristics of college students who use psychoactive drugs for nonmedical purposes. *Journal of American College Health, 33,* 189–192.

Perkins, H.W. (1985). Religious traditions, parents, and peers as determinants of alcohol and drug use among college students. *Review of Religious Research, 27*(1), 15–31.

Perkins, H.W. (1987). Parental religion and alcohol use problems as intergenerational predictors of problem drinking among college youth. *Journal for the Scientific Study of Religion, 26*(3), 340–357.

Rohrbaugh, J., & Jessor, R. (1975). Religiosity in youth: A personal control against deviant behavior. *Journal of Personality, 43,* 136–155.

Schlegel, R.P., & Sanborn, M.D. (1979). Religious affiliation and adolescent drinking. *Journal of Studies on Alcohol, 40*(7), 693–703.

Spilka, B., Hood, R.W., & Gorsuch, R.L. (1985). *The psychology of religion: An empirical approach.* Englewood Cliffs, NJ: Prentice-Hall.

Steffenhagen, R.A., McAree, C.P., & Nixon, H.L. (1972). Drug use among college females: Socio-demographic and social psychological correlates. *The International Journal of the Addictions, 7*(2), 285–303.

Vener, A.M., Zaenglein, M., & Stewart, D.B. (1977). Traditional religious orthodoxy, respect for authority and nonconformity in adolescence. *Adolescence, 12*(45), 43–56.

Wechsler, H., Demone, H.W., Thum, D., & Kasey, E.K. (1970). Religious-ethnic differences in alcohol consumption. *Journal of Health and Social Behavior, 11,* 21–29.

Weinstein, R.M. (1976). The imputation of motives for marijuana behavior. *The International Journal of the Addictions, 11,* 571–595.

Whitehead, P.C. (1970). Religious affiliation and use of drugs among adolescent students. *Journal for the Scientific Study of Religion, 9*(2), 152–154.

Wuthnow, R. (1978). *Experimentation in American religion.* Berkeley: University of California Press.

Zucker, R.A., & Harford, T.C. (1983). National study of the demography of adolescent drinking practices in 1980. *Journal of Studies in Alcohol, 44*(6), 974–985.

17

Religious Orientation and Mental Health

Kevin S. Masters and Allen E. Bergin

Historical Perspective

The relation between religion and mental health has long been a topic of debate among psychologists. Some of the most famous names in psychological history have taken a stance on this issue. Sigmund Freud, G. Stanley Hall, B. F. Skinner, Carl Rogers, Carl Jung, and many others had much to say, both pro and con. In addition, William James (1902) noted that there are both healthy and unhealthy ways of being religious, and Gordon Allport (1950) stated that the way one is religious may have mental health implications.

More recent authors have continued the debate. Bergin (1980) noted that theistic values could have beneficial effects and may be useful in psychotherapy, but others disagreed (Ellis, 1980; Walls, 1980). Albert Ellis (1986) has been unequivocal in asserting that "devout religiosity" (p. 104) leads to emotional disturbance; while more probabilistic religious beliefs may have ". . . psychotherapeutic value to some of the people some of the time . . . " (p. 101).

Although there is no clear consensus regarding the impact of religion on mental health (Jensen & Bergin, 1988), it does appear that there is agreement on one thing: religion is not a homogeneous, unidimensional construct. A uniformity approach simply does not allow for precise differentiation of the role of religion in the life of the believer and consequently leaves many important questions unaddressed. Therefore, if researchers are interested in seriously studying the psychological impact of religion, they need to go beyond asking "Is the person religious?" and move to the question "How is the person religious?" There may be many ways to do this. Some writers have looked at religious affiliation or denomination. These studies provide a more differentiated level of investigation. But knowing that people are, for example, Presbyterians tells us very little about what being Presbyterian means to them, what their personal theological beliefs actually are, or how they experience their "Presbyterianism." The level of analysis remains too broad to allow for understanding of the impact and relation of specific religious factors on psychological mechanisms.

Definition of Intrinsic and Extrinsic Religious Orientations

Currently the most important and comprehensive body of literature pertaining to the relationship between religious orientation and mental health is grounded in Allport and Ross's (1967) analysis. This includes two major divisions; intrinsic and extrinsic. The intrinsic orientation is guided by a sincere commitment that operates as the navigating motivation in a person's life. People who are intrinsically motivated internalize their beliefs and live by them regardless of the external consequences. For example, a person intrinsically committed to the ideal of sexual relations only in marriage may refuse premarital or extra-marital sexual advances. Gorsuch and McPherson (1989) reported that the single best item from the Religious Orientation Scale (ROS; Allport & Ross, 1967) to measure intrinsic religion is "My whole approach to life is based upon my religion."

The extrinsic orientation, on the other hand, is basically utilitarian. Extrinsically motivated people use their religion as a means of obtaining status, security, self-justification, and sociability. Obviously a more selfish element is involved in this approach. Gorsuch and McPherson (1989) found that the item "I go to church mainly because I enjoy seeing people I know there" best measures the extrinsic orientation. Extrinsic individuals may view their religion as a means to a happy life. So they may pray in order to feel better or alleviate fears.

Recent research (Kirkpatrick, 1989) has suggested that the extrinsic approach, as currently measured, may actually consist of two orientations: (1) extrinsic-social (i.e., using religion toward social gain); and (2) extrinsic-personal (i.e., using religion toward gaining comfort, security, and protection). This differentiation may prove useful in future research (Gorsuch & McPherson, 1989; McFarland, 1989).

A former neighbor of one of the authors inadvertently provided a vivid illustration of the difference between intrinsic and extrinsic orientations, and of how knowing a person's denominational allegiance does not adequately describe that person's religious orientation. Both he and his wife were Catholic. One night he, an extrinsically religious individual, complained to her, saying, "The problem with you, Jane, is that you let your religion run your life."

Definition of Mental Health

While defining terms like "religion" and "religious orientation" has proved to be very difficult (Kirkpatrick & Hood, 1990; Masters, 1991), defining mental health has been only slightly easier. Singular definitions of mental health rooted in narrow theories are inadequate. However, there may be more agreement among professionals than theoretical differences in terminology would suggest.

To determine empirically what values professional therapists consider important to mental health, Jensen and Bergin (1988) conducted a national survey of 425 mental health professionals in the United States. Surprisingly, the sample was largely in agreement that the following are important for mental health: (1) competent perception and expression of feelings; (2) freedom, autonomy, and responsibility; (3) integration and coping ability; (4) self-maintenance and physical fitness;

(5) self-awareness and personal growth; (6) human relatedness and interpersonal commitment; (7) mature frame of orientation; and (8) forgiveness. However, diversity of opinion was found on the themes of spirituality/religiosity and sexual fulfillment. Thus while it is difficult to state exactly what is meant by mental health, it seems that practicing professionals do at least generally agree on many of the important aspects of it. Nevertheless, disagreement remains concerning the impact of religiosity.

Mental Health and Religious Orientation: An Overview

Over the last 20 years there has been a plethora of research on the intrinsic/extrinsic orientation. Gorsuch (1988) commented that this approach has provided the most empirically useful definitions of religion so far, while Donahue (1985) noted that 70 published studies had used Allport's ROS, making it one of the most frequently used measures of religiousness. What follows will be a representative, but not exhaustive, review of this literature as it pertains to mental health. We will also briefly discuss the "quest" dimension (Batson & Ventis, 1982).

A few words of caution are in order before proceeding. Most of the research to be presented has been conducted on college students, church members, or others who were not seeking psychological intervention, and who would not be considered to be suffering from a clinical disorder at the time of the study. Certainly, the findings are useful in providing information about mental health, but there are limits to what can be said regarding mental illness. Additionally, much of the research is short-term, cross-sectional, and correlational in nature. Consequently, it is not possible to confirm causal inferences, although refutation remains theoretically plausible. Finally, to facilitate the readability of the chapter, we will not report the numerous individual correlation coefficients. Generally speaking, the magnitude of the correlations is modest, ranging from the high teens into the .40s.

Freedom from Pathology

A frequently cited definition of mental health is the absence of pathology. Bergin, Stinchfield, Gaskin, Masters, and Sullivan (1988), in a study of intrinsically religious college students, found that subjects' scores on the MMPI were all within normal ranges. More specifically, several studies have looked at religious orientation as it relates to two of the most common forms of pathology, depression and anxiety. For example, Watson, Morris, and Hood (1988a,b,c) conducted a series of investigations finding that intrinsic religiousness correlated negatively with depression scales, whereas extrinsic religiousness was positively correlated with them.

Many authors have investigated religious orientation and anxiety. Again the findings generally indicate less anxiety among the intrinsically religious and more among the extrinsically religious. Baker and Gorsuch (1982) found a negative correlation between intrinsic scores and trait anxiety, and a positive correlation between extrinsic scores and anxiety. Similar findings were reported by Lovekin and Malony (1977), and Bergin, Masters, and Richards (1987). Sturgeon and Hamley (1979) reported that intrinsically oriented Christians were less anxious on trait and existential anxiety than were their extrinsic counterparts. Finally, Watson, Morris, and Hood (1988c) reported that there was no relation between intrinsic scores and anxiety, but there was a positive relation between extrinsic scores and anxiety.

A third area of pathology that has been the object of empirical investigation concerns obsessive–compulsive symptoms. Dixon, Alexander, and Anderson (1990) argued that level of obsessional-compulsive symptoms can be considered one index of mental health in college populations. They also noted that those taking a negative view of religiousness have often hypothesized a link between religion and obsessions and compulsions. Dixon et al. found that increases in extrinsic religiousness were associated with increases in obsessive–compulsive symptoms, while increases in intrinsic religiousness were associated with decreases in symptoms. These findings, along with those of Bergin et al. (1987), provide evidence contrary to Wiebe and Fleck's (1980) concern that intrinsic religiousness may degenerate into pathological rigidity and obsessive compulsivity.

Positive Mental Health

There are a number of studies relating intrinsic and extrinsic religiousness with a variety of dimensions of personality and emotional functioning that are considered positive. The breadth, and to some extent the lack of depth, of this research makes it difficult to organize. For our purposes, the characteristics of mental health cited above (Jensen & Bergin, 1988) will serve as an orienting framework.

Competent Perception and Expression of Feelings. This dimension concerns being sensitive to others and being open and accepting of one's own feelings. A series of studies by Watson et al. (1988a,b; Watson, Hood, Morris, & Hall, 1987) revealed that intrinsic religiousness correlated positively with empathic concern, self-consciousness, and internal state of awareness whereas the opposite was true for extrinsic religiousness. Additionally, intrinsic religion correlated negatively with measures of narcissistic personality disorder, whereas extrinsic religion was positively related with these measures. Intrinsic religion was unrelated to measures of superiority/arrogance and self-absorption/self-admiration. Chau, Johnson, Bowers, Darvill, and Danko (1990) found intrinsic scores to be positively correlated with altruism, and Wiebe and Fleck (1980) found intrinsically religious subjects to be empathetic and open to their emotions.

In the area of helping behavior, however, Batson and colleagues (Batson & Gray, 1981; Batson & Flory, 1990) have argued that intrinsic subjects are motivated by egoistic goals of gaining social and self-rewards, rather than altruistic or empathic concerns for the victim. This position has been convincingly attacked on logical as well as methodological grounds by Gorsuch (1988) and Watson et al. (1987). Presently, it is fair to say that the motivation of intrinsically religious individuals in helping situations is an area still open to further investigation.

Freedom, Autonomy, and Responsibility. Mental health professionals agree that healthy individuals are characterized by the aptitude to develop alternatives at choice points, the capacity for self-control, and the assumption of responsibility for their actions. Several studies have addressed these areas.

Pargament, Steele, and Tyler (1979) noted that intrinsic individuals were characterized by an active, flexible approach to dealing with life situations, and Kahoe (1974) found that intrinsic scores were consistently related to grade point average (with college aptitude held constant). In a related finding, Bergin et al. (1987) found that intrinsic scores were positively related to tolerance and self-control, whereas extrinsic scores related negatively with tolerance. Donahue (1985) reports that intrinsic scores are relatively unrelated to dogmatism, whereas extrinsic scores show a positive relation. These findings all suggest that intrinsic individuals have the ability to work flexibly in problem-solving situations and to develop reasonable alternatives.

A consistent finding is that intrinsic individuals score high on measures of responsibility. Wiebe and Fleck (1980) noted that intrinsic subjects showed greater concern for moral standards, conscientiousness, discipline, and responsibility than did extrinsic or nonreligious subjects. Likewise, Bergin et al. (1987) found high positive correlations between measures of responsibility and measures of intrinsic religiosity, whereas the opposite was true of extrinsic scores. In fact, the .44 correlation between intrinsic religiosity and responsibility on the California Psychological Inventory is one of the strongest correlations in the literature. Another sample, reported in the same study, demonstrated that intrinsic individuals tend to reject the notion that the past is an all-important determinant of present behavior. This suggests a greater likelihood for behavior change.

Integration and Coping. The abilities to cope with stress and to have an integrated cognitive approach to understanding are characteristic of mentally healthy individuals. In an interesting study utilizing Protestant, Jewish, and Roman Catholic subjects, Pargament et al. (1979) found that high intrinsic members had more active coping skills than did low intrinsic members. In a more recent study, Hathaway and Pargament (1990) suggest that the way intrinsic religiosity and mental health relate may be mediated by a third variable called psychoreligiousness, which deals with how one's faith influences one's life. This study is exemplary because it proposes a detailed model to explain the relationships involved, while also defining, measuring, and clarifying specific mediating variables that have been largely unexplored.

Albert Ellis and other cognitively oriented psychologists have observed that irrational thought patterns and beliefs lie at the core of many psychopathological conditions. But how does religious orientation relate to this dimension of functioning? Studies by Watson et al. (1988c) and Bergin et al. (1987) indicate that intrinsic religiosity is not related to irrational thinking, but the extrinsic approach tends to show positive relations.

Self-Awareness and Personal Growth. Psychologists believe that being aware of one's own motives, personality patterns, and behaviors is highly desirable. The same is true with regard to one's ability to alter these in a positive manner. Studies relating religious orientation to self-esteem, self-efficacy, ego strength, and insecurity are all relevant to this discussion.

Several writers (Payne, Bergin, Bielema, & Jenkins, 1991; Watson, Hood, Morris, 1985) have noted that findings relating religiousness and self-esteem have been equivocal. However, they point out that the humanistic language of many self-esteem scales is incompatible with orthodox concepts, such as sin and guilt. When these value biases and the guilt language of sin have been controlled, positive relationships between self-functioning and intrinsic religiosity have been found. Additionally, Bergin et al. (1988) obtained normal scores for an intrinsically religious sample of college students on the Tennessee Self-Concept Scale. Other authors (e.g., Pargament et al., 1979) have noted that intrinsically oriented people are characterized by both efficacy and self-esteem. Minton and Spilka (1976) revealed that powerlessness was affiliated with extrinsic religion but not with intrinsic religion. Finally, Baker and Gorsuch (1982) showed positive relations between intrinsic religion and ego strength, and negative relations between intrinsic religion and insecurity. The opposite pattern was found for the relationship between extrinsic religion and the same variables.

Mature Frame of Orientation. Therapists agree that having a purpose for living and being guided by higher level principles of living are beneficial to mental functioning. In this regard, Frankl (1985) has provided a vivid portrayal of the importance of meaning and purpose.

Many writers have noted an increase in religiosity later in life, in what Erikson (1963) has described as the stage of integrity versus despair. At this time, individuals are looking for purpose and meaning to their existence. In a study of elderly people, Van Haitsma (1986) found that intrinsic scores correlated with a life satisfaction index. Both Bolt (1975) and Soderstrom and Wright (1977) found that intrinsically motivated subjects had significantly higher purpose-in-life scores than did extrinsically motivated subjects.

In a related area, Donahue (1985) has noted that research may indicate a trend for fear of death to be negatively related to intrinsic religion, and to be positively related with extrinsic religion. Finally, several authors (Alker & Gawin, 1978; Bergin et al., 1987; Chamberlain & Zika, 1988; Payne et al., 1991) have noted a small but reliable relationship demonstrating that intrinsic religion is related to well-being. In a study of the elderly, however, Koenig, Kvale, and Ferrel (1988) found that only health accounted for more of the explained variance in morale and well-being measures than did religious variables (which included intrinsic measures).

Challenge to the Healthiness of Intrinsic Religiosity

Keeping methodological constraints in mind, it seems a straightforward matter to conclude that intrinsic religion is associated with positive mental health, while extrinsic religion is associated with poor mental health. However, Batson and his colleagues (Batson, 1976; Batson, Flink, Shoenrade, Fultz, & Pych, 1986; Batson, Naifeh, & Pate, 1978; Batson & Ventis, 1982) have consistently offered a strong challenge to this conclusion. Their research is primarily based in the areas of prejudice and helping behavior, but it has implications across the intrinsic–extrinsic spectrum of research. Essentially, they conclude that (1) intrinsic religion, as presently measured, fails to incorporate an important aspect of Allport's original conceptualization (i.e., doubt), (2) measures of intrinsic religion are hopelessly confounded by social desirability, and (3) self-reported helping behavior of religious subjects has failed to correlate with specific helping behavior. Thus, positive correlations between intrinsic religion and favorable mental health variables may simply be due to the desire to appear healthy on the part of the intrinsic individuals. Batson and his colleagues have produced correlational and experimental evidence to support this position. In addition, as described below, they also introduced a third style of religious orientation, namely quest.

Several writers (Chau et al., 1990; Donahue, 1985; Gorsuch, 1988; Morris, Hood, & Watson, 1988; Watson, Morris, Foster, & Hood, 1986) have criticized the social desirability hypothesis on both theoretical and empirical grounds. Specific points of rebuttal include the following: (1) not all studies have found a relation between intrinsic religiosity and social desirability; (2) certain measures of social desirability may be confounded by a religious relevance dimension; (3) it is unreasonable to expect aggregated variables to relate to an individual variable because the level of aggregation is inappropriate; (4) there is evidence that intrinsically religious people may actually be more desirable socially; (5) a historical perspective indicates that what is socially desirable at one time and place may not be at another time and place, something that proponents of the social desirability hypothesis have failed to consider; and (6) other equally persuasive theoretical interpretations of the literature are possible. These arguments are compelling, and readers are encouraged to study the original articles in order to draw their own conclusions. Our opinion is that intrinsic religiousness has withstood the social desirability challenge, and therefore the conclusion that this orientation is related to better mental health functioning remains legitimate.

Quest

Batson's third religious orientation has been termed *quest*. He feels that it is more true to Allport's original conceptualization of intrinsic religion since it includes aspects that he believes have been left out of the later writings and scale of measurement. These include complexity, doubt, and tentativeness (Batson & Ventis, 1982). Subsequently, the Interactional Scale (Batson & Ventis, 1982) was designed to measure quest by capturing the "readiness to face existential questions without reducing their complexity . . . , self-criticism and perception of religious doubts as positive . . . , and openness to change" (p. 154). Batson and Ventis theorize that, since this approach more adequately captures the essence of healthy religion, it will ultimately produce the strongest relations with positive mental health. Indeed, he and others (e.g., Sapp & Jones, 1986) have provided empirical evidence to support their position for such variables as integration, self-criticism, flexibility in dealing with existential concerns, principled moral reasoning, and prejudice.

Once again, however, there have been numerous criticisms of this research (Donahue, 1985; Watson, Morris, & Hood, 1989). Some authors contend that quest has been found to relate positively to indicators of *poor* mental health. For example, Spilka, Kojetin and McIntosh (1985) found that quest was positively related to anxiety and conflict. Kojetin, McIntosh, Bridges, and Spilka (1987) reported similar findings, although they hypothesized that this may indicate negative functioning or, alternatively, a constructive phase of doubt leading to intrinsic faith. Other writers (e.g., Watson, Morris, & Hood, 1989) have suggested that the Interactional Scale (measuring quest) is more representative of a rejection of traditional religion than an existentially complex attempt to find meaning in life. They also reject the idea that orthodox beliefs, which correlate with intrinsic scores, are indicative of ontological simplicity. Finally, from a theoretical perspective, Donahue (1985) argues that quest is not in the historical Hebrew tradition (as stated by Batson) and that it is not the essence of what Allport (1950) had in mind when discussing mature religion. Rather, quest more likely indicates a phase in the development of a mature/intrinsic religious orientation.

Conclusion and Suggestions for Future Research

If intrinsic religiousness is indeed related to mental health, what is it about being intrinsically religious that is beneficial? This is certainly a difficult question to answer. Those who are intrinsically religious (at least as they have been studied within the Judeo-Christian tradition) have a comprehensive world view that has tremendous explanatory power. It provides them with a sense of purpose and meaning to life. But perhaps it is their strength of conviction to this world view that is most important.

In an interesting study, Ross (1990) found that stronger religious beliefs related to lower levels of psychological distress. She also found that people with no religion had low levels of distress. Similarly, Shaver, Lenauer, and Sadd (1980), in a study of 2500 American women, found a curvilinear relation between religiousness, on the one hand, and health and happiness on the other. Again it appears that certainty of belief, or lack of conflict, may be more important to well-being than religion per se. Other authors have noted that intrinsic and nonreligious individuals often score similarly on various measures of mental health.

It also seems important that one actually behaves in synchrony with one's religious values in order for there to be beneficial mental health consequences. For example, Pargament et al. (1979) found that those who attended church frequently, but were less intrinsically religious, showed the worst psychological profiles on such dimensions as coping skills, self-attitudes, and world attitudes. A little religion may be a bad thing. As an old-time evangelist used to say, "Some people have just enough religion to bug them rather than bless them." The extrinsic approach is essentially pragmatic and may therefore be confusing in terms of behavioral proscriptions. Intrinsic approaches seem more straightforward and therefore behavioral admonitions are more clearly defined and perhaps more capable of being followed.

If strength of commitment and subsequent behavior are important, then what is the role of doubt in religious faith? The empirical evidence shows that doubt may be related to worse functioning. However, several writers have observed that doubt may be essential to the development of intrinsic faith. They propose the following developmental sequence: extrinsic-quest-intrinsic. A period of doubt may be necessary to move from the utilitarian and limited extrinsic approach to a broad and principled intrinsic religiousness. For individuals to accept certain ways of being religious as their own, they may need to question the very principles that they eventually embrace. Cognitive dissonance theory would suggest that those who initially struggle with their faith may, once having accepted it, be more likely to hold strongly (and intrinsically) to it. However, some individuals may get stuck in the doubting stage and not progress to the point of being comfortable with their beliefs.

Support for the progression over time toward intrinsic religiousness was supplied by Masters, Bergin, Reynolds, and Sullivan (1991) in their longitudinal study of 60 religious college students. Longitudinal studies are, however, few and far between. The field could certainly benefit from research that more thoroughly investigates the role of religion and ways of being religious in individuals as they grow through the life cycle. Prospective research that asks penetrating questions about how one is religious and relates this to adjustment and behavior will prove to be most useful.

If strength of commitment is important, does it matter what one is committed to? What are the behavioral and psychological ramifications, if any, of believing, for example, in predestination, free will, salvation by grace, salvation by works, and so forth? This area is wide open for future investigation. Donahue (1989) has argued that an understanding of theology is important to the psychology of religion and that "future research should examine the cognitive structure and ramifications of religious beliefs, and which belief structures are associated with which effects" (p. 334). Kirkpatrick and Hood (1990) have similarly called for studies investigating specific belief content. Certainly these recommendations are worthy of careful consideration and implementation.

Finally, there are many important topics pertaining to religious orientation that have not been considered in this brief chapter. For example, we have not discussed measurement issues, conceptual purity problems, or alternative perspectives for viewing religious orientation. Other investigators may wish to pursue these topics in order to come to a more complete understanding of the role of religious orientation in mental health functioning.

References

Alker, H.A., & Gawin, F. (1978). On the intrapsychic specificity of happiness. *Journal of Personality, 46,* 311–322.

Allport, G.W. (1950). *The individual and his religion.* New York: Macmillan.

Allport, G.W., & Ross, J.M. (1967). Personal religious orientation and prejudice. *Journal of Personality and Social Psychology, 5,* 432–443.

Baker, M., & Gorsuch, R. (1982). Trait anxiety and intrinsic-extrinsic religiousness. *Journal for the Scientific Study of Religion, 21,* 119–122.

Batson, C.D. (1976). Religion as prosocial: Agent or double agent? *Journal for the Scientific Study of Religion, 15,* 29–45.

Batson, C.D., Flink, C.H., Shoenrade, P.A., Fultz, J., & Pych, V. (1986). Religious orientation and overt versus covert racial prejudice. *Journal of Personality and Social Psychology, 50,* 175–181.

Batson, C.D., & Flory, J.D. (1990). Goal-relevant cognitions associated with helping by individuals high on intrinsic, end religion. *Journal for the Scientific Study of Religion, 29*, 346–360.

Batson, C.D., & Gray, R.A. (1981). Religious orientation and helping behavior: Responding to one's own or to the victim's needs? *Journal of Personality and Social Psychology, 40*, 511–520.

Batson, C.D., Naifeh, S.J., & Pate, S. (1978). Social desirability, religious orientation, and racial prejudice. *Journal for the Scientific Study of Religion, 17*, 31–41.

Batson, C.D., & Ventis, W.L. (1982). *The religious experience.* New York: Oxford University Press.

Bergin, A.E. (1980). Psychotherapy and religious values. *Journal of Consulting and Clinical Psychology, 48*, 95–105.

Bergin, A.E., Masters, K.S., & Richards, P.S. (1987). Religiousness and mental health reconsidered: A study of an intrinsically religious sample. *Journal of Counseling Psychology, 34*, 197–204.

Bergin, A.E., Stinchfield, R.D., Gaskin, T.A., Masters, K.S., & Sullivan, C.E. (1988). Religious life-styles and mental health: An exploratory study. *Journal of Counseling Psychology, 35*, 91–98.

Bolt, M. (1975). Purpose in life and religious orientation. *Journal of Psychology and Theology, 3*, 116–118.

Chamberlain, K., & Zika, S. (1988). Religiosity, life meaning and well-being: Some relationships in a sample of women. *Journal for the Scientific Study of Religion, 27*, 411–420.

Chau, L.L., Johnson, R.C., Bowers, J.K., Darvill, T.J., & Danko, G.P. (1990). Intrinsic and extrinsic religiosity as related to conscience, adjustment, and altruism. *Personality and Individual Differences, 11*, 397–400.

Dixon, W., Alexander, J., & Anderson, W. (1990, May). *The relationship between intrinsic and extrinsic religious orientation and obsessions and compulsions.* Paper presented at the 62nd Annual Meeting of the Midwestern Psychological Association, Chicago, Illinois.

Donahue, M.J. (1985). Intrinsic and extrinsic religiousness: Review and meta-analysis. *Journal of Personality and Social Psychology, 48*, 400–419.

Donahue, M.J. (1989). Disregarding theology in the psychology of religion: Some examples. *Journal of Psychology and Theology, 17*, 324–335.

Ellis, A. (1980). Psychotherapy and atheistic values: A response to A.E. Bergin's "Psychotherapy and religious values." *Journal of Consulting and Clinical Psychology, 48*, 635–639.

Ellis, A. (1986). Do some religious beliefs help create emotional disturbance? *Psychotherapy in Private Practice, 4*, 101–106.

Erikson, E.H. (1963). *Childhood and society.* New York: Norton.

Frankl, V. (1985). *Man's search for meaning.* New York: Washington Square Press.

Gorsuch, R.L. (1988). Psychology of religion. In M.R. Rosenzweig & L.W. Porter (Eds.), *Annual review of psychology: Vol. 39* (pp. 201–221). Palo Alto: Annual Reviews.

Gorsuch, R.L., & McPherson, S.E. (1989). Intrinsic/Extrinsic measurement: I/E-revised and single-item scales. *Journal for the Scientific Study of Religion, 28*, 348–354.

Hathaway, W.I., & Pargament, K.I. (1990). Intrinsic religiousness, religious coping, and psychosocial competence: A covariance structure analysis. *Journal for the Scientific Study of Religion, 29*, 423–441.

James, W. (1902). *The varieties of religious experience.* New York: Longmans Green.

Jensen, J.P., & Bergin, A.E. (1988). Mental health values of professional therapists: A national interdisciplinary survey. *Professional Psychology: Research and Practice, 19,* 290–297.

Kahoe, R.D. (1974). Personality and achievement correlates of intrinsic and extrinsic religious orientations. *Journal of Personality and Social Psychology, 29,* 812–818.

Kirkpatrick, L.A. (1989). A psychometric analysis of the Allport-Ross and Feagin measures of intrinsic-extrinsic religious orientation. *Research in the Social Scientific Study of Religion, 1,* 1–31.

Kirkpatrick L.A., & Hood, R.W., Jr. (1990). Intrinsic-extrinsic religious orientation: The boon or bane of contemporary psychology of religion? *Journal for the Scientific Study of Religion, 29,* 442–462.

Koenig, H.G., Kvale, J.N., & Ferrel, C. (1988). Religion and well-being in later life. *The Gerontologist, 28,* 18–28.

Kojetin, B.A., McIntosh, D.N., Bridges, R.A., & Spilka, B. (1987). Quest: Constructive search or religious conflict? *Journal for the Scientific Study of Religion, 26,* 111–115.

Lovekin, A., & Malony, H.N. (1977). Religious glossolalia: A longitudinal study of personality changes. *Journal for the Scientific Study of Religion, 16,* 383–393.

Masters, K.S. (1991). Of boons, banes, babies and bathwater: A reply to Kirkpatrick and Hood's discussion of intrinsic/extrinsic religious orientation. *Journal for the Scientific Study of Religion, 30,* 312–317.

Masters, K.S., Bergin, A.E., Reynolds, E.M., & Sullivan, C.E. (1991). Religious life-styles and mental health: A follow-up study. *Counseling and Values, 35,* 211–224.

McFarland, S.G. (1989). Religious orientations and targets of discrimination. *Journal for the Scientific Study of Religion, 28,* 324–336.

Minton, B., & Spilka, B. (1976). Perspectives on death in relation to powerlessness and form of personal religion. *Omega, 7,* 261–267.

Morris, R.J., Hood, R.W., Jr., Watson, P.J. (1988). A second look at religious orientation, social desirability, and prejudice. *Bulletin of the Psychonomic Society, 27,* 81–84.

Pargament, K.I., Steele, R.E., & Tyler, F.B. (1979). Religious participation, religious motivation and individual psychosocial competence. *Journal for the Scientific Study of Religion, 18,* 412–419.

Payne, I.R., Bergin, A.E., Bielema, K.A., & Jenkins, P.H. (1991). Review of religion and mental health: Prevention and the enhancement of psychosocial functioning. *Prevention in Human Services, 9,* 11–40.

Ross, C.E. (1990). Religion and psychological distress. *Journal for the Scientific Study of Religion, 29,* 236–245.

Sapp, G.L., & Jones, L. (1986). Religious orientation and moral judgment. *Journal for the Scientific Study of Religion, 25,* 208–214.

Shaver, P., Lenauer, M., & Sadd, S. (1980). Religiousness, conversion, and subjective well-being: The "healthy-minded" religion of modern American women. *American Journal of Psychiatry, 137,* 1563–1568.

Soderstrom, D., & Wright, E.W. (1977). Religious orientation and meaning in life. *Journal of Clinical Psychology, 33,* 65–68.

Spilka, B., Kojetin, B., & McIntosh, D. (1985). Forms and measures of personal faith: Questions, correlates and distinctions. *Journal for the Scientific Study of Religion, 24,* 437–442.

Sturgeon, R.S., & Hamley, R.W. (1979). Religiosity and anxiety. *The Journal of Social Psychology, 108,* 137–138.

Van Haitsma, K. (1986). Intrinsic religious orientation: Implications in the study of religiosity and personal adjustment in the aged. *The Journal of Social Psychology, 126,* 685–687.

Walls, G.B. (1980). Values and psychotherapy: A comment on "psychotherapy and religious values." *Journal of Consulting and Clinical Psychology, 48,* 640–641.

Watson, P.J., Hood, R.W., Jr., & Morris, R.J. (1985). Religiosity, sin and self-esteem. *Journal of Psychology and Theology, 13,* 116–128.

Watson, P.J., Hood, R.W., Jr., Morris, R.J., & Hall, J.R. (1987). The relationship between religiosity and narcissism. *Counseling and Values, 31,* 179–184.

Watson, P.J., Morris, R.J., Foster, J.E., & Hood, R.W., Jr. (1986). Religiosity and social desirability. *Journal for the Scientific Study of Religion, 25,* 215–232.

Watson, P.J., Morris, R.J., & Hood, R.W., Jr. (1988a). Sin and self-functioning, Part 1: Grace, guilt, and self-consciousness. *Journal of Psychology and Theology, 16,* 254–268.

Watson, P.J., Morris, R.J., & Hood, R.W., Jr. (1988b). Sin and self-functioning, Part 2: Grace, guilt, and psychological adjustment. *Journal of Psychology and Theology, 16,* 270–281.

Watson, P.J., Morris, R.J., & Hood, R.W., Jr. (1988c). Sin and self-functioning, Part 3: The psychology and ideology of irrational beliefs. *Journal of Psychology and Theology, 16,* 348–361.

Watson, P.J., Morris, R.J., & Hood, R.W., Jr. (1989). Interactional factor correlations with means and end religiousness. *Journal for the Scientific Study of Religion, 28,* 337–347.

Wiebe, K.F., & Fleck, J.R. (1980). Personality correlates of intrinsic, extrinsic, and nonreligious orientations. *The Journal of Psychology, 105,* 181–187.

18

Mental Health of Cult Consumers: Legal and Scientific Controversy

James T. Richardson

Considerable controversy has erupted within the American context about the mental health status of participants in new religions, sometimes referred to as cults (Bromley & Richardson, 1983). Some people have claimed that participants are "brainwashed" into joining, and that "mind control" is used to retain members, leading to severe mental disorders (Singer, 1979; Singer & West, 1980; Clark, 1979; Shapiro, 1977). Others have adopted the view that participation is usually voluntary (Richardson, 1985a), lasts for a short time for most of those involved (Bird & Reimer, 1982; Richardson, van der Lans, & Derks, 1986), and that the experience is often ameliorative in its consequences (Kilbourne & Richardson, 1984; 1988).

Two recent reviews reveal the results of considerable scholarly research that has been done on the effects of participating in the new religions (Richardson, 1985b, 1990). The first of these reviews reported on psychological and psychiatric studies of participants in a number of new religions, including the Unification Church, a major Jesus Movement organization, the Divine Light Mission, Ananda Cooperative Village (an Eastern-oriented communal group in California), European segments of some groups (Unification Church, Ananda Marga, and the Children of God), deprogrammed members of several groups, and a campus fundamentalist group. It closes with the statement:

> The personality assessments of these groups reveal that life in the new religions is often therapeutic instead of harmful. Other information suggests that these young people are *affirming* their idealism by virtue of their involvement in such groups. Certainly there is some "submerging of personality" in the groups which are communal or collective, simply because they do not foster the individualistic and competitive lifestyle to which we are accustomed, particularly in American society. However, there is little data to support the almost completely negative picture painted by a few psychiatrists and psychologists who have been involved in the controversy over new religions. (Richardson, 1985b, p. 221)

The more recent review focused mainly on the controversial Rajneesh group, which has been studied in depth by a team from the University of Oregon psychology and sociology departments, and the Hare Krishna, which has seen more personality assessment research than any other new religion. It also included some follow-up work on the Jesus Movement group reported on in the earlier review. Both the Hare Krishna and the Rajneesh group have been the focus of tremendous controversy, including legal actions, making the research on them of special importance. In spite of the allegations about life in those two groups, the second review closed with this assessment:

> I see no reason to modify the conclusion statement from the earlier review. Indeed, the statement can be made even stronger, based on the thorough and sophisticated research that has been done. . . . The Rajneesh group has developed a lifestyle with more emotional openness and gender equality than exists in normal life, and some quite well-educated and relatively high status people have chosen to be a part of that lifestyle. This seems particularly the case for some women. The Hare Krishna have developed a rigorous, but apparently satisfying lifestyle for a few people, attracted by the very attributes that bring criticism from some detractors. Male Hare Krishna members seem to fare particularly well, in spite of their "compulsivity." The (Jesus Movement) group members, who had displayed traits that might have been dysfunctional in normal society, have apparently overcome any possible problems and adapted well to their new noncommunal lifestyles. (Richardson, 1990, p. 38)

Despite the overwhelming weight of research on participants in the new religions, some people (most notably, a few in the therapeutic community) refuse to accept the findings, and claim that the new religions are harmful. One major statement in *The American Psychologist,* after examining several commonalities between new religions and many types of psychotherapy, concluded that the controversy within the therapeutic community over new religions can best be explained by applying sociological conflict theory to the situation (Kilbourne & Richardson, 1984). There is a conflict between some therapists and new religions for clientele, and for ideological hegemony in American pluralistic culture.

The extent of the controversy over new religions or cults should not be underestimated (Robbins, 1988; Robbins, Shepherd, & McBride, 1985).[1] There have been congressional hearings on the matter, numerous attempts to pass state laws limiting the activities of such groups, and hundreds of court cases concerning various aspects of the groups, including several that have reached the U. S. Supreme Court (Bohn & Guttman, 1989; Richardson, 1986, 1991a, 1991b). There has also been a huge amount of media attention, usually taking a negative approach when describing the new groups and their participants (van Dreil & Richardson, 1988).

While it will never be possible to discern completely the roots of this controversy, it is important to make efforts to understand the history of events that brought us to the present state. This brief paper will examine one key episode in this history that made a major contribution to the development of what if referred to as the "anti-cult" position concerning cults and their consumers. The episode involved a series of legal actions brought by a father in an effort to gain legal and physical control over his son, who had chosen to join one of the new groups, popularly called "cults." The episode is important because (1) it attracted a large amount of publicity at the time, particularly in New York, the media center of the country, and (2) it involved some key mental health professionals in terms of the effort to define cult participation as a mental health problem.

The father in the case was a psychiatrist named Eli Shapiro, whose experiences with his son's involvement led him to write what may have been the first article in a scholarly journal defining cult participation as a significant mental health problem (Shapiro, 1977). He coined the term "destructive cultism" (the title of the article) as a name for a new mental health syndrome, which has been used since as a way to describe participation as a mental health problem by those opposed to such participation. The person used by the father as an expert to make an assessment of his son and to testify in court about the mental health of the son was Dr. John Clark, a prominent figure in anti-cult circles for the past two decades. He has written one prominent, even if brief, paper (Clark 1979), as well as widely distributed materials for anti-cult organizations (e.g., Clark, Langone, Schechter, & Daly, 1981), and has served as a leader and spokesman for those opposed to the new religions. His involvement in this case is important to consider in some depth, for it reveals both the substance of belief of those who would define cult participation as *ipso facto* a mental health problem, and it shows the strength of those beliefs and feelings among some in the mental health community in America.

The Shapiro Litigation

The litigation on which we focus involves efforts made by the father of Edward Shapiro to gain temporary and permanent guardianship over him through the use of conservatorship laws. The novel psychiatric theory presented by Dr. Clark in the case will be examined in depth, through the use of a transcript of the trial to determine if a Temporary Guardianship should be extended to allow more psychiatric testing of Edward Shapiro. The fact that two weeks of testing at a reputable mental hospital (McClean Hospital in Boston) had not revealed mental illness did not deter Dr. Clark from insisting on more testing of the son.

Edward Shapiro had suffered for some time from a diabetic condition. His father was concerned, as well, for his economic well-being. Edward had stock (over $30,000 worth, registered in his name) which had been given to him by his father, and over which he would gain control when he reached 21. His father wanted his son to leave ISKCON (International Society for Krishna Consciousness) and live a more normal life, and did not want the stock transferred to ISKCON.

Because of these concerns, the father, Eli Shapiro, in 1973 sought appointment of himself and his wife, Edward's stepmother, as Temporary Conservator of Edward's estate. The conservatorship law in Massachusetts allowed such proceedings for reasons of "advanced age or mental weakness," and it was on the latter point that the action hinged. The mental weakness allegedly derived from mind control used against the younger Shapiro by ISKCON recruiters, according to arguments advanced in legal briefs and in open court later in the proceedings. The Temporary Conservatorship was granted by the court, and not dissolved until 1977.

In 1976, in further legal action, the father sought to be appointed as Temporary and Permanent Guardian of his son. This occurred after Edward's arrest in New

York as a material witness in the bizarre case in which ISKCON was indicted by a grand jury for the false imprisonment and brainwashing of its members. The Temporary Guardianship was granted and, using that authority, Dr. Shapiro brought his son to Boston and placed him in a mental hospital for a thorough psychiatric evaluation. The intent was to have Edward declared mentally incompetent to manage his own health and financial affairs, which would support the father's petition for permanent guardianship.

As a part of the proceedings for Temporary Guardianship, Dr. John Clark signed an affidavit which stated:

> Edward David Shapiro demonstrates psychotic thinking and extremely poor judgment which renders him incapable of managing his very severe and long-standing juvenile diabetes; thus he is in immediate and constant danger to himself because he is mentally ill.

This analysis was reached on the basis on conversations with the father, the observation of a conversation between the father and the son, and a 15-minute interview with Edward by Clark some nine months before at a police station in New York. (Edward had been arrested in conjunction with the earlier-mentioned indictment of ISKCON members for "illegal imprisonment through mind control," and was being held there as a material witness. The New York case, which grew out of an earlier affidavit by Dr. Clark that Edward Shapiro was "incompetent as a result of mind control," was eventually dismissed.)

Thus, because of two affidavits signed by Dr. Clark, Edward Shapiro was forcibly taken away from his chosen religious group, transported to another state, incarcerated in a mental hospital, and forced to undergo psychiatric examinations. Edward Shapiro lost control of his finances, some of which funds were then used for expenses in the action, which attempted to prove him mentally ill (even to pay Dr. Clark's fee).

Theories Presented by Clark in the Shapiro Matter

Dr. Clark presented some rather unique ideas during the Shapiro litigation. He assumed that "cults" "brainwash" their members and use "mind control" techniques to maintain discipline and membership in the group.[2] Clark had espoused his brainwashing/mind control ideas in other forums. However, the strength of his defense of the theory was unexpected, especially in light of information available to Clark prior to his testimony. This concerned the two-week evaluation and observation at the mental hospital which led the team of doctors there to conclude that Shapiro was *not* mentally ill, and that he was capable of taking care of his physical health and financial affairs.

Clark took the unusual position that regular methods of detecting mental illness would not suffice in cases of mind control, because the mind control would cause the person being evaluated to give inaccurate responses. In other words, *mental illness could be concealed through use of mind control techniques.* Logically, this could mean that the more normal the responses to standardized evaluation methods, the more likely that the subject was under mind control. This seems an absurd position to hold, but it also makes the theory incapable of disproof. Supposedly, only an expert like Clark can tell if responses are real, or are influenced by mind control.

Clark proposed to the court that Edward Shapiro be retained in the hospital for an additional period of up to a month to undergo "stress testing" to determine if he was under mind control. During these tests the subject would not be allowed to see members of his religion or his attorneys, and he would be supervised constantly by a member of the hospital staff. He would not be allowed to retain his prayer beads or any religious literature, and he could not avail himself of a tape-recorder if he intended to use it "for reinforcement" (apparently this meant playing tapes of religious events or talks). Clark agreed that during this time "the relationship between him and his religion would be cut off . . . " (trial transcript, p. 44).

Other quotations from Clark's testimony illustrate development of his theory. Concerning the alleged difficulty of telling if someone was mentally ill, Clark said, ". . . if he has been subject to mind control, it might not be possible for an ordinary, customary evaluation to identify the nature or extent of mental illness" (trial transcript, p. 19). When discussing ways in which he could tell whether Shapiro was mentally ill, among other things Clark cited the fact that "He looked like he was hallucinating, ceaseless chanting, reading a book. This went on essentially without interruption. . . . At that time he looked as though he was struggling to hold his mind and thoughts of his own self together" (trial transcript, p. 21). Clark ignored the possibility that Shapiro's chanting and reading of religious literature was a reaction to incarceration by the New York police, and to the distressing nature of the overall situation.

When probed by the court about why inquiry into mind control should be undertaken, Clark stated: "What I'm trying to get at is, all the time he was talking until he began to relax after an hour and a half, he was even then playing with his prayer beads" (trial transcript, p. 24). In response to further questioning by the judge about whether his interviews with Shapiro had led him to develop a theory of mind control, Clark responded at length in a very incoherent fashion, closing with this assessment of cults and ISKCON:

> The cults themselves in many, many ways impose their will to the point where individuals can no longer be taken up about anything. Their actions are stereotyped, controlled, obedient to the leader, to anything that is said by the leaders. . . .
> The Hare Krishna cult very clearly does not believe in modern science, does not believe in the scientific thought that affects the diabetic condition at all. . . . It is true of almost every other aspect of the cult, whether it is food or whether it is even language of the Hare Krishna cult; it also changes all language. (trial transcript, p. 25–26)

Clark agreed that he was something of an expert on ISKCON, and claimed expertise on other groups, mentioning the Unification Church, Scientology, and the Church of Armageddon. He stated, "The theories are all vaguely similar. They are playing mind games. The individuals are locked in them, cannot get out. Those that have left, they have gotten twisted. . . . (trial transcript, p. 27).

The judge then asked if Clark had any independent basis aside from Hare

Krishna membership for saying that Shapiro was mentally ill. Clark replied affirmatively and explained that Shapiro was an isolated and troubled young man without friends, and that he had changed dramatically in his behaviors, particularly related to treating his medical problem.

The judge pressed Dr. Clark to say what kind of mental illness Shapiro had, and Clark replied, "Borderline personality." Then the judge and Eli Shapiro's attorney both asked Clark what this meant, to which he responded in a very incoherent way. When asked if "borderlines" could be legally helped in an institution, Clark replied at length that they could be helped, but that they were sometimes dangerous to others, and that they lived a "disordered life," especially when under "mind control."

Later, when commenting on Edward Shapiro's test results, Clark said:

> It should be said in describing him that with relatively no argument, he is under outside control, primarily even to the point of being given rather conventional responses on the date he took his psychological tests. . . . Without having been there, I'd suggest that the psychological tests were manipulated. He is very bright, and I say tests were interfered with. . . . (trial transcript, p. 32)

Responding to the same question, Clark stated that Shapiro was having extreme difficulty in managing very strong feelings, and that "he wished to be contained" (trial transcript, p. 33). Clark also claimed that Shapiro's stick-like drawing of a man:

> simply indicates again that the evaluation was not taken because of outside pressures and indoctrination is so complete, so total, that he cannot spend any serious number of hours during the day away from the individuals allegedly controlling or other members of the cult, or away from the constant chanting, of reading the books, or some other way of reinforcement of mind control. (trial transcript, p. 34)

Then, in response to a question by the judge about how this condition could be cured, Clark talked about the need for a "stress test," done "away from controlling agencies and persons." He claimed that such testing was "not cruelty."

After this rather rambling initial testimony, Eli Shapiro's attorney asked pointed questions about mind control and related matters. He asked Clark to describe the signs of mind control demonstrated in Edward Shapiro. Clark said:

> Constant need for reinforcement, contact with persons of his cult, a compulsive use of language of the cult, even in some situations which are not altogether appropriate under slight stress. A wandering away from stressful situations, a return back to the rituals by chanting and a complete turning away from the established, well-organized intellectual understanding of reality. . . . (trial transcript, p. 35)

The attorney then asked if an inability to care for one's physical self "manifests itself as a kind of mind control to you?" (trial transcripts, p. 36). Clark agreed and noted that some cults believe that "the body is totally without importance." The attorney asked about personality types who might be more susceptible to mind control. Clark described one type that is basically hopeless and will inevitably return to the cult. He added that these constituted about 30 percent, but he did not say 30 percent of what. The other type Clark labeled "seekers," who engage in all types of experiences, including criminal ones, and who have "structural ego problems," including "borderline states" and "some varieties of schizophrenia" (trial transcript, p. 37).

The attorney for the father then asked Clark if mind control was "a concept that is emerging in the psychiatric field today" (p. 37). Clark agreed and attempted to equate the terror experiences of Korean prisoners of war with the group pressures of ISKCON. The attorney then asked:

> It is your testimony that one who is subject to or under the influence of mind control could respond in an otherwise normal fashion and appear to have no mental illness or disorder to the usual evaluation, such as was used at McClean Hospital in this instance? (trial transcript, p. 38)

Clark replied affirmatively, saying he felt there was evidence in the record of this effect.

The discussion shifted again to the "stress testing." The attorney asked if underlying mental illness or mental disorder would be revealed by stress testing? Clark responded, "Very likely much more possible. I can't say. Very likely. It has happened" (trial transcript, p. 39). Clark then admitted that he had used stress testing earlier on another person in the same hospital. However, he admitted that the testing was not completed because someone in authority in the ward stopped him.

The closing question in the direct examination concerned whether Edward Shapiro showed signs of being under mind control which warranted his being detained for a longer period for more testing. Clark responded: "Yes. As a doctor I see signs. I'd like to have confirmation one way or the other. At this moment there is no confirmation" (trial transcript, p. 40).

During cross-examination by Edward Shapiro's attorney, Clark indicated that the type of environment for stress testing would be "whatever would be legally possible." He stated that the period could be for "up to a month" for the testing. Then, in response to a series of well-put questions, Clark admitted that a person undergoing stress testing would be completely cut off from any outside contact, including his religion, as earlier mentioned. He also added that it was possible that mind control had been "programmed by the monasteries," although he would not state that monks were therefore mentally ill (but he came close).

The attorney for Edward Shapiro then asked Clark:

> With respect to what you've said today, you still don't know whether Mr. Shapiro is incompetent or mentally ill because you don't know yet, even today, whether he is under the control of the Hare Krishnas, is it fair to say? (trial transcript, p. 47)

Clark replied, "I'm saying I think he is, but it needs further testing. I'm taking a medical stance" (trial transcript, p. 47).

The attorney then produced a copy of an affidavit filed in September which led to the apprehension of Edward Shapiro by the New York City police. He asked Clark to read the statement he had made in those proceedings, and Clark complied:

> On the basis of witnessing a lengthy conversation in January, 1976, between Edward Shapiro and his parents, Dr. and Mrs. Eli Shapiro, I have the opinion that he is incompetent as a result of being under the influence of mind control. Because

of this, Edward is rendered incapable of managing his own affairs and seeking the proper care, and is injurious to his physical health. (trial transcript, p. 51)

Clark then admitted that he still agreed with this statement, even though it had been made without the benefit of an interview with Edward Shapiro. He also admitted that his more recent affidavit concerning incompetence made for the present trial was based on a nine-month-old conversation observed with the parents.

During redirect testimony, Clark was asked why he disagreed with the conclusions of the panel of doctors who had not found evidence of mental illness during Edward Shapiro's two-week stay in the hospital. He said that the testing was not complete, and that the stress testing needed to be done. He also claimed that the subject was suppressing information, and insisted several times that he thought the subject was mentally ill.

Reaction of Other Psychiatrists to Clark's Ideas

The reaction of psychiatrists from McClean Hospital was strongly negative to what Clark was promoting. They testified after Clark, stating that they did not think Shapiro was mentally ill, based on the use of standard testing methods and considerably more time in testing and interviews than Clark had spent with the subject. These other mental health professionals also stated that they thought Shapiro could take care of his own financial affairs and physical health. In fact, they admitted that they had allowed Shapiro to self-administer his insulin with a needle while in the hospital. His diabetes was described as "well-controlled."

Significantly, the other mental health experts also refused to collaborate with Clark on the use of terms such as "mind control," with one expert indicating, "That phrase, mind control, does not appear to be in my standard nomenclature for diagnosing" (trial transcript, p. 64). They also denied that it was an "emerging psychiatric field."

Eli Shapiro's attorney forced an admission that they were not experts in the field of mind control, and that they were not familiar with the stress-testing procedures Clark had advocated. However, these admissions were made after the discussion in which they denied the existence of such diagnostic categories and procedures. Also, the hospital representatives disagreed that a patient could mask underlying mental illness by being brainwashed or under mind control. When pressed as to whether they had reached a conclusion about what type of treatment Edward Shapiro should receive, one hospital expert stated: "Well, what is it we are treating, since we've found no evidence of disorder?" (trial transcript, p. 76). When asked why the hospital did not administer the requested stress test, the response was that such testing would raise severe questions about the patient's legal and civil rights, as well as ethical concerns about the practice of medicine.

The eventual outcome of these proceedings was denial of a continuation of the Temporary Guardianship for the purposes of further evaluation. A few months later, in a three-day hearing on the motion for Permanent Guardianship, Eli Shapiro was again unsuccessful in gaining legal control of his son. Thus this bizarre legal episode was finally over, although most of the assets that Edward had (the $30,000 in stock) were used to pay for the effort to have him declared incompetent. The repercussions of this episode continued, however.

Aftermath and Repercussions

I have been unable to ascertain the exact sequence of events that followed the trial, but apparently someone associated with the litigation filed a complaint with the Disciplinary Board of Medicine in Massachusetts. This resulted in a letter that was very critical of Clark for his actions in the Shapiro matter. The letter particularly focused on his improper use of thought reform and mind control as a diagnostic category in psychiatry, and criticized Clark for basing his diagnosis on "mere membership" in a religious organization. Clark was also criticized for making his diagnosis after having had so little contact with the subject, and for his failure to present in either of the affidavits any factual basis for his diagnosis of Shapiro as being unable to care for himself. The last paragraph of the letter bears quoting in its entirety.

> In summary, it is the Committee's opinion that it is not good medical practice to certify a patient as mentally ill and dangerous without setting forth the factual basis of these conclusions. It is also improper and unlawful to base a finding of mental illness solely on membership in a religion, regardless of one's personal opinion as to the merits of that religion.

Thus it seems that Massachusett's legal and psychiatric circles did not give credence to Clark's crude theory about mind control being a direct result of membership in a new religion. Also, support was not forthcoming regarding the position that mind control could be used to suppress mental illness even when sophisticated tests were used (thus requiring special stress testing).

It remains to be seen whether there would have been a different outcome in the Shapiro case had Clark been a better witness (more articulate and convincing), and had Clark spent more time with the subject prior to his far-reaching testimony. Other cult/brainwashing cases using brainwashing/mind control theories have been more successful (Richardson, 1991a).[3]

It should be noted that the Shapiro case did not make use of the Diagnostic and Statistical Manual, Third Edition (DSM-III) (American Psychiatric Association, 1980), which has become a successful tool for brainwashing theorists in other cases similar to this one (Anthony, 1990; Richardson, 1991a). The DSM-III had not appeared at the time of the Shapiro case, and the earlier edition did not contain specific references to mental disorders allegedly associated with cults. Those people opposed to participation in new religions now have a powerful tool to use in their pronouncements about effects of religions on mental health, because the DSM-III contains several references to cults and cultic leaders (Kilbourne & Richardson, 1984; Richardson, 1989).

Clark himself has not been deterred from taking an active role in the anti-cult movement, and in continuing to make pronouncements about the dangers of mind control. He published a paper in 1978, "Problems in Referral of Cult Members" (Clark, 1978). In that paper, Clark complained about difficulties in getting psychiatric hospitals to accept and properly handle cult members. Reading this paper, after examining the Shapiro case, helps one understand Clark's grounds for complaint.

Although Clark has not succeeded in publishing any articles of which we are aware in scholarly, refereed journals, he does continue to turn out papers for anti-cult conferences promoting his ideas. Also, Clark's ties with the major anti-cult organization, American Family Foundation, gain him a ready audience for his theories. He is listed first on one major American Family Foundation publication entitled, "Destructive Cult Conversion: Theory, Research and Treatment" (Clark et al., 1981), which purports to present the latest findings on mind control. It is widely cited by anti-cultists, even though the report ignores the research referred to in the two reviews mentioned earlier (Richardson, 1985b, 1990). Thus, Clark continues to present theories that were roundly rejected in the Shapiro trial, and that virtually all the scholarly community has concluded are not valid.

In 1990, Clark was honored by the American Family Foundation by having a major annual award named after him. Also, in 1984, he received the Cult Awareness Network's "Leo J. Ryan Award," which is named after the congressman killed in the Jonestown tragedy in Guyana. In late 1990, the Cult Awareness Network announced establishment of a "John Gordon Clark Fund" to assist former members of "destructive cults" (the term coined first by Eli Shapiro in his seminal article). Thus, John Clark's ideology and ideas thrive in certain quarters, even if he has been somewhat discredited within his profession.

Regrettably, Clark's crude theories appear to have become quite widely accepted within American society, even if they have been discredited among most scholars (Barker, 1984; Robbins, 1984; Anthony, 1990; Richardson, 1990, 1991a). Clark, Eli Shapiro, and a few others appear to have been relatively successful in defining cult consumers as deviants who may be mentally ill, with the illness caused by the groups to which they are attracted. Participation has become "medicalized" (Robbins & Anthony, 1982; Richardson & Stewart, 1990), and participants may be defined as in need of intervention to help them deal with their disorder. The groups themselves, which are thought by many to either cause or take advantage of mental disorders, have become much more subject to social control efforts by the state and its agencies. Thus certain types of religious groups and experiences have become equated with mental health problems, a situation with considerable significant implications in our society.

Notes

1. The controversy is illustrated by a statement made by editors of a collection on cult participation published in the journal, *Marriage and Family Review,* in 1981. The editors, themselves therapists, had solicited papers from representatives of several disciplines and seemed somewhat surprised when they received a divergence of opinion. They state in the foreword:

We as editors and publisher disclaim any responsibility for the particular authors. The articles represent solely the reports of individual contributors. Neither the publisher nor the editors have conducted independent research to confirm or disprove any of their statements or reports. We have requested that the authors document their particular statements and have given them the freedoms guaranteed under the U.S. Constitution to state freely their analyses as they see them from their particular perspectives. They alone are responsible for the authenticity of the material.

2. Clark's position does not comport well with the extremely high attrition rates for new religions (Bird & Reimer, 1982; Richardson, et al., 1986), but these rates were not brought up by opposing counsel to undercut Clark's theories. Instead the defense focused on Clark's meager contact with Shapiro, and the fact that mind control and brainwashing are not acceptable diagnostic categories in psychiatry.

3. Clark has not been a major player in legal actions since the Shapiro case, possibly because he could be impeached so easily because of his involvement in the Shapiro case. The major burden of testifying to brainwashing/mind control theories in legal matters involving cult recruitment has fallen to psychologist Dr. Margaret Singer, who has testified now in over 40 such cases, including several in which multimillion-dollar verdicts have been rendered in favor of plaintiffs espousing theories similar to those of Clark. However, her work and testimony have come under increasing scrutiny (Anthony, 1990; Richardson, 1991a), and she has been precluded from testifying to her views in one recent federal court case in California.

References

American Psychiatric Association (1980). *The diagnostic and statistical manual, Third edition.* New York: American Psychiatric Association.

Anthony, D. (1990). Religious movements and "brainwashing" litigation. In T. Robbins & D. Anthony (Eds.), *In gods we trust* (pp. 295–344). New Brunswick, NJ: Transaction Books.

Barker, E. (1984). *The making of a "Moonie": Choice or brainwashing.* Oxford: Basil Blackwell.

Bird, F., & Reimer, B. (1982). Participation rates in new religions and para-religious movements. *Journal for the Scientific Study of Religion, 21,* 1–14.

Bohn, T., & Guttman, J.S. (1989). The civil liberties of religious minorities. In M. Galanter (Ed.), *Cults and new religious movements* (pp. 257–290). Washington, DC: American Psychiatric Association.

Bromley, D.G., & Richardson, J.T. (1983). *The brainwashing/deprogramming controversy.* New York: Edwin Mellen.

Clark, J.G. (1978). Problems in referral of cult members. *Journal of the National Association of Private Psychiatric Hospitals, 9,* 19–21.

Clark, J.G. (1979). Cults. *Journal of the American Medical Association, 242,* 281–297.

Clark, J.G., Langone, M.D., Schechter, R.E., & Daly, R. (1981). *Destructive cult conversion: Theory, research and treatment.* Weston, MA: American Family Foundation.

Kilbourne, B.K., & Richardson, J.T. (1984). Psychotherapy and new religions in a pluralistic society. *American Psychologist, 39,* 237–251.

Kilbourne, B.K., & Richardson, J.T. (1988). A social psychological analysis of healing. *Journal of Integrative and Eclectic Psychotherapy, 7,* 20–34.

Richardson, J.T. (1985a). The active vs. passive convert: Paradigm conflict in conversion/recruitment research. *Journal for the Scientific Study of Religion, 24,* 163–179.

Richardson, J.T. (1985b). Psychological and psychiatric studies of new religions. In L.B. Brown (Ed.), *Advances in psychology of religion* (pp. 209–223). New York: Pergamon Press.

Richardson, J.T. (1986). Consumer protection and deviant religion. *Review of Religious Research, 28,* 168–179.

Richardson, J.T. (1989). The psychology of induction. In M. Galanter (Ed.), *Cults and new religious movements* (pp. 211–238). Washington, DC: American Psychiatric Association.

Richardson, J.T. (1990). *Mental health, religion, and the law.* Paper presented at conference on Religion, Mental Health, and Psychopathology, Cracow University, Cracow, Poland.

Richardson, J.T. (1991a). Cult brainwashing cases and freedom of religion. *Journal of Church and State, 33,* 55–74.

Richardson, J.T. (1991b). Religion on trial: New religions in Oregon. In M. Goldman (Ed.), *Religion in the rain.* Corvallis: Oregon State University Press.

Richardson, J.T., & Stewart, M.W. (1990). *Medicalizing participation in new religions.* Paper presented at annual meeting of the Association for the Sociology of Religion, Washington, D.C.

Richardson, J.T., van der Lans, J., & Derks, F. (1986). Leaving and labeling: Voluntary and coerced disaffiliation from religious social movements. In K. Lang & G. Lang (Eds), *Research in social movements, conflicts and change* (pp. 97–126). Greenwich, CT: JAI Press.

Robbins, T. (1984). Constructing cultist "mind control." *Sociological Analysis, 45,* 241–256.

Robbins, T. (1988). *Cults, converts, and charisma.* Beverly Hills, CA: Sage.

Robbins, T., & Anthony, D. (1982). Deprogramming, brainwashing and the medicalization of new religious movements. *Social Problems, 29,* 283–297.

Robbins, T., Shepherd, W., & McBride, J. (Eds.) (1985). *Cults, culture, and the law.* Chico, CA: Scholars Press.

Shapiro, E. (1977). Destructive cultism. *American Family Physician, 15,* 80–83.

Singer, M.T. (1979). Coming out of the cults. *Psychology Today, 12,* 72–82.

Singer, M.T., & West, L.J. (1980). Cults, quacks, and nonprofessional psychotherapies. In H. Kaplan, A. Freedman, & B. Sadock (Eds.), *Comprehensive textbook of psychiatry.* Baltimore: Williams & Wilkins.

Transcript. (1976). Temporary guardianship of Edward Shapiro, Middlesex County, Massachusetts Probate Court, Case No. 471805.

van Driel, B., & Richardson, J.T. (1988). Print media coverage of new religious movements: A longitudinal study. *Journal of Communication, 38,* 37–61.

19

Religious Diagnosis in Evaluations of Mental Health

H. Newton Malony

Religious diagnosis has been a part of the evaluation of mental *illness* for many years. The address of Henry M. Hurd before the Ninth International Medical Congress in 1887 is but one example of this longstanding tradition. Hurd, the superintendent of Eastern Michigan Asylum, spoke to the gathered physicians on "The religious delusions of the insane." He stated, "The predominant characteristics of religious sentiments being hope and fear—a hope of eternal reward and a fear of lasting punishment—it is evident that when these sentiments are deranged there must be morbid hope and morbid fear" (Hurd, 1888, p. 1).

As can be seen in the title of Hurd's speech, he felt that "delusions" were the dominant symptoms of religious psychopathology. He reported that the mental hospitals of his day were filled with "Gods," "Saints," "Virgin Marys," as well as "Fiends," "Devils," and "Dragons." He discussed how to make a differential diagnosis among the religious delusions of precocious children, troubled adolescents, compulsive masturbators, hypersensitive adults, and substance abusers.

Hurd had nothing to say about how religious sentiments would be expressed in the lives of those who were *not* in asylums. If they did not claim to be Gods, Saints, Devils, or Dragons, what did nonpatient religionists claim? Was their faith a force for justice, a buttress against tragedy, a relief from boredom, a stimulant to achievement, a statement of goodness, or a benefit to their self-esteem? Did the religion of the nonhospitalized citizens of the late nineteenth century contribute to their mental health? Hurd did not answer these questions, because he was concerned primarily with the involvement of religion in mental illness.

Hurd is but one in a long line of those who have overemphasized the not-too-infrequent appearance of religious symptoms among the mentally ill. Wayne Oates, well-known American pastoral educator, wrote two complete volumes on the subject, *Religious Factors in Mental Illness* (1955) and *When Religion Gets Sick* (1971). Edgar Draper and his colleagues continued the Hurdian tradition by proposing a method by which religious ideation could be used in the diagnosis of different mental illnesses (Draper, Meyer, Parzen, & Samelson, 1965). Perhaps it is unfair to discount Hurd, Oates, and Draper for their neglect of the contribution of religion to mental *health*. After all, they were professionals whose job it was to heal the sick, not promote wellness. Their failure to "diagnose" the symptoms of healthy religion is not surprising. In the past, diagnosis has been something one did to determine the causes of pathology. Typically, we have not thought of diagnosing the reasons for health. A broadened understanding of "diagnosis," however, would logically include an investigation into how religion contributes to being, staying, and getting well in addition to what happens when people become ill.

This chapter deals with the issue unattended to by Hurd, Oates, and Draper; namely, the place of religious diagnosis in evaluations of mental *health*. Although some of the research reported here shows the relationships between religion and mental health as studied among groups of people, the emphasis in this chapter is on diagnosing how religion can be used in the treatment, prevention, and self-development processes of individuals.

In a sense, this chapter can best be thought of as a prolegomena to the study of these more positive functions of religion. Although both Lovinger (1984) and Spero (1985) have written treatises on dealing with religious issues in counseling, only Propst (1988, 1991) has demonstrated that religious tenets can be utilized effectively in treatment. In a controlled study of therapy with depressed Christian women, she demonstrated that cognitive-behavioral therapy that utilized Christian themes was more effective than nonreligious cognitive-behavioral procedures, even when utilized by nonreligious therapists. She also recommended the use of religious themes in helping clients go beyond symptom reduction to achieve life change, and to become more spiritual. Although she did not propose that religious activity and mental health were synonymous, she did take issue with such writers as William James who implied in his description of "saintliness" that too much religion was a dangerous thing. However, since research on religion and mental health has found both positive and negative relationships (see Batson & Ventis, 1982, p. 211–251), there is a need to reconsider the basic assumptions and definitions on which claims of the positive value of faith can be based.

While much of the chapter will describe a specific program of research aimed at developing standardized measures of religious maturity used by mental health professionals (Malony, 1985, 1988, 1990, 1991), this description will be preceded by a discussion of the foundations on which such an attempt has been made. This program of research and test development has been limited to demonstrating how diagnosing the ways in which *Christian* faith can enhance mental health. However, the processes are thought to have heuristic value for the functioning of other major religions as well.

Defining Religion

In their meta-analysis of the research on religion and mental health, Batson and Ventis (1982) suggested that a significant amount of the data supports a negative relationship between amount of religious involvement and mental health. Using a sevenfold definition of mental health and comparing data across 57 studies, they concluded that there were over twice as many negative as positive or neutral findings. These conclusions were the same as those reached almost fifteen years earlier by Dittes (1969). Batson, Ventis, and Dittes defined religion as adherence to conservative religious beliefs and some degree of institutional involvement. The weakness in these data lies in this limited definition of religion.

There is a need for more sophisticated and sensitive measures of religious functioning than institutional activity or simple belief affirmation. What is needed is a definition of religion that reflects how one applies the teachings of one's faith to the affairs of daily life. As will be shown in a subsequent section of this essay, mental health is unavoidably understood to mean successful functioning within one's culture. Religion should be similarly defined. Most religions are a culture unto themselves. Thus, successful living-out of the implications of a set of religious beliefs in everyday existence would appear to be more important than agreement with certain beliefs and/or attendance at religious gatherings—the criteria used by Batson, Ventis, and Dittes.

Paul Pruyser (1968) perceived this definitional deficiency and chided his fellow/ sister psychologists for their disinclination to take the theologies of their clients seriously. "Theology" was understood to mean the systematized thinking of the leaders of the religions to which people belonged. He was joined in this critique by Hood (1989) and by Spilka and Mullin (1977). Each of these authors concluded that to ignore the way in which the thought-out content of faith (i.e., its dogma) was intended to be acted upon often meant that researchers were defining religion in ways that insiders would judge to be inconsequential.

As can be seen, Pruyser understood theology as something more than religious beliefs or religious activity. Theology is the systematic way in which beliefs are put together in a cosmology (the nature of the universe), an ontology (the essence of reality), an anthropology (the understanding of human nature), a teleology (the purpose of life), a soteriology (the way the world and humans can be changed), an eschatology (the meaning of history), an ecclesiology (the relative importance of group activity), an epistemology (how one can know what is to be known), and an ethic (what it means to be faithful, just, and moral).

More importantly, Pruyser suggested these components of theology were intended to result in a plan for living which, if practiced, could bring joy and self-satisfaction to the believer. Every religion has these elements in its theology, even when the basic belief is nontheistic, as in Buddhism. Integrating these assumed, but often unstated, theological components into a style of life was thought by Pruyser to be a valid measure to use in determining if religion is positively related to mental health. Such components are multidimensional. They are obviously more comprehensive than simple attendance at religious meetings and more complex than conformity to certain beliefs. In our research we have termed these components "functional theology" (Malony, 1988).

In his book *The Minister as Diagnostician,* Pruyser (1968) suggested that there were seven implications to these components of Christian "functional theology." These include (1) awareness of God: the degree to which people experience a sense of awe and creatureliness in relationship to the divine (i.e., reverence versus idolatry); (2) acceptance of God's grace and steadfast love: the degree to which people understand and experience God's benevolence and unconditional love (i.e., trust and a sense of providence versus exaggerated independence and helplessness); (3) being repentant and responsible: the degree to which people take responsibility for their own feelings and behavior (i.e., redemption, justification, forgiveness, and change versus lack of awareness, irresponsibility, bitterness, and vindictiveness); (4) knowing God's leadership and direction: the degree to which people trust in, hope for, and live out God's direction in their lives (i.e., faith versus despair); (5) involvement in organized religion: the degree to which people are involved quantitatively, qualitatively, and motivationally in the church (i.e., commitment and association versus isolation and aloneness); (6) experiencing fellowship: the degree to which people relate to and have a sense of interpersonal identity (i.e., communion with others versus self-centeredness and pride); (7) being ethical: the degree to which people are flexible in, and committed to, the application of ethical principles in their daily living (i.e., a sense of vocation and the living of life by values versus a loss of meaning and a lack of a feeling of oughtness).

Because we felt that mature Christians were tolerant and not prejudgmental, we added a category not mentioned by Pruyser. It is termed "affirming openness in faith" and refers to the degree to which people are growing, elaborating, and being open to newness in their faith (i.e., humility and interest in changing versus closed-mindedness and authoritarianism).

Our presumption has been that if a composite measure of these eight dimensions could be made, then a comprehensive assessment of lived religion would be forthcoming. Thus, we would measure the ways in which Christian theology functioned in daily life. It has been our presumption that where functional theology was high there would be a positive relation with mental health. We have further presumed that the previously reported negative relationships of religion to mental health were due to inadequate assessments of religion and that the above comprehensive assessment could correct for this deficiency.

As noted, this kind of functional theology is tradition-specific. It is focused on, and limited to, the Christian religion. Our conviction has been that optimal religious functioning was most often a style of life related to the prescriptions of a given religious tradition, whether that tradition be Hindu, Moslem, Jewish, Christian, Buddhist, or astrological. Thus, dimensions of individual spirituality divorced from the tenets of a given tradition would not be expected to relate systematically to mental health. Each tradition should construct comprehensive measures of its own functional theology.

The unique features of the Christian tradition are that it is (1) historical: it is based on a God who acts in history and in individual lives; (2) revelational: it is grounded in a truth given from a supernatural source; (3) interpersonal: it is primarily concerned with human relationships; (4) transactional: it intends that people interact with others and the world in a prescribed manner; and (5) communal: it requires that people come together in the church. Thus, Pruyser's dimensions are explicitly Christian. Such dimensions as awe, awareness, acceptance of love, dependency, repentance, forgiveness, church involvement, being ethical, and tolerance are distinctively Christian. They apply only to those people who answer yes to the question, "Are you a Christian?"

Designing the Religious Status Interview and the Religious Status Inventory

(Malony, 1988) to measure Pruyser's dimensions was not intended to discount religions other than Christian, but rather to focus attention on one culturally defined way that people are religious. These dimensions of functional theology are clearly compatible with Western culture. Yet one could presume that Western culture is becoming so pluralistic and cosmopolitan that measures designed to assess functional theology in other religious traditions might also be legitimately related to mental health. There is a need for scholars from other traditions to accomplish this task. However, in their present form, the above measures are intended to assess mature Christian living in a manner that is transdenominational and ecumenical. We have assumed that they measure functional theology in a way that affirms the basics that unify all Christians, while leaving unmeasured those unique features that divide them.

Having defined religion, I now turn to a definition of mental health. I hope I have demonstrated how crucial it is to assure that the definition of religion used in studies relating religion to mental health is valid and comprehensive. In his treatise "The Case against Religion," Albert Ellis (1971) merged a definition of bad religion and a definition of good mental health in deducing that religion and mental health were antithetical. I challenged this far-too-easy tendency to discount religion by focusing on its aberrations, rather than its ideals (Malony, 1982). However, in spite of his contention that being religious in any manner should be related to lower mental health, a survey of admissions to Ellis's own counseling center in New York found no correlation between number of problems and religion (Sharkey & Malony, 1986). His admission procedures have clients rate the importance of religion in their lives—yet another example of an insufficient measure.

Defining Mental Health

It is just as critical to be clear about definitions of mental health as definitions of religion. In an earlier publication I noted that there were three available options: negative, normal, and positive (Malony, 1983). Negative mental health pertains to the absence of illness. For example, a person can be said to be mentally healthy who is no longer depressed. Normal mental health pertains to average adjustment. For example, a person can be said to be mentally healthy who is not sick and has a good self-concept, a satisfying job, friends, and is happy most of the time. Positive mental health pertains to the development of a state of mind that feels like one has gone beyond the average adjustment and is "weller than well."

Jahoda (1958) listed six criteria for positive mental health: (1) an accurate perception of reality, which includes seeing what is really there in spite of pressures from the environment to distort; (2) mastery of the situation, including a sense of control and success in love, work, and play; (3) autonomy, which includes a sense of independence, self-determination, acceptance or rejection of influence, and the ability to surrender or commit oneself if one so desires; (4) having a positive attitude toward oneself, which includes self-acceptance, self-awareness, strong self-identity, and a lack of self-consciousness; (5) personal integration, which includes an adequate balance of inner forces and a philosophy of life; and (6) self-actualization, which includes a sense that one is growing and developing toward self-realization and long-range goals that one has set for oneself. Where Jahoda's criteria consistently characterize life, it can easily be said that positive mental health has been achieved. It should be obvious that when one attempts to relate religion and mental health, one should specify whether one is using a negative, a normal, or a positive definition of mental health.

Each of these options is appropriate when made explicit. However, it is unacceptable always to use a positive definition of mental health and conclude that religion is nonfunctional. It is possible that religion could function to make one mentally healthy in the sense of avoiding, tempering, or relieving the symptoms of emotional disturbance. This would result in a strong relation between religion and mental health, *negatively* defined. Furthermore, it is possible that religion could function to make one mentally healthy in the sense of adjusting and accommodating oneself to the reality in which one lived. This would result in a strong relation between religion and mental health, *normally* defined.

For example, in utilizing the aforementioned Religious Status Interview measure of Pruyser's dimensions of functional theology, it was found that those Christians who were committed to a psychiatric hospital had lower scores than visitors who came to see them. In a subsequent study, outpatient psychiatric Christian patients received higher interview scores than inpatients, yet lower scores than Christian nonpatients (Malony, 1988). In yet another investigation, higher interview scores in a general population were observed to be related to less guilt proneness and lower anxiety on the 16 Personality Factors Test (Malony, 1988). In all of these studies a negative definition of mental health (i.e., absence of disease) was utilized. By contrast, a normal definition of mental health was utilized in another study involving elderly Christian women. Controlling for number and recency of stressful life events, women with higher Religious Status Interview scores reported less current distress, less anxiety, and less depression in their lives. Although these women differed greatly in the number of situationally stressful events to which they had been exposed in their lives, when these were controlled statistically, there was a strong positive relationship found between their adjustment and their functional theology (Malony, 1988).

We have also used a positive definition of mental health in some of our research on the relationships between diagnoses of religious status and mental health. In a general population sample assessed by the Religious Status Interview and the 16 Personality Factors Test, higher functional theology was found to be related to several positive personality traits: intelligence, bold venturesomeness, and imaginativeness (Malony, 1988). These personality characteristics could be conceived to be indices of positive mental health. They go beyond simple average adjustment.

To reiterate, in studies of the relationship between religion and mental health, it is just as important for researchers to specify whether they are utilizing negative, normal, or positive definitions of mental health as it is to have a definition of religion that is multidimensional and valid. I trust I have illustrated these concerns in suggesting how differing definitions of mental health can be used in research involving relationships with measures of optimal Christian functioning (e.g., the Religious Status Interview and the Religious Status Inventory). Most of our research has found that there was a positive relationship between religion and mental health when these definitions are taken into account. These results are contrary to the negative relationship reported by Dittes (1969) and the mixed relationships reported by Batson and Ventis (1982).

Diagnosis as Distinct from Research

Up to this point I have been describing *research* comparing religion to mental health. Yet the title of this chapter suggests that I will discuss *diagnosis* rather than research. The two terms are not synonymous. Typically, research has meant the comparison of traits or behaviors among groups of people, while diagnosis has referred to the comparison of traits or behaviors within an individual. In research, we usually study a few things in many individuals, while in diagnosis we study many things in one individual. My intent here has been to deal with diagnosis rather than research. In spite of the fact that most of the data validating our measures of functional theology (the Religious Status Interview and the Religious Status Inventory) has involved research, our prime concern in these endeavors has been to design a measure to be used in the assessment of individuals.

Designing such an individual diagnostic tool was definitely the intent of Pruyser (1968) when he proposed the categories on which the Religious Status Interview and the Religious Status Inventory have been based. He was concerned about the deference with which clergypersons acceded to psychological and psychiatric pronouncements. Pruyser wanted to provide the chaplains at Topeka State Hospital, near to the Menninger Foundation where he worked, with procedures they could use in reporting individual religious assessments at patient case-conferences. He felt that these procedures could be used by parish ministers in their pastoral counseling.

I have been convinced that mental health professionals as well as parish ministers and chaplains needed to have a tool for evaluating religious functioning. In the United States, at least, religion is modal; it is part of most people's lives. Over 90 percent of the population say they believe in God and over 50 percent belong to some church or synagogue. There are over 341,000 congregations in the United States. In fact, one denomination claims to have a church in every zip code in the country. Fifty-six percent of the population say that religion is very important, and 58 percent of the population say that religion is an answer to most of today's problems. Mental health professionals evaluate individuals on such things as personality traits, type of psychopathology, intelligence, psychodynamics, vocational interests, marital adjustment, cognitive functioning, brain damage, and environmental stress. Yet they have not routinely evaluated their clients' religious functioning. The omission of an assessment of such a commonly appearing characteristic would not be tolerated in any other aspect of life.

Yes, there is a need for mental health professionals to have a measure of optimal religious functioning that they can trust to represent the best thinking of religious leaders and that meets basic psychometric standards. We have been trying to meet that need through the development of the Religious Status Interview and the Religious Status Inventory (for details of this project, see Malony, 1988). With these tools we now have measures that have interrater and test-retest reliabilities. While total scores appear to be much more reliable than subdimension scores, we have found these measures capable of predicting pastor nominations of mature and immature Christians. They are also able to discriminate among people of varying levels of pathology as noted above. Also as previously described, these measures have been demonstrated valid in predicting who would suffer more distress and who would exhibit positive personality traits (Malony, 1988). The Religious Status Inventory has been found to have a stable factor structure that matches, in part, the Pruyser dimensions on the basis of which it was constructed.[1]

The task remaining is to illustrate ways in which these measures of functional theology can be effectively used in the three-fold diagnostic task in which mental health professionals typically engage. This three-fold task involves diagnosis of symptoms, mental status, and treatment plans. Figure 19.1 identifies the diagnostic options available at each of these steps.

As Figure 19.1 shows, the first question to ask is, "Is religion a part of the symptom pattern or not?" In the examples of Superintendent Henry Hurd with which this essay began, religion was a definite part of what appeared pathological even to the untrained eye. Those who thought themselves to be "saints" or "demons" were obviously religiously deranged. However, this is not always so, as many mental health professionals will attest. A paranoid person who feels that a homosexual conspiracy torments him each night via broadcasts in his pillow does not evidence overt religious pathology. In Figure 19.1, the line is dotted between the presence and absence of religious distortion in the diagnosis of symptoms. This indicates that, while there may be no obvious religious involvement in cases like that of the paranoid person just described, underneath such symptoms may be deep-seated guilt and a feeling that one is being punished for some previously committed sin. Obviously, where religion does not appear in explicit or implicit symptoms, one could infer that there is no correlation between religion and mental illness. This illustrates the use of a "negative" definition of mental health.

This leads us to the second step usually taken by mental health professionals, namely a diagnosis of the mental status of the patient or client. Here the question

Religion

DIAGNOSIS I: Symptoms	PRESENT	ABSENT
DIAGNOSIS II: Mental Status	STRENGTH	WEAKNESS
DIAGNOSIS III: Treatment	HELPFUL	HARMFUL

Fig. 19.1. Relationship of Religion to Diagnostic Decisions

is one of determining the personality traits of the individual before they became ill or disturbed. If the clinician discovers that the person is religious, then an assessment of the way in which that religion is being expressed would be appropriate. Here is where such assessments of functional theology as the Religious Status Interview and Inventory would be valuable adjuncts to the diagnostic process.

The primary question being asked here is, "Is this individual's religion a strength or a weakness in his/her underlying personality structure?" If religion is diagnosed as a weakness, it functioned as an indirect provoker of the pathology or it was not a strong enough component of the personality to prevent the disturbance from occurring. If religion is diagnosed as a strength, it functioned to redirect the pathology toward less serious symptoms or it buffered the disturbance when it occurred and kept the disturbance from getting worse. Once again, the line separating the two options in the diagram is dotted to indicate that the diagnostic judgment exists along a continuum of more or less strength and weakness. There is always the possibility that religion plays no part in the individual's mental status. But where religion is assessed by such comprehensive measures as the Religious Status Interview and Inventory, a clear diagnostic judgment can be made. We assume that a strong functional theology as measured by these instruments will be related to strengths in patients' premorbid personalities. This illustrates the use of a "normal" definition of mental health.

The prior assessment of religion in relation to the symptom pattern and overall mental status leads us to treatment planning, the last step in the diagnostic process. It should be apparent that, where religion does not appear among the symptoms and where it is diagnosed to be a personality strength, it can become an asset rather than a liability, in treatment. Diagnosing how religion can be utilized in treatment includes evaluating whether an individual's religion is (1) important or unimportant, (2) active or inactive, (3) good or bad, and (4) helpful or harmful (Malony, 1991).

For religion to be a utilizable asset in treatment, it should be important, active, good, and helpful. We have contended that not all religion would be related to mental health. Specifically, religion can be expected to be a useful resource for treatment planning if it (1) has significance for the individual (i.e., is important); (2) evokes a modicum of energy from the individual (i.e., is active); (3) is aligned with the best thinking of a given tradition (i.e., is good); and (4) functions to increase the individual's autonomy, self-esteem, and self-control (i.e., is helpful).

Of course, all of these characteristics of religion exist along continua. Religion can be more or less important, more or less active, more or less good, and more or less helpful. Where diagnosticians judge a person's religion to be entirely devoid of all positive qualities, they can choose to disregard or annihilate it in treatment planning. Disregarding religion may appear reasonable to mental health professionals because that is what they have tended to do anyway. Furthermore, all clinicians know that there is only a limited amount of treatment time, and that all treatment involves emphasizing some issues and ignoring others. Annihilating a person's religion may be a less familiar option but it should not be rejected automatically. A person's religion may be such a liability that the clinician judges the person to be better off with no religion than with the one he or she has. In neither disregarding nor annihilating religion is there any chance that religion will be related to mental health.

Other treatment options, however, stand good chances of finding religion to be related to mental health. These options are to correct, to reinstate, and to encourage a person's religion. I have described these options elsewhere as follows:

> To take the "correct" option would be to assume that parts of the person's functional religion were weak or erroneous and should be changed or else they would handicap treatment. The "reinstate" option would be to assume that while the person's functional religion was potentially helpful, it was not consciously operative, and, therefore, should be made more explicit, self-conscious, and intentional. The "encourage" option would imply that the person's functional religion was adequate, active, and a definite strength to be supported and enhanced. (Malony, 1991, p. 8)

Where individual's religion is corrected, reinstated, or encouraged, there is present the assumption that religion can be part of the healing and self-actualization process. While all mental health professionals are interested in symptom reduction, most are likewise concerned to help people become who they could be if they realized their potential. This combines an understanding of mental health as both normal and positive. Helping a person to readjust and to get back into life with renewed vigor illustrates a normal definition of health. Strong functional theology, as measured by such tools as the Religious Status Interview and Inventory, can assist in this process. Assisting people in overcoming their difficulties and surmounting stress to the point of becoming transformed illustrates a positive definition of health. Strong functional theology can also promote this process.

As Oates (1955) said, "The patient has no right, however, to expect his psychiatrist to be a trained theologian any more than he has to think of his pastor as a diagnostician of nervous and mental diseases" (p. 154). However, it can be expected that mental health professionals take seriously the religion of their patients while relying on the informed content of such measures as the Religious Status Interview and Inventory. These instruments were designed in collaboration with theologians who judged them to contain the criteria of good Christian functional theology. Where such respect and reliance occurs, it can be assumed that good mental health will, indeed, be found to relate positively to religion.

Conclusion

This discussion has been a prolegomena to the relation of mental health to the diagnosis of religious functioning. It proposes a research program that has yet to be undertaken. Although our research has concluded that the measures we have designed are comprehensive and valid tools for use by mental health professionals, there is little evidence to prove that diagnoses based on these scales is positively related to mental health—defined negatively, normally, or positively. Yet we are convinced that they are. In fact, we are convinced that the assessment of functioning from within a religious tradition, such as Christianity, is the best way to approach the issue. We perceive, along with Wayne Oates (1955):

> the character of the god before whose shrine the patient worships to be of primary importance. . . . Weaning the patient from his [sic] household god, his confusion of loyalties, his cherished grudges, and his worship at the shrine of his own omnipotence is the religious part of his getting well and staying well. But more than that, doubly important to the healing of the patient is his discovery of a God who "fainteth not and neither is weary," "whose love is broader than man's mind," . . . "who has granted that we may become like him in love," "who emptied himself for us that we might become sons of God," . . . "who forgives us of our sins and enables us to forgive each other and bear one another's burdens." (p. 168–169)

This is good religion at its best. We wager that good mental health is to be found where a diagnosis reveals the presence of such faith, or where such faith is the consequence of counseling. In fact, this is what Pollner (1989) found in an exploratory study of the extent to which relationships with "divine others" affected psychological well-being. Although his study was a research survey of samples ranging from 1300 to 2700 participants, rather than diagnostic case studies, the results are extremely suggestive. Pollner found that symbolic relationships with a divine being, such as God, was a better predictor of well-being than race, income, age, marital status, and church attendance. Those who reported ongoing relations with God reported more general happiness, life satisfaction, and life excitement. We predict that this would also be true for individuals who differ in terms of race, income, age, marital status, and the index that Batson and Ventis (1982) and Dittes (1969) found was not predictive—church attendance.

Notes

1. Those desiring copies of the Religious Status Interview and the Religious Status Inventory as well as the standardization data underlying each of these measures can write to the author at 180 North Oakland, Pasadena, California, USA, 91101.

References

Batson, C.D., & Ventis, W.L. (1982). *The religious experience: A social-psychological perspective.* New York: Oxford University Press.

Dittes, J.E. (1969). Psychology of religion. In G. Lindzey & E. Aronson (Eds.), *The handbook of social psychology* (vol. 5). Reading, MA: Addison Wesley.

Draper, E., Meyer, G.E., Parzen, Z., & Samelson, G. (1965). On the diagnostic value of religious ideation. *Archives of General Psychiatry, 13,* 202–207.

Ellis, A. (1971). *The case against religion: A psychotherapist's view.* New York: Institute for Rational Living.

Hood, R. (1989). The relevance of theologies for the psychology of religion. *Journal of Psychology and Theology, 17,* 336–342.

Hurd, H.M. (1888). The religious delusions of the insane. *American Journal of Insanity,* April, 1–17.

Jahoda, M. (1958). *Current concepts of positive mental health.* New York: Basic Books.

Lovinger, R.J. (1984). *Working with religious issues in therapy.* New York: Jacob Aronson.

Malony, H.N. (1982). The case for religion: A counter to Albert Ellis. Unpublished manuscript. Fuller Theological Seminary, Graduate School of Psychology, Pasadena, California.

Malony, H.N. (1983). *Wholeness and holiness: The psychotheology of mental health.* Grand Rapids, MI: Baker Book House.

Malony, H.N. (1985). Assessing religious maturity. In M. Stern (Ed.), *Psychotherapy and the religiously committed patient* (pp. 25–33). New York: Haworth.

Malony, H.N. (1988). The clinical assessment of optimal religious functioning. *Review of Religious Research, 30,* 3–15.

Malony, H.N. (1990, December). *How counselors can help people become more spiritual through religious assessment.* Paper presented at the conference on Religion, Mental Health, and Mental Pathology, Cracow, Poland.

Malony, H.N. (1991). The uses of religious assessment in counseling. In L.B. Brown (Ed.), *Religion and mental health.* New York: Springer.

Oates, W.E. (1955). *Religious factors in mental illness.* New York: Association Press.

Oates, W.E. (1971). *When religion gets sick.* Philadelphia: Westminster.

Pollner, M. (1989). Divine relations, social relations, and well being. *Journal of Health and Social Behavior, 30,* 92–104.

Propst, L.R. (1988). *Psychotherapy in a religious framework.* New York: Human Sciences Press.

Propst, L.R. (1991, January). Christian contributions to the treatment of clinical depression. *John G. Finch Symposium on Theology and the Human Sciences.* Conducted at Fuller Theological Seminary, Pasadena, California.

Pruyser, P.W. (1968). *The minister as diagnostician.* New York: Scribners.

Sharkey, P.W., & Malony, H.N. (1986). Religiosity and emotional disturbance: A test of Ellis's thesis in his own counseling center. *Psychotherapy, 23,* 640–641.

Spero, M.H. (1985). *Psychotherapy of the religious patient.* Springfield, IL: C.C Thomas.

Spilka, B., & Mullin, M. (1977). Personal religion and psychological schemata: A research approach to a theological psychology of religion. *Character Potential, 8,* 57–66.

IV

CROSS-CULTURAL
PERSPECTIVES

20

Religion as a Mediating Factor in Culture Change

Erika Bourguignon

"In the autumn of 1984 a wave of rumors about mad Balanta women spread across the south of Guinea Bissau." So begins a fascinating account by the Dutch psychiatrist Joop T.V.M. de Jong (1987, p. 77) in his book *A Descent into African Psychiatry*. Guinea Bissau is a small West African country that had obtained its independence from Portugal only ten years before, and the Balanta are its largest ethnic group. What de Jong is referring to in the quotation cited above is a movement that came to be called Jangue Jangue. Young women who had lost children or who were unable to conceive were, it was said, being helped by an inspired woman healer. She supposedly received spirit messages that gave her knowledge of medicinal plants, as well as a new code of living. This code included an anti-witchcraft movement, of which there had been several in the past. In particular, one was associated with the struggle for liberation from colonial rule. Additionally, the leader's teachings rejected many traditional practices, including arranged marriages and expensive mourning ceremonies involving much drinking and slaughtering of cattle. The founder's original inspiration (which followed on a serious illness) and the conversions of new members involved such features as dreaming, hearing voices, head shaking, and running off into the bush.

Is this mental illness? Is it religion? What is its relation to culture change?

Here is another account, from another part of the world: Aihwa Ong (1987) reported from Malaysia that, in 1975, 40 Malay women were seized by spirits in a large American electronics plant. In 1978 this happened to 120 women operators in the microscope section of a factory. In the same year, another 15 women were afflicted by spirit possession in an American microelectronics plant, as a result of which production was disrupted for three days. Numerous other cases of mass attacks on young women have appeared in boarding schools as well as in factories. To the women and their families these were attacks by spirits called *hantu,* which had to be exorcised. Some factories hired shamans to purify the premises. Newspaper accounts spoke of "mass hysteria," "examination stress," "stress of urban living," and such.

Both versions recognized that there was something wrong, that the young women workers and students were in some manner incapacitated. The newspaper version was tinged with Western psychiatric interpretations, but those of the women and their families were cast in traditional religious terms. Ong (1987) agreed that, indeed, something was the matter. She wrote: "The eruption of spirit possession episodes in transnational companies discloses the anguish, resistance and cultural struggle of some neophyte factory workers" (p. 220). Furthermore, Ong suggested an interpretation: "The *hantu* symbolism, shifting in and out of their consciousness, spoke of the right to be treated as *human beings.* Spirit attacks were indirect retaliation against coercion and demands for justice in personal terms in the industrial milieu" (p. 220, emphasis in original). Ong saw the conditions of factory work as dehumanizing, and the seizures experienced by the women were a response in traditional terms to these conditions.

A comparison of the two cases is instructive. In the case of the Jangue Jangue of Guinea Bissau, we find one individual whose personal distress led her to become a social movement leader who introduced substantial changes into a society in distress. In many ways, this movement resembled the classic case of what the American anthropologist A.F.C. Wallace (1956) has called a "revitalization movement," a movement through which people seek to construct a more satisfying way of life for themselves. Wallace (1970) described such a movement and its course over time in detail in the case of the Seneca (Iroquois) Indians and their prophet Handsome Lake. He, too, drew his message for this disturbed society from the depth of his own distress. Both N'Tombikte, the Jangue Jangue founder, and Handsome Lake heard the message of change as coming from a supernatural source, the authority of powerful spirits. For both, the message called for a major reorientation of the society. What was initially experienced as illness became part of the founder's own cure and of the power to cure others. De Jong visited N'Tombikte on two occasions, in 1985 and again in 1987, and found her to be a stable personality, with a sincere commitment to her mission. However, certain of her initial "symptoms" or spirit manifestations (auditory pseudohallucinations, running off into the bush, compulsive behavior) seem to fit various psychiatric categories.

From the perspective of the present discussion, it is important to note the actual sequence of these events. It proceeds from social as well as personal distress to a revelation of orders, with authority, from gods or spirits. Although the execution of these orders is therapeutic for the prophet, the message is meant not only to heal others similarly afflicted but also to renew the society. For the Jangue Jangue, this renewal constituted in effect a revolt of young women against the rule of old men. The personal and social distress is phrased in the familiar terms of religion, and so is the solution to the problems on the individual as well as the social level.

The case of the young Malay women, thrust into the urban institutions of industrial Malaysia, is quite different. Personal distress is experienced in traditional, familiar terms, as spirit possession. However, there is no prophet, no message or program for the revitalization or transformation of society, and, indeed, no initial, broad social disorganization. The language of spirit possession is used by many of the victims, and their families and friends because it is the familiar way of expressing distress. In fact, there is a long history in Malaysia of female spirit possession (e.g., Kessler, 1977). But there is also a competing, Western psychiatric interpretation, which has been adopted by newspapers, factory managers, and even some of the workers, as reported by Ong. Ong, herself, saw the factory discipline as coercive and the work schedule and life demands and opportunities faced by the young women as totally alien to their village environment. There is no healing of self and society incipient in these attacks, whether they be phrased as due to spirits or to hysteria. Being taken back to their villages and families to recover gives these young women a brief time out, a respite from the factory work that requires such intense attention to fine detail, and an organized routine of effort. However, such a return to the family setting also exposes the young women to a renewed sense of local values and meanings, ones that are at great variance with those of the city and the factory. There is, in other words, a continuous pull between the two cultures.

What, then, can we say about religion, culture change, and mental health on the basis of these two small examples?

In the case of the Balanta of Guinea Bissau we find social disorganization and dissatisfaction followed by call for reorganization and renewal. The founder's illness and spontaneous healing are rooted in her culture. The cure she proposes for her society, de Jong (1987) suggests, draws on profound underlying psychological forces, such as the deep hostility between men and women, and the young and old as they have existed in traditional Balanta society. In fact, the movement was not a resistance to modernization, but rather a *furthering* of modernization of a special kind. Instead it represented the rejection of such practices as arranged marriages, the waste and destruction of cattle at extensive and expensive funerals, demand for the schooling of girls as well as boys, and so forth. The movement was not directed against colonial powers or colonialism, or against the central government. This is despite the fact that government forces became suspicious of it and fearful that the movement did, in fact, constitute a conspiracy and a source of potential insurrection. In its healing aspects, the movement also expressed a need in the absence of medical services in the region. The movement, then, was therapeutic, and takes its authority from tradition. It was also modernizing, as modernization was understood on the local, rural level. Seen from this perspective, we do indeed see religion here at work as a mediating factor in dealing with the stresses of change by promoting change in its own way through the use of traditional metaphors, values, and symbols.

Again, the Malaysian case was quite different. Distress was expressed in a traditional idiom. It was distress at aspects of modernizations, rather than directed at the traditional society. Moreover, no ultimate solutions were proposed, nor were any solutions to the conflicts at issue for the victims of the attacks. The interpretation of the "spirit attacks" (or "mass hysteria") as resistance and retaliation was not the emic, local interpretation, but that of the observer. The transnational companies appeared to have accommodated to these periodic events by giving victims some time off, hiring exorcists, "cleansing" the premises of polluting influences, etc. In other words, it was all part of the cost of doing business in that part of the world. Nothing fundamental was changing, and the young women needed and wanted the jobs. Consequently, one expected that, in time, they or their younger sisters would adjust to the new conditions of work, and the *hantu* would lose their power. Stress-related disorders can take other forms, of a secular variety. (In America it is now popular to speak of "Yuppie" diseases, such as "chronic fatigue syndrome," for example.) From the perspective of the *hantu,* one might say that these ancient local spirits were fighting a rear-guard action against modernization and the shifting of populations from villages to cities, from farms to factories. Guinea Bissau is a long way from that stage of modernization.

Even though both of our examples use a religious idiom to express distress, they are actually opposites in a number of important respects. Jangue Jangue is a movement of modernization, while the Malaysian *hantu* attacks are a response to, and perhaps and expression of, resistance against (some aspects of) modernization. Jangue Jangue is its own therapy, while Malaysian *hantu* possessions are pathological, both as seen from the local perspective and from a biomedical point of view. Jangue Jangue constitutes a social movement, while *hantu* possession, though at times contagious, occurs on the individual level and has no further development into anything beyond the specific incident. Jangue Jangue is innovative, while *hantu* possession is traditional, although it occurs in a novel setting. Jangue Jangue can be seen as an innovative religious and sociopolitical movement, rooted in the old religious and cultural tradition and world view. Here religion may indeed be said to act as a mediating factor in culture change. By taking culture change introduced from the outside and deriving their own program from it, the women turned it into a weapon for ameliorating their situation in society, and for providing a degree of therapy and reassurance for themselves. None of this is true for the *hantu*-possessed young women. For them the traditional beliefs merely serve to provide an explanatory device, one that does not address the conditions from which they suffer. The ailment itself gives them time out, but no more. The stresses from which they suffer and to which they react are, indeed, those of modernization, urbanization and industrialization, as well as the changes in the status of young women that accompany these processes. The changes themselves are ambivalent. They provide a degree of personal and financial independence. But they also impose on them the discipline of factory work or of Western schooling, and the routines of urban life. Religion, in this instance, does not serve to mediate or facilitate culture change.

Instances of both of the types described here can be found throughout the world and throughout history. The case of Handsome Lake, the Seneca prophet, was cited earlier (Wallace, 1970). Weston La Barre (1971) collected an imposing list of what he has called "crisis cults," which are religious responses to social and cultural disruption. Such movements are not limited to small-scale traditional societies as they might be found in the Third World. Primitive Christianity and the Protestant Reformation in its various forms, were also movements to create a better society phrased in religious terms and based on forms of religious inspiration. Throughout Latin America, Pentecostalism (e.g., Glazier, 1980) and various forms of *espiritismo* (spiritualism) are the fastest growing forms of religion (see, Bastide, 1978). These, too, have many of the aspects of revitalization movements and crisis cults. Compared to such movements, which often involve large masses of people, small numbers are concerned in the periodic outbreaks of "hysterical attacks" among individuals under intolerable stress. Generally, they are not given much attention by historians and other students of political and religious phenomena, although the events themselves may indeed be expressed in the language of religion.

Belief in spirit possession, linked to altered states of consciousness (ASC), is a very widespread phenomenon. Jangue Jangue and the young women workers in Malaysia show that it can take very different forms in diverse social and cultural settings. I have suggested elsewhere (Bourguignon, 1973) that such behavior may serve as a safety valve both for individuals and societies under stress. In addition, these can act as a marker indicating where, in a given society, certain types of stress are to be found. In both the Balanta and the Malaysian cases, stresses are particularly strong for young women. For the Balanta, the issues are barrenness and male dominance in the family setting. For the Malaysian women, the issues are urbanization, industrialization, and the displacements and disciplines of factory work. The issues, in other words, are quite different, associated as they are in the one instance with a traditional society and in the other with a modernizing one.

Human beings live in a world that is culturally constructed and culturally variable. Human experience, however uniquely personal, is shaped and lived in the context of ongoing and evolving cultural traditions. Yet this diversity of cultures is framed within the limits of a common human nature. It is in this context that we must consider the widespread phenomenon of revitalization movements and crisis cults as responses to situations in which personal and social distress are combined. Moreover, visions, trances, "voices," are common features of these situations whether or not there is a previous cultural or social warrant for them. If the person who experiences these states (or an associate with organizational talent) can interpret them as socially relevant messages and if a social echo is aroused, the conditions for the birth of a movement exist. On the other hand, there are innumerable cases where stress produces seizures and perhaps visions and voices, but no distinct messages are formulated, no receptive audience accepts or elaborates a nucleus of a message, and no revitalization or renewal results. The Malaysian factory workers may represent an example of such a case.

Having taken our examples this far, we must now address the two basic questions that we have so far ignored. What is meant by "religion?" What is meant by "mental health?"[1]

Despite their apparent simplicity, these are in effect difficult questions, and much ink has been spilled in dealing with one and the other. For example, from an anthropological point of view, Spiro (1987/1966) wrote that "the belief in superhuman beings and their power to assist or harm man . . . is the core variable [defining] religion" (p. 94). Later in the same discussion he defined religion as "an institution consisting of culturally patterned interactions with culturally postulated superhuman beings" (p. 96). In the context that concerns us here, religion stands as a shorthand for the whole of a given culture; its world view, its culturally constituted behavioral environment, its values (including those involved in human interactions) and its meanings and symbols. *Hantu* are an element of Malaysian traditional culture, of the villagers' behavioral environment, and belief in their manifestations is part and parcel of village level relationships. The god and the ancestors who speak to the Balanta women are to be understood in similar terms, for even traditional spirits, under certain circumstances, may give their faithful new messages. Spirit belief, like the rest of the culture, may undergo transformations in periods of crisis, culture contact, and modernization.

In modern mass societies the subject is in some ways more complicated. There is no one-to-one correspondence between a specific religion and national culture. Rather than a single religion, there are many. Also, not all individuals participate in religion in any sense of the word. Here religion is an institution among others, with its own legal status. It can be defined as taking shape in the form of a church, with its theology, its staff, its group of faithful, its rules and rituals, its buildings and material aspects, its finances, and so forth. But although the majority of people in the United States, for example, who identify themselves as "religious" are associated in some manner with Christian denominations, there are many different churches, some mainstream and some marginal. Moreover, in addition to Christians, there are Jews, Muslims, Buddhists, Hindus, members of Native American Indian groups, and numerous innovative religious groups, some of which are short-lived. The list is open-ended, with new religious groups springing up continuously. One person's religion, then, may be another's superstition, heresy, nonsense or madness.

This is a situation that is produced not only by locally developed innovations but also by streams of immigrants from other parts of the world. As such it is now a familiar phenomenon in what were relatively homogeneous societies such as Great Britain.

The topic of "mental health" is equally complicated, if not more so. The term is eschewed by modern psychiatry. The latest version of the Diagnostic and Statistical Manual of Mental Disorders (DSM-III-R) of the American Psychiatric Association (1987) does not use the term and speaks only of "mental disorders." It notes in the Introduction (1987, p. xxii) that "no definition adequately specifies precise boundaries for the concept 'mental disorder.'" The emphasis is on clinical syndromes or patterns that are presented by the patient: "Whatever its cause, it must currently be considered a manifestation of a behavioral, psychological or biological dysfunction in a person" (p. xxii). The text goes on to note that deviant behaviors in various areas, including specifically religion, are not mental disorders unless they are "a symptom of a dysfunction in a person" (p. xxii). A specific caution is expressed with regard to normative behaviors in other cultures. In other words, what may appear mad in one place may be entirely sane in another. In the case of the Balanta, for example, it would appear that an initial pathological ("dysfunctional") state in the founder and of (some) individual followers has been replaced by a ritual, pathomimetic (or pathomorphic) state. That is, ritual behavior is patterned on a pathological model. Roland Littlewood (1984) elaborated this point in an interesting paper titled "The imitation of madness: The influence of psychopathology on culture."

Clearly, defining what is pathological across cultural boundaries may at times be difficult. Littlewood and Lipsedge (1989) cited a number of cases illustrative of such difficulties taken from their clinical experience with immigrants to Britain. One such case is that of a Jamaica-born woman whose life in London centered on her Pentecostal church. She was referred to the psychiatrist when, on one occasion, she began to behave oddly during her work as a nurse's aide, singing loudly, neglecting her patients, and so forth. Littlewood, the attending psychiatrist, wondered whether her behavior was not that of "speaking in tongues," normal in the context of her church. However, to her fellow church members, her behavior was deviant. They told Littlewood that she was "sick in the head" and that he should "give her an injection immediately" (Littlewood and Lipsedge, 1989, p. 173). Yet he continued to wonder whether her behavior might not have been acceptable to a more "extreme" sect, reasoning that she might be "too enthusiastic" for that particular group. Littlewood went on to speculate about the group's motivation: "To protect themselves from being seen by society as deranged, her group had perhaps labelled her as ill. If that was the case, the medical profession was being used to delineate ritualistic differences between the churches" (Littlewood and Lipsedge, 1989, p. 174).

Despite the above-mentioned DSM-III-R warnings, it seems that it is not always clear to observers (including psychiatrists) what is religion and what is pathology, and, perhaps, what is both. There is, however, an important further point to be noted here. Littlewood and Lipsedge (1989) dealt with aliens, immigrants to Britain, people who brought unfamiliar ways to their new environment. They were involved in a special case of culture change, in which the psychiatrist had no familiar baseline with which to compare the behavior under observation. Moreover, the traditional ways of immigrants are often modified in new situations. Also, if we are concerned with "deviancy," deviant with respect to the behavior of which group? And on the matter of "dysfunction," dysfunctional in the context of what or whose social demands?

The issue of the "normalcy" of religious behavior, then, is much more easily dealt with in the context of a stable society. Wolf (1990) presented the fascinating case of a woman in a relatively isolated village in Taiwan who "didn't become a shaman." She described how this woman, who exhibited forms of shamanistic behavior, was eventually judged by her neighbors not to be possessed by a god but rather to be "crazy." It is rare that such a case is described in some detail by an observer. In fact, it is likely that decisions about the authenticity of aspirant shamans have to be made where shamanism, possession trance, or other forms of institutionalized altered states of consciousness exist. That is, there has to be a differential diagnosis, a decision as to whether the person's "odd" behavior has a religious, supernatural origin. If so, it must also be decided whether it is of a positive (socially valued) or negative (socially abhorred) kind, and whether the individual is to be restored to an ordinary life. In the latter instance, traditional societies generally provide rituals of healing, whether or not the issue is phrased in terms of health ("madness") or, for example, of negative possession. This is the case with the Malay women, possessed by *hantu,* who must be pacified and exorcised to bring the women back to ordinary functioning. From a biomedical perspective, they are temporarily disabled, dysfunctional, and suffering from a disorder of a dissociative type.

The beliefs in the possessing spirits do not "cause" the attacks but provide an idiom through which distress is expressed. In terms of the traditional world view, however, the spirits do indeed cause the attacks because they are angered by the polluted conditions of the factories or other breaches of traditional norms. Or so it is said.

In Malaysia, as in most modernizing societies, there exist multiple systems of healing, with diverse "explanatory models" (Kleinman, 1980). Decisions about where to seek help, and in what order of priority, must be made by the "therapy-managing group" (Janzen, 1978), which includes the afflicted person and his or her family and friends. In the traditional sector, healing is a function of what, from a Western perspective, we are likely to call religious experts. This is because spirits, ancestors and other superhuman entities are likely to be involved.

In modernizing societies, religious healing often occurs in syncretistic groups, that is, groups whose beliefs and rituals can be traced to a variety of sources. When they are of recent origin, as in the case of the Jangue Jangue among the Balanta of Guinea Bissau, the strong presence of the founder is likely to be felt. This is the case, for example, of the prophet Albert Atcho, whose activity in the Ivory Coast was studied by a French team of anthropologists in the 1960s (Piault, 1975). His principal means of healing was confession, through which penitents/patients accused themselves of deeds of witchcraft. Religion, as well as healing and politics through the adjudication of disputes, all came into play here. This, however, was a society where Western medicine, as well as other forms of religious healing were also available.

Krippner (1987) has shown how certain Brazilian spiritists deal with cases of Multiple Personality Disorder (MPD), using both psychiatric and spiritist concepts, and how they make differential diagnoses. Here beliefs in spirits, which we classify as religious, constitute a world view that accommodates certain aspects of biomedicine but, essentially, represents an alternative to it. By contrast, biomedicine, as represented in the DSM-III-R strictly separates its practice from that of religion of any kind, whatever the private beliefs of practitioners might be.

Syncretistic religions, which appear under conditions of rapid culture contact and culture change, are of particular interest for several reasons. They represent creative attempts at developing new cognitive and perceptual structures and modified affective and motivational orientations. Often they remain open-ended and show evidence of continuing modification over time.

Those who create these syntheses probably draw not only on their own conscious as well as unconscious sources of stress and energy for their new systems, but also on such sources in their communities. As such they may be viewed as deviant, and even as dangerous, by the larger society and the powers that be. Yet when the creative innovations are successful, and when they speak to the fundamental issues that concern people, these innovations may be bulwarks against stress and anxiety as well as a means of redress for individuals and groups. As such they can have both political and therapeutic dimensions.

Earlier, we spoke of "mental disorders," "dysfunctional behavior," and "disturbed" individuals. We have not spoken of "mental health," a term not much used in contemporary psychiatry.[1] Yet this is a relatively recent development. Fifteen years ago, DeVos (1976, p. 6) said that "psychiatrists and psychologists are principally interested in 'mental health,' [a term whose] definition reflects consensus about what constitutes normal, 'healthy' behavior *within a particular value system*" (emphasis added). DeVos, following Clyde Kluckhohn (1944), preferred to distinguish between "adjustment" and "adaptation" on the one hand, and "maladjustment" and "maladaptation" on the other. "Adjustment," he wrote, "refers to an ideal progression of maturation, which is potential for all human beings," while adaptation "refers to social and behavioral responses . . . of the individual in his social nexus" (DeVos, p. 4). According to DeVos, adjustment involves personality, whereas adaptation refers to social structure. Given these definitions, it is then possible for an individual to be both adapted and maladjusted or maladapted and adjusted. It is "adjustment" that appears to correspond to a culture-free concept of optimal mental health. As such, "adjustment" is a supra-cultural, etic concept, the content of which, has to be specified in cultural terms. The difficulties of identifying such adjustment (or, in humanistic terms, "self-realization") are great in the concrete, individual case, since such a person may be deviant in social and cultural terms. The difficulties are particularly great under conditions of rapid social change, where traditional values and conditions of life are no longer fully available as reliable guideposts, and where conflicting world views and demands may expose individuals to particular stresses. Under such circumstances, ideals or models against which the maturing individual is measured (or measures himself or herself) are often contradictory and shifting.

Under conditions of stress, conflict, and confusion, religion may play an increasingly important role. Whether it assists either adjustment or adaptation, or both or neither, will have to be judged in the individual case. Moreover, there are likely to be important differences between leaders and followers, men and women, young and old. Religion may provide security and act as a shield against mental disorders, as a reflection or expression of stress and distress, and even as a promoter of stress. It may do this by insisting on strict conformity to traditions or even to reinvigorated traditions, which may be in conflict with a larger society. At the same time, new religions or religious innovations may provide coping strategies for their members.

Religious change both reflects and expresses change and provides, at times, impetus and motivation for change. However, this change is not always in the direction of "modernization." The religious revival and increased fundamentalism in the major divisions of Islam represent a well-known case in point. The Khomeini revolution in Iran was, in many ways, a reaction against the type of modernization practiced under the regime of the Shah (Naipaul, 1981). The presence of American and European forces in Saudi Arabia in 1990 and after appears to have stimulated a wave of religious conservatism in that country. The growth of Christian fundamentalism in the United States in the 1980s, and of the Jewish fundamentalism in Israel, all speak to the fears engendered in the modern and post-modern world. Indeed, the various forms of fundamentalism and religious revival that are such a characteristic phenomenon of the late twentieth century appear to constitute a broad reaction against the trend of secularization of the preceding one hundred years or more.

It is interesting to note that these developments are taking place at all levels of modernization and economic development. A wide range of emotions fuel these movements, including rage, fear, dissatisfaction, and hope. Therefore, while religion may support modernization or ease its strains under certain circumstances, it may also be a conservative force, opposing change. Or it may do so in its rhetoric. In fact, in many instances, as illustrated in the Islamic countries visited by Naipaul

(1981)—Iran, Pakistan, Malaysia, and Indonesia—the Islamic past to which an appeal is made never existed in quite the form in which it is presented. What is being attempted, in the name of the past, is indeed a kind of utopia, something new and quite different.

These religious movements are notable for their political dimensions. The Pentecostalism spreading so rapidly in Latin America represents a different approach, a religious quietism attempting to disregard the "world." Though this religious movement may be said to represent a response to rapid culture change and the distress and dislocation caused by it, and to be expressive of that change, it focuses on individual salvation rather than on political action. Salvation involves a personal, spiritual, and psychological transformation, and often healing, whether mental or physical.

While it may be possible to argue that some of these religious movements are adaptive for their members who feel themselves threatened by the modern world, it may yet be questioned whether they offer opportunities for personal growth that foster adjustment.

Culture change, whether resulting from migration, development, revolution, or other factors, involves transformations in many aspects of living. This produces stress which, in turn, has an impact on mental health. Religion may provide forms of accommodation, new groups providing personal support, explanatory systems, restructuring of values, opportunities for social action, healing rituals, and more. It may support change or resist it, and it may alleviate stress or increase it. Religion is a multiform phenomenon, and its relation to mental health, however defined, is complex and variable. No easy generalizations are possible. The specific consideration of examples, however, may shed some light on the kind of research required to answer larger questions.

Notes

1. Where the term is used, as in the names of organizations such as the World Federation for Mental Health or various Mental Health Associations or Federations on the local level, this really refers to organizations fighting for the prevention and cure of mental ill-health. Similarly, the broader term "health care" refers to the prevention and cure of disease.

References

American Psychiatric Association (1987). *Diagnostic and statistic manual of mental disorders* (DSM-III-R) (third edition). Washington, D.C.
Bastide, R. (1978). *The African religions of Brazil: Toward a sociology of the interpenetration of civilizations.* Translated by H. Sebba. Baltimore, MD: The Johns Hopkins Press.
Bourguignon, E. (1973). Introduction: A framework for the comparative study of altered states of consciousness. In E. Bourguignon (Ed.), *Religion, altered states of consciousness and social change* (pp. 3–35). Columbus, Ohio: Ohio State University Press.
DeVos, G.A. (1976). Introduction: Change as a social science problem. In G.A. DeVos (Ed.),

Response to change: Society, culture, and personality (pp. 1–11). New York: Van Nostrand.

Glazier, S.D. (Ed.) (1980). *Perspectives on Pentecostalism: Case studies from the Caribbean and Latin America.* Washington, DC: University Press of America.

Janzen, J.M. (1978). *The quest for therapy in lower Zaire.* Berkeley: The University of California Press.

Jong, J.T.V.M. de (1987). *A descent into African psychiatry.* Amsterdam: Royal Tropical Institute, The Netherlands.

Kessler, C.S. (1977). Conflict and sovereignty in Kelantanese Malay spirit seances. In V. Crapanzano & V. Garrison (Eds.), *Case studies in spirit possession* (pp. 295–327). New York: Wiley-Interscience.

Kleinman, A. (1980). *Patients and healers in the context of culture.* Berkeley: University of California Press.

Kluckhohn, C. (1944). *Navaho witchcraft.* Boston: Beacon Press.

Krippner, S. (1987). Cross-cultural approaches to multiple personality disorder: Practices in Brazilian spiritism. *Ethos, 15,* 273–296.

La Barre, W. (1971). Materials for a history of studies of crisis cults: A bibliographic essay. *Current Anthropology, 12,* 3–44.

Littlewood, R. (1984). The imitation of madness: The influence of psychopathology upon culture. *Social Science and Medicine, 19,* 705–715.

Littlewood, R., Lipsedge, M. (1989). *Aliens and alienists: Ethnic minorities and psychiatry* (second edition). London: Unwin Hyman.

Naipaul, V.S. (1981). *Among the believers: An Islamic journey.* New York: Knopf.

Ong, A. (1987). *Spirits of resistance and capitalist work discipline: Factory women in Malaysia.* Albany, NY: State University of New York Press.

Piault, C. (Ed.) (1975). *Prophétisme et thérapeutique: Albert Atcho et la communauté de Bregbo.* Paris: Hermann.

Spiro, M.E. (1987). Religion: Problems of definition and explanation. In B. Kilbourne & L.L. Langness (Eds.), *Culture and human nature: The theoretical papers of Melford E. Spiro* (pp. 187–222). Chicago: University of Chicago Press. (Original work published 1966.)

Wallace, A.F.C. (1956). Revitalization movements. *American Anthropologist, 58,* 264–281.

Wallace, A.F.C. (1970). *The death and rebirth of the Seneca.* New York: Knopf.

Wolf, M. (1990). The woman who didn't become a shaman. *American Ethnologist, 17,* 419–430.

21

Buddhism and Mental Health:
A Comparative Analysis

Gary Groth-Marnat

Buddhism is a group of beliefs and practices for attaining enlightenment. All assumptions, conceptions, and implications related to mental health can center on this one basic orientation. Indeed, the Buddha himself continually tried to keep his teaching simple, concise, and straightforward; when asked why he was different from other people, his reply was simply "I'm awake." However, the different Buddhist understandings of mental activity can become highly complex and varied. Should this complexity become overwhelming, the student can create clarity by coming back to the basic goal of what it means to seek enlightenment.

In Buddhist countries there is little separation between mental and spiritual health. If an individual experiences pain and suffering, a spiritual answer is typically given. In a general way, this would involve understanding the person's craving and attachment in combination with explaining how their past actions (karma) had led them into the present state of their lives. In the past, Buddhist monks frequently served as psychotherapists and used such techniques as meditation, ritual ceremonies, and support (Way, 1985). Any future mental health services in Buddhist countries are likely to incorporate both these Buddhist concepts and Western concepts of psychopathology (Way, 1985; Wig, 1990). In contrast, most Western mental health services have attempted to remain independent of religious beliefs. Despite the influence of pastoral counseling, most mental health practitioners regard religious influences as being overly prescriptive and moralistic. They are also inclined to associate them with superstitious and outmoded beliefs. Some have even argued that mental and spiritual health may not necessarily be associated (Cohen, 1977). Highly religious people in the West may even be expected to have poorer mental health since they might be highly sensitive, feel as if they need to have their faith tested through suffering, feel a sense of persecution, and experience a painful sense of longing for a relationship with God (note the story of Job).

The contrast between Eastern and Western conceptions of suffering are explained in part by their striking difference in the understanding of the nature of the mind. In Buddhist beliefs, the mind, and indeed a person's sense of ego identity, are perceived as an illusion based on ignorance. It is this ignorance that ultimately leads to suffering and a sense of separateness and alienation between people. A Buddhist would even perceive our "normal" sense of identity as being so distorted that we are unaware that it is a distortion. Thus, normality might even be conceptualized as a culturewide neurosis, a "consensus trance," a collective psychosis, or even an immortality construct fueled by death denial (Becker, 1973; Schumaker, 1990; Tart, 1986). The Buddhist cure for this state is by training the mind to go beyond the distortions and limits of normality and into a deeper sense of Truth. Buddhism is not so much a religion (there is no belief in a God), but more a technology for changing consciousness. On the other hand, traditional Western approaches toward increasing mental health are through a *strengthening* of a person's ego, *enhancing* faith in some external God, and *increasing* ties with the external world. It is this belief in the ultimate reality (or unreality) of the self and the external world that so clearly distinguishes Eastern and Western formulations of mental health.

The key assumptions of Buddhism are contained in the Four Noble Truths. These principles serve as a brief summary of the personal discovery of the Buddha. He also intended them to be an invitation to any person wanting to follow the path suggested by the Truths in order to reach enlightenment.

The First Noble Truth is that life is imperfection, suffering (dukkha), empty, insubstantial, and impermanent (Rahula, 1974). On the surface, this seems like a pessimistic, and hopeless belief. However, it is easy to misinterpret. The First Noble Truth does not mean that there is no such thing as human happiness, but rather that life is necessarily a transitory state, and this impermanence will be associated with suffering. Buddhist practice is more ambitious in that it is concerned with an ultimate and lasting sense of clarity and wisdom. While Western psychology is concerned with *relative* mental health, Buddhism is more concerned with *ultimate* mental health. A person's relative happiness (and thus unhappiness) is maintained in that the more a person tries to cling to the transient states of happiness, the more unlikely it is that the person will be able to maintain them. This is the case because, contrary to our wishes, existence is based on change. It is the clash between what is and what we would like things to be that contributes to suffering. This first essential principle is supported by the Second Noble Truth which is that, at the core of all suffering, is clinging, craving, desire, thirst, and greed (tanha). A rigorous Buddhist analysis of all mental health difficulties would center on understanding how this attachment, this fighting against the changeableness of existence, is at the core of human unhappiness.

The Buddha did not merely describe what he believed to be at the core of human suffering, but also proposed a solution. The Third Noble Truth states that, when the nature of suffering is understood, it can be ended through nonattachment. While the formula is simple, achieving it requires an extremely high level of commitment, discipline, and practice. The end result is to enter into a state of enlightenment, or Nirvana. However, nonattachment should not be misunderstood as being a state of apathy, pessimism, or depression. There is an essential paradox with the Buddhist prescription to attain a state of stillness or emptiness, in that when this state has been achieved there is a tremendous sense of fullness. By becoming "empty," people become filled with a deep sense of connection with others. They are also filled with compassion and a sense that nothing is lacking, while participating in "all thingness" (Dubs, 1987). By truly wanting nothing, the person achieves everything. They become fully awake to the present moment. Suffering (dukkha) and attachment (tanha) disappear.

The Fourth Noble Truth is a description of the Eightfold Path, which includes specific guidelines on how enlightenment can be achieved. These are Right Understanding, Right Thought, Right Speech, Right Action, Right Livelihood, Right Effort, Right Mindfulness, and Right Concentration (meditation). Much of Buddhist teaching is an elaboration of how these guidelines can be incorporated into daily life. They result in a life that is characterized by ethical conduct, mental discipline, and wisdom.

The above portrait of the ideal life contrasts sharply with most Western beliefs of what constitutes happiness. On a collective, mundane level, most Westerners believe that happiness derives from what they *have*. If a person is not quite happy enough, it is often believed that it is because a few more things are necessary, such as material objects, personal qualities (i.e., a stronger ego), a better therapist, or better relationships. Even religious faith might be perceived as one more thing that people need to *acquire* because they do not have "enough of it." In a much different way, the Buddhist ideal is to discover what we *are* rather than what we need to acquire (Walsh, 1989). The Buddhist "practitioner" must sit and experience, rather than acquire, control, and try. In fact, according to the Second Noble Truth, the very act of trying to acquire and control is what causes human suffering.

Buddhist Definition of Mental Health

The Buddhist view of mental health can, in part, be explained by describing what it is not. The healthy person is clearly not someone who merely has an absence of psychopathology. Also, it does not involve a person who has high ego strength or high self-esteem. Instead, the ego is seen as a hindrance to ultimate mental health, since it is an illusion that, like the mind itself, is built on attachment. Western therapy does not really address what Buddhism would consider to be the core issue, namely the ego's fear of nonexistence. It is this fear of nonexistence (and the ego's corresponding dread of existence) that Buddhism attempts to address. Buddhist mental health is also not dependent on faith in an external unquestioned God or cosmology. Rather, Buddhist psychology emphasizes the questioning of everything, including the Buddha himself. Buddhist belief, especially Zen, emphasizes that the Buddha merely points a direction toward enlightenment and that the goal should not be confused with the pointing finger. Thus Buddhist mental health is more consonant with humanistic beliefs, which emphasize self-realization, self-awareness, self-fulfillment, and self-mastery. However, there is one overriding paradox in that there is ultimately no belief in the self.

Descriptions of the Buddha (or enlightened people) portray an image of the mentally healthy person. This image is not so much a person with certain qualities (things), but more a way of perceiving, experiencing, and interacting with the world. What emerges are the following partially overlapping characteristics:

Nondualistic World View

Events, things, and people in the world are not perceived as a subject encountering an object; there is no valid separation to be made between good-bad, enlightened-unenlightened, and self-nonself. Truth simply emerges, even though there is no meaningful distinction between truth and nontruth. If mental illness can be seen as the struggle between opposing internal forces, then it too would cease to exist. Things in the world simply "are." The person is a perfect mirror reflecting everything as it is.

Sense of Emptiness/Nothingness

Letting go of the self results in a sense of emptiness. For example, there is no sense of giving since there is no real difference between the giver, the gift, and the receiver. There is also no distinction between nongiving and nonreceiving, since such a distinction would lead to attachment, craving, and ultimately to suffering.

No Dread of Experience

Since fear of existence is based on the dualism between being and nonbeing, there is no fear of either death or life. Since there is no ego, there can be no anxiety regarding death. The person is both free *from being* and free *to be.*

Timelessness

The enlightened person lives from moment to moment, completely in the present. Since there is no need to grasp onto events in order to make them stand still, they flow from one experience to the next.

Spontaneous Expression of Love and Wisdom

Paradoxically, the enlightened person's detachment from desire results in the spontaneous development of unconditional love (karuna), wisdom (prajna), and compassion. These qualities emerge when the person "lets go." They are not goals, but by-products. The Buddha himself had the qualities of the "Supreme Healer" in that he was serene, detached, selfless, and compassionate in the course of devoting his life to the alleviation of suffering. This is counter to many Western stereotypes of Buddhism, which consider the Buddhist ideal to be withdrawn and solitary (Buddhists would believe that withdrawal is necessary for enlightenment, but that this withdrawal is temporary).

Humility

The person struggling toward enlightenment acknowledges that to be human means to have weaknesses. The personal acknowledgement of one's own weaknesses leads to tolerance of the shortcomings of others. This leads to better and less demanding relationships.

Flexibility

The less people are attached to their cravings, the more able they are to change. The act of clinging makes the world static, thus preventing change. Moreover, clinging to life results in a clinging to death, and this results in the dread of existence. The essence of life is change, and yet change often appears as suffering. If a person does not grasp and cling, then there is no sense of pain or loss when things disappear. The person can be flexible to the changes of the world.

Whereas very few people actually attain full enlightenment, Buddhist cultures portray the above characteristics as models of mental health. In addition, there is a clear path by which Buddhist practitioners attempt not only to live up to these qualities but also to discover them within themselves.

Buddhism and Personal Change

The most frequently discussed Buddhist methods for developing mental health are meditation, understanding the causes of suffering (consequential analysis), stories, and, among Zen practitioners, the koan. Each of these methods provides a somewhat different way of dealing with the Five Hindrances of lust, anger, torpor, worry, and skepticism. They are intended to develop the Seven Factors of Illumination, which include Mindfulness, Investigation of Doctrine, Energy, Joy, Relaxation, Concentration, and Equanimity (Rahula, 1974). Each one of the methods has some parallels with Western approaches, and, in some cases, there is a body of available research.

Meditation has sometimes been referred to as the royal road to mental health. It is both a tool for exploring consciousness and a means of transforming it. Practitioners state that it is able to purge the mind of "mental toxins" (hostility, envy, greed, anger, etc.), create psychological harmony, and, as a result, enhance physical health. In addition, meditation is believed to increase personal control and self-restraint, while also facilitating right knowledge. It is the opposites of these characteristics (lack of control, lack of restraint, lack of right knowledge) that are often associated with poor mental health (de Silva, 1979). The two basic strategies are to focus one's concentration (usually on a chant or on breathing), or to observe one's reactions in a mindful manner. Watching one's reactions during meditation requires that the practitioner note mental contents but suspend judgment over them. The contents are neither accepted nor rejected, and they are not placed into any categories of good or evil. For example, if people experience angry mental contents, they avoid identifying with them. Rather, anger or confusion simply occurs. Eventually, the practitioner lets go of dysfunctional beliefs, self-statements, and assumptions (Mikulas, 1978). The mental contents, many of which are emotionally charged, gradually become desensitized as the practitioner stops identifying with them (Dubs, 1987).

A number of empirical studies support the beneficial effects of meditation. For example, Alexander, Langer, and Newman (1989) found that meditators had an increased sense of well-being, increased cognitive performance, and greater longevity. They have also been found to have increased subtlety and speed of information processing (Brown, Forte, & Dysart, 1984), and greater levels of empathy (Lesh, 1970). Carrington and Ephron (1975) showed that meditators were less critical, had fewer paranoid ideas, and had increased levels of insight. Dubs (1987) reviewed studies on short-term meditators (six months or less) and concluded: (1) prior to commencing meditation, they were somewhat more anxious and neurotic than the overall population; (2) assuming they were not extremely disturbed, meditation helped to reduce neurotic symptoms, especially anxiety; and (3) anxiety levels were reduced to at least normal levels and quite possibly were reduced to levels below the overall population. The above sample of studies suggests that meditation is effective in producing a number of effects consistent both with Buddhist theory and with Western conceptions of mental health.

Buddhist psychology asserts that the mind, in any ultimate sense, does not exist. However, there is faith in the intellect's ability to recognize the nature of suffering and to see through the illusion created by the ego. In this way, the mind is used to achieve liberation by dissolving itself. An essential step in this process is a clear analysis of the consequences of disturbing emotions. Buddhists believe that these emotions will eventually be seen to lack a true basis. One of the major teaching techniques is through the use of short, succinct stories (Groth-Marnat, in press). Bodhidharma, the alleged founder of Zen was approached by his student Hui-k'o,

"I have no peace of mind," said Hui-k'o. "Please pacify my mind."
"Bring out your mind here before me," replied Bodhidharma, "and I will pacify it!"
"But when I seek my mind," said Hui-k'o, "I cannot find it."
"There!" snapped Bodhidharma, "I have pacified your mind!" (Watts, 1957, p. 107)

Hui-k'o immediately attained enlightenment. The practitioner who thoroughly recognizes the illusion of mental suffering creates a state of mind in which mental contents become depotentiated in that they are impotent to cause emotional conflict. Through rational analysis, Buddhist practitioners can work on such areas as hatred, anger, greed, aggression, or egotistical desires. For every unhealthy thought or action, there is an opposing healthy one. Greed can be countered by nonattachment, avarice by nonaversion, envy by impartiality, and delusion by insight. The end result would be a state of mindfulness (the opposite of ignorance) in which the person can clearly perceive an object, event, or person. Thus emotions can be purified through a clear, mindful analysis. The problems in living, then, are based on ignorance, a lack of intrinsic awareness, and misconceptions.

The above beliefs are consistent with current cognitive theories of emotions. Both Buddhist practitioners and cognitive behavior therapists would agree that dysfunctional thoughts attract mental attention, which then lead to dysfunctional emotions (Fenner, 1987). The beginning point is to change inner thoughts. For example, Ellis (1979) recommends that clients challenge different irrational beliefs, such as the need to be loved by everyone, the need to be perfect, the tendency to exaggerate the negative aspects of events, and the belief that happiness is dependent on external events. The consequence of rational, realistic cognitions would be an increase in positive emotions such as self-pride, a sense of control, ego strength, and happiness.

However, there are notable differences between cognitive behavior therapy and Buddhist rational analysis. Buddhists believe that all emotions, including happiness, result in further suffering because they are transient and based on attachment. The Buddhist goal is therefore more ambitious in that the end result is based on selflessness and nonattachment, which leads to unconditional freedom, liberation, and happiness (nirvana). In addition, cognitive therapies (and most other psychotherapies) have narrower goals, such as resolving a specific problem (e.g., eliminating a phobia), adjusting to society, or being successful (Fenner, 1987).

One of the unique features of Zen Buddhism is the use of puzzles known as koans. For example, students might be asked what their essential nature was before they were born, or how you would get a goose out of a bottle without breaking the bottle or hurting the goose. The student usually struggles with any number of abstract, philosophical, and intellectual answers. But the teacher inevitably indicates they are incorrect. The student becomes more and more filled with doubt and confusion until the usual mode of perceiving the world collapses. Ideally, this gives way to a new clarity of vision which enables the student to answer the koan in a manner that the teacher perceives as indicating a greater sense of enlightenment.

Rossi (1986) explains that the koan initially produces a high level of sympathetic activation which is associated with the student's confusion, frustration, and anxiety. When the "answer" (i.e., new perception) is realized, there is a strong sense of relaxation, dissolution of the ego, and sense of fullness, which is consistent with heightened parasympathetic nervous system dominance. It is this contrast between initial tension and the subsequent relief and relaxation that propels the student into a new understanding of the world. However, this occurs within the context of the student-teacher relationship which is a function of specific cultural beliefs and expectations.

Internality

Buddhism, probably more than any other belief system, emphasizes that people are responsible for their own condition. This is true both because of the principle of karma (cause and effect) and because of belief in the potential for mental control. The law of karma states that, for each thought and behavior, there is a corresponding effect at some future time. If a person is in a certain situation, then it must be the result of some past action. By fully understanding these past actions, people can better perceive why they are involved in their current condition. This can also be understood through the principle of attachment. The reason for continued cause-effect occurrences is because the person has not been able to achieve freedom. This freedom is directly dependent on cognitions, since the mind is the only creator Buddhism recognizes. Thien-An (1975) illustrates this point:

> A Zen master once said that water is of one essence, but if it is drunk by a cow, it becomes milk, while if it is drunk by a snake, it becomes poison. In the same way whether life is blissful or sorrowful depends on our state of mind, not on the world. (p. 43)

Although the teacher (including the Buddha himself) is initially helpful, even he will eventually be a hindrance. An ancient Buddhist saying is "Look within, you are the Buddha." Thus, no one can save another person other than oneself. This is in marked contrast to most Western or Near Eastern religions, which believe that a person's life is controlled by fate or some divine force.

The above views present a unique conception of personal difficulties. The Buddhist would say that, strictly speaking, there are no problems. Any problems are based on the ego's divisive thinking. The ego is ultimately an illusion, and therefore the problems it creates are also illusions. Furthermore, the solution to all problems is through enlightenment, something that is always there despite our ignorance of it. In a sense, we are unenlightened about our enlightenment.

It is difficult to make definitive conclusions regarding the relation between the above extreme views of internality and its impact on mental health. In general, internality provides people within Western cultures with a sense of competence and control over their lives (Phares, 1976). However, there may also be the risk that the person feels more alone and isolated. Additionally, they may be more susceptible to depression since they must take a greater degree of responsibility for what has happened to themselves. However, this potential "abandonment of the individual" into self-responsibility is counteracted by a strong tradition of compassion within Buddhist cultures. Perhaps the development of this compassion was necessary to neutralize the person's potential sense of isolation. The individual is also psychologically supported in most Buddhist cultures in that they emphasize the importance of the community and family.

Reduction of Death Anxiety

One of the major functions of religious beliefs are to reduce a person's fear of death. It has even been hypothesized that religions were developed and maintained mainly as a means of offsetting the increased fear of death that has resulted from the development of reflective consciousness (Schumaker, 1990). Each of the different religions use somewhat different strategies for reducing death anxiety. There also seem to be differences between how effectively they accomplish this goal.

Buddhism conceptualizes death anxiety as originating from the artificial distinction between the subject and object, the knower and the known. Since the self (knower, or subject) stands apart from its world, it is separate. Since it is separate, it can then perceive that if it can exist, it can also not exist. The Buddhist practitioner tries to confront and change this potential sense of nothingness by working to eliminate the distinction between self and not self (Kara, 1979). This is quite different from most Western religious traditions, which believe in an afterlife, as well as a personal savior who guides or determines a person's existence in this life. The Buddhist strategy is highly present-oriented, whereas most Western traditions look ahead into some believed-in future. Western traditions are also more likely to stress belief and faith, whereas Buddhist traditions emphasize experience and enlightenment through such techniques as meditation and rational analysis. The Buddhist reduces, or even eliminates, fear of death by realizing that death neither exists nor does it not exist. It is an illusion just as the ego is. When the ego ceases to exist, so too does death.

Whereas the above strategy is based on religious teaching, these teachings have also been translated into specific cultural messages. In particular, Buddhist cultures teach a sense of internal control, detachment, and acceptance of life events, including death itself. They also encourage a strong sense of being an extension of, and being connected with, a world community (Westman & Canter, 1985). Whereas Western culture can be characterized as being death-denying (Becker, 1973), Buddhist cultures are more death-accepting. In fact, one technique of meditation is to concentrate on the fact that death is inevitable. This is believed to enrich life by reducing people's greed and attachment and making them aware of the importance of each moment. Such a confrontation might be similar to a less intense version of a near-death experience (Groth-Marnat & Schumaker, 1989).

Many Buddhist cultures even believe that death, like any other complex activity, requires training and preparation. Life itself is perceived as a dissociated, fragmented state and death presents itself as an opportunity to awaken from the illusion of life. Quite oppositely, most Westerners would perceive this as a morbid preoccupation with death, something that threatens the Western need for external control. In part, this explains the Western taboo on discussions of death (Groth-Marnat, 1977). However, this denial and avoidance of death is likely to isolate the dying person, thereby making dying more traumatic and anxiety provoking than it might otherwise be. The above cross-cultural comparisons of death anxiety are consistent with empirical research which suggests that cultures influenced by Buddhist beliefs seem to be more effective at reducing death anxiety (McMordie & Kumar, 1984; Schumaker, Baraclough, & Vagg, 1988; Schumaker, Warren, & Groth-Marnat, 1991).

Conclusion

Buddhism is not so much a religion as it is a practical method for achieving change. Many of these changes are consistent with traditional conceptions of mental health. The basic tenets of Buddhism are essentially clear and simple; due to attachment, life is necessarily filled with suffering. By eliminating attachment, we eliminate suffering and realize Truth. Although, on the surface, such a perspective may appear negative and even nihilistic, the cessation of the self paradoxically creates a sense of compassion, fullness, connection with other people, flexibility, timelessness, joy, equanimity, and acceptance. It is these characteristics that comprise the Buddhist model of the mentally healthy person. The specific techniques of enlightenment (e.g., mental health) include various forms of meditation, rational analysis, teaching stories, and koans. The available empirical evidence suggests that these beliefs and practices have some clear mental health benefits such as greater acceptance of death, greater empathy, reduction of general anxiety, increased insight, greater cognitive performance, and an enhanced sense of well-being.

References

Alexander, C., Langer, E., & Newman, R. (1989). Aging, mindfulness, and transcendental meditation. *Journal of Personality and Social Psychology, 57,* 950–964.

Becker, E. (1973). *The denial of death.* New York: Free Press.

Brown, D., Forte, M., & Dysart, M. (1984). Visual sensitivity and mindfulness meditation. *Perceptual and Motor Skills, 58,* 775–784.

Carrington, P., & Ephron, H.S. (1975). Meditation and psychoanalysis. *Journal of the American Academy of Psychoanalysis, 3,* 43–57.

Cohen, E.J. (1977). Holiness and health: An examination of the relationship between Christian holiness and mental health. *Journal of Psychology and Theology, 5,* 285–291.

de Silva, M.W.P. (1979). *An introduction to Buddhist psychology.* New York: Harper & Row.

Dubs, G. (1987). Psycho-spiritual development in Zen Buddhism: A study of resistance in meditation. *Journal of Transpersonal Psychology, 19,* 19–87.

Ellis, A. (1979). *Reason and emotion in psychotherapy.* Secaucus, NJ: Citadel Press.

Fenner, P. (1987). Cognitive theories of the emotions in Buddhism and Western psychology. *Psychologia, 30,* 217–227.

Groth-Marnat, G. (1977). The phenomenon of dying as seen through the individuals with a reduced life expectance. Doctoral dissertation, California School of Professional Psychology, San Diego. *Dissertation Abstracts International, 38.*

Groth-Marnat, G. (in press). Past traditions of therapeutic metaphor. *Psychology.*

Groth-Marnat, G., & Schumaker, J.F. (1989). The near-death experience: A review and critique. *Journal of Humanistic Psychology, 29,* 109–133.

Kara, A. (1979). The ego dilemma and the Buddhist experience of enlightenment. *Journal of Religion and Health, 18,* 144–159.

Lesh, T.V. (1970). Zen meditation and the development of empathy in counselors. *Journal of Humanistic Psychology, 10,* 39–74.

McMordie, W.R., & Kumar, A. (1984). Cross-cultural research on the Templer/McMordie Death Anxiety Scale. *Psychological Reports, 54,* 959–963.

Mikulas, W. (1978). Four noble truths of Buddhism related to behavior therapy. *Psychological Record, 28,* 59–67.

Phares, E.J. (1976). *Locus of control and personality.* Morristown, NJ: General Learning Press.

Rahula, W. (1974). *What the Buddha taught.* New York: Grove Press.

Rossi, E. (1986). Altered states of consciousness in everday life: The ultradian rhythms. In B. Wolman (Ed.), *Handbook of altered states of consciousness.* New York: Van Nostrand Reinhold.

Schumaker, J.F. (1990). *Wings of Illusion.* Cambridge, UK: Polity Press (also Buffalo, NY: Prometheus Books).

Schumaker, J.F., Barraclough, R.A., & Vagg, L.M. (1988). Death anxiety in Malaysian and Australian students. *Journal of Social Psychology, 128,* 41–47.

Schumaker, J.F., Warren, W.G., Groth-Marnat, G. (1991). Death anxiety in Japan and Australia. *Journal of Social Psychology, 131,* 511–518.

Tart, C. (1986). *Waking up.* Boston: New Science Library/Shambala.

Thien-An, T. (1975). *Zen philosophy, Zen practice.* Emeryville, CA: Dharma Publishing.

Walsh, R. (1989). Toward a synthesis of Eastern and Western psychologies. In A.A. Sheikh & K.S. Sheikh (Eds.), *Eastern and Western approaches to healing* (pp. 542–555). New York: Wiley.

Watts, A. (1957). *The way of Zen.* New York: Penguin.

Way, R.T. (1985). Burmese culture, personality, and mental health. *Australian and New Zealand Journal of Psychiatry, 19,* 275–282.

Westman, A.S., & Canter, F.M. (1985). Fear of death and the extended self. *Psychological Reports, 56,* 419–425.

Wig, N.N. (1990). Indian concepts of mental health and their impact on care of the mentally ill. *International Journal of Mental Health, 18,* 71–80.

22

Religious Experience and Psychopathology: Cross-Cultural Perspectives

Raymond H. Prince

By religious experiences I mean states of mind which their subjects invest with supernatural or preternatural meaning (interpreting the experiences as related to such agencies as spirits, gods, devils, or magical influences). Defined in this way, we can immediately see a significant kinship between psychiatric disorders and religious experiences. Functional psychoses, including both schizophrenia and manic-depressive psychoses are often interpreted by patients in this way (Boisen, 1936; Custance, 1951). Swedenborg, George Fox, and many other religious leaders experienced states of mind which they believed were of supernatural origin. But, for the psychiatrist, these are very difficult to distinguish from psychotic states. For example, reactions to bereavement include melancholia in some individuals (Freud, 1925/1917) and mystical experiences among others (Aberbach, 1987). Also, Westerners who have been subject to mystical or other types of religious experiences commonly believe them to indicate mental illness and, for this reason, avoid speaking of them (Prince, 1979).

Outside the Western world, this kinship between religious experiences and psychiatric disorders becomes even more striking. Within the Western world view, the interpretation of unusual events as the result of the activities of supernatural agencies has increasingly lost favor; only scientific explanations are held in high regard (Prince & Reiss, 1990). In many other world cultures, however, supernatural agencies retain their central importance in interpreting life events. States of mind and behavior that we in the West designate psychiatric disorders are commonly seen as religious phenomena, both by their subjects and by members of their social group. Under these circumstances, religious institutions are activated for interpretation and socialization rather than medical institutions.

In this chapter I will illustrate these views about the kinship between psychiatric disorders and religious experiences by contrasting examples from the Western world with examples from Korean and Indian cultures. I should note here that to provide at least some degree of objectivity in discussing these notoriously slippery subjective states, I have drawn upon well-documented case examples reported by others rather than cases from my own records.

Psychiatric Disorder and Religious Experience in the Western World

Tart (1969) noted that "Within Western culture we have strong negative attitudes towards ASCs (altered states of consciousness): there is the normal (good) state of consciousness and there are pathological states of consciousness" (p. 2). Indeed it has often been claimed that contemporary Western cultures actively discourage the experiencing, labeling, discussion, and utilization of altered states of consciousness (Bourguignon, 1985). Nonetheless, survey research in recent years suggests that a large proportion of Western populations have religious experiences. Dating back to the 1970s, several well-conducted studies of populations at large both in the United States and Britain have reported some 20–40 percent of representative samples as experiencing religious experiences at some time in their lives, and some 5 percent as experiencing them often (Back & Bourque, 1970; Greeley & McCready, 1973; Hay & Morisy, 1978). These findings were based on positive responses to such survey questions as, "Have you ever felt as though you were very close to a powerful, spiritual force that seemed to lift you out of yourself?" or "Have you ever been aware of or influenced by, a presence or power, whether referred to as God or not, which is different from your everyday self?"

But what kinds of experiences were respondents actually referring to when they answered positively to such questions? To find out, Valla and Prince (1989) conducted detailed interviews with subjects who had previously responded positively to such questions. Some 183 experiences were reported by 49 self-selected subjects in a high-income Montreal suburb. The authors found that the experiences were rather undifferentiated and difficult to classify. The features of the experiences showed a good deal of overlap. Three types of experiences were most common: ecstatic (subjects reported standing outside themselves and their life situations so that they could see the world in a detached or objective manner); aesthetic (intensifications of their responses to beauty); and hallucinatory (short-lived illusions or visual hallucinations). They found very few typical "nature" mystic experiences (loss of ego boundaries with a euphoric feeling of fusion of self-with-world) of the type described by William James (1902) and no "introvertive" mystic experiences (the world disappears and consciousness is filled with one thing or with oneness in the presence of God), as described by Stace (1960).

Valla and Prince (1989) concluded that:

> Almost all of the experiences were of very brief duration—from a few moments to a few minutes. But in spite of their brevity, they were almost all of great significance to the subjects. They were extraordinary states of consciousness that had occurred only a few times in a lifetime and were highly memorable. Many of the subjects spoke of their experiences with considerable intensity and affect, even though they had occurred long before. (p. 163)

As regards the lack of differentiation among the Montreal experiences, the authors believed this was the result of the above-mentioned Western denigration and general neglect of altered states of consciousness. Since religious experiences lacked acceptable institutionalization or acceptable settings for their validation (except perhaps in the Pentecostal church, or within charismatic Catholic groups), most subjects kept them secret and were unable to integrate them into their view of themselves or of the world.

In this context, it is interesting to consider the case of Henry James, Sr., to demonstrate how an individual in the Western world may sometimes deal with religious experiences. This case is also of interest because the experience was negative and frightening, one that today would almost certainly be managed in a psychiatric context.

Henry James, Sr. (1811–1882), was the father of several famous Americans, William James (psychologist), Henry James, Jr. (novelist), and Alice James (diarist). Henry James, Sr., grew up in a highly repressive Presbyterian family. His father was a self-made millionaire who emphasized work and a punitive God. Henry spent his childhood in revolt against this joyless and gloomy world view. Soon after his marriage when he was 33 years old, Henry experienced a remarkable episode of fearfulness, which had a profound life-long effect.

At the time, Henry, his wife, and two children were living on the outskirts of London. As described by Henry James Jr.'s biographer, Leon Edel (1953), he had eaten a good meal and was contentedly sitting alone by the fire "feeling only the exhilaration incident to a good digestion" (p. 30). Without warning he suddenly experienced a "day-nightmare." It seemed to him that there was an invisible shape squatting in the room "raying out from his fetid personality influences fatal to life" (p. 30). James recognized that "to all appearance it was a perfect insane and abject terror, without ostensible cause" (p. 30). But the effect upon him was profound: "the thing had not lasted ten seconds before I felt myself a wreck; that is, reduced from a state of firm, vigorous, joyful manhood to one of almost helpless infancy" (p. 30). He felt like running to the foot of the stairs and calling to his wife as if she were his mother, or running to the roadside to appeal to the public to protect him. Following this episode, he entered a state of depression and despair, which led him to consult eminent London physicians who told him that he had overworked his brain and urged that he should give up reading, get out into the open air, and cultivate cheerful company. They also recommended a water-cure. In compliance with medical instructions, he went to a watering place but the waters did not help. He discovered that he no longer wanted to study the scriptures and that his melancholy and despair were so intense that to go for a walk or to sleep in strange surroundings required as much effort as "to plan a military campaign or write an epic" (p. 31).

At the watering place however, he met a certain Mrs. Chichester whom he described as "a lady of rare qualities of heart and mind, and of singular personal loveliness as well" (Edel, 1953, p. 32). When she asked him what had brought him to seek the water-cure he was very willing to pour out to her the story of his episode of horror and his subsequent melancholia. Remarkably, she seemed to understand him:

> It is then, very much as I had ventured to suspect from two or three previous things you have said; you are undergoing what Swedenborg calls a *vastation;* and though,

naturally, you yourself are despondent or even despairing about the issue I cannot help take an altogether hopeful view of your prospect. (Edel, 1953, p. 32)

Mrs. Chichester explained that according to Swedenborgian teachings Henry's *vastation* represented one of the stages in the regeneration of man which included the awakening, purgation, illumination, and the new birth. Mrs. Chichester directed him to a source of information about Swedenborg (a Swedish scientist turned mystic). Reading Swedenborg's account of the spirit world and the nature of Swedenborg's concept of God as an all-forgiving, all-loving Father, he rapidly recovered his peace of mind and spent the rest of his life interpreting Swedenborg and writing difficult books on Swedenborg's world view.

William James, Henry's son, referred to his father's *vastation* experience in his famous *Varieties of Religious Experience* (1902). The medical practitioners of his day seemed to have very little understanding of his experience of terror or of his melancholy, though it is interesting that James consulted physicians rather than clergymen about them. In any case, with the help of Swedenborg, he was able subsequently to formulate his problem in religious terms. Had Henry James, Sr. consulted a psychiatrist today he would probably have been diagnosed as suffering a panic attack followed by a major depressive disorder, and prescribed a tricyclic antidepressant.

Sinbyong (Spirit Sickness) in South Korea

Unlike the Western world, Korea today has a pervasive living tradition of belief in the spirit world and in the potentiality for spirits and humans to interact. Spirits may also create unusual mental states among humans by possessing them. Koreans with odd experiences, such as those of Henry James or some of those reporting religious experiences in Montreal, live in a cultural milieu that provides an interpretation within a widely accepted world view.

Shamanism in Korea has a venerable history. According to legend, the first king of Korea was a shaman, and recent archaeological excavations of burial mounds in Kyongju, the ancient southern capital, have discovered gold crowns and burial goods incorporating a rich shamanic symbolism, including the cosmic tree, reindeer horns, and flying horses, which are reminiscent of the contents of burial mounds of prehistoric Siberian shaman-chieftains (Adams, 1986; Covell, 1986). Over the centuries, however, shamanism has been repeatedly suppressed by foreign religious intrusions: by the Buddhists (after 500 A.D.), the Confucianists of the Yi dynasty (1392–1900), Japanese Shintoism (1910–1945); by Christian missionaries, and by recent politicians who saw the beliefs constituting the shamanic world as incongruous with the rational and technological aspirations of modern Korea. An important result of suppression during the Yi dynasty was that, whereas in earlier times shamans were almost always men, shamanism was forced underground and the shamanic role was taken over by women. Today Korean shamans are almost 95 percent women, and they serve an almost entirely female clientele.

According to Korean anthropologist Harvey (1979), estimates of the numbers of shamans in South Korea today range from one shaman per 1616 population, to one per 314. Of course estimates are problematic because of differing opinions as to who should be designated a shaman, and because enumerations during eras of persecution are unreliable. In any case, all observers agree that there are very significant numbers today. Shamans are called upon to treat illnesses, solve problems such as infertility or loss of wealth, or just general bad luck. Today a shamanic *kut* (one of the more elaborate rituals) which may last for 24 hours, costs the participating family as much as the Korean equivalent of $5000 (U.S.).

Regarding the focus of this chapter, the important aspect of Korean shamanism is the belief that spirits who wish to recruit a woman as a shaman indicate their intention by afflicting her with a spirit sickness (*sinbyong*). It should be noted that the role of shaman is regarded with ambivalence in Korea. In many ways the role of a shaman is outside the social pale. The family will often be ashamed when one of their daughters enters the shamanic role, and they may even disown her. Because women as shamans tend to dominate the household and no longer experience sexual pleasure with their husbands (sexual pleasures are transferred to trance experiences, which are viewed as possession by spirits), husbands are ashamed to have shamans as wives. Women inflicted by *sinbyong* are therefore often reluctant to accept the call. On the other hand, shamans have great prestige and power within the female Korean world. Quite a number of detailed biographical studies of shamans in Korea have been published (Harvey, 1979; Kendall, 1985, 1988). The following abbreviated case history from Harvey (1979) illustrates the kinds of emotional disturbances attributed to *sinbyong,* as well as the life context in which they may occur.

P.M. was born in 1925 in the capital of today's North Korea. Her father sold dry goods in one of the city's open markets. During her childhood she was cared for by her grandmother because her mother worked at the market with her father. P.M.'s father died unexpectedly when she was thirteen. Soon after her father's death she experienced her first of four episodes of spirit sickness (*sinbyong*):

> She began to feel unwell but without any well defined symptoms. She suffered from a general condition of malaise. Every doctor her mother consulted said there was nothing the matter with her physically. In desperation her mother consulted a *mudang* (female shaman) who diagnosed the illness as *sinbyong.* She also prophesied that P.M. would become a *mudang.* Alarmed, her mother kept the information secret. (Harvey, 1979, p. 98)

P.M. recovered from her mysterious illness shortly after. At eighteen, she graduated from high school and worked as a typist for a Japanese printing firm. At the age of nineteen, she began to feel unwell:

> She was able to work most of the time but suffered from an inner terror bordering on panic. Unlike before, she was hearing voices, and her hallucinatory experiences were so frightening that she was afraid to confide even in her mother. (Harvey, 1979, p. 99)

Her mother interpreted this illness as her second call to become a shaman. After World War II, the family fled from North Korea to Seoul, South Korea, where P.M.

found a job and met her husband. Her husband had been an office clerk before he was drafted into the army during the Korean war. They married because P.M. had become pregnant. Although her daughter had broken the rules of the community, P.M.'s mother was secretly pleased with the pregnancy and marriage because she felt that her daughter might thereby escape her shamanic destiny. But her husband's family was enraged. When she and her husband moved in with her in-laws, severe family tensions developed. It was after the death of her second son when he was a few months old that her third episode of *sinbyong* occurred (at age twenty-three):

> This time her symptoms were more sharply defined and more severe as well. She was not only hearing things but seeing things as well. Her ears rang a lot and she could hear voices whispering in them; and when she yielded to the urge to talk she uttered prophetic statements. Neighbours and relatives began to speculate that she had been "caught by the spirit" and was possessed. She suffered from terrible palpitations of the heart, indigestion, and dizzy spells, sometimes alternately and sometimes in combinations. She was constantly afraid of being caught hallucinating by her husband or his family. She was determined to overcome these symptoms and began to read a lot of novels as a way of fighting off the hallucinations. Her in-laws however pointed to her engrossed reading as additional proof of her laziness and were severely irritated. (Harvey, 1979, p. 105)

P.M.'s mother finally urged her to become a *mudang* since she preferred to have a live *mudang* than a dead daughter. In 1955, P.M. gave birth to her fifth child. She suffered severe post partum haemorrhage and her fourth and final episode of *sinbyong:*

> She would awaken abruptly from sleep sometimes and rush out of the house, heading towards a Buddhist temple. At other times, she was just going to the mountains. Or sometimes she would start jumping up and down vigorously stopping only when someone in the family restricted her. (Harvey, 1979, p. 107)

If her family questioned her as to her whereabouts she would answer "Oh to see Sim Jang-Nim" a well-known shamanic spirit army general. It was after this episode of spirit sickness that P.M. finally succumbed to her calling and became initiated as a *mudang.* She described her feelings in the initial weeks after her initiation as "intoxicating and being afloat on a cloud" (Harvey, 1979, p. 111). Subsequently she became a highly successful shaman and made a good living. Her husband was unemployed and occupied himself in pasting labels on matchboxes and making paper bags at home. For the most part he looked after the children while his wife carried out her shamanic duties. Having a shaman for a wife was embarrassing to him in the society of men, and therefore he liked to stay at home.

From a psychiatric point of view, it would appear that P.M.'s episodes of spirit sickness were rather typical psychiatric disorders. Perhaps the initial episode would be regarded as a depression and the subsequent episodes as hysterical psychoses. Although the content of her hallucinatory experiences and some of her unusual behavior are clearly related to shamanic imagery, the symptomatology is not otherwise unusual. The episodes often seem responsive to life stresses such as the death of her father and infant son. From an intensive study of the life histories of a number of shamans, Korean psychiatrist Kwang-Iel Kim (1972, 1973) concluded that shamans often grew up under painful and deprived circumstances. Hostility towards parents and incestuous fantasies were common, and there was a frequent history of mental illness including schizophrenia, hysteria, or psychosomatic disorder prior to initiation as a shaman.

It should be noted that not all Korean psychiatrists agree with Kim's assessment. For example, the Jungian analyst and psychiatrist Bou-Yong Rhi (1989) differentiates *sinbyong* subjects from psychiatric cases:

> From the moment such suffering is endowed with the meaning of a divine call, it ceases to have a clinical dimension. It is now neither disease nor illness but a divine suffering which incessantly urges the individual to a religious life. There, it is not only difficult but also inadequate to interpret initiation disease solely from a clinical or medical psychological viewpoint without taking the religious meaning of the suffering into consideration. (p. 8)

Rhi, however, does not provide us with a convincing symptomatology that would differentiate *sinbyong* from mental states regarded as psychopathological.

Religious Experience and Psychosis in the Brahmanic Tradition

As in Korea, many Indian cultures are characterized by world views permitting the interpretation and integration of religious experiences. Korea and India, however, have had different historical exposures to Western psychiatry. Concomitant with British colonization, lunatic asylums appeared in India as early as 1787 (Rao, 1975). But, as Rhi (1973) observes, significant intrusions of Western medicine and psychiatry appeared in Korea only with the Japanese invasion in the early twentieth century. Again it is instructive to consider a specific Indian example to demonstrate the kinship between psychiatric disorder and religious experience.

Sri Bhagavan Maharshi (1879–1950) is an important Tamil saint. He is one of several holy men who have a wide following outside India. Extensive biographical details of Bhagavan's life are provided by British historian Arthur Osborne (1954), who lived in Bhagavan's ashram in Tiruvannamalai during the last five years of the saint's life. Bhagavan (under the name Shri Ganesha) is perhaps most familiar to Westerners in the pages of Somerset Maugham's novel *The Razor's Edge;* Maugham had visited him briefly in March 1938 (Maugham, 1949, p. 273).

Venkataraman (later called Sri Bhagavan, an epithet indicating complete oneness with God) was the son of a Brahmin lawyer who practiced near Madurai in South India. Born in 1879, Venkataraman attended high school until the age of sixteen when one day he was overcome by a sudden and violent fear of death:

> I just felt I am going to die and began thinking about what to do about it. It did not occur to me to consult a doctor, or my elders or friends; I felt I had to solve the problem myself, there and then. (Osborne, 1954, p. 18)

He described how he tried to find out what death really meant. He stretched himself out as a corpse and then held his breath and imagined himself being carried for cremation and burial. As a result of this charade-of-death, he was able to confront his terror of death and prove to his own satisfaction that death was not death of the self but only of the body. According to his own account, fear of death vanished once and for all (Osborne, 1954).

Shortly after this experience, he lost interest in his school work and his former friends and activities. Leaving a farewell note to his family which did not say where he was going, he set off for Tiruvannamalai where he took up his abode in the thousand-pillared hall of the temple in that city. He spent the next two and a half years in almost complete silence, immobility, and trance. He moved around from temple to temple in the vicinity and was cared for and fed by the gradually increasing circle of devotees who sensed his profound spirituality. He neglected his body in the extreme. For example, six months after arriving at Tiruvannamalai, Venkataraman moved in to the "shrine of Gurumurtam" where:

> the floor of the shrine was infested with ants but he seemed oblivious to their crawling over him and biting him. After some time a stool was placed in the corner for him to sit on and its legs immersed in water to keep them away, but even then he leaned back against the wall and so made a bridge for them. From constant sitting there his back made a permanent imprint on the wall. . . . (His) body was utterly neglected. He ignored it completely. It was unwashed; his hair had grown again and was thick and matted; his finger nails had grown long and curled over. . . . His body was weakened to the limit of endurance. When he needed to go out he had barely the strength to rise. He would raise himself up a few inches and then sink back again, weak and dizzy, and would have to try several times before he could rise to his feet. (Osborne, 1954, p. 35–36)

During this period of silence and withdrawal, his family finally succeeded in locating him. But he ignored their attempts to persuade him to move closer to home where they could at least attend to his physical needs. Toward the end of these two and a half years of withdrawal, he began to show signs of return to the world. Instead of depending on others to feed him, he began to go regularly around the town begging for food. He also began to speak a little. For instance, one of his devotees could not understand certain holy books because they were written in Tamil, so Bhagavan read them and explained them to him.

As he gradually returned to the social world, an increasing number of followers collected around him to seek his advice and bask in his spirituality. In 1916 Sri Bhagavan's mother and her eldest son came to live in the vicinity of the cave in which he had set up his abode. Bhagavan's mother herself became one of his devotees and, after his mother's death in 1922, Bhagavan had an ashram built over her burial place. He became widely known as a great spiritual master, both within India and around the world through the writings of Brunton (1934).

Bhagavan remained in what appears to have been a psychotic withdrawal state from the age of sixteen to nineteen. After recovery, he had no further such episodes during his life. He evidently had no sexual experience during his life, and during adulthood his only possessions were a loin cloth and a drinking gourd. For the outside observer, it is difficult to understand how Bhagavan, during his psychosis, would appear any different from other Indian psychotics at the time. Yet it is clear that many other psychotics in the same part of the country were being concurrently hospitalized in Western-style psychiatric facilities.

Conclusions

Through these examples, I have tried to demonstrate that highly similar mental and behavioral states may be designated psychiatric disorders in some cultural settings and religious experiences in others. These examples also suggest that, within cultures that invest these unusual states with meaning and provide the individual experiencing them with institutional support, at least a proportion of them may be contained and channeled into socially valuable roles.

These are by no means isolated phenomena. Well-known European mystics such as Suzo, Catherine of Genoa, Guyon, and Saint Theresa have also been discussed from the psychopathological point of view (Leuba, 1925). Lenz (1974) outlined the similarities and differences between five religiously oriented psychotics and the Catholic saint, Ignatius of Loyola. He concluded that differences could only be observed when the long-term picture was known. The psychotics became more and more withdrawn and bizarre, whereas the saint recovered from his visionary state and went on to become an energetic and revered innovator within the Catholic church. However, their acute psychiatric disturbances were very similar. Wapnick (1972) compared in detail the experiences of Saint Theresa with those of a female schizophrenic patient and concluded that "though the mystic and the schizophrenic ostensibly share the same flight from the social world, the mystic's abandonment is merely of his own dependent attachments to it" (p. 172). According to Wapnick, the religious leader achieves freedom from life habits and customs that were adopted as protection against the anxieties that accompany growth toward independence. On the other hand, the purpose of the schizophrenic's withdrawal is total escape from the social world within which he/she is unable to function. We might also add that such factors as the intensity or duration of the religious experience, as well as the degree of personal disorganization and incapacitation associated with it, determines whether the episode will finally be regarded as religious and positive, or psychotic and negative.

References

Aberbach, D. (1987). Grief and mysticism. *International Review of Psycho-Analysis, 14,* 509–526.

Adams, E.B. (1986). *Korea's Kyongju: Cultural spirit of Silla in Korea.* Seoul: Seoul International Publishing.

Back, K.W., & Bourque, L.B. (1970). Can feelings be enumerated? *Behavioural Science, 15,* 487–496.

Boisen, A.T. (1936). *The exploration of the inner world: A study of mental disorder and religious experience.* New York: Willett Clark.

Bourguignon, E. (1985). Multiple personality, possession trance, and psychic unity. In H.P. Duerr (Ed.), *Die wilde Seele.* Frankfurt: Syndikat.

Brunton, P. (1934). *A search in secret India.* London: Rider.

Covell, A.C. (1986). *Folk art and magic: Shamanism in Korea.* Seoul: Hollym.

Custance, J. (1951). *Wisdom, madness and folly: The philosophy of a lunatic.* London: Golancz.

Edel, L. (1953). *Henry James: The untried years: 1843–1870.* Philadelphia: Lippincott.

Freud, S. (1925). Mourning and melancholia. In *Collected papers,* Volume 4 (pp. 152–170). London: Hogarth Press. (Original work published 1917.)

Greeley, A.M., & McCready, W.C. (1973). *The sociology of mystical ecstasy: Some preliminary notes.* Paper presented at the meeting of the Society for the Scientific Study of Religion, San Francisco.

Harvey, Y.K. (1979). *Six Korean women: The socialization of shamans.* New York: West Publishing.

Hay, C., & Morisy, A. (1978). Reports of ecstatic, paranormal or religious experience in Great Britain and the United States: A comparison of trends. *Journal for the Scientific Study of Religion, 17,* 225–268.

James, W. (1902). *The varieties of religious experience.* New York: Longmans Green.

Kendall, L. (1985). *Shamans, housewives, and other restless spirits: Women in Korean ritual life.* Honolulu: University of Hawaii Press.

Kendall, L. (1988). *The life and hard times of a Korean shaman.* Honolulu: University of Hawaii Press.

Kim, K.I. (1972). Psychoanalytic consideration of Korean shamanism. *Korean Neuropsychiatric Association Journal, 2,* 121–129 (in Korean with English summary).

Kim, K.I. (1973). Psychodynamic study of two cases of shaman in Korea. *Korean Journal of Cultural Anthropology, 6,* 45–65 (in Korean with English abstract).

Lenz, H. (1974). Faith and delusion. *Transcultural Psychiatric Research Review, 11,* 18–19.

Leuba, J.H. (1925). *The psychology of religious mysticism.* London: Routledge and Kegan Paul.

Maugham, W.S. (1949). *A writer's notebook.* London: Heinemann.

Osborne, A. (1954). *Ramana Maharshi and the path of self-knowledge.* New York: Samuel Weiser.

Prince, R.H. (1979). Religious experience and psychosis. *Journal of Altered States of Consciousness, 5,* 167–181.

Prince, R.H., & Reiss, M. (1990). Psychiatry and the irrational: Does our scientific world view interfere with the adaptation of psychotics? *Psychiatric Journal of the University of Ottawa, 15,* 137–143.

Rhi, B.Y. (1973). A preliminary study of medical acculturation problems in Korea. *Korean Neuropsychiatric Association Journal, 12,* 15–22 (abstracted in *Transcultural Psychiatric Research Review* (1974) *21,* 42–44).

Rhi, B.Y. (1989, May). *Psychotherapeutic aspects of shamanism with special reference to Korean mudang.* Mimeo, 33 pages, presented at a conference on "Shamanism and Mental Health," Seoul, Korea.

Stace, W.T. (1960). *The teachings of the mystics.* New York: Mentor.

Tart, C.T. (1969). Introduction. In C.T. Tart (Ed.), *Altered states of consciousness: A book of readings* (pp. 1–6). New York: John Wiley.

Valla, J.P., & Prince, R.H. (1989). Religious experiences as self-healing mechanisms. In C. Ward (Ed.), *Altered states of consciousness and mental health: A cross-cultural perspective* (pp. 149–166). London: Sage.

Rao V.A. (1975). India. In J.G. Howells (Ed.), *World history of psychiatry* (pp. 624–649). New York: Brenner/Mazel.

Wapnick, K. (1972). Mysticism and schizophrenia. In J. White (Ed.), *The highest state of consciousness* (pp. 153–174). New York: Anchor Books.

23

Religious Ritual and Mental Health

Janet L. Jacobs

The cross-cultural study of religious ritual has typically been approached from a sociocultural perspective in which the rites of religious ceremonies are examined through the lens of functionalist theory. An exception to this approach is found in the work of Scheff (1979), who more than a decade ago initiated a debate on the emotional value of ritual from the standpoint of catharsis and the reduction of anxiety. According to Scheff, ritual allows for the recognition of emotional distress in a socially sanctioned milieu that provides secure boundaries in which to relive and experience emotional pain and suffering. This release of feeling reverses a tendency toward repression by facilitating the acknowledgment and expression of that which is painful, fearful, sad, or humiliating.

Scheff's theory of ritual catharsis is distinguished by the concept of *emotional distancing*. In effect, Scheff argues that ritual offers a form of cathartic release by creating conditions under which the participant can become actively involved in the expression of feeling, while distancing himself or herself from the intensity of the emotional experience. Emotional distance is manifested in the dual role that the individual assumes as both participant and observer in a religious rite, a split that leads to a contradictory set of responses as the participant is at the same time believer and skeptic. Accordingly, Scheff concludes that the ritual of prayer serves to distance the communicant, thus making that individual both a participant and an observer. This occurs "so long as the communicant both believes and disbelieves the he or she is in communication with a supernatural being" (Scheff, 1979, p. 119).

While Scheff's interpretation of emotional distance offers an interesting perspective on ritual and emotion, this chapter presents an alternative understanding of the relationship between ritual, catharsis, and mental health. As an interactive process, ritual engages the participant in behaviors that reinforce connection and attachment to significant others. The subject of such attachment may be a divine being, a spiritual leader, a religious community, or an entire society. However, it is the sense of connectedness that facilitates the cathartic response through which painful emotion can be brought to consciousness, and relived or expressed for the first time.

Returning to Scheff's example of prayer, the cathartic value of the religious rite is derived from the interpersonal connection between the communicant and God.

Rather than skepticism and emotional distance, it is the attachment to the divine, the supernatural, and significant others that gives ritual its power to engender potentially overwhelming emotions, which are then resolved through a relational act of religious observance. Within this interactive framework, a cross-cultural analysis of ritual and catharsis will be presented here. Drawing on anthropological data and social-psychological theory, the emotions of shame, grief, and anger will be examined through ceremonial rites of confession, mourning, and confrontation.

Shame and Confession

Shame, perhaps one of the most pervasive of human emotions, is intrinsic in an understanding of the value of ritual as catharsis. In discussing the significance of shame in the development of personality and social relations in Western society, Giddens (1984) notes the high prevalence of shame-related terms as they emerge in the course of everyday language. He observes that shame threatens the foundations of self-esteem and comments that "the motivational components of the infantile and adult personality derive from a generalized orientation to the avoidance of anxiety and the preservation of self-esteem against the 'flooding through' of shame and guilt" (Giddens, 1984, pp. 55–57).

That shame and guilt have cross-cultural relevance is evidenced by the public and private rites that inform a variety of religious systems, from the tribal practices of scapegoating to the Catholic confessional. The universality of ritual confession has been observed by Reik (1959), who perceives in humankind "a compulsion to confess" (p. 180), which alleviates suffering and anguish. Such a perspective on ritual suggests that self-esteem and self-acceptance are at the core of the confessional act, the goal of which is to reduce the shame and self-loathing that accompanies perceptions of sin and wrong-doing.

Through acts of confession, the penitent is engaged in an emotional expression of self-blame. This is culturally contextualized by definitions of sinfulness and evil that govern human societies and, in particular, religious cultures. Forgiveness and understanding thus form the basis on which confession is undertaken, as individuals seek absolution through attachment to spiritual authority. This attachment is expressed through ceremonial confessions, such as "Forgive me, Father, for I have sinned," which are most commonly directed at a divine being or a representative of God endowed with the power to forgive. The reduction of anxiety, crucial to the ritual process, therefore emerges out of the unburdening of sin in the presence of a forgiving other. Thus, as a cathartic release, confession ends the penitent's moral isolation, reducing the effects of alienation on a shamed member of society.

Within an interactive framework, confessional rites offer a ritualized context through which the silence of shame is broken by an act of disclosure that connects the individual to the social and spiritual world outside his or her subjective reality. The presence of others, either in the form of a divinity, a spiritual leader, or a social reference group, contributes to reclaiming that part of the self that is diminished by guilt.

The relational aspects of ritual catharsis may be carried out in a private act between penitent and confessor, or a more public ceremony where the community as a whole participates in a rite of confession. Among the Nicaraguan Indians, the private act of confession is similar to that found in the Catholic church,[1] as members of the community individually confess their sins to a tribal elder who is empowered to absolve those who confess. Here a member of the society describes the emotional impact of the ceremonial rite:

> We tell him when we have broken any of our feast days, and have not kept them, or when we have spoken ill of our gods for not sending rain, and when we have said that they are not good; and the old men impose a penance upon us for the temple, and when we have confessed it, we depart, feeling much relieved and pleased at having told them, and as though we had not done wrong. . . . (La Barre, 1964, p. 39)

Among the Huichol of southern Mexico, the confessor is Grandfather Fire, a sacred flame to which all sins are cast. In the following account, La Barre (1964) describes the confession of sexual sins in preparation for a pilgrimage:

> Each woman prepares at home a string of palm leaf strips, with a knot for each lover, omitting none. She brings this string to the temple, and, standing before Grandfather Fire, mentions their names one by one, then throws the cord on the fire to be consumed. It is said that no hard feelings result from this confession, as otherwise the men would not find a single *hikuli* plant. The men similarly knot strings as they go along recalling their sins, and at a certain camp they "talk to all the five winds" and deliver their "roll call" to the leader to be burned by Grandfather Fire. (p. 41)

A more public form of confession has been found among Native Americans in the Untied States as exemplified by the confessional rites of the Plains Ojibway, who declare their sins openly in the presence of the entire society. In the early twentieth century, Skinner (1914) provided the following account of the confessional ceremony:

> It was formerly the custom to call a public confession of illicit sexual intercourse at intervals. Some man, given the right in a dream to call such an assembly, gathered the people together in his lodge, where they owned up. First the elders, then the youths, and then the women. A large painted spirit rock was present, placed in the center of the floor, to render the occasion one of solemnity. The stone heard their words, and disaster overtook all liars. Men who did not tell the truth were certain to be slain on their next war party. (p. 540)

Similarly, the Jewish Day of Atonement is celebrated with a communal fast for twenty-four hours accompanied by religious services in which members of the congregation together repent the wrong-doings of the year before. The confession of sins is recited aloud in unison, emphasizing the collective responsibility of the Jewish community. At designated times in the religious service, the participants rise and say to God:

> We have sinned against You by being heartless,
> And we have sinned against You by speaking recklessly,

We have sinned against You openly and in secret,
  and we have sinned against You through offensive talk.
We have sinned against You through impure thoughts,
  and we have sinned against You through empty confession. . . . (Harlow, 1978,
  p. 407)

Public confession of this sort involves the collective expression of sin, which creates a consciousness of shared guilt. The effect is to reduce even further the sense of isolation that is attached to feelings of shame. The use of the inclusive "we" suggests that no one person is more or less culpable than another as the sins of one become the sins of all. In this public ritual, as in all of the confessional rites discussed thus far, ritual disclosure enhances the cathartic expression of emotion by externalizing the guilt and shame that might otherwise be turned inward against the self. Therefore, rites of confession become one means to release the internalized suffering of emotional distress. In a similar fashion, public rituals of mourning provide a ritualized structure through which feelings of grief and sorrow are openly acknowledged and validated within a supportive religious community.

Grief and Rites of Mourning

The study of ritualized mourning has for the most part been associated with anthropological investigations into the social function of death ceremonies. Within this framework communal rites for the dead have been explained in terms of group solidarity and the interaction that characterizes the mourning process (Mandelbaum, 1959). In comparison with the functionalist approach, far less emphasis has been placed on the psychological value of ceremonial mourning, although the research documents the intense expression of grief that often accompanies the social aspects of religious rituals for the dead.

Among the Cocopa, a Native American culture, Kelly (1949) reports that, upon the announcement of death, family members enter into a period of grieving in which they cry, wail, and scream almost to the point of complete exhaustion. Such cathartic release, which is interrupted with ceremonial song and dance, may continue for two days before the cremation of the deceased. The expression of grief during rituals such as these engages the individual in an open exchange of feelings. According to Pincus (1974), this contributes to the mental health of participants who might otherwise suffer from the effects of denial and an "impoverishment of personality" found in more repressive cultures. In this respect, the absence of ritualized grieving can lead to norms of cultural denial and callousness in which suffering and violence are treated with indifference (Gorer, 1965).

Part of the cathartic value of ritualized grieving is contained in those aspects of mourning that facilitate the survivor's identification with the suffering of the deceased. The Cocopa, for example, impersonate the dead relative before burning his or her possessions in an elaborate cremation ceremony. The Catholic funerary mass provides a similar association to the dead through the symbolic representation of the crucifixion. Jackson (1959) describes the identification among Catholic mourners in this way:

> In the ritualized memorial service the person identifies himself [herself] with Jesus, a deceased individual of religious importance, in such a way that his [her] whole being, conscious, unconscious, and superconscious, is engaged in a rite that involves both thought and action, along with other persons. So it has social and religious acceptance at the same time it has personal efficacy. . . . Thus it becomes a safe channel for the deep feelings. (pp. 223–224)

Since World War II, the memorial service for the Day of Atonement in the Jewish tradition reminds the participants not only of the loss of their loved ones but also of the death of the six million Jews who died in the Holocaust. An excerpt from this service reads as follows:

> Exalted, compassionate God, grant perfect peace in Your sheltering Presence, among the holy and the pure, to the souls of all our brethren, men, women and children of the House of Israel who were slaughtered and burned. May their memory endure, inspiring truth and loyalty in our lives. May their souls thus be bound up in the bond of life. (Harlow, 1978, p. 691)

Each year, the Jewish mourners' identification with the deceased assumes a personal as well as a social dimension as the reminder of the Holocaust engenders deep emotions of grief and a collective sorrow. Through ritualized mourning, the symbolic connection to the dead contextualizes the release of emotion, creating an empathic bond with those who have died. Through emotional attachment to the deceased, feelings of despair and longing are expressed as death represents a final separation that is both mourned and feared.

Fear, as well as sorrow, informs the individual's response to death. This is evidenced in the prevalence of mythologies and beliefs that surround the unknown fate of those who have died. As such, rituals of mourning provide a framework for coping with fear and grief by incorporating taboos and customs to ensure the safe migration of the soul. In the Christian tradition, such precautions are found in the administration of last rites, while the Hindu faith takes great care in freeing the soul for reincarnation. Among the Kota in India, only a young boy may light the funeral pyre during cremation, as all other members of society are considered impure. This particular custom ensures that the spirit will not linger and cause harm among the living, and also that it will find safe passage to the world beyond corporeal life (Mandelbaum, 1959).

Rituals of mourning therefore reduce anxiety through the imposition of ceremonial rites that govern interaction with the deceased. The effects of catharsis are thus enhanced under those circumstances in which protection and security inform the relational framework of the ritual process. In the ritual expression of anger, concerns over safety are particularly significant as the release of hostility is potentially harmful to the self and to others. As such, ritualized anger, which has been studied far less extensively than rites of confession or mourning, offers insight into the process of catharsis from the perspective of conflict and ceremonial power relations.

The Ritual Expression of Anger

Research on anger and catharsis indicates that the expression of hostile emotions is most cathartic when the target of hostility is in an equal or subordinate relationship to the angered individual (Tavris, 1982). When anger is expressed by someone in a less powerful position, the effects of catharsis are reduced by the anxiety that surrounds fear of reprisal. Furthermore, because of the association of anger with aggression, the benefits of cathartic release may be mitigated by tensions that surround the open expression of rage.

Because of the difficulties that characterize the cathartic release of anger, ritualized acts of aggression provide a structured interaction in which hostility is expressed and controlled by the boundaries of ceremonial rites that mediate the social relations of power among the participants. Turner (1969) defines such rituals as rites of status reversal wherein low status members of society engage in the ceremonial expression of rage against more powerful members of the community. In his work on *Ritual and Process,* Turner describes at length the Holi Festival in India, a spring rite dedicated to Lord Krishna in which the weak aggress against the strong. The following account illustrates this ritualized form of role reversal:

> Who were those smiling men whose shins were being most mercilessly beaten by the women? They were the wealthier Brahman and Jat farmers of the village, and the beaters were those ardent local Radhas, the "wives of the village," figuring by both the real and fictional intercaste system of kinship. The wfe of an "elder brother" was properly a man's joking mate, while the wife of a "younger brother" was properly removed from him by rules of extreme respect, but both were merged here with a man's mother-surrogates, the wives of his "father's younger brothers," in one revolutionary cabal of "wives" that cut across all lesser lines and links. The boldest beaters in this veiled battalion were often in fact the wives of the farmers' low-caste field-laborers, artisans, or menials—the concubines and kitchen help of the victims. "Go and bake bread!" teased one farmer, egging his assailant on. "Do you want some seed from me?" shouted another flattered victim, smarting under the blows, but standing his ground. Six Brahman men in their fifties, pillars of village society, limped past in panting flight from the quarter staff wielded by a massive young Bhangin, sweeper of their latrines. (Turner, 1969, p. 186)

According to Turner (1969), such rituals are cathartic since they cleanse society of "structurally engendered 'sins'" (p. 185) through legitimated norm violations that allow the powerless to vent their anger and hostility at those who oppress and abuse them. At the same time, the powerful must sustain the physical and verbal assaults of their social subordinates.

In a somewhat different approach to ritualized power reversal, Wallace (1966) discusses what he terms *saturnalia rituals,* rites of rebellion that violate norms of social propriety. In the Zuni culture, for example, clowns play an important ceremonial role in satirizing the Catholic mass of the missionaries. Norbeck (1961) provides this account of the mock ritual:

> The dancers suddenly wheeled into line, threw themselves on their knees before my table, and with extravagant beatings of breast began an outlandish and fanciful

mockery of a Mexican Catholic congregation at vespers. One bawled out a parody upon the pater-noster, another mumbled along in the manner of an old man reciting the rosary, while the fellow with the India-rubber coat jumped up and began a passionate exhortation or sermon, which for mimetic fidelity was incomparable. This kept the audience laughing with sore sides for some moments. . . .

The dancers swallowed great draughts (of urine), smacked their lips, and amid the roaring merriment of the spectators, remarked that it was very, very, good. The clowns were now upon their mettle, each trying to surpass his neighbors in feats of nastiness. . . . (p. 208)

Although Wallace suggests that this type of ritual rebellion is more secular than religious in nature, his interpretation fails to take into account the spiritual role of the clown in Native American tradition (Cameron, 1981) as that member of society who reveals truth and brings wisdom to the tribe. In the example cited here, such wisdom is communicated through the feelings of humiliation and anger that have been the experience of Native people whose culture and heritage have been devalued and destroyed through colonization.

Healing rites found among feminist spirituality groups in the United States offer still another perspective on ritualized anger and the cathartic expression of revenge and hostility. Within this movement, women who have been physically and sexually abused find strength in goddess-centered healing rites that avenge the violator through an act of symbolical aggression. A rape victim describes the catharsis of shared hostility in this manner:

When we threw the eggs and shouted I felt my own anger come to the surface so strongly, so immediately there, and I was crying and I could see it there, coming with the other women too, and it felt like something you could reach out and touch, a really charged atmosphere. I could see this other woman's pain and feel the similarity between her pain and mine. . . . I guess there were two elements there, feeling the anger, feeling it come to the surface so quickly, and feeling in the larger sense that this is something all women have, that we all need to get out, that we all need to process. (Jacobs, 1989, pp. 269–270)

In these rituals of healing, participants report that the release of tension and anxiety is enhanced by the presence of others who validate the emotional experience. Also, as in the status reversal rites described by Turner and Wallace, participants receive "permission" to feel hate and anger without fear of consequence or retaliation. Catharsis thus occurs as emotions are validated in a ritual structure that legitimates aggression without fear of inflicting real harm. Through these ritual acts the victim achieves a sense of mastery over the victimizer.

As the examples of status reversal rituals suggest, the emotion of anger is more likely to be ritually expressed among those members of society who experience powerlessness and domination. The act of catharsis thus becomes a means for coping with the reality of oppressive social relations as the ritual act of power reversal alleviates momentarily the psychological effects of subordination and social stratification.

While some scholars contend that contemporary industrial society suffers from an absence of religious ritual (Mandelbaum, 1959; Klapp, 1969; Goffman, 1971), it is important to point out that such views do not take into account the prevalence of ritual practices among marginalized groups in modern cultures such as the United States. Within African American, Hispanic, and Native American populations, rituals and religious ceremonies continue to provide a social identity and emotional connection for disenfranchised and alienated members of society. The cathartic aspects of revivalist traditions in the black church in the United States are particularly evident in the experiences of Angelou (1969), who describes the effects of revival meetings on the black participants:

> Everyone attended the revival meetings. Members of the hoity-toity Mount Zion Baptist Church mingled with the intellectual members of the African Methodist Episcopal and African Methodist Episcopal Zion, and the plain working people of the Christian Methodist Episcopal. . . .
>   They basked in the righteousness of the poor and the exclusiveness of the downtrodden. Let the whitefolks have their money and power and segregation and sarcasm and big houses and schools and lawns like carpets, and books, and mostly—mostly—let them have their whiteness. It was better to be meek and lowly, spat upon and abused for this little time than to spend eternity frying in the fires of hell. No one would have admitted that the Christian and charitable people were happy to think of their oppressors turning forever on the Devil's spit over the flame of fire and brimstone. (pp. 103–111)

In the prayers of the African American congregants, the rage of oppression and subordination is ameliorated by the belief in a just and righteous God who will punish the wicked and redeem the faithful.

The relationship between social status and ritual practice thus calls into question Goffman's conclusion that "in contemporary society rituals performed to stand-ins for supernatural entities are everywhere in decay" (1971, p. 63). Rather, a more pluralistic approach to the study of modern culture indicates that, for women and ethnic and racial minorities, religious rites remain an important vehicle for the release of emotions that might otherwise be denied and repressed by the dominant culture.

Conclusion

As a cross-cultural analysis, the study of religious ritual and mental health includes an assessment of religious practices throughout the world, as well as those within diverse cultures such as the United States. Such an assessment suggests that religious ceremonies play a significant role in reducing anxiety and isolation as emotions are acknowledged, expressed, and resolved within a social milieu of attachment and connection to significant others. This perspective on catharsis emphasizes the relationship between the release of feeling and the interactive social relations that characterize rituals of mourning, confession, and confrontation. The psychological benefits of ritual thus emerge out of the relational aspects of ceremonial acts that validate and give expression to the emotional reality of human experience.

Notes

1. According to La Barre (1964) and Darlington (1937), ritual confession among Native Americans was not imposed by missionary authority but is indigenous to these cultures.

References

Angelou, M. (1969). *I know why the caged bird sings.* New York: Bantam Books.
Cameron, A. (1981). *Daughters of copper woman.* Vancouver, BC: Press Gang Publishers.
Darlington, H.S. (1937). Confessions of sins. *Psychoanalytic Review, 24,* 150–164.
Giddens, A. (1984). *The constitution of society.* Berkeley, CA: University of California Press.
Goffman, E. (1971). *Relations in public.* New York: Basic Books.
Gorer, G. (1965). *Death, grief and mourning in contemporary Britain.* London: The Crosset Press.
Harlow, J. (Ed.). (1978). *Mahzor for Rosh Hashanah and Yom Kippur.* New York: The Rabbinical Assembly.
Jackson, E. (1959). Grief and ritual. In H. Feifel (Ed.), *The meaning of death* (pp. 213–218). New York: McGraw-Hill.
Jacobs, J.L. (1989). The effects of ritual healing on female victims of abuse: A study of empowerment and transformation. *Sociological Analysis, 50,* 265–279.
Kelly, W.H. (1949). Cocopa attitudes and practices with respect to death and mourning. *Southwestern Journal of Anthropology, 5,* 151–165.
Klapp, O.E. (1969). *Collective search for identity.* New York: Holt, Rinehart & Winston.
La Barre, W. (1964). Confession as a cathartic therapy in American Indian tribes. In A. Kiev (Ed.), *Magic, faith, and healing* (pp. 36–49). Glencoe, IL: Free Press.
Mandelbaum, D.G. (1959). Social uses of funeral rites. In H. Feifel (Ed.), *The meaning of death* (pp. 189–217). New York: McGraw-Hill.
Norbeck, E. (1961). *Religion in primitive society.* New York: Harper & Row.
Pincus, L. (1974). *Death and the family: The importance of mourning.* New York: Vintage.
Reik, T. (1959). *The compulsion to confess.* New York: Farrar, Straus, & Cudahy.
Scheff, T.J. (1979). *Catharsis in healing, ritual, and drama.* Berkeley, CA: University of California Press.
Skinner, A. (1914). Political organizations, cults, and ceremonies of the Plains Ojibway and Plains Cree Indians. *Anthropological Papers, American Museum of Natural History, 11,* 540.
Tavris, C. (1982). *Anger: The misunderstood emotion.* New York: Simon & Schuster.
Turner, V.W. (1969). *The ritual process.* Chicago: Aldine.
Wallace, A.F.C. (1966). *Religion: An anthropological view.* New York: Random House.

24

Content and Prevalence of
Psychopathology
in World Religions

David Greenberg and Eliezer Witztum

Religious affiliation involves a perpetual commitment to a body of beliefs and practices for all moments and situations, and includes a belief in a superior controlling being. But what are the effects of religious affiliation on mental health? Does a commitment to unprovable beliefs and the practice of repetitive rituals aid us by giving legitimized expression to irrational and compulsive elements in us? Alternatively, do these practices encourage the development of psychiatric disorders? Does participation in a close religious group protect against the stress of social and ideological isolation (e.g., Durkheim, 1972), thereby preventing mental illness, or does it precipitate disorder by subordinating the members' individual needs to the common good? Could it be that this either-or choice is too simplistic, and that religious affiliation may be pathogenic for some while being therapeutic for others? Or could it be that these religious factors are trivial in their capacity to influence the emergence of mental illness (e.g., Siskind, 1971), in contrast to such powerful factors as heredity (Mullan & Murray, 1989) and major life events (Day et al., 1987)?

While considering these questions, confusion arises over the distinction between religious affiliation and religiosity. Membership in a religious group is a passive process for many, handed down from parents. Many continue to consider themselves affiliated with a particular religion while sharing none of its beliefs and performing none, or only a comfortable vestige, of its practices. The association between religiosity and mental health was examined by Batson and Ventis (1982), who showed that differing conceptions of mental health partially determine whether religiosity is considered to have therapeutic or pathogenic effects. Religiosity tends to have a negative correlation with mental health when mental health is defined as personal competence, self-actualization, and freedom from guilt. On the other hand, if mental health is defined as absence from illness, then the correlation from the available data is more likely to be positive.

In this chapter we consider the association between the presence of psychiatric disorder and different religious affiliations. Affiliation will be defined as the person's declaration of belonging to a particular religion, with no attention to the degree of attachment, whether social or religious. The following issues will be considered: (1) is mental illness *more common* in particular religions? (2) do religious beliefs affect the *distribution* of diagnoses? and (3) do religious practices affect the actual *content* of mental illness? We will also consider the role of religious belief systems in determining the form of disturbance and in devising its healing (e.g., evil spirits in spiritism, santeria, and kabbalah).

Prevalence of Mental Illness in Different Religions

There have been few studies on the comparative rates of mental illness in different religions. Slater's (1947) study of soldiers hospitalized at one English hospital during World War II found that Jews and Salvation Army members were much more likely than all other religious groups to have a psychiatric admission: while 61 percent of the Protestànt soldiers hospitalized were admitted to the neuropsychiatric ward, the same figure for Jewish solders was 92 percent. Dayton (1940) found that 9.5 percent of all neurotic inpatients in Massachusetts in the 1920s were Jewish, although Jews were only 3.9 percent of the general population. Among psychotic inpatients, Catholics had more alcoholic and schizophrenic psychoses. Protestants had more senile psychosis, and Jews had more manic-depressive psychosis.

In a one-day prevalence study in New Haven, Connecticut, Roberts and Myers (1954) found that 24 percent of all neurotics in inpatient and outpatient psychiatric care were Jewish, compared to 9.5 percent of the general population. There were no cases of addiction among the Jewish patients; religious affiliation was not discriminatory for other diagnoses. In a study of psychiatric hospitalizations of white and nonwhite Protestants and Catholics in Philadelphia, Kleiner, Tuckman, and Lovell (1959) found that Catholics were more likely to be admitted with schizophrenia, whereas Protestants showed a higher rate of organic syndromes. Catholics and blacks were more likely than other groups to be diagnosed as psychotic. Malzberg (1962) studied all first psychiatric admissions in New York State in 1949–1951 and found that Jews were underrepresented among organic psychoses and overrepresented for manic-depression and neuroses in comparison with Catholics and Protestants.

In the Midtown Manhattan Study, Srole and Langner (1962) noted the religious origins (Catholic, Protestant, or Jewish) of psychiatric inpatients and outpatients of public and private institutions on one day in New York. They found fewer Jews in public hospitals than expected, although this was almost compensated by their overrepresentation in private hospitals. Jews were nearly four times more likely than others to be in outpatient treatment. The same study included an early epidemiological community survey of over 1660 residents, which supported the results of the clinic sample, finding less severe impairment and more mild impairment among Jews. This study included the question, "To whom would you turn for help for a disturbed individual?" Jewish respondents were far more willing than others to turn to a psychotherapist.

Burgess and Wagner (1971) found that Catholics and Baptists were overrepresented in admissions to public psychiatric hospitals, with Methodists and Lutherans underrepresented, and Episcopalians and Jews proportionately represented. Larson et al. (1989) reviewed seven community studies and eight studies of psychiatric patients published in the years 1978–1982 and found Jews to be overrepresented, Protestants underrepresented, and Catholics proportionately represented. The specific studies were not cited, and details of the measures or types of psychopathology were not provided.

MacDonald and Luckett (1983) studied 7000 discharges at a Midwestern outpatient service in the United States during 1977–1980. They found that religious affiliations were associated with particular diagnoses: mainline Protestants had more marital maladjustment and less alcoholism, nonmainline Protestants had more adjustment reactions of childhood and less alcoholism, and Catholics had more obsessive-compulsive disorder. It was also found that patients with "no religious preference" had more alcohol and drug addiction, less marital maladjustment, and a lower rate of obsessive-compulsive symptoms. The authors even suggested that religious "subgroups" (e.g., Presbyterian, Lutheran, United Methodist, Episcopal, etc.) have their own psychiatric diagnostic profile. However, the validity of their profile of the distribution of 40 possible diagnoses (based on subgroups of 30 or more patients) is questionable. Nevertheless, the study is unique and deserves replication.

The above studies found religious affiliation to be a significant variable in the distribution of mental illness. The most consistent finding was of more neurosis and less psychosis among Jews, in comparison with other Western religions. Nevertheless, caution is necessary in interpreting the results. With the exception of Slater (1947), the studies were carried out in the United States where each religion has its own social status and immigration history. The findings of Slater (1947), Kleiner, Tuckman, and Lovell (1959), and Burgess and Wagner (1971) can all be explained by lower social status being associated with increased psychopathology rather than religious affiliation per se (Argyle & Beit-Hallahmi, 1975).

It is also likely that the attitude of a particular religious affiliation toward mental health services influences their willingness to seek help. This limitation was overcome by Srole and Langner (1962), who included a community survey of psychiatric morbidity. Their study also revealed the inaccuracy of reporting public hospital admissions alone, showing that some religious groups were unwilling to use public psychiatric facilities and more willing to use private ones. Comparative community surveys of religions in countries where the social status of the religious affiliation may be different (e.g., Catholics in Italy versus the United States, Jews in Israel versus the United States), would help to determine whether the factor influencing the distribution of mental illness is religious affiliation itself, social status, or another factor. Rahav, Goodman, Popper, and Lin (1986) divided all psychiatric inpatients in Jerusalem in 1977 into socioeconomic status and ethnic origins and found that socioeconomic status and local social support were more critical factors than religious ethnicity.

In a recent study of depression and readiness to use mental health services in a community sample of 800, it was found that lower socioeconomic status was associated with increased depression, less social support, and greater unwillingness to seek professional help. However, ethnicity (Mexican American versus Anglo-American), including minority status, was not associated with these factors (Briones et al., 1990). While ethnicity and religious affiliation are not synonymous, this study does demonstrate the importance of socioeconomic status as a factor affecting both the incidence of psychiatric disorder and the willingness to seek professional help.

In conclusion, although all the studies suggest that certain religious affiliations are associated with more or less psychopathology, it is not clear if affiliation is a secondary factor. Returning to a question posed at the outset, it appears that belonging to, and being supported by, a social matrix is protective against the development of psychiatric disorders. These factors may be critical in determining psychopathology and willingness to seek help. Membership in a religious group does not automatically provide these factors, and it remains unclear to what extent these factors protect against, or cause, psychiatric disorders.

Religion and the Distribution of Psychiatric Disorders

Meadow and Kahoe (1984) outlined three components of religion that may be assumed to influence one's cognitions, emotions, and behaviors. These are (1) creeds—the beliefs concerning the world and its maker; (2) cultus—the ceremonies and rituals that give symbolic expression to religious feelings; and (3) code—the demands concerning daily behavior. Religions place varying emphases on these components, and may consequently have selective impact on the thoughts, feelings, and behaviors of their followers. If every religion has its idiosyncratic creeds, cultus, and code, one might speculate that different religions will have their own specific psychopathological conditions.

The major psychiatric disorders have been shown to be present in similar proportions throughout the world. However, certain psychiatric conditions are culture-specific, and are molded by local beliefs and practices. In the ensuing sections, we will evaluate the influence of two widespread religious beliefs upon psychopathology. In both cases we will show that normative beliefs are associated with psychological states that are themselves normative, but that would be considered pathological at other times and in other religions. Once these beliefs are no longer normative, the presentation as a mild psychological state will become rare, and will instead be a feature of severe psychopathology.

Psychopathology and Religious Beliefs

Possession in Hinduism, Christianity, and Judaism

Dissociative states, especially possession states, feature prominently in many religions (Lewis, 1986). Bourguignon (1973) found that 437 (90 percent) of 488 societies throughout the world had culturally patterned forms of altered consciousness, notably trance and possession states. Janet interpreted possession as the inevitable consequence of a religious person's conflict with his God, while paranoia served the same function between people and society (see Horton, 1924). All religious rituals have an accepted format, and their details must be familiarized before they are performed. Possession states, while seemingly uncontrolled and spontaneous, undergo the same process. Before entering a possession state, the person learns what is likely to be experienced, and also how to interpret what is perceived. The possession is then induced with drumming, dancing, crowd contagion, or drugs. The possession state (an active process, in contrast with the relatively passive trance state) is followed by amnesia for the event (Bourguignon, 1979).

Saxena and Prasad (1989) described possession disorder in a sample of psychiatric outpatients as involving (1) a sudden and brief change of voice, mannerisms, and behavior; (2) the incorporation of the identity of a known dead person, or culturally accepted demon, spirit, or god; (3) associated attention-seeking and dramatic behavior. There is complete or partial amnesia for the episode. In nearly all cases the average duration of an episode was less than four hours.

Despite the normative status of possession states in religions, Yap (1969) observed that possession behavior can become so extravagant and uncontrolled that the subject is taken to a psychiatrist. This seemingly arbitrary criterion of social acceptability is reiterated by Wing, Cooper, and Sartorius (1974), who differentiated "subcultural" and "hysterical" possession states. In the latter type of possession, the motivation for the symptoms is unclear, and it tends to lack societal endorsement. Similarly, Ward (1980) distinguished between "ritual" possession, which was ceremonially and socially appropriate, and "peripheral" possession, which was part of a chronic condition or a reaction to personal conflict.

Belief in transmigration of souls is an important part of the Hindu and Buddhist religions. The soul of every living being is believed capable of transmigrating into another being. Spirit possession is recognized throughout India, having a special religious name in every language (Rao, 1986). In an epidemiological study in West Karnataka, India, 90 percent of respondents believed in possession, while the one-year prevalence rate for possession states was 3.7 percent (Rao, 1986). Possession states are also common in Bangladesh, Sri Lanka, and Nepal (Stirrat, 1977; Hoenig & Wijesinghe, 1979). In a study of 2651 psychiatric outpatients in India in 1986, 62 cases (2.3 percent) had dissociative disorder, of whom six had possession disorder, diagnosed as atypical dissociative disorder in the DSM-III (Saxena & Prasad, 1989). This demonstrated that normative beliefs and states are associated with mild overt psychopathology.

With the decline of belief in magic and the supernatural (Thomas, 1978), so too have possession states become rare in modern Christian Europe. However, as Garrett, (1987) wrote:

> In the 17th century, the rivalry of Protestants and Catholics generated profound religious excitement. . . . All wars were religious wars and the Millennium seemed to be at hand, spirit possession manifested itself in many forms. Possession by demons occasionally reached epidemic proportions, and the testimony of the possessed was taken to be evidence that God and Satan were manifesting themselves. (p. 24)

The dramatic disappearance of possession states presumably reflects changes in modern belief systems. The impact of culture and history on the changing face of mental illness was demonstrated by Kroll and Bachrach (1982), who compared the religious symptoms of 23 hospitalized psychotics with the symptoms of visionaries of the Middle Ages. Eight psychotics described possession experiences (e.g., angels speaking through one's voice, the Holy Spirit taking over one's thoughts). This symptomatology would not have been considered pathological in the Middle Ages, when mental illness manifested itself differently in babbling, howling, biting, tearing oneself to pieces, and when possession was not considered abnormal. It has been suggested that possession states are most comparable to multiple personality disorder in the West. Initially considered to be rare, the latter is now being defined more broadly and reported more often. The phenomena are analogous, although the latter lacks a religious cultural setting, and runs a more chronic course (Adityanjee & Khandelwal, 1989).

The Jewish Talmud (third to fifth centuries) referred to spirits, while kabbalists (Jewish mystics) of the twelfth century described transmigration of the soul of a dead person into a newborn as a punishment, especially for sexual sins. Later times saw the development of the concept of the Dybbuk, which resembles the descriptions of possession in other religions in that the soul of a dead person enters the body of someone during their life (Bilu & Beit-Hallahmi, 1989). While possession states are rarely encountered in Judaism today, a study of 560 Jewish adolescents in Israel found that 46 percent believed in transmigration of souls (Zeidner & Beit-Hallahmi, 1988). These beliefs were particularly common among adolescents of African origin. Although the belief in possession is widespread among Jews, cases are rare and they tend to appear as severe psychopathology.

Case Vignette: Spirit Possession

A young ultraorthodox Jewish man, recently married, had been behaving strangely over the last four months, becoming increasingly withdrawn until he ceased his studies and was nearly mute. In the preceding months, he had visited cemeteries around Jerusalem with invisible companions in order to study kabbalah, and complained that the soul of a dead friend had transmigrated into his body, saying: "I have been impregnated by a spirit." He pronounced the ineffable names of God and carried out prayers of unification with God, which he had collected from kabbalistic books. But he gradually became depressed and introverted, and withdrew from all social contact.

Glossolalia

While possession states are no longer a feature of the religious behavior of the modern European Christian, glossolalia (or speaking in tongues) remains active among the revivalist Christian groups in the United States. It has also become common among white American Lutherans, Presbyterians, and Catholics, to the extent that it is estimated that there are two million practitioners of glossolalia in the United

States today (Littlewood & Lipsedge, 1989). Believed by its practitioners to be one of the gifts of the Holy Spirit, May (1956) noted that St. Paul spoke in tongues, and that the practice predated Christianity. Littlewood and Lipsedge (1989) noted that glossolalia is a dissociative state of a highly controlled form, in that it will only occur at particular moments in a church service. While a Western observer may view glossolalia as a regressive experience and glossolalists as emotionally unstable, researchers report glossolalists to be well-adjusted (Boisen, 1939; Kiev, 1964; Pattison & Casey, 1969). Littlewood and Lipsedge (1989) found glossolalia to be less common among their West Indian Pentecostal patients than in religious congregations, while concluding that glossolalia has an important expressive role in society.

Possession and glossolalia are presented here to demonstrate the effect of the state of a religious belief: currently possession and glossolalia are considered normative in many parts of the world. When brought to the attention of mental health workers in those areas, they are seen as mild psychopathological disorders. In Western religions where possession states are no longer normative, they are seen as serious psychopathology. Therefore, "irrational" religious beliefs do not encourage the development of psychiatric disorder. Instead, their normative role means that they feature in normal religious expression and in mild psychopathology.

World Religions and the Content of Mental Illness: Obsessive-Compulsive Disorder

We have noted the relationship between two religious creeds and psychiatric diagnoses. We will now present the varying picture of one condition, obsessive-compulsive disorder, in the major world religions in order to demonstrate the impact of religious cultus on the content of a condition in which rituals feature prominently.

According to the Islamic law, "Al Woodo" is a cleansing ceremony in which parts of the body are washed three times prior to the five-times daily prayers, with particular emphasis on cleanliness of the anal region. Performed after micturition, defecation, and ejaculation, clothes must be changed if they have been in contact with urine or feces, and underwear is changed before prayer. A menstruating woman is forbidden to fast, pray or touch the Koran, and her underwear is washed separately. In a study of 84 cases of obsessive-compulsive disorder in Egyptian Moslems, Okasha (1970) found that the excessive performance of "Al Woodo" was the most common compulsive ritual. One patient fell asleep in the bath during her endless washes at the onset of menstruation, while another spent hours cleaning himself before prayer. His sample was based on the work of Okasha, Kamel, and Hassan (1968), who diagnosed obsessive-compulsive disorder in 2.6 percent of Egyptian psychiatric outpatients, reflecting the ability of the population to discriminate successfully between ritual and compulsion. In a sample of 32 cases of obsessive-compulsive disorder in Saudi Arabian Moslems, the most common topic of obsession was religion: 16 concerned prayer and washing, 13 concerned body contamination, while a further 11 concerned faith. Similarly, the most common topic of compulsions was religion: 16 had repetition rituals, mainly the repetition of prayers, and

12 had washing compulsions concerning religion (Mahgoub & Abdel-Hafeiz, 1991).

The Hindu religion in India was described by Berkeley-Hill (1921) as having a "pollution complex," exemplified by the class of the "untouchables," the importance of bathing in Hindu festivals, the view of the body as dirty, and its emphasis on repeated washing. Chackraborty (1975) described "suchi-bai," a ritual in India based on a fear of contamination and a desire to remain clean. He considers it a form of obsessive-compulsive disorder that is tolerated in India as it is an exaggeration of religious attitudes to cleanliness and purity. Akhtar, Wig, Varma, Pershad, and Verma (1975) studied 82 cases of obsessive-compulsive disorder in India and found nine cases of symptoms that involved religious beliefs and practices. The symptoms of a further 38 cases involved contamination from semen, menstrual blood, and excreta, which are also features of religious taboo (Akhtar, Wig, Varma, Pershad, & Verma, 1978). Ray (1964) studied 42 cases of obsessive-compulsive disorder in India, predominantly Hindu, and found ideas of impurity and uncleanliness in 14 of those cases.

Roman Catholicism has two sacraments that must be repeated frequently, one of which, confession, has featured repeatedly as a symptom of obsessive-compulsive disorder. Ignatius of Loyola father of the Jesuit order, and Martin Luther, a devout Catholic monk before founding Protestant Christianity, both spent many hours ruminating over their transgressions and recounting them in detail in confession (Greenberg, Witztum, & Pisante, 1987). Vergote (1988), a Catholic philosopher and psychoanalyst, described a patient tormented by the anxiety of committing "mortal sins." He went to confession twice daily. Every incident became an occasion for torturous doubts of conscience, the themes of which were predominantly sexual. He described the man meeting an attractive married woman, looking at her and desiring her, but then feeling that, according to Christ's words, he was guilty of "sinning in one's heart" (p. 49). Vergote noted the central role of guilt in such cases, describing it as the "religious neurosis of culpability" (p. 48). Weisner and Riffel (1960) reported 23 Roman Catholic referrals to a Child Guidance Center, who were "continually consulting the priest . . . they felt past sins were either not properly confessed or not properly understood by the priest. . . . Many found it difficult going to Communion because of their inability to resolve their doubt about sin on their soul" (p. 315). No data are available regarding the prevalence of such problems.

Protestant Christianity places less emphasis on ritual and greater value on prayer, as expressed by James (1982/1902): "Prayer is religion in act; that is, prayer is real religion . . . wherever this prayer rises and stirs the soul, even in the absence of forms or of doctrines, we have living religion" (p. 464). Consistent with this prime role of prayer, Enoch and Trethowan (1979) described "a compulsion to blaspheme or swear aloud in church . . . referred to as the 'devil in the tongue'" (p. 168). In his treatise *Of Religious Melancholy,* John Moore (1963/1692), the Bishop of Norwich, wrote about good moral worshippers who were assailed by "naughty and sometimes blasphemous thoughts . . . (which) start in their minds, while they are exercised in the worship of God . . . (despite) all their efforts to stifle and suppress them" (pp. 252–253). Similarly, we have found that the religious symptoms encountered by Protestant Christians with obsessive-compulsive disorder include thoughts that arise during prayer of blasphemy or of illness and harm coming to other people.

The Jewish religion has many rituals whose similarity to compulsive symptomatology may well have influenced Freud in his famous likening of religion to a "universal obsessional neurosis" (Freud, 1959/1907). A concern with purity and contamination are prominent in the Jewish dietary laws. Meat can only come from certain animals (known as kosher), which must be slaughtered and prepared in a particular way. Milk and meat foods must be prepared and eaten separately, and all bread must be removed from every Jewish home before the festival of Passover. Menstrual purity is surrounded by ritual: "No woman can divest herself of her ritual impurity or cease being forbidden from having relations unless and until she immerses herself in a ritual bath . . . if she does not, she is liable to excision" (Maimonides, Mishne Tora, Laws of Forbidden Relations, 11:16). Certain thrice-daily prayers are given special significance and require particular devotion. Strictly religious Jewish female patients with obsessive-compulsive disorder commonly show symptoms involving washing of the hands and food utensils, and compulsive checking before and during menstrual immersion. Male patients often display excessive perianal washing before prayers, as well as compulsive and repetitive praying in response to self-doubt concerning the adequacy of their devotion (Greenberg, 1984; Greenberg, Witztum, & Pisante, 1987).

While the symptoms of obsessive-compulsive disorder are, by definition, in excess of accepted religious standards, the above review of the religious sources and clinical presentations of obsessive-compulsive disorder in different religions demonstrates the influence of religious rituals on obsessions and compulsions. The valued rituals of a religion are the focus of obsessive-compulsive disorder, especially those rituals emphasizing cleanliness, impurity, and precision. An intriguing exception is Protestant Christianity, with few religious rituals, but sufficient emphasis on prayer for this to be the focus of obsessive thoughts. Societies without demands for religious ritual are by no means free of obsessive-compulsive disorder (Robins et al., 1984): their role as the focus for obsessions is taken by secular symptoms such as excessive house pride and fear of germs, rabies, and AIDS. It is not known if societies relatively free of religious rituals have less obsessive-compulsive disorder. The authors suspect that this is not the case. Every society, secular or religious, has its rules and taboos, and these are the setting, but not the cause, of obsessive-compulsive disorder.

Religious Beliefs, Psychopathological Forms, and Healing: Evil Spirits in Spiritism, Santeria, and Kabbalah

Belief in the existence of a world of spirits was a component of the earliest forms of religion and is the basis of the animistic theory of the role of religion in society (Malinowski, 1954). In this section, we will discuss examples of beliefs in spirits, how these beliefs affect the content of local psychopathology, and how local religion also provides a therapeutic response.

The predominant religion in the Caribbean island of Puerto Rico is a local variant of Catholicism characterized by praying, burning candles, and bringing personal offerings as part of special relationships with the Virgin Mary and other saints. Known as *spiritism* (*espiritismo*), it describes an invisible world of spirits surrounding the visible world. Some spirits attach themselves to human beings, while others remain disembodied. They maintain contact through people with spiritual propensities (spiritists) who can intervene with the incarnated spirits (Ramos-McKay, Comas-Diaz, & Rivera, 1988; Koss, 1977).

Spiritism is also a form of mental health care. The spiritist works in a group setting, receiving messages or being possessed by spirits in order to diagnose, prognosticate, advise, and prescribe herbal or ritual remedies (Koss, 1977). A recent epidemiological study found that 18 percent of Puerto Ricans, mainly from low-income groups, visit a spiritist at some time in their lives (Hohmann et al., 1990). However, the covert nature of spiritist practices may lead people to deny participation. One-third of Puerto Ricans now living in New York visit spiritists, while 50–75 percent of New York Puerto Rican mental health care users have turned to a spiritist (Torrey, 1986). Approximately 80 percent of a small community sample of Puerto Ricans now living in Connecticut, and 90 percent in a psychiatric outpatient sample, believed that spiritism can cause mental illness, while 30 percent of the patient sample believed their own illness to be the result of spiritism (Gaviria & Wintrob, 1976). Hohmann et al. (1990) found that Puerto Ricans who had seen a spiritist were less likely to have schizophrenia and more likely to have subclinical depressive symptoms. It was also found that they had no increased lifetime risk of diagnosable psychopathology. This research did not record the effects of the visit to the spiritist, nor whether people approached the spiritist before or after visiting mental health specialists. Nevertheless, it is apparent that people with mild psychopathology tend to seek help from spiritists. Harwood (1977) has regarded the spiritist's attribution of distress as "spirit-induced" as an effective form of psychotherapy. It was even seen as the treatment of choice since it enabled the spiritist and the *centro* (the treatment group led by the spiritist) to bring dissociative disorders under social control. Koss (1987) reported greater satisfaction among spiritists' patients than among therapists' patients.

Santeria is a Cuban variant of spiritism, incorporating a belief in Olodumare-Olofi, creator of the universe, and his attendant "oricha," whose identities are a combination of African gods and Catholic saints. Illnesses are believed to be caused by supernatural forces, and a sufferer will turn to his group, containing up to 100 members led by a priest, who may sacrifice an animal or fruits to the "oricha" saints. The sacrifice invites the saints to possess one of the members, usually the priest. The possessed person suddenly collapses, then becomes agitated, touching group members while speaking gibberish. A second group member translates, and finally the group calls the possessed member by his/her own name so that the soul returns (Alonso & Jeffrey, 1988). Rarely is professional health care sought (Koss, 1987), although the presentation of *santeria* beliefs and rituals in psychoses has been described (Alonso & Jeffrey, 1988). There are belief systems that resemble Cuban *santeria* and Puerto Rican spiritism throughout Latin America, such as *Curandreas* in Mexico (Torrey, 1986) and *Umbanda* in Brazil (Pressel, 1974). It is estimated that over 50 percent of the Brazilian population, irrespective of socioeconomic group, visit spiritists (Hohmann et al., 1990).

Judaism, while known for its pragmatism and comfortable coexistence with modern Western values, nevertheless has an elaborate system of angels and demons. The kabbalah accorded demons an important role in the cosmic design. To this day, amulets are sought from Rabbis to drive away spirits, and many daily practices in Judaism have been shown to have originated in their ability to deal with the forces of evil (Trachtenberg, 1974). In our own clinical practice, patients refer to demons, punishing angels, and *sitra ahra* (meaning "the other side," referring to the forces of evil) not in a metaphysical sense, but as something concretely threatening and persecutory. Below is a case from Judaism of a young man, the victim of evil spirits, guided and supported by his mystical mentor.

Case Vignette

A 29-year old father of three had become strange, withdrawn, and aggressive. Born into a Kurdish Jewish family, he started to study kabbalah with a leading Jewish mystic. After three years, during a visit to the tomb of a saint with the mystic and his followers, the group prayed and then went to sleep. He was awakened suddenly by a vision of a man with a white beard, who instructed him to light a candle. He fainted from fright and did not carry out the request. The mystic rebuked him for not having lit the candle, as he was sure that it was the buried saint who had appeared. Subsequent to this experience, he was visited regularly for two years by good spirits. Following the death of the mystic, these good spirits were replaced by fearful and persecutory demons. He said that they came to him because of his sinful life and also because of his previous soul's sinfulness. He became increasingly isolated and spent his time studying kabbalist texts and visiting the tombs of saints. His comfort was that the mystic had assured him that his suffering meant that his soul was being repaired. This case involved a gradual withdrawal from work, study, and all social contacts, as well as an immersion in paranoid hallucinations. Initially, the mystic gave religious meaning and respectability to his psychotic experiences (a process described as "symbolic inversion" by Littlewood, 1983). The death of the mystic removed this support, the spirits became overpowering, and he became overtly psychotic.

Puerto Rican spiritism, *santeria,* and Jewish mysticism have been shown here to provide a framework for people to understand and manage visitations from spirits. There are no clear data on the therapeutic capacity of these religious systems. It seems likely that mild psychopathology is significantly helped by support, a sense of belonging, and a religious meaning for their distress, and this seems to be particularly true of dissociative disorders. However, the role of these factors in the management of psychotic disorders is yet to be specified.

Conclusion

Our review of mental illness in different world religions revealed that religious affiliation is associated with varying frequencies of psychopathology. However, most of the studies were carried out in 1940–1965 in the United States. At that time and place, each affiliation had its own social status and immigration history, which may have influenced the results. Furthermore, only one study was community based. The rest were inpatient or outpatient samples, and are therefore flawed in that their findings reflect the willingness to come for help rather than the frequency of psychopathology. Recent studies suggest that socioeconomic status and support may be more critical than religious affiliation per se. Further research will need to be community based and multinational. The mental illness profile of one religious affiliation in several countries will help discriminate between affiliation and other social factors. While this chapter has related to "religious affiliation" as if it were a unitary factor, future research should challenge this position.

Certain beliefs and rituals of different world religions were evaluated for their impact on the content of psychopathology. If possession and glossolalia are normative beliefs, they will be found among normal people as mild psychopathology. Once considered abnormal, they are more likely to appear as a feature of psychosis. The rituals of cleanliness, purity, and exactness were presented in some of the major world religions, and they form the content of obsessive-compulsive disorder in these religions. We know of no comparative studies of the incidence of obsessive-compulsive disorder in different religions. An epidemiological study of all psychiatric disorders in different religions is necessary to evaluate if religions emphasizing ritual have more obsessive-compulsive disorder specifically, or more or less psychopathology generally. It may be that ritualized religion, or a particular religious affiliation, predisposes people to obsessive-compulsive disorder. Another possibility is that a member of such a religious group will tend to develop this condition rather than other psychiatric disorders.

Finally, spiritism, *santeria,* and Jewish mysticism were presented as religious belief systems that not only populate their adherents' minds with spirits of good and evil, but have also developed methods of therapy. Their widespread use suggests that many people with mild psychopathology find meaning and support within these belief systems. The roles of religious and secular healers are important issues for providers of mental health care. Systematic outcome studies are both unlikely to occur or to be strictly comparable. Nevertheless, assessment of the psychopathology of participants before and after referral to both systems will increase understanding. It may also improve respect and cooperation, while decreasing suspicion and antagonism among those involved in the mental health care of the population.

References

Adityanjee, G.S.P., & Khandelwal, S.K. (1989). Current status of multiple personality disorder in India. *American Journal of Psychiatry, 146,* 1607–1610.

Akhtar, S., Wig, N.N., Varma, V.K., Pershad, D., & Verma, S.K. (1975). A phenomenological analysis of symptoms in obsessive-compulsive neurosis. *British Journal of Psychiatry, 127,* 342–348.

Akhtar, S., Wig, N.N., Varma, V.K., Pershad, D., & Verma, S.K. (1978). Socio-cultural and clinical determinants of symptomatology in obsessional neurosis. *International Journal of Social Psychiatry, 24,* 157–162.

Alonso, L., & Jeffrey, W.D. (1988). Mental illness complicated by the santeria belief in spirit possession. *Hospital and Community Psychiatry, 39,* 1188–1191.

Argyle, M., & Beit-Hallahmi, B. (1975). *The social psychology of religion.* London: Routledge & Kegan Paul.

Batson, C.D., & Ventis, W.L. (1982). *The religious experience.* Oxford: Oxford University Press.

Berkeley-Hill, O. (1921). The anal-erotic factor in the religion, philosophy and character of the Hindus. *International Journal of Psychoanalysis, 2,* 306–329.

Bilu, Y., & Beit-Hallahmi, B. (1989). Dybbuk possession as hysterical symptom: Psychodynamic and socio-cultural factors. *Israel Journal of Psychiatry, 26,* 138–149.

Boisen, A.T. (1939). Economic distress and religious experience: A study of the holy rollers. *Psychiatry, 2,* 185–194.

Bourguignon, E. (1973). *Religion, altered states of consciousness and social change.* Columbus: Ohio State University.

Bourguignon, E. (1979). *Psychological anthropology.* New York: Holt, Rinehart & Winston.

Briones, D.F., Heller, P.L., Chalfant, H.P., Roberts, A.E., Aguirre-Hauchbaum, S.F., & Farr, W.F. (1990). Socioeconomic status, ethnicity, psychological distress, and readiness to utilize a mental health facility. *American Journal of Psychiatry, 147,* 1333–1340.

Burgess, J.H., & Wagner, R.L. (1971). Religion as a factor in extrusion to public mental hospitals. *Journal for the Scientific Study of Religion, 10,* 237–240.

Chackraborty, A. (1975). Ritual, a culture specific neurosis, and obsessional states in Bengali culture. *Indian Journal of Psychiatry, 17,* 211–216, 273–283.

Day, R., Neilsen, J.A., Korten, A., Ernberg, G., Dube, K.C., Gebhart, J., Jablensky, A., Leon, C., Marsella, A., Olatawura, M., Sartorius, N., Stromgren, E., Takahashi, R., Wig, N., & Wynne, L.C. (1987). Stressful life events preceding the acute onset of schizophrenia: A cross-national study from the World Health Organization. *Culture, Medicine and Psychiatry, 11,* 123–205.

Dayton, N.A. (1940). *New facts on mental disorders.* Springfield, IL: Charles C Thomas.

Durkheim, E. (1972). Religion and ritual. In A. Giddens (Ed.), *Emile Durkheim: Selected writings* (pp. 219–238). Cambridge: Cambridge University Press.

Enoch, M.D., & Trethowan, W.H. (1979). *Uncommon psychiatric syndromes* (2nd ed.). Bristol: Wright.

Freud, S. (1959). Obsessive acts and religious practices. In J. Strachey (Ed. and Trans.), *The standard edition of the complete psychological works by Sigmund Freud* (vol. 9, pp. 115–127). London: Hogarth Press. (Original work published 1907.)

Garrett, C. (1987). *Spirit possession and popular religion.* Baltimore: Johns Hopkins University Press.

Gaviria, M., & Wintrob, R.M. (1976). Supernatural influence in psychopathology: Puerto Rican folk beliefs about mental illness. *Canadian Psychiatric Association Journal, 21,* 361–369.

Greenberg, D. (1984). Are religious compulsions religious or compulsive? A phenomenological study. *American Journal of Psychotherapy, 38,* 524–532.

Greenberg, D., Witztum, E., & Pisante, J. (1987). Scrupulosity: Religious attitudes and clinical presentations. *British Journal of Medical Psychology, 60,* 29–37.

Harwood, A. (1977). Puerto Rican spiritism: Part 1—Description and analysis of an alternative psychotherapeutic approach. *Culture, Medicine and Psychiatry, 1,* 69–95.

Hoenig, J., & Wijesinghe, C. (1979). Religious beliefs and psychiatric disorder in Sri Lanka. *Confinia Psychiatrica, 22,* 19–33.

Hohmann, A.A., Richeport, M., Marriott, B.M., Canino, G.J., Rubio-Stipec, M., & Bird, H. (1990). Spiritism in Puerto Rico: Results of an island-wide community study. *British Journal of Psychiatry, 157,* 328–335.

Horton, W.M. (1924). The origin and psychological function of religion according to Pierre Janet. *American Journal of Psychology, 35,* 16–52.

James, W. (1982). *The varieties of religious experience.* London: Penguin. (Original work published 1902.)

Kiev, A. (1964). Psychotherapeutic aspects of Pentecostal sects among West Indian immigrants to England. *British Journal of Sociology, 15,* 129–138.

Kleiner, R.J., Tuckman, J., & Lovell, M. (1959). Mental disorder and status based on religious affiliation. *Human Relations, 12,* 273–276.

Koss, J.D. (1977). Religion and science divinely related: A case history of spiritism in Puerto Rico. *Caribbean Studies, 16,* 22–43.

Koss, J.D. (1987). Expectations and outcome for patients given mental health care or spiritist healing in Puerto Rico. *American Journal of Psychiatry, 144,* 56–61.

Kroll, J., & Bachrach, B. (1982). Medieval visions and contemporary hallucinations. *Psychological Medicine, 12,* 709–721.

Larson, D.B., Donahue, M.J., Lyons, J.S., Benson, P.L., Pattison, M., & Worthington, E.L. (1989). Religious affiliations in mental health research samples as compared with national samples. *Journal of Nervous and Mental Disease, 177,* 109–111.

Lewis, I.M. (1986). Religion in context. Cambridge: Cambridge University Press.

Littlewood, R. (1983). The antinomian hasid. *British Journal of Medical Psychology, 56,* 67–78.

Littlewood, R., & Lipsedge, M. (1989). *Aliens and alienists* (2nd ed.). London: Unwin Hyman.

MacDonald, C.V., & Luckett, J.B. (1983). Religious affiliation and psychiatric diagnoses. *Journal for the Scientific Study of Religion, 22,* 15–37.

Mahgoub, O.M. & Abdel-Hafeiz, H.B. (1991). Pattern of obsessive-compulsive disorder in Eastern Saudi Arabia. *British Journal of Psychiatry, 158,* 840–842.

Malinowski, B. (1954). *Magic, science and religion.* New York: Doubleday Anchor.

Malzberg, B. (1962). The distribution of mental disease according to religious affiliation in New York State, 1949–1951. *Mental Hygiene, 46,* 510–522.

May, L.C. (1956). A survey of glossolalia and related phenomena in non-Christian religions. *American Anthropologist, 58,* 75–96.

Meadow, M.J., & Kahoe, R.D. (1984). *Psychology of religion.* New York: Harper & Row.

Moore, J. (1963). Of religious melancholy. In D. Hunter & I. Macalpine (Eds.), *Three hundred years of psychiatry 1535–1860* (pp. 252–253). London: Oxford University Press. (Original work published 1692.)

Mullan, M.J., & Murray, R.M. (1989). The impact of molecular genetics on our understanding of the psychoses. *British Journal of Psychiatry, 154,* 591–595.

Okasha, A. (1970). Presentation and outcome of obsessional disorders in Egypt. *Ain Shams Medical Journal, 21,* 367–373.

Okasha, A., Kamel, M., & Hassan, A. (1968). Preliminary psychiatric observations in Egypt. *British Journal of Psychiatry, 114,* 949–955.

Pattison, E.M., & Casey, R.L. (1969). Glossolalia: A contemporary mystical experience. In E.M. Pattison (Ed.), *Clinical psychiatry and religion* (pp. 133–148). Boston: Little, Brown.

Pressel, E. (1974). Umbanda trance and possession in San Paulo, Brazil. In I.I. Zaretsky (Ed.), *Trance healing and hallucination* (pp. 113–225). New York: Wiley.

Rahav, M., Goodman, A.B., Popper, M., & Lin, S.P. (1986). Distribution of treated mental illness in the neighborhoods of Jerusalem. *American Journal of Psychiatry, 143,* 1249–1254.

Ramos-McKay, J., Comas-Diaz, L., & Rivera, L.A. (1988). Puerto Ricans. In L. Comas-Diaz

& E.E.H. Griffith (Eds.), *Clinical guidelines in cross-cultural mental health* (pp. 204–232). New York: Wiley Interscience.

Rao, V. (1986). Indian and Western psychiatry: A comparison. In J.L. Cox (Ed.), *Transcultural psychiatry* (pp. 291–305). London: Groom Helm.

Ray, S.D. (1964). Obsessional states observed in New Delhi. *British Journal of Psychiatry, 110,* 181–182.

Roberts, B.H., & Myers, J.K. (1954). Religion, national origin, immigration, and mental illness. *American Journal of Psychiatry, 110,* 759–764.

Robins, L.N., Helzer, J.E., Weissman, M.M., Orvaschel, H., Gruenberg, E., Burke, J.D., & Regier, D.A. (1984). Lifetime prevalence of specific psychiatric disorders in three sites. *Archives of General Psychiatry, 41,* 949–958.

Saxena, S., & Prasad, K.V.S.R. (1989). DSM-III subclassification of dissociative disorders applied to psychiatric outpatients in India. *American Journal of Psychiatry, 146,* 261–262.

Siskind, G. (1971). Denominational membership, expression of religious sentiments and status upon admission to a psychiatric hospital. *Mental Hygiene, 55,* 246–247.

Slater, E. (1947). Neurosis and religious affiliation. *Journal of Mental Science, 93,* 392–398.

Srole, L., & Langner, T. (1962). Religious origin. In L. Srole, T.S. Langner, S.T. Michael, M.K. Opler, & T.A.C. Rennie (Eds.), *Mental health in the metropolis: The midtown Manhattan study* (pp. 300–324). New York: McGraw-Hill.

Stirrat, R.L. (1977). Demonic possession in Roman Catholic Sri Lanka. *Journal of Anthropological Research, 33,* 133–157.

Thomas, K. (1978). *Religion and the decline of magic.* London: Peregrine.

Torrey, E.F. (1986). *Witchdoctors and psychiatrists.* Northvale: Jason Aronson.

Trachtenberg, J. (1974). *Jewish magic and superstition: A study in folk religion.* New York: Atheneum.

Vergote, A. (1988). *Guilt and desire: Religious attitudes and their pathological derivatives.* New Haven: Yale University.

Ward, C. (1980). Spirit possession and mental health: A psycho-anthropological perspective. *Human Relations, 33,* 149–163.

Weisner, W.M., & Riffel, P.A. (1960). Scrupulosity: Religion and obsessive-compulsive behavior in children. *American Journal of Psychiatry, 117,* 314–318.

Wing, J.K., Cooper, J.E., & Sartorius, N. (1974). *The measurement and classification of psychiatric symptoms.* Cambridge: Cambridge University Press.

Yap, P.M. (1969). The culture-bound reactive syndromes. In W. Caudill & T-Y, Lin (Eds.), *Mental health research in Asia and the Pacific.* Honolulu: East-West Center Press.

Zeidner, M., & Beit-Hallahmi, B. (1988). Sex, ethnic, and social class differences in parareligious beliefs among Israeli adolescents. *Journal of Social Psychology, 128,* 333–343.

Index

Advisory function of religion, 203
Affective distortion, 4
Aging, and mental health, 177–88
  in Judeo-Christian tradition, 178–79
Agnosticism, 56, 61–62
Alcohol. *See* Substance use
Ananda Cooperative Village, 233
Anger, 274, 292, 295
  in elderly, 181, 184
  repression of, 3
  and ritual, 296–98
  in women, 48
Anxiety, 13, 18, 98–109, 129, 179, 223–24,
  289
  and Buddhism, 275, 277–78
  and Catholics, 58
  in children, 99
  creation of, 3
  death, 102–4, 277–78
  existential, 123
  interpersonal, 50
  and irreligion, 58
  and Jews, 58
  prevalence of, 98
  prevention of, 104
  and Protestants, 58
  and repentance, 99
  and ritual, 292
  and socioeconomic factors, 183
  and women, 50
Aquinas, Thomas, 44
Asceticism, Christian, 74–76
Atheism. *See* Irreligion
Attitudes, religious, 18, 182–83, 185,
  201
Attributions, and beliefs, 166–70
Augustine's *Confessions,* 117–18
Autonomy, 224–25

Baptists, 134, 298, 301–2
  evangelical, 92
Belief
  in afterlife, 3, 213
  and attributions, 166–70
  dogmatic type of, 18, 126–27, 225
  dysfunctional aspects of, 126–28
Blood pressure, and religion, 102
Borderline personality, 238
Buddhism, 43, 44, 54, 109, 119, 124, 262,
  273, 278, 286
  and internality, 276–77
  and mental health, 270–80
  and personal change, 274–76

Catholicism, 48, 134, 225, 283, 293, 295,
  301–2, 304–5, 307, 309
  and marital adjustment, 194
  and sexuality, 76–77, 79–81
  and stress, 100
  and suicide, 12, 87–89, 91–93, 100
  and substance use, 216–17
  and well-being, 143–45
Channeling, 129
Children
  and anxiety, 99
  and religion, 163–76
  and religious affiliation, 170–72
Children of God, 233
Christian Scientists, 113
Church attendance, 12–13, 18, 255
  and blood pressure, 102
  and crime, 204–8
  and delinquency, 199–204
  and substance use, 212–13, 215–17
  and well-being, 182, 184
Cognition
  crisis of, 59–62

Cognition (*continued*)
  unreasonable types of, 59
Cognitive dissonance, 229
Cognitive distortion, 4
Confession, 117–18, 292–94, 295, 307
  and self-esteem, 292
Consciousness, altered states of, 282
Consensual religion, 8, 111
Coping, 11–12, 14, 167, 183, 225
Creativity, 13, 59
Crime, 215
  and church attendance, 204–8
  and moral communities, 207–8
  and religion, 12, 199–210
  and social class, 12
Cultism, destructive, 235, 242
Cults, crisis, 262
Cult consumers, mental health of, 233–44
Cult of self-worship, 135
Culture change, 259–69
Curandreas, in Mexico, 309

Death anxiety, 102–4, 277–78
Delinquency
  and church attendance, 199–204
  and religiosity, 13, 15, 18, 199–210
Dependency, 4, 12, 18
Depression, 18, 87–97, 101, 113, 116, 179,
    271, 302
  in elderly people, 184–85
  and socioeconomic factors, 183
  in women, 45, 48–50, 94
Desexualization of women, 47
Dissociative disorders, 310
Distrust, 14
Divine Light Mission, 233
Divorce, 88
Drug use. *See* Substance use
Durkheim's integration model, 88–89, 94
Dysfunctional religion, 8–9, 126–28, 172–
    73, 249

Ego strength, 12, 226
Elderly people, 15, 102, 142, 145, 177–88
Episcopals, 302
Espiritismo, 262
Esteem, need for, 47
Extrapunitiveness, 12
Extrinsic religion. *See* Religion

Family functioning, 17
Fear of death. *See* Death anxiety
Female empowerment, 49–50
Freedom, 224–25
Functional religion, 8
Fundamentalism
  and marital adjustment, 191
  and self-actualization, 134–35
  and substance use, 213–14

Glossolalia, 264–65, 305–6
God
  domestication of, 60
  images of, 50–51, 100, 111–12, 115–16,
    165–66, 170–73
  punitive, 118–19
Grief, 294–95
Guilt, 3, 15, 39, 47–49, 50, 127, 225, 294
  phychoanalytic view of, 114–15
  sexual, 81

Hantu spirits, 259–62, 265
Hare Krishna movement, 234–37
Healthy religion, 7
Hebrews, 44, 100
Hedonism, 201–2
Hinduism, 43, 44, 54, 124, 262, 295, 303–
    4, 307
Homosexuality, 76, 81–82, 72–73
Hostility, 4, 70–71, 172, 181
Huichol, of Mexico, 293
Hutterites, 48–49

Images of God. *See* God
Immature religion, 7, 184
Impulse control, 18
Inadequacy, 11–14, 128
Intellectual inadequacy, 12
Interfaith marriages, 194–5
Internality, and Buddhism, 276–77
Intolerance, 65, 127–28
Intrinsic religion. *See* Religion
Intropunitiveness, 12, 48
Irreligion
  and crisis of cognition, 59
  and deliquency, 201
  developmental type of, 54
  and emotional distance, 64–65
  as an interpretive system, 61

mental health consequences of, 54–69
prevalence of, 54
reactive type of, 54
and religious substitutionism, 62–64
and ritual, 59, 64–65
sources of, 55
and transcendence, 59–61
Islam, 43–44, 54, 167, 262, 306–7

Judaism, 38, 43, 48, 92, 100, 225, 264, 293,
  301–5, 308, 310–11
and marital adjustment, 194
and sexuality, 71, 79
and substance use, 217

Korea, 284–87
Koran, 306
Kabbalah, 308–10

Life satisfaction
and irreligion, 57
and prayer, 180
and religion, 141–46, 183
Loneliness, 14, 48, 94
Luther, Martin, 44, 77
Lutherans, 302

Magical thought, 125–26
Manic-depressive disorder, 301
Marijuana. *See* Substance use
Marital adjustment
and Catholicism, 194
and divorce, 88
and fundamentalism, 191
and interfaith marriages, 194–95
and Protestantism, 194
and religion, 17–18, 189–98, 222
and religious homogamy, 194–95
secularization hypothesis of, 189–190
and sexual gratification, 192
Masturbation, 72, 77–81
Mature religion, 7
Meaning in life, 103, 138–48
need for, 46
Mental health
and aging, 142, 145, 177–88
and agnosticism, 61–62
and Buddhism, 270–80
as composite, 10

and culture change, 259–69
definition of, 9–11, 222–23, 249–51,
  263–64
diagnostic biases in, 45
and religious experience, 281–90
sex differences in, 45–46
of societies, 66
of women, 43–53, 80, 297
Methodists, 302
and suicide, 93
Moral communities, 207–8
Moral crisis, 55–56
Morality, 13, 15, 167–68, 207–8
medicalization of, 77–78
Mourning, 294–95

Narcissism, 224
Nazarenes, and suicide, 93
Near-death experience, 278
Neurotic religion, 8, 184
Neuroticism
and extraversion, 154
and introversion, 154
and religion, 149–60
Neutralized religion, 8
New religions, and parapsychology, 128–
  30
Nirvana, 271

Obsessive-compulsive disorder, 224, 306–
  8, 311

Pagan asceticism, and sexuality, 72–74
Paranoia, 4, 50, 252, 310
Paranormal beliefs, 62–63, 129
Parapsychology, 128–30
Pentecostals, 268, 283
and well-being, 143
Perceptual distortion, and religion, 4
Personal growth, 225–26. *See also* Self-
  actualization
Pilgrimage, religious, 102
Possession, 37, 260–61, 265, 304–6
Prayer, 179, 184, 292, 306–8
and life satisfaction, 180
Prejudice, 13, 18, 127–28, 181, 227
Presbyterians, 221, 302
Protestants, 136, 225, 262, 304, 307–8
and marital adjustment, 194

Protestants (*continued*)
  and substance use, 216–17
  and suicide, 12, 87–89, 100
Psychicists, 35–36
Psychoanalysis
  and anxiety, 98
  and guilt, 114–15
  and religion, 4, 37–38, 114–17
  and sexuality, 78
  and superego functions, 115–16
Psychopathology of religion, 12, 13, 33–42
  cross-cultural perspectives on, 281–90
  history of, 34–39
  and phenomenology, 38
  and psychoanalysis, 37–38
  in world religions, 300–14
Psychoticism, 149–60

Quest religion, 7, 15–16, 227–28

Racism, 127
Rape, 76, 205–7, 297
Rationality, 59, 122–31
  and magical thought, 125–26
Religion
  advisory function of, 203
  and affective distortion, 4
  and anxiety. *See* Anxiety
  and autonomy, 224–25
  and blood pressure, 102
  and cognitive distortion, 4
  committed type of, 8, 111
  consensual type of, 8, 111
  and coping, 11–12, 14, 167, 183, 225
  and crime, 12, 199–210. *See also*
    Delinquency
  and culture change, 259–269
  and death anxiety, 102–4, 277–78
  definition of, 5–9, 15, 163, 177–78, 199,
    246–49, 252, 263–64, 272–74
  and delinquency, 13, 15, 18, 199–210
  and dependency, 4, 12, 18
  and depression. *See* Depression
  and distrust, 14
  and dogmatic belief, 18, 126–27, 225
  dysfunctional aspects of, 8–9, 126–28,
    172–73, 249
  in elderly people, 15, 102, 142, 145, 177–
    88
  and extrapunitiveness, 12

  extrinsic type of, 7–8, 13, 15, 17–18, 111,
    138–39, 140, 142–43, 153, 172–73,
    213, 221–232
  and family functioning, 17
  and female empowerment, 49–50
  and freedom, 224–25
  functional alternatives to, 62–63
  functional type of, 8–9
  functions of, 3, 61, 122–24
  Glock's five-part model of, 5
  and grief, 294–95
  and guilt, 3, 15, 47–49, 50, 81, 110–21,
    127, 225
  healthy type of, 7
  and hostility, 4, 70–71, 172, 181
  as ideological system, 33
  immature type of, 7, 184
  and impulse control, 18
  and inadequacy, 11–14, 128
  and intellectual inadequacy, 12
  and intolerance, 65, 127–28
  intrinsic type of, 7–8, 13, 15–18, 102,
    111–14, 134–35, 138–39, 140, 142–43,
    145, 153, 172–73, 180–81, 183, 213,
    221–32
  and intropunitiveness, 12, 48
  and life meaning, 138–48
  and life satisfaction, 141–46, 180, 183
  and loneliness, 14, 94
  masculinization of, 44–45
  and marital adjustment, 17–18, 189–98,
    222
  mature type of, 7, 145, 184, 226
  and mental health of children, 99, 163–
    76, 170–72
  and mental health in later life, 15, 102,
    142, 145, 177–88
  as mental sickness, 4
  as model for identity, 167
  and morality, 13, 15, 167–68, 207–8
  multidimensional nature of, 5–8, 145
  and neuroticism, 149–60
  neurotic type of, 8, 184
  neutralized type of, 7
  New Age type of, 129
  and orientation, 221–32
  and parapsychology, 128–30
  and positive impact on women, 50–51
  and prejudice, 13, 18, 127–28, 181, 227
  and premarital sex, 17

private type of, 62–64, 94
and psychoanalytic theory, 37–38, 98,
 114–17
and psychoticism, 149–60
quest type of, 7, 15–16, 227–28
and racism, 127
and rape, 205–7, 297
and rationality, 59, 122–31
as rescue operation, 3
and responsibility, 224–25
and ritual, 3, 59, 64–65, 183, 291–99,
 309
and self-actualization, 8–10, 15, 18, 59,
 132–37, 254, 272
and self-esteem, 3, 12, 17–18, 47, 50–51,
 110–21, 127, 215, 225–26
serious type of, 8
and sexism, 127–28
and sex roles, 43–44
and sexual adjustment, 4, 15, 70–84
and sexual performance of women, 45
and sexual revolution, 78–82
and shame, 112–13, 115–18, 292–94
and sick soul, 7
and social behavior, 3, 167–68
and social support, 172
as source of disturbance in women, 45–
 53, 80
and stress, 47, 50, 100, 172, 181, 184–85,
 261–63
and substance use, 11–13, 17–18, 102,
 200–1, 211–20
and suggestibility, 4, 12, 18, 65
and suicide. *See* Suicide
and superego functions, 115–16
and symbols, 6, 48, 139, 310
and tolerance, 65, 127–28, 225
unhealthy type of, 7
as universal neurosis, 4
and well-being, 3, 13, 17–18, 138–48,
 168, 180–81, 184, 275, 279
and women, 43–53, 70–82, 297
Reformed Churches, and suicide, 92
Religious attitudes, 18, 182–83, 185, 201
Religious diagnosis, in mental health
 evaluations, 245–56
Religious experience, and psychopathology,
 281–290
Religious meanings, 48–50
Religious privatization, 62–64

Religious substitutions, 62–63
Repentance, and anxiety, 99
Responsibility, social, 15
Revitalization movement, 260, 262
Ritual, 3, 59, 183, 309
 and anger, 296–98
 and catharsis, 292–93
 eclipse of, 64–65
 and emotional distance, 64–65, 291–92
 and mental health, 291–99

Santeria, 309–11
Schizophrenia, 184, 287, 289, 302
Secularization hypothesis, 189–90
Self-absolutization, 59–60
Self-actualization, 8–10, 15, 18, 59, 132–
 37, 254, 272
 and fundamentalism, 134–35
 measurement of, 134–35
 and society, 135–36
Self-esteem, 3, 12, 17–18, 50, 63, 110–21,
 127, 135, 215
 and intrinsic/extrinsic religion, 17, 111–
 12, 225–26
 and ritual, 292
 of women, 47, 50–51
Self-realization, 8–10, 59. *See also* Self-
 actualization
Seventh Day Adventists
 and substance use, 214–15
 and suicide, 92
Sex, premarital, 17
Sex guilt, 81
Sex roles, 43–44
Sexism, 127–28
Sexual adjustment, 192
 in ancient societies, 71–77
 and Catholic orthodoxy, 81–82
 and Christian asceticism, 74–76
 and Christianity, 70–71
 and medicalization of morality, 77–78
 and pagan asceticism, 72–74
 and religiosity, 4, 15, 70–84
Sexual feelings, inhibition of, 4
Sexual gratification, and marital
 adjustment, 192
Sexual performance in women, 45
Shame, 112–13, 115–18, 292–94
Shapiro legislation, 235–36
Sick soul, 7

Sin, 4, 15, 45, 47, 73, 76, 100, 110–21, 123,
    127, 226, 292, 307, 310
Sinbyong in Korea, 284–87
Social cohesion, 3
Somaticisits, 35–36
Stark effect, 200–201
St. Augustine, 75–76, 117–18
St. Paul, 44, 74
St. Theresa, 39, 289
St. Thomas Aquinas, 76
Stress, 172, 261–63
    in Catholics, 100
    in elderly people, 181, 184–85
    and women, 47, 49–50
Substance use
    measures of, 213
    and religion, 11–13, 17–18, 200–201,
        211–20
Substitutionism, religious, 62–64
Suggestibility, 4, 12, 18, 65
Suicide, 12, 17–18, 50, 100, 179
    and Catholicism, 12, 87–89, 91–93, 100
    and evangelical Baptists, 92
    and evangelical Methodists, 93
    and Nazarenes, 92
    and Protestants, 12
    and Reformed Churches, 92
    and religion, 87–97
    and Seventh Day Adventists, 92
    in social context, 91–93
    and Unitarians, 93
Superego functions, 115–16
Symbols, religious, 6, 39, 48, 310

Timelessness in Buddhism, 273, 278
Tobacco. *See* Substance use
Tolerance, 65, 127–28, 225
Tongues, speaking in, 264–65, 305–6
Transcendence, 59–61, 140
Transcendental temptation, 129

Umbanda in Brazil, 309
Unhealthy religion, 7
Unification Church, 233
Unitarians, and suicide, 93

Well-being, 3, 13, 17–18, 138–48, 168,
    180–82, 184, 275, 279
Women
    cultural desexualization of, 80
    as culture-bearers, 55
    and depression, 94
    and guilt, 47
    and helplessness, 50
    and mental disorder, 45–46
    and religion, 43–53, 297
    and self-esteem, 50
    and stress, 47
    and sexual performance, 45
    and sexual subjugation of, 74–75
    socialization of, 47

Worry, 15

Zen Buddhism. *See* Buddhism
Zuni culture, 296